W9-AOK-904

THE MODERN VEGETARIAN KITCHEN

THE MODERN VEGETARIAN KITCHEN

Peter Berley

with Melissa Clark

Photographs by Beth Galton

Illustrations by Laura Hartman Maestro

1⊕ ReganBooks
Celebrating Ten Bestselling Years
An Imprint of HarperCollinsPublishers

A hardcover edition of this book was published in 2000 by ReganBooks, an imprint of HarperCollins Publishers.

THE MODERN VEGETARIAN KITCHEN. Copyright © 2000 by Peter Berley. All rights reserved. Printed in the United States of America. No part of this book may be used or reproduced in any manner whatsoever without written permission except in the case of brief quotations embodied in critical articles and reviews. For information address HarperCollins Publishers Inc., 10 East 53rd Street, New York, NY 10022.

HarperCollins books may be purchased for educational, business, or sales promotional use. For information please write: Special Markets Department, HarperCollins Publishers Inc., 10 East 53rd Street, New York, NY 10022.

First paperback edition published 2004.

Designed by Leah Carlson-Stanisic
Illustrations by Laura Hartman Maestro
Photographs by Beth Galton

Kitchen courtesy of VarennaPoliform
150 East 58th Street
New York, NY 10155
1-877-VARENNA
www.varenna.com

Cookware courtesy of Bridge Kitchenware
214 East 52nd Street
New York, NY 10022
212-688-4220

www.bridgekitchenware.com

The Library of Congress has cataloged the hardcover edition as follows:

Berley, Peter.
    The modern vegetarian kitchen/Peter Berley with Melissa Clark.—1st ed.
        p.   cm.
    Includes bibliographical references and index.
    ISBN 0-06-039295-9
    1. Vegetarian cookery.   I. Clark, Melissa.   II. Title.
TX837 .B478 2000
641.5'636—dc21   00-042524
ISBN 0-06-039295-9

ISBN 0-06-098911-4 (pbk.)

04   05   06   07   08   RRD   10 9 8 7 6 5 4 3

For my parents,

Daniel and Frances

Contents

List of Illustrations

Acknowledgments

First, thanks to my grandparents, Bill and Anna Berley and Esther and Yussell Rotholz, for having the courage and pluck to come to America as immigrants with next to nothing and build a life filled with love, joy, and wonderful food for me and my sisters, Karen, Lisa, and Barbara.

To my parents, for my appetite for good food, music, art, and literature.

To my loving wife, Meggan, and my daughters, Kayla and Emma, my greatest treasures.

To Ellen Schiff, for her loving support and encouragement.

To my mentor and music teacher, Lennie Tristano, who helped me find my voice. Cooking, like jazz, is a creative, highly personal, and communicative art form. Lennie taught me that technique, study, and practice should never be an end in themselves but the tools through which we can express our feelings and intuition. Cooking is a performance art, and just like jazz, it is always about change.

To George Ohsawa, Michio Kushi, and Annemarie Colbin, whose courage, daring, and vision inspired me to change my career and become a cook.

To Richard Olney, Angelo Pellegrini, Alice Waters, Giuliano Bugialli, and Patience Gray, whose incredible books have for years stoked the fires of my imagination and serve as benchmarks by which I will always measure mine.

Special thanks to Judith Regan, gifted publisher and angel, whose wise counsel and belief in me from the beginning have probably changed my life forever. To Chuck Verrill, for helping me sort through my ideas and make some sense of publishing contracts and legalese. Without Chuck, I don't know if this book would ever have actually gotten off the ground.

To my cousin John Rotholz, my computer guru—and the brother I never had.

If I had a ton of rose petals I would shower them on Melissa Clark, writer, partner, friend, and one of Brooklyn's true treasures. Melissa gave wings to my ideas and recipes. Without Melissa, *The Modern Vegetarian Kitchen* would have been just another puddle on the boulevard of broken dreams.

To my agent, Caroline Krupp, for her support, wisdom, and encouragement.

To Cassie Jones, my editor, cheerleader, and guide, whose great patience and gentle support kept the project right on target.

To the great people at ReganBooks and HarperCollins who helped pull this book together: Heather Locascio, Leah Carlson-Stanisic, Lucy Albanese, and Lorie Young.

To Laura Hartman Maestro, whose delightful drawings grace these pages and contribute clarity, lively imagination, and soul. Laura is a true master.

To Andrea "Tough Love" Chesman, my copy editor, for her relentless and painstaking attention to detail. I've never eaten humble pie with so much flavor.

To my friend Corinne Colin, proprietor of the beautiful Culinary Loft in SoHo, New York, for providing a dream test kitchen and classroom laboratory.

To Diane Carlson, Mark Mace, Susan Kauffman, and all my friends at the Natural Gourmet Institute for Food and Health in New York City, for the opportunity to teach on a regular basis and work out many of these ideas and recipes.

To Deborah Madison, Michael Romano, and Mollie Katzen—incredible chefs and authors who all took time out of their insanely busy schedules to read over the manuscript and offer support, encouragement, and honest feedback.

To Diane Lallone for her recipe testing and assistance in the early going, and to my friend Mike Perrine for contributing some of his awesome vegan desserts.

To my dear friend—and great vegan chef—Peter Cervoni, for being there.

To friends and teaching assistants Jennifer, Seth, Michelle, Nadine, and Mark for schlepping, cleanup, and putting up with my merry pessimism and bad jokes.

To Leslie McEachern and all the folks at Angelica Kitchen restaurant.

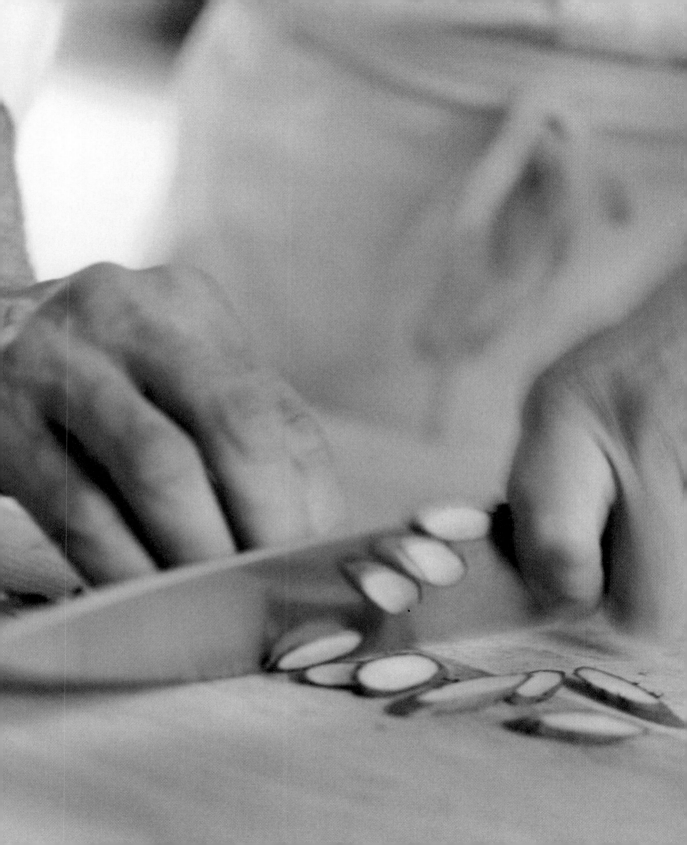

Introduction

For the past thirty years, I have been involved with food and cooking in one way or another. When I think back, I can recall the culinary adventures I've had and how I have changed as a cook, but I also notice that I still feel essentially the same about food. Cooking has served as an endless source of pleasure that not only sustains my body but constantly tunes and sharpens all of my senses. I can't imagine a day in which I have not touched, smelled, seen, heard, and tasted the results of my cooking.

Cooking is an essential domestic ritual that anchors us in time and gives a rhythm to life's cycles and changes. We live in an age in which the center of our primary relationship to the world is moving away from a domestic setting and toward the workplace. We are at a point where we are in danger of losing a great source of intimacy and connection to the world and the people around us. This book is designed to help you bring one of the most fundamental, soul-satisfying experiences back into your home.

My history is rooted in memories of my grandparents, Bill and Esther, who were my two major influences in terms of food and cooking. My grandfather was an aspiring organic gardener who had dreams of moving west from his home in Brooklyn to start an organic farm. When the Depression hit, he set his sights on smaller goals and purchased a small plot of land in upper Westchester County, where he built a home and planted a garden. I spent summers there from the time I was born until my early teens: weeding and chasing after garter snakes, chopping earthworms in half to watch them wiggle, and hanging out in the tool shed with Catutti, the old Italian gardener who helped my grandfather. My grandmother spent nearly every day until just a few years before her death at age ninety-five baking and cooking the traditional foods of her Russian village. I cherish the time I spent by her side, watching her in the kitchen, helping her, and tasting as she worked.

After high school, I enrolled at Berklee College of Music in Boston in an attempt to follow my lifelong dream of becoming the next Charlie Parker. I wrote big-band arrangements and lived on take-out food. One day, in a frenzy of Good Jewish Boyness, I finally threw away the huge pile of crusty take-out containers and scrubbed the three-foot-high mound of dirty dishes. Afterward, feeling curiously calm, I noticed that I was really hungry, but not for anything from the local Blimpie's or chop suey joint.

Suddenly, in a blinding flash, I remembered the bag of lentils that my grandmother had sent to me in a care package and which I had promptly stowed on the top shelf of my kitchen cabinet, safely out of sight. I felt the compulsion deep within my gut to do what hundreds of generations of Eastern European Jews before me had done. Recalling my grandmother in her kitchen, I whipped out a heavy enamel soup kettle and added some oil, celery, carrots, onions, and garlic. I tossed in the lentils and some seasonings, added water, and *voilà!* Admittedly, my very first pot of lentil soup wasn't all that good, but I took joy in the fact that I had created it from scratch to nourish myself. I had discovered my true calling.

I fell wholeheartedly into my new love of healthy eating and cooked for myself and my friends whenever I could. After starting yoga classes (this was the seventies), I decided to become a vegetarian, although the only real dietary change I made was to simply stop eating meat. I happened to injure myself during one of my yoga classes and was referred to a Japanese acupuncturist, who, after examining me, recommended that I change my diet. She laid a book in my hand that would completely change my life: *Zen Macrobiotic Cooking* by George Ohsawa. His book was my bible, and I became a card-carrying macrobiotic.

Two of Ohsawa's disciples, Michio and Aveline Kushi, began teaching in Boston, and I studied with them for three very intense months. The Kushis were a charismatic couple who taught astrology, shiatsu, and philosophy as well as macrobiotic cooking. After filling my brain with their teachings and my stomach with Oriental pickles, seaweed, and brown rice, I returned to New York and made the decision to focus on food instead of pursuing a music career.

So, I began hosting a supper club on Friday nights in my Upper West Side apartment. Twenty to twenty-five people would pay a few dollars each to eat my homemade macrobiotic dinners. It was truly rewarding, and I was excited to successfully connect to the world through food. After a year, I realized I needed a bigger place. I had met Annemarie Colbin, a terrific cook and teacher (and the founder of the Natural Gourmet Institute for Food and Health) through a mutual friend. She let me rent out her space, and I was able to feed fifty to sixty members of the macrobiotic community two nights per week. Those suppers were my laboratory—I got to experiment with all sorts of techniques and ingredients, building my repertoire and creating new dishes. At the same time, I started the Macrobiotic Community Home Food Service, which delivered food to homebound people with cancer and AIDS, and began teaching classes at the Natural Gourmet.

One day, from out of the blue, Lorenzo Mitchell, my friend and former sidekick in the kitchen, called me up to ask if I was interested in becoming the chef at a restaurant he was considering buying in Blue Hill, Maine, in the Penobscot Bay area. Looking for a new challenge, I decided to accept his offer and headed to Maine with my wife, Meggan, and our two baby girls, Emma and Kayla.

The Firepond was a great restaurant. It was right by pristine fishing water, forests full of wild mushrooms and berries, a winery, and three organic farms. I worked in the kitchen with a classically trained French chef, and with my natural foods/macrobiotic background and his technique, we created a fantastic menu. But, after the 1987 crash, businesses throughout Maine were suffering, and we eventually sold the restaurant. I moved my family back to New York.

There, Annemarie invited me back to the Natural Gourmet to teach and to develop a curriculum for the chef training program. Little by little, I also built up my own clientele, taught private classes, and did some catering. In 1992, I accepted the position of executive chef at Angelica Kitchen, a vegan restaurant in New York.

During my time at Angelica, from 1992 to 1999, my primary goal was to create the most unique, sophisticated, and dazzling food for our guests. However, "wowing" people soon began to wear thin. The more notice I received, the more unhappy and dissatisfied I became. Instead of constantly having to impress people, I wanted to share with them the pure joy and happiness I feel when I cook. I wanted to show people how to feed themselves and enjoy the process of cooking.

To remedy this, I began to teach a series of Sunday evening classes at the restaurant, which led to the development of recipes for *The Angelica Home Kitchen*. While these recipes are wonderful reflections of Angelica, I still felt only partially satisfied—I wanted to reach people on a more fundamental level.

I wanted to demonstrate the techniques and principles behind what lands on the customer's plate. In my classes, students would ask very basic questions: What kind of pot should I use? What kind of knife? How do I clean my pots and sharpen my knives? What tools do I really need to equip my kitchen? I went into my own home kitchen and started to cook with a beginner's mind-set. I began to notice what the essentials were, in terms of tools, techniques, and basic recipes, keeping in mind that few of us have the time or space for much else besides work, the kids, and the computer.

Soon I felt I had gathered enough insight and momentum to write my own cookbook. Undertaking this project was also great for me on a personal level, because I wanted to learn how to communicate my culinary experience with words. In some ways, writing this book was like cooking—it was very improvisational and seemed to flow naturally.

As you go through the chapters and try out some of the recipes, ideas and images will begin to blossom according to your own senses and tastes. As you gather tools and techniques, you will become comfortable with the knowledge that you are free to create according to the whims and desires of your own imagination as you are pulled by the awesome forces of the changing seasons. You will be able to admire the first glossy pumpkins of fall and know intuitively what you want to make of them. When you see perfectly fresh purple eggplants, they will spark ideas. And when those ideas become embedded in the culture of your domesticity, they will sprout and grow into a dish that will sustain and bring joy to you and your loved ones.

A Word About Vegetarianism

During my seven years at Angelica Kitchen, a strictly vegan venue, I learned a great deal about coaxing out the maximum flavor and concentrating on the essence of foods without the use of dairy products or eggs. When I left, I refocused and decided to open up my cuisine to include some animal products. I began looking to strike a balance where healthy eating is also the most pleasurable eating. I wanted my diet to be based on my needs, preferences, and desires—one that would maintain my body, spirit, and mind, keeping me healthy and vibrant.

This book is about modern seasonal vegetarian cuisine. It is about home cooking—everyday meals as opposed to feasts. While the recipes and menus in this book are primarily concerned with vegetable foods, some do use dairy and eggs. But I am always mindful of where I add dairy and eggs and only use them when it is going to make a positive difference in the dish.

Diet is a very personal and subjective thing. We all respond to foods in idiosyncratic ways based on our genetic and cultural backgrounds. I feel it is dangerous to subscribe to any particular philosophy that dictates what is right or wrong for a population. For example, most Westerners have not been raised on soy and might not adapt to it well or ever find tempeh to be a satisfying source of protein. However, in the West, there is a huge tradition of dairy farming and more of a predisposition to include those products in our diets than there is in most Eastern countries.

For twelve years, I avoided dairy products because I reacted badly to some of them. Eventually, I found that uncultured dairy products, such as milk, seem to affect me, but cultured dairy products, such as yogurt and sour cream, do not. While my diet is by no means dairy-based, it does include some dairy products, and I find that my body feels healthier and stronger since I have broadened my scope to include them. I have noticed that when we decide to totally eradicate certain foods from our diet, we become less flexible in what we are able to eat and less adaptable to new foods. If we expand our range, as long as the quality is very good, we become better able to digest and benefit from a wider variety of foods.

I designed this book to be vegan-friendly, but not exclusively vegan. It is a book for people who are not opposed to eggs and dairy; but those who prefer not to eat animal products will not have to scavenge for a few recipes that they can use. Since all my recipes that call for butter use it in its melted form, vegans can easily substitute oil. And since I use cheese and yogurt primarily as garnishes and condiments, vegans can easily omit them or substitute soy creams. My recipes are not all soy-based and there is nothing exclusive or weird about them. You can be confident that the meals you cook from this book will please your meat-eating, vegetarian, and vegan friends and family alike.

A Word About Seasonal, Organic Ingredients

It's wonderful that organic foods are no longer regarded as fringe or fanatical and are rapidly moving into the mainstream. Studies have shown that organically grown foods have an even higher vitamin and mineral content than their conventionally farmed counterparts. Fresh fruits and vegetables, grains, and legumes keep your blood replenished with vital nutrients, but how much you get from them depends on the quality of the plants. And the quality of the plants in turn depends on the quality of the soil. The interconnectedness of all living things means that the health of the soil will always reflect the health of the people.

Conventional farming relies heavily on chemical fertilizers, pesticides, and fungicides, all because of poor soil health. Healthy soil is alive with microorganisms, bacteria, and fungi that make nutrients available to the plants above, keeping them strong and better protected from pests and disease. Farmers who practice sustainable agriculture bolster the soil with additions of compost, follow a schedule of crop rotation (since different plants require and use up different nutrients), use insects and plants as natural pest controls, and plant nitrogen-fixing cover crops in fields not in production.

I heartily encourage you to support sustainably managed organic farms and your local growers, as well as supermarkets that stock organic or local produce. But, beware—just because a bag of carrots is labeled organic, that doesn't necessarily mean they were grown in a sustainable way. There are plenty of large agribusinesses that plant acres and acres of fields with a single crop, which can lead to poor soil quality, although they might not spray their crops with toxic chemicals.

Large corporations that have a vested interest in controlling what is grown have been hoarding seeds, basically taking certain varieties of vegetables out of circulation. Unfortunately, vegetables that have been bred to hold up to the rigors of shipping and to be of uniform shape and color often lack the most important thing of all—flavor! There are some organizations, such as the Seed Savers' Exchange, that are collecting heirloom seeds and trying to recover agricultural diversity. And, although most supermarkets generally carry only a few of the commercially popular varieties of potatoes and lettuce, demand for diversity is rising, and more and more heirloom varieties are appearing at farmers' markets and in health food stores.

Local, seasonal eating is also becoming more mainstream as more and more people are realizing that food grows in both place and time. It is now fashionable for restaurants to construct their menus around the seasons and buy produce from local farmers' markets. Common sense should tell you that if you eat something grown close to where you live and in its proper season, it will have the best flavor since it hasn't been subjected to packaging and refrigeration. We pay a heavy price for eating out-of-season produce, both in terms of the environment and flavor and freshness. There is a profound difference between a head of lettuce that was picked days ago in California and shipped in a refrigerated semi to the supermarket, and one that was picked the same morning you bought it at the farmers' market. Before fossil fuels, refrigerated trucks, and hothouses, people were more connected to the land and ate only what grew around them. Maybe you had a large variety of vegetables available to you, maybe you didn't. To this day, even though I live in New York City and can get almost any vegetable at almost any time of the year, I just can't bring myself to eat kiwi fruit from New Zealand, fresh basil in February, or those all too ubiquitous hothouse tomatoes. I'd rather eat what is grown nearby and wait until each fruit's and each vegetable's proper season, when the flavors are the best and I can pick them up fresh at the farmers' market.

Welcome to

Your Kitchen

Making your own meals can be a frightening and intimidating experience if you did not grow up cooking by your grandmother's side, tugging on her apron strings and watching her every move. Although hunger is probably the most powerful human appetite and food the most basic need, cooking does not necessarily come naturally.

One of the most important parts of cooking is having, and using, the proper tools. In my classes, I like to ask my students what crafts they enjoy besides cooking and try to relate the importance of proper tools to the jobs they do. A dull knife is like an out-of-tune musical instrument. A stove that does not burn cleanly and evenly is like a crooked loom. Cooking with old, lifeless spices is like trying to spackle a wall with dried plaster. Working with a poorly conceived recipe is like trying to build a piece of furniture with a faulty blueprint.

Good cooking requires a basic love for life, appreciation for good food, and a deep desire to share this love with others. Good cooking does not exist in a vacuum. It is reflected in a celebration of the miracles and mysteries of nature. I love amusing myself with food; however, it is always better when there is someone to share it with. That said, good cooking need never impress others. It should be an act of graceful, natural self-assurance and self-expression. Think of it as though you were writing simple thank-you notes to the universe for having received the gifts of life, liberty, and the pursuit of happiness.

Good cooking requires a clean, well-lit, amply ventilated, organized, and comfortable space. When getting started, choose a time when you are relaxed to attempt a new or more complicated dish. Make sure you have a basic working knowledge of techniques and the basic hand tools to ensure your ease in the kitchen. Start off with a fresh, local supply of wholesome, preferably organic, ingredients and clean water. Finally, supply yourself with solid, durable pots and pans of the correct size and shape and a reliable source of heat, preferably with a live flame.

I have cooked in hundreds of kitchens in private homes and apartments, catering facilities, and restaurants, and I know that I cannot invoke the Spirit of Nourishment until I feel right where I am cooking. The kitchen has to be a place where I feel free. I cannot cook when my spirit is dragged down by cluttered work surfaces that are dirty or disorganized; dim or cold lighting; or poorly maintained pots, pans, and utensils.

Give yourself a moment to take a good look around your kitchen and notice how you feel. Does your kitchen invite you or repel you? Do you feel inspired and relaxed or overwhelmed and tense? Pick up your tools and utensils—do they make you feel good? Are your counters clean and uncluttered? Is your stove working? Will you be happy spending time in this room? If not, it's time to act!

Put on some good music, invite a friend over, and organize your kitchen. Survey your counters and cabinets, take inventory of your pots, pans, and utensils, and see what's lurking at the back of your cabinets. Throw out any dried spices, herbs, flour, cereals, grains, or beans that have been in your kitchen for more than a year. Check your oils for rancidity. Clean out the refrigerator and freezer. Clean the stove and oven and check to see if all your burners are working. Buy an oven thermometer (you should be able to pick one up for a couple of bucks at your local hardware store or supermarket) and see if your oven is accurate. If your tap water is chlorinated or funky tasting, buy a filter.

If you are new to cooking, leaf through the recipes and choose one or two that strike your fancy. Read through the recipe carefully, noting procedures and the ingredients list. See if you have the necessary equipment. If you purchase what you need to execute a dish, over time you will accumulate a well-outfitted kitchen.

A few well-chosen, properly maintained hand tools are all that is necessary. Whatever tool can serve as an extension of your body and mind, amplify your feelings, and articulate your vision is the proper one for you. I am not much of a gadget freak, and I would rather find ways of using one tool to perform many tasks than clutter my kitchen with novel inventions. I love the primal rituals and rhythms of pounding, kneading, and chopping that add so much to the taste and personality of the food and to the cook's pleasure and connection to the ingredients. An organized collection of essential tools makes me more focused and gives me greater enjoyment and pleasure in cooking.

Equipment Essentials

BAKING EQUIPMENT

I recommend using heavy baking dishes made from black baker's steel, tin, glass, or ceramic. I don't recommend lightweight aluminum nonstick pans, which will warp over time.

- Several 2-quart glass or ceramic baking dishes
- 9-inch tart pan with removable bottom
- 9- or 10-inch springform cake pan
- 9- or 10-inch glass, ceramic, or tin pie plate
- 8-inch square pan
- 8-by-4-inch loaf pan
- 2 or 3 baking sheets or jelly-roll pans
- Baker's stone (aka pizza stone)
- Long-stemmed instant-read thermometer for testing water and bread dough temperature
- Plastic spray bottle
- Scale that measures ounces and pounds

BLENDER

I really recommend investing in an immersion blender—a motorized wand that purées foods in a bowl or pot. They are handy, relatively inexpensive, and eliminate a lot of cleanup. If you use a traditional blender for puréeing soups or other hot liquids, never fill it more than halfway, to avoid splatter burns.

BOWLS

Lightweight, all-purpose, stainless-steel stackable mixing bowls make it easy for you to choose the right size. I also use these nonbreakable bowls for storing and organizing prepped ingredients. You will also need a large, heavy glass or crockery mixing bowl for making bread dough.

BOX GRATER

A sturdy four-sided grater is the best tool for shredding vegetables and grating cheeses.

CHEESECLOTH

Purchase a supply of unbleached cheesecloth for kitchen use. If you are using it to strain liquids, dampen it before using. Cheesecloth is also a great tool for making bouquets garnis (little bundles of herbs and spices). You can drop these herb bundles into sauces, soups, and stews for easy retrieval later.

Peeling and grating tools: box grater, swivel peeler, and rasp.

COFFEE MILL

I use my electric coffee mill for hard-to-grind spices, such as cinnamon sticks, whole cloves, cardamom pods, and bay leaves.

COLANDER

Use a 12-inch-wide colander for draining pasta and greens.

CUTTING BOARD

Wood is the best and most hygienic surface for cutting. Plastic and polyethylene boards breed bacteria and require bleach to keep clean. Modern science has recently validated what cooks have intuitively known for thousands of years: Bacteria cannot thrive on natural, untreated wood. In fact, resins in the wood act as natural antibacterial agents. Another big advantage of wooden cutting boards is that they don't dull the blades of your knives like most synthetic materials do.

FLAME TAMER

On some stoves, low just isn't low enough. If you are simmering a dish for a long time, this inexpensive tool will prevent foods from sticking and burning on the bottom of a pan.

FOOD MILL

A hand-cranked food mill is handy for puréeing soups and sauces, as well as for removing the seeds and pits from cooked tomatoes and other vegetables. Look for one with three removable disks rather than the common one-piece variety. This will allow you to make purées of different consistencies.

FOOD PROCESSOR

The modern electric food processor has been both a blessing and a curse for those who love to cook. I find that it severs the physical connection to ingredients. However, that said, I do possess a small food processor that I use for creaming tofu and making custards, mousses, and other smooth, savory dips and spreads.

Blending and puréeing tools: hand-cranked food mill, food processor, and immersion blender.

KITCHEN TIMER

Essential for timing baked goods.

KNIVES

More than any other tool, a knife connects the cook to the food. Learning to use a knife properly is similar to learning how to write. A properly honed and maintained knife is the essential instrument by which you will inscribe your personality, thoughts, and feelings on most of the foods that you cook, eat, and share. Any experienced cook will have his or her favorite knives.

Knives forged from carbon steel used to be considered state-of-the-art and are excellent but for the fact that they can rust and stain. Stainless-steel knives will not rust or stain; however, they are very difficult to sharpen and tend to dull quickly. Most chefs use knives made from high-carbon steel, a blend of carbon steel and stainless steel that gives a great, sharp edge without the rust.

There are really just four essential knives:

- **10-inch serrated bread knife**
- **8-inch, heavy, all-purpose chef's knife of either Western or Asian design for most cutting, chopping, and mincing chores**
- **2- or 3-inch paring knife for delicate slicing, peeling, and garnishing**
- **4- to 6-inch knife with a fine serrated edge for slicing acidic foods like tomatoes and citrus fruits, which tend to dull straight-edged blades rather quickly**

KNIFE SHARPENER

There is no point in owning a good set of knives without having the tools to keep them sharp. If you properly maintain your knives, everything will feel right and your hands will be able to move with a lightness and freedom that is impossible with a dull edge. A sharp blade is also safer, since dull knives will not glide through the fibers and tissues of food without some degree of clumsy, forceful exaggeration. The tough, shiny peels of fruits and vegetables are especially treacherous to cut with a dull edge, since they can cause the knife to slip and wound the cook.

I always keep a steel handy and use it to touch up the blade every time I cook. A sharpening stone will hone and reconstruct the edge when it has

The essential knife set: bread knife, chef's knife, paring knife, small serrated knife, sharpener, stone, and oil.

become too dull to revive on the steel—I use one every couple of months. I like either an old-fashioned whetstone that requires oil (better for harder types of steel), or a whetstone that uses water for lubrication (excellent for softer metal and thinner blades). A diamond-embedded stone does an excellent job with both stainless-steel and high-carbon steel knives.

LADLES

I like to have several sizes of wooden and metal ladles. A 6- to 8-ounce ladle is good for soups and stews, while a 2- to 4-ounce ladle is useful for sauces.

MEASURING CUPS AND SPOONS

Heavy-duty dry measuring cups and spoons; 1-, 2-, and 4-cup glass measures for liquids.

MORTAR WITH PESTLE

A heavy marble mortar with a wooden pestle is a tool of awesome beauty and ancient design. It is also the best device for grinding spices and coarse sea salt; pounding toasted nuts; and making pesto, tapenade, and other rustic sauces.

PARCHMENT PAPER

Parchment is great for lining baking sheets. You don't have to grease the pan, and it saves on cleanup time. If you have aluminum pans, a piece of parchment layered between the pan and the food will prevent reactions with the aluminum. Also, I use a layer of parchment between aluminum foil and the food it is covering to prevent the aluminum from having direct contact with the acids in foods, which can cause it to deteriorate. You can also cover a cooking dish or pot with a circle of parchment to keep your food submerged and prevent air from browning it.

Tools for measuring weight, volume, and temperature are essential for successful baking: dry measuring cups and spoons, liquid measuring cups, a scale, and a long-stemmed instant-read thermometer.

Tools for grinding spices, seeds, and nuts: large Mediterranean marble mortar and pestle, Asian suribachi, and electric coffee mill.

POTS AND PANS

Heavy-bottomed pots and pans are essential. Look for ones made from cast iron and thick stainless steel. I find Le Creuset to be a good make as well as All-Clad's Master Chef line. I also like Sitram, a line from France. My list of essentials includes:

- 8- to 10-inch stainless-steel slope-sided skillet
- 8- to 10-inch cast-iron skillet
- 10-inch stainless-steel sauté pan with lid (3-quart capacity)
- 1-quart stainless-steel saucepan with lid
- 2-quart stainless-steel saucepan with lid
- 8-quart stainless-steel stockpot with steamer insert
- 3- to 4-quart stainless-steel pressure cooker
- 2-quart enamel-coated cast-iron pot for porridge
- 3-quart enamel-coated cast-iron pot for soups and stews
- 4-quart flameproof earthenware casserole with lid for baking and oven braising
- 5- to 6-quart cast-iron Dutch oven for bread baking and stews

Well-made, properly maintained pots and pans will last a lifetime.

RASP

A rasp can be very useful for grating citrus zest.

SALAD SPINNER

A salad spinner dries delicate greens very effectively. My favorite is the kind that has a string to pull.

SALT AND PEPPER MILLS

A pepper mill is essential, because peppercorns, like all spices, lose their pungency relatively quickly after being ground.

If you use moist, gray Celtic sea salt, regular mills won't work—they jam and corrode if they have metal parts. You'll need to get a ceramic mill that has a blade and sort of chops the salt instead of one that grinds (see Sources on page 434). You can also use a mortar, which is really quick. I like to grind about ¹/₄ cup sea salt and keep it in a little bowl by my stove. If it does recrystallize, you can just pound it up again.

SIEVE OR STRAINER

Use metal sieves and strainers to drain grains and pasta, rinse vegetables, strain purées, and sift dry ingredients. I have a 3-inch-wide fine sieve that I use for dusting bread and pasta doughs with flour,

The evolution of hand tools. They bring efficiency and pleasure to cooking.

and 6-inch and 8-inch medium sieves for rinsing vegetables and grains and straining purées.

SPATULA

No tool will empty a bowl or pot more effectively than a rubber spatula. Not to be confused with a plastic spatula, which is brittle, the synthetic rubber spatula is heat resistant and extremely flexible. The ingredients for delicate batters are best folded together gently with a rubber spatula.

CLEANING SUPPLIES

Distilled white vinegar and baking soda make an effective, inexpensive, safe, and totally biodegradable cleanser. Use chemical cleansers only for extra-tough jobs.

- **Frequently changed, good-quality sponges**
- **Baking soda**
- **Distilled white vinegar**
- **Gentle scouring powder, such as Bon Ami, that is safe for scouring stainless-steel or enamel surfaces**
- **Phosphate- and chlorine-free dishwashing lotion**
- **Elbow grease**

SPIDER

This tool resembles a rigid, round fishing net with a long bamboo handle. I always reach for my spider when I need to fish something out of boiling water or hot oil. The angle of the handle makes a spider much more versatile than a slotted spoon.

SPOONS

The wooden spoon is probably one of the oldest-known tools. Wood is the best material for moving food around. Unlike metal spoons, smooth wooden spoons feel good in your hands. They do not transfer heat as metal does, so their handles stay cool. Spoons made of metal tend to have thin, straight edges that can tear and bruise delicate foods as well as damage the cooking surfaces of stainless-steel and enamel-coated pots and pans.

STORAGE CONTAINERS

Heavy plastic or glass storage containers with tight-fitting lids are perfect for storing prepped ingredients or leftovers. Get a variety of 1-cup, 1-quart, and 2-quart sizes.

TONGS

Spring-action stainless-steel tongs act like fingers and provide the cook with amazing dexterity and comfort when handling hot foods. They are great for plucking herb sprigs and bay leaves from simmering stews and for turning fried, roasted, or grilled vegetables. The 8- to 10-inch-long tongs are the most handy and easiest to use.

VEGETABLE PEELER

Use a carbon-steel swivel peeler, because stainless-steel peelers tend to dull quickly.

WHISKS

Stainless-steel whisks are used to smooth and homogenize mixtures such as vinaigrettes, sauces, and polentas. They are also good for combining the dry ingredients of batters and doughs.

Pantry Essentials

CHILI PEPPERS

If you buy chili peppers in their whole, dried form they will have much more flavor and character than if you bought them preground. Toasting activates the flavor and lends a nuttiness to the chilies. To toast them, place them in a dry skillet over medium heat, turning frequently for 2 to 3 minutes, so that they just begin to puff. Take care not to burn them. After they are toasted, let them cool and crisp up. Then break open the chilies, and discard the seeds (which are believed to be bad for your kidneys) and stem. Now you can grind them into a powder or add them to a dish. If you want to make hot sauce, toast a handful of chili peppers, seed and stem them, put them in a saucepan with water to cover, simmer until soft, and purée them with some of their cooking water—*voilà*, chili paste!

CITRUS

I cannot stress enough the importance of using freshly squeezed lemon juice rather than bottled juice. The difference in taste is just astounding. All citrus fruits juice best at room temperature and will release even more juice if you roll them firmly on a counter to break down the cell structure. I do not strain my lemon juice unless I have extra left over. In that case, removing the pulp will make the juice keep longer, since the pulp can turn bitter over time.

The zests of all citrus fruits contain the essential oils and concentrated aromas of that fruit. They add immensely to the flavor of foods, since a lot of what we taste is actually what we smell.

DRIED SEA VEGETABLES

Hiziki, dulse, arame, wakame, and nori are all excellent sources of a wide variety of essential trace minerals, calcium, and iron. Commonly found in health food stores (or see Sources, page 434), they all keep indefinitely in a cool, dry place. I have included some of my favorite soups, salads, and side dishes that feature these handy staples.

DRY GOODS

As a basic rule of thumb, any substance that contains oil should be kept away from light, heat, and humidity. This includes all whole grains and grain products such as cracked or flaked cereals, whole-grain flours, and meals. Seeds, nuts, and, to a lesser extent, dried beans are also perishable. I keep whole grains and beans in lightproof canisters or in glass jars behind closed cupboard doors. Seeds and shelled nuts are more susceptible to rancidity, so I keep them in the freezer. I keep my whole-grain flour in the refrigerator.

HERBS

When you buy fresh herbs, you often end up with more than you can actually use. To keep herbs fresh, put them in a glass filled with water as soon as you get them home, just as you would a bouquet of flowers. Cover the bouquet with a plastic bag and store in the refrigerator. In general, hardy herbs like thyme, rosemary, and sage will last for up to 3 weeks this way. Change the water every 3 or 4 days to keep them fresh.

Fresh herbs will stay healthy and green for up to 3 weeks refrigerated in a glass of water covered with a plastic bag. Change the water every 3 or 4 days.

The other alternative is to dry them. Spread the fresh herbs out on a sushi mat or a bread rack—anything that will allow air to circulate—and let them dry. When they become fully dried and brittle, rub the leaves off of the stems, put them in a jar, and store them in your cupboard, away from light. They will keep their flavor for a couple of months.

KOMBU

Kombu is a sea vegetable that has been used in Asia for thousands of years as a flavor enhancer and as a mineral supplement. The secret is the white power on the surface, which contains glutamic acids (so don't rinse kombu). These acids are unrefined and naturally balanced by the abundance of calcium and other trace minerals present and will not cause the headaches that affect some people who consume it in its refined state: monosodium glutamate (MSG). Using kombu is a great way to get some minerals into your diet, and it doesn't have a very strong seaweed flavor. Kombu also helps beans cook faster. (See Sources, page 434, for sea vegetables.)

MIRIN

Mirin is a sweet Japanese rice wine. It has an alcohol content of about 8 percent, but when you cook it, most of the alcohol evaporates. Mirin mellows out salty dishes and rounds out acidic dishes such as tomato sauces. It is the classic partner of soy sauce, ginger, garlic, and sesame oil. You can find high-quality mirin made without caramel color and sugar at most health food stores.

MISO

Miso is a fermented soy product that has been inoculated with several different strains of beneficial bacteria. Unpasteurized miso is a living thing and must be kept refrigerated. Since salt controls the rate of fermentation, misos made with more salt are fermented for longer and have more of a chance to develop darker, richer, and more complex flavors. These include dark barley miso and red rice miso. Sweeter, lighter misos such as chickpea and sweet white miso have less salt and are fermented for a shorter time.

OILS

Olive oil does not need to be refrigerated, unless you don't plan to use it for some time (say a few months), but I do recommend that you keep it in a can or dark glass container and store it away from extreme heat. Over the years I have stored my olive oil in cans, special stainless-steel pitchers, ceramic vessels, and glass bottles. My absolute favorite is a heavyweight dark glass Grand Marnier bottle that my friend and colleague Melissa Clark gave me. I fashioned a stopper by cutting a V notch down the side of a wine cork so I can pour the oil in a thin stream. The neck is especially nice, and the bottle has a beautiful shape.

Basic ingredients that make food both pleasurable and digestible include fresh herbs; citrus; traditional vinegar; extra-virgin olive oil; coarse, unrefined sea salt; and fresh pepper.

Seed and nut oils are highly perishable and should be stored in the refrigerator. I only purchase these oils when they come in dark glass or opaque metal canisters.

PEPPER

Pepper should be used in a sensitive way: too much can ruin a dish; not enough means that the flavors won't be as bright as they can be. Preground pepper, like all spices, loses its potency over time—the essential oils dissipate and the pepper becomes bitter. So you should grind your own pepper as you go. Generally, I add pepper at the end of the cooking process, since it becomes more aggressive and concentrated as it cooks.

PRODUCE

Green leafy vegetables are best kept in a cold, relatively humid environment and should be purchased in small quantities. Mushrooms and cucumbers should be kept in paper bags in the refrigerator away from humidity. Members of the onion family such as garlic and shallots keep well in a dark, dry, ventilated area (as do potatoes and tomatoes). I have several wooden baskets that I use to store vegetables outside of the refrigerator.

SALT

Salt is the most important seasoning of all—there is no cuisine without it. It catalyzes, energizes, and harmonizes the flavor of foods and improves texture. Salt can tone down the acid in a dish, bring out and balance the flavors, or punch up the sweetness. Chemically, it dehydrates and preserves.

As far as I'm concerned, refined table salt is terrible. It lacks flavor except for bitterness, contains hardly any minerals, and basically ruins food. Real, unrefined, coarse gray Celtic sea salt contains the eighty-four mineral elements originally in the ocean, which, when rehydrated and mixed with food, completely harmonize with the human body's own fluids. Cooking with sea salt supplements your diet, since some of the essential minerals present in sea salt are not naturally present in the plant world, and even more have been depleted from the soil in which today's crops grow. Celtic sea salt is not harsh and even has a sweetness to it. You can get it for about $2.50 per pound at health food and specialty stores (see Sources, page 434). I also use less expensive kosher salt for salting water that I'm going to be discarding eventually, such as water for cooking pasta. It's also good for scrubbing cutting boards and copper or cast-iron pots and pans.

Because heat allows salt to be absorbed, salt changes the nature of the food, in terms of flavor and texture, throughout the cooking process. I find it best to taste foods as they cook and adjust the salt as necessary. When boiling water for cooking pasta or vegetables, I put salt in only after the water has come to a boil, since it takes salted water longer to come to a boil. Fine sea salt is what I generally use for cakes, cookies, and pies, although kosher salt will work as well.

SOY SAUCE

Soy sauce used to be a great condiment, but today most of it is made with refined salt. I once participated in a blind taste test of twenty-five soy sauce brands for *Cook's Magazine,* and I learned how bitter and harsh most of them are. The traditionally fermented, unpasteurized soy sauces were everyone's favorite. My brand of choice is Nama Shoyu, which has a wonderful, mellow flavor, is a good source of beneficial bacteria, and aids in digestion.

SPICES

It is more economical and you will get much better flavor if you buy your spices whole, not ground. Of course, some, such as turmeric or powdered ginger, are impossible to buy whole, but most are easy to find and grind yourself. I grind hard spices in a clean electric coffee mill; the rest I grind in my mortar.

If you want to get the most flavor from your spices, toast them whole for several minutes in a dry skillet over medium heat (or in a 350°F oven for about 5 minutes) before you grind them. Toasting tenderizes the spices and releases their essential oils. The skins will have parched, and they will be much easier to grind by hand.

UMEBOSHI

Umeboshi is a paste made from plums that have been picked while immature and pickled in brine. I use umeboshi as nonvegetarians would use anchovies or fish paste. It is salty, intense, and complex, with a fruity note.

VINEGAR

Some staples to keep on hand are red and white wine vinegars, unpasteurized cider vinegar, naturally brewed brown rice vinegar, and high-quality balsamic vinegar.

Soups

and Stews

Seasons come and go, and with them the earth reveals different sides of her personality.

I feel that it is important to follow these patterns, so many of my soup recipes use vegetables that correspond to different times of the year. It is a way to celebrate each season and its unique gifts. Some of the soup recipes, like Kamut Berry, Kidney Bean, and "Wild" Mushroom Soup (page 54) are hearty, dark, and full of grains and pulses—perfect for a brisk fall day or a cold winter's night. Others, like Yellow Pepper and Almond Soup (page 44) are lighter, refreshing, and well suited for the spring and summer months.

When I create a soup, I first think of the result. I think about what I'm in the mood to eat. Do I want a hearty, warming soup, or one that's light, zesty, and spicy? Maybe I'm in the mood for something cool and tangy. I think of what is in season, what I will find at the market, which herbs are growing in my backyard, and what leftovers are in my refrigerator. Once my stomach has made up my mind and I have all my ingredients together, I can begin.

In general, there are three basic methods of creating the foundation of any soup: simmering, sautéing, and sweating. To make a typical Western-style soup base, I sweat or sauté aromatic vegetables, most often onions and garlic, in oil or butter. Sautéing is done in hot oil over medium-high heat. It quickly seals in flavors and produces vegetables that are crisp and lightly browned. Sweating, on the other hand, is a slow-cooking process done over low heat, in which you add the fat and the aromatic vegetables at the same time. With Asian-style soups, the vegetables are simmered in their own juices without any fat, and the flavoring comes at the end, with the addition of miso or soy sauce. For most of these soups, I prefer sweating, because it results in vegetables that are tender, sweet, and mild.

There are a couple of keys to successful sweating. First, use a heavy-bottomed pan that conducts heat evenly. If you have a thin pan, it will be difficult to control the heat and the vegetables can easily scorch and stick. Second, it is very important to keep the heat low and the environment moist. I always add a pinch of sea salt, which aids in drawing out the water in vegetables and helps to prevent them from browning. Covering the pan also helps by allowing the steam to condense on the lid so that the vegetables stew very gently in their own juices. If, after all precautions have been taken, the vegetables do start to brown, simply reduce the heat and add a minimal amount of water (1 or 2 tablespoons) to prevent sticking.

My next step is to add the liquid. Now, this can be a light broth, a slightly richer stock, or just plain water. Although the definitions for broth and stock overlap, I differentiate between them by their intensity. I think of broth as an infusion made with the trimmings of the vegetables that you are using in the soup. It's cooked quickly, and the flavor is not concentrated by reducing. Stocks are usually left to simmer for a longer time and allowed to reduce, giving them a more robust taste.

It is a good idea to make your own broths and stocks for several reasons. Let's say you are making an asparagus soup. Normally, you would trim and throw out the bottoms of the stalks, which tend to be tough and woody. Why not throw them into a pot with some water and make a broth? It is an economical and healthful way to get the most out of the asparagus and to intensify the flavor of the resulting soup. On the more esoteric side, by using the whole asparagus, you also become more connected to the garden. You end up having had an enriched experience, and an enriched soup built upon layers of flavor. Granted, we don't always have the time or inclination to do this. Using water is a perfectly acceptable alternative.

If you would like to make your own stock or broth, vegetables that work well include all members of the allium family, such as onions, shallots, leeks, garlic, chives, and scallions; and most mild root vegetables, including parsnips, carrots, burdock, and turnips. Also good are mushrooms, celery, fennel, squash, and tomatoes. I just have a few words of warning. Avoid all cruciferous vegetables (cabbage, broccoli, mustard greens), which are in the mustard family and have strong flavors. Also, you generally want to have a greater proportion of mild vegetables to bolder-tasting ones, because even broths tend to reduce a bit when they're cooked and you don't want the strong-flavored vegetables to dominate. If you're serving the stock or broth on its own, you can season it with sea salt and pepper to taste just before serving. However, if you are using it as a base for a soup, you will have greater control of the finished product if you add your seasonings to the finished soup.

After the stock or broth is ready, create the body of the soup. This simply involves adding the main elements to the liquid. Chunks of vegetables, peas, beans, lentils, and any kind of grain or pasta may be thrown into the pot and left to simmer and soften while they soak up the flavors of the soup base. If you are improvising a soup, think about which vegetables, grains, or beans would taste good together, and try to add the longer-cooking ingredients, like the beans or grains, first, before the vegetables.

To make a puréed soup, I always pass the cooked soup through a hand-cranked food mill. Food mills are very convenient tools. They are easy to use and easy to clean. You can set the mill over your pot and purée anything right into the soup. Using a food mill will result in a slightly coarse-textured purée; if you want a very satiny, smooth soup, it is best to use a food processor or a blender, preferably a hand-held immersion blender. They are relatively inexpensive and very handy. You can also purée soup in several batches using a regular blender or food processor. To avoid painful splatter burns, never fill a blender more than halfway when puréeing hot liquids.

The final two steps in soup making are to decide on a seasoning that will help define the soup and give it character and to come up with an appropriate garnish. I like to season things simply, and not use too many different herbs and spices all at once (except when I'm making a soup that uses a spice blend, such as a harissa or curry powder). I think salt is the most important seasoning, and I use sea salt for its excellent taste and mineral value. I choose a garnish that complements the flavor and texture of the soup. Depending on the soup, and my mood, I might use chopped parsley, a chiffonade of basil, a tangy pesto, a dollop of creamy yogurt, a homemade spice oil, or some chopped, toasted nuts or seeds.

The method I use to make stews is slightly different from the one I use for soups, since most stews are not based on a stock or broth. This is because the main ingredients in stews tend to be heartier and more flavorful, so all you really have to do is throw them together and let them simmer. In fact, the most basic stews simply require cutting up vegetables; adding any beans, pulses or grains, water, and seasonings; and letting the whole thing simmer until dinnertime. More complex stews are based on a sautéed base of vegetables onto which the other ingredients and liquid are added. Compared to soups, stews are generally thicker (using less added liquid to start), cook for a longer time, and usually star as the main course in a meal. I find that stews are best suited for autumn and winter meals, when your body craves foods that are warming and filling.

Stocks and Broths

All-Season Vegetable Stock

This basic stock can be used year-round for practically any soup or stew.

1 large onion, cut into $1/2$-inch pieces
2 carrots, cut into $1/2$-inch pieces
1 celery rib, cut into $1/2$-inch pieces
1 parsnip, cut into $1/2$-inch pieces
8 ounces white mushrooms, cut into $1/2$-inch pieces
1 whole garlic bulb, unpeeled and cut in half
6 cups water
2 bay leaves
2 sprigs fresh thyme or 1 teaspoon dried thyme

1. In a 3-quart soup kettle, combine the onion, carrots, celery, parsnip, mushrooms, and garlic. Add the water and bring to a boil. Skim the foam. Add the bay leaves and thyme.

2. Reduce the heat and simmer, uncovered, for 1 hour.

3. Strain.

YIELD: ABOUT 1 QUART

LEFTOVER BROTH OR STOCK

When you prepare any broth or stock, you can always make more than you need and either serve the broth on its own or reserve it for later use. Vegetable broths and stocks are best used within 2 days. They don't freeze very well because they lack gelatin, found in stock made with animal bones, and aren't really worth freezing anyway, because they're relatively quick to make.

Kombu Dashi

This is an all-purpose broth that enhances the flavors of whatever is cooked in it. Kombu dashi is the traditional basis for all Japanese soups.

1 (6-inch) piece kombu
4 cups cold water

In a saucepan over medium heat, combine the kombu and water and bring to a boil. Reduce the heat to low and simmer for 1 minute. Remove the kombu and reserve it for another use. It will keep 2 days in the refrigerator in an airtight container. The kombu can be chopped into bite-sized pieces or thin strips and simmered with beans or grains or in soup.

YIELD: 4 CUPS

Seasoned Dashi

This is a delicate yet intensely flavored broth that is excellent served either hot or cold. It makes a wonderful light meal when poured over soba noodles, tofu, and lightly cooked vegetables.

4 cups Kombu Dashi (page 30)
2 cups dried shiitake mushrooms
1 (2-inch) piece gingerroot, thinly sliced
4 cups water
$3/4$ cup naturally brewed soy sauce
$1/2$ cup mirin
6 tablespoons brown rice vinegar
Nori strips for garnish
Chopped fresh scallions,
     white and green parts, for garnish
Chopped fresh cilantro for garnish

1. In a 3-quart saucepan, bring the Kombu Dashi to a boil. Add the mushrooms and ginger, reduce the heat, and simmer, covered, for 1 hour.

2. Strain the broth and add the water. Stir in the soy sauce, mirin, and vinegar.

3. Garnish with nori strips, scallions, and cilantro and serve.

YIELD: 2 QUARTS, OR 6 TO 8 SERVINGS

Spring Tonic

This tonic is a wonderful way to renew our bodies after a long winter of heavy food and drink. Traditionally, people used to prepare all kinds of healthful spring tonics—broths made from different plants that would help to cleanse the blood, stimulate the gallbladder, clean the liver, and enhance vision. This soup really showcases the quality and freshness of the ingredients and is best when locally grown, freshly picked, briefly cooked vegetables are used.

> 1 small onion, thinly sliced
> 3 or 4 ramps (wild leeks) or scallions, roots trimmed,
>   green and white parts thinly sliced
> 1 bunch red radishes with tops, roots trimmed
>   and thinly sliced, greens coarsely chopped
> 1 tablespoon extra-virgin olive oil
> Coarse sea salt
> 4 cups water
> 1 bunch watercress, tough stems removed
> Freshly squeezed lemon juice
> Snipped chives for garnish

1. In a medium saucepan over medium heat, sauté the onion, ramps, and radish root slices in the oil with a pinch of salt for 2 to 3 minutes, until softened.

2. Add the water, raise the heat, and bring to a boil. Reduce the heat to low and simmer, uncovered, for 15 minutes.

3. Add the watercress and radish greens and simmer for 5 minutes.

4. Remove the pan from the heat, and season with salt and lemon juice to taste.

5. Serve garnished with chives.   YIELD: 4 TO 6 SERVINGS

RAMPS

Also known as wild leeks, delicious, tender ramps grow underneath the forest canopies of the East Coast from Canada to South Carolina and California. These greens have a sweeter, milder flavor than scallions and are becoming increasingly easy to find at farmers' markets. Look for them in late May and early June.

Sweet Corn, Tomato, and Basil Broth

I like to think that if Moses had received an eleventh commandment on Mount Sinai, it surely would have been something like: Thou shalt not eat basil, corn, or tomatoes in the winter, spring, or fall. When summertime comes and these ingredients are at their peak, you will be glad you waited!

Serve this broth seasoned with sea salt or soy sauce to taste and garnished with chopped parsley, or reserve for soup stock.

6 ears sweet corn
1 pound (3 to 4 medium) ripe tomatoes, quartered
1 large sweet white onion, sliced into thin rings
$1/2$ cup fresh basil, roughly chopped
2 quarts cold water

1. Husk the corn and scrape off the kernels. Reserve the kernels for another dish.

2. Place the cobs and silks, tomatoes, onion, and basil in a 3-quart saucepan. Add the water and bring to a boil over high heat. Reduce the heat to low and simmer, partially covered, for 1 hour.

3. Strain the broth and discard the solids.

YIELD: ABOUT 1 $1/2$ QUARTS

Roasted Root Vegetable Stock

I call this a stock because it is much stronger than any of the previous broths. First, a batch of roots is roasted to caramelize their complex sugars. Then, after these are simmered in water, a second round of roots is cooked in the roasted root broth to create a rich and savory stock. This stock is particularly suitable as the base for a hearty mushroom gravy or risotto. It can also play a supporting role in a hearty onion soup or be served on its own, garnished with minced parsley and seasoned with a dash of soy sauce.

2 pounds carrots, cut into 1-inch chunks
2 pounds onions, cut into 1-inch chunks
1 whole garlic bulb, separated into cloves (unpeeled)
2 tablespoons olive oil
3 quarts cold water
$1/2$ pound burdock root, cut into 1-inch chunks (see Note)
$1/2$ pound parsnips, cut into 1-inch chunks
1 small turnip, cut into 1-inch chunks
1 celery rib with its leaves,
    cut into 1-inch chunks
1 (1-inch) piece gingerroot,
    sliced into $1/8$-inch rounds

1. Preheat the oven to 400°F.

2. In a medium bowl, toss together half of the carrots, onions, and garlic cloves with the oil and spread them in an even layer over 1 or 2 baking sheets. Roast for 40 to 50 minutes, stirring occasionally, until they are well caramelized.

3. In a 4- to 6-quart soup pot, combine the roasted vegetables with 2 quarts of the water and bring to a boil over high heat. Reduce the heat to low and simmer, uncovered, for 1 hour.

4. Strain the broth into another pot and discard the vegetables. Add the remaining vegetables, ginger, and 2 quarts water. Bring to a boil over high heat. Reduce the heat to low and simmer for 1 hour.

5. Strain the stock and discard the solids.

NOTE: If you can't find burdock, just use more carrots, turnips, and parsnips to equal a total of 3½ pounds root vegetables.   YIELD: ABOUT 6 CUPS

Preparing Onions

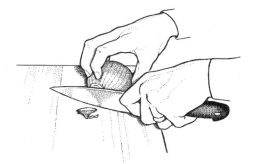

Slice off the stem of the onion.

Place the onion cut side down and slice through the root.

Peel the onion halves.

For slices, cut the onion along the meridian lines.

Cut the sliced onion crosswise to dice.

Pumpkin, Fennel, and Leek Broth

With the cool days of autumn comes the second wave of leeks, which I make good use of here. Sage rounds out the flavors of this broth with its earthy, robust taste.

Serve this broth seasoned with sea salt or soy sauce to taste and garnished with chopped parsley, or reserve for soup stock.

1 pumpkin or other winter squash (about 2 pounds)
2 large or 3 small leeks, split in half lengthwise
1 large fennel bulb with top, roughly chopped
2 or 3 sprigs fresh sage
2 quarts cold water

1. Slice the pumpkin in half. Peel off the rind and scoop out the seeds and pulp. Reserve the pulp for another dish.

2. Add the pumpkin rind, pumpkin seeds, leeks, fennel, and sage sprigs to a soup pot. Add the water and bring to a boil over high heat. Reduce the heat to low and simmer, uncovered, for 1 hour.

3. Strain the broth and discard the solids.

YIELD: ABOUT 1 1/2 QUARTS

Seasonal Miso Soups

Miso soups are great during any time of the year. You can easily change the kind of miso you use with the seasons: try the darker, richer misos in the fall and winter, and the lighter, less-salted ones for spring and summer. Then add whatever vegetables are at their peak.

Spring Miso Soup

2 scallions, trimmed

2 sprigs dill

1 teaspoon light sesame oil

1 bunch (8 to 10) red radishes with tops,
roots thinly sliced, greens coarsely chopped

1 small carrot, grated

3 cups Kombu Dashi (page 30)

10 ounces green peas in the pod (about 2/3 cup shelled)

About 7 tablespoons unpasteurized light barley miso

1 teaspoon freshly squeezed lemon juice

1. Slice the scallion greens into thin diagonals and reserve them for garnish. Slice the white parts into thin rings.

2. Pluck the dill leaves from their stems. Reserve the stems for soup stock.

3. In a medium saucepan over medium heat, warm the oil. Add the scallion whites, radish root slices, and carrot. Sauté for 3 to 4 minutes, until softened.

4. Add the Kombu Dashi, raise the heat, and bring the soup to a boil. Reduce the heat to low and simmer, uncovered, for 5 minutes, or until the vegetables are crisp-tender.

5. Add the radish greens, peas, and dill. Increase the heat and return the soup to a simmer. Continue to cook, uncovered, for 3 minutes.

6. Pour $1/4$ cup of the soup stock into a small bowl. Add the 7 tablespoons miso and stir to dissolve. Add the miso mixture to the soup and simmer for another minute. Season with more miso if desired or add a bit of water if the soup is too strong.

7. Stir in the lemon juice and serve immediately garnished with the scallion greens.

YIELD: 4 SERVINGS

TECHNIQUES FOR DISSOLVING MISO

A suribachi is one of my favorite tools. It is somewhat like a mortar, but the inside of the bowl is unglazed earthenware with grooves. Its tradition and design are perfect for dissolving miso as well as for crushing toasted seeds and puréeing soft cooked foods. Otherwise, the miso can be dissolved in a small bowl using the back of a wooden spoon to break it up and combine it with the liquid.

Summer Miso Soup

1 teaspoon extra-virgin olive oil
Kernels from 1 ear sweet corn
1 small onion, cut into thin crescents
1 garlic clove, minced
4 cups Kombu Dashi (page 30) or Sweet Corn, Tomato, and Basil Broth (page 33)
1 cup tender green beans,
    sliced diagonally into 1-inch lengths
1/4 pound soft tofu, rinsed, dried,
    and cut into 1/2-inch cubes
1 small head tender lettuce, such as Bibb,
    Oakleaf, or Lolla Rossa, cut into thin strips
About 7 tablespoons unpasteurized sweet white rice
    or chickpea miso
6 basil leaves, torn into strips
Snipped chives for garnish

1. In a medium saucepan over medium heat, warm the oil. Add the corn kernels, onion, and garlic. Turn the vegetables over with a wooden spoon to coat with oil and sauté for 3 to 5 minutes, until the onion softens and begins to release its juices. Do not allow to brown.

2. Pour the Kombu Dashi into the pan, raise the heat, and bring to a simmer. Add the green beans and cook for 8 to 10 minutes, until the vegetables are tender. Add the tofu and lettuce and cook for 3 minutes more.

3. Pour 1/4 cup of the soup broth into a small bowl. Add the 7 tablespoons miso and stir to dissolve. Add this mixture to the soup along with the basil and simmer gently for another minute. Add more miso to taste, or water if the soup flavor is too strong.

4. Serve immediately, garnished with snipped chives.   YIELD: 4 SERVINGS

REHEATING MISO SOUPS

In general, miso soups do not reheat well and should be served immediately. The living bacteria in unpasteurized miso is delicate and will quickly lose its subtle flavor and powers of promoting digestion. However, in the interest of time, the soup base can be made ahead and refrigerated for up to 2 days before the miso is added.

Autumn Miso Soup

1 (3-inch) piece wakame (see Sources, page 434)
1 quart water, Kombu Dashi (page 30), or Pumpkin, Fennel,
    and Leek Broth (page 36)
4 dried shiitake mushrooms
1 (1-inch) piece gingerroot,
    sliced into thin rounds
1 onion, diced
1 cup peeled and chopped winter squash
    (bite-sized pieces)
1 cup chopped savoy cabbage
1 turnip, peeled and cut into bite-sized pieces
About $1/2$ cup unpasteurized red (genmai) miso
Finely chopped flat-leaf parsley for garnish

1. In a medium saucepan, soak the wakame in the water for 15 minutes, or until softened. Transfer the wakame to a cutting board, chop into bite-sized pieces, and set aside.

2. Add the mushrooms and ginger to the water and bring to a boil over high heat. Reduce the heat to low, cover, and simmer for 15 minutes.

3. With a slotted spoon, remove the mushrooms and set aside to cool. Remove and discard the ginger.

4. Add the onion, squash, cabbage, and turnip to the broth. Simmer, uncovered, for 10 minutes.

5. Trim and discard the stems of the mushrooms, or reserve for another use. Slice the caps into thin pieces and return them to the soup. Continue to simmer for 15 to 20 minutes, until all the vegetables are tender. Add the wakame and cook for 5 minutes more.

6. Pour $1/4$ cup of the broth into a small bowl. Add $1/2$ cup miso and stir to dissolve. Add the miso mixture to the pot and simmer for 1 to 2 more minutes. Sample and add more miso to taste, or water if the soup is too strong.

7. Serve immediately, garnished with parsley.

YIELD: 6 SERVINGS

Winter Miso Soup

1 burdock root, grated
1 carrot, grated
1 parsnip, grated
1 onion, cut into thin crescents
4 cups Kombu Dashi (page 30) or Roasted Root Vegetable Stock (page 34)
$1/4$ pound firm tofu
$1/2$ cup light sesame oil
$1/2$ cup unpasteurized dark barley (mugi) miso
1 scallion, trimmed and thinly sliced

1. In a medium saucepan over high heat, combine the burdock, carrot, parsnip, onion, and Kombu Dashi and bring to a boil. Reduce the heat to low and simmer, covered, for 25 to 30 minutes.

2. While the soup simmers, drain the tofu and pat dry with a clean towel. Cut the tofu into $1/2$-inch cubes. In a heavy sauté pan over medium heat, warm the oil. Add the tofu and fry 8 to 10 minutes, stirring frequently, until golden brown. Remove the tofu and drain on a paper towel.

3. When the vegetables are tender, add the tofu to the soup. Pour $1/4$ cup of the broth into a small bowl. Add $1/2$ cup miso and stir to dissolve. Add the miso mixture to the soup and simmer for 1 minute longer. Add more miso to taste, or water if the soup is too strong.

4. Serve immediately, garnished with scallions.

YIELD: 6 SERVINGS

Vegetable and Bean Soups

Summertime Corn and Vegetable Chowder

Making this soup always takes me back to my childhood, where I spent many an evening sitting in my grandmother Esther's tiny kitchen. Until she turned ninety-two, she cooked every day of her life and would often serve soup as a first course at dinner. Sometimes she'd purée half of the soup and return it to the pot. That way she could make a textured soup with a velvety smooth background. From a culinary perspective, potato purées are a very simple way to create a creamy base for a soup that is full of flavor and body, yet low in fat.

3 ears sweet corn, kernels scraped, cobs reserved

2 cups peeled and diced new potatoes, about half a pound

1 (3-inch) piece kombu

4 cups cold water, or Sweet Corn, Tomato, and Basil Broth (page 33)

2 tablespoons unsalted butter or extra-virgin olive oil

1 tablespoon extra-virgin olive oil

1 sweet onion, such as Vidalia or Walla Walla, diced

Coarse sea salt

2 garlic cloves, minced

1 carrot, quartered and thinly sliced

1 small celery rib, stem and leaves thinly sliced

1 pound ripe tomatoes, peeled, seeded, and chopped

1 small head tender lettuce, such as
    Bibb or Boston, cut into ribbons

1/4 cup chopped fresh basil

Freshly milled black pepper

1. In a medium saucepan over high heat, combine the corn cobs, potatoes, kombu, and water and bring to a boil. Remove the kombu and reserve for another use. Reduce the heat to low and simmer for 20 minutes, or until the potatoes crush easily with the back of a spoon when pressed against the side of the pot. Remove and discard the corn cobs.

2. While the broth simmers, warm the butter and oil in a 3-quart saucepan over medium heat. Add the onion and a pinch of salt and sauté for 5 to 7 minutes, until the onion is softened. Stir in the reserved corn kernels, garlic, carrot, celery, and tomatoes. Reduce the heat to low, cover, and cook for 15 minutes, stirring occasionally, until the vegetables are tender.

3. Pass the potatoes through the fine holes of a food mill directly into the saucepan, or purée with a handheld immersion blender, and add to the soup. Thin with water if desired. Raise the heat and bring to a boil. Stir in the lettuce and basil. Reduce the heat to low and simmer for 2 more minutes.

4. Season with salt and pepper to taste, and serve.

YIELD: 4 TO 6 SERVINGS

Yellow Pepper and Almond Soup

I came up with this soup after reading a book on Spanish cooking, which inspired me to use almonds as a thickener. It's a spicy late-summer soup with a festive color and can be served either hot or cold.

1 cup whole almonds, peeled
    (see How to Peel Almonds, page 377)
2 tablespoons extra-virgin olive oil
1 large red onion, chopped
Coarse sea salt
1 tablespoon minced garlic
2 sprigs fresh thyme
2 bay leaves
1/4 teaspoon hot red pepper flakes
2 pinches saffron threads
    (about 1/2 teaspoon)
2 cups peeled and seeded tomatoes (canned or fresh)
    with their juice
2 large yellow bell peppers, diced
2 carrots, chopped
Water
Freshly milled black pepper
Snipped fresh chives, basil, or
    cilantro for garnish

1. In a heavy-bottomed 3-quart saucepan over medium heat, combine the almonds and oil and stir with a wooden spoon for 5 to 7 minutes, until the almonds turn a lovely golden color and smell toasty and sweet. With a slotted spoon, remove the almonds to a plate. Drain any oil back into the pan.

2. Add the onion and a pinch of salt, turning the onion pieces over in the oil to coat. Cook gently, covered, for 15 minutes, or until very tender. Do not allow the onion to brown.

3. Stir in the garlic, thyme, bay leaves, red pepper flakes, and saffron, and cook for 3 minutes. Add the tomatoes, yellow peppers, carrots, and enough water to barely cover the vegetables. Raise the heat and bring to a boil. Reduce the heat to low, cover, and cook for 20 minutes, or until the vegetables are tender.

4. While the soup simmers, pound the almonds to a fine meal using a mortar and pestle. Add a few tablespoons of the broth from the simmering soup to the almonds to make a paste. With a rubber spatula, scrape the almond paste into the soup and continue to cook for a few minutes more, until the soup thickens.

5. If the soup seems too thick, add more water. Add salt and pepper to taste. Simmer for another minute to let the flavors meld.

6. Serve sprinkled with fresh herbs.

YIELD: 4 TO 6 SERVINGS

Butternut Squash Soup

This is the quintessential autumn soup, with its pale orange color reflecting the season's falling leaves. In it, winter squash is seasoned with an array of spices that make it taste like a savory, liquid pumpkin pie.

2 tablespoons light sesame oil, olive oil,
  or unsalted butter
1 large onion, chopped
Coarse sea salt
1 tablespoon peeled and
  minced gingerroot
3 garlic cloves, peeled and left whole
1 small handful celery leaves
3 to 4 fresh sage leaves
1 (2-inch) cinnamon stick
3 whole cloves
1/2 cup apple cider or
  apple juice
4 cups All-Season Vegetable Stock
  (page 29), Pumpkin, Fennel, and Leek Broth
  (page 36), or water
3 pounds butternut squash, peeled, seeded,
  and chopped
Freshly milled black pepper
1 tablespoon unsalted butter (optional)
Freshly ground cinnamon for garnish
Minced parsley for garnish

1. In a heavy 3- to 4-quart soup kettle over medium-high heat, warm the oil. Add the onion and a pinch of salt. With a wooden spoon, turn the onion over in the oil a few times. Reduce the heat to low, add the gingerroot and garlic, cover the kettle, and cook gently for 15 minutes.

2. Make a bouquet garni by tying together with kitchen twine or wrapping in cheesecloth the celery leaves, sage, cinnamon stick, and cloves.

3. Add the bouquet garni to the kettle. Then add the apple cider, stock, and the squash. Raise the heat and bring the soup to a boil. Reduce the heat to as low as possible and simmer, covered, for 30 to 40 minutes, until the squash crushes easily against the side of the kettle when pressed with a wooden spoon.

4. Remove the bouquet garni and pass the soup through the fine holes of a hand-cranked food mill or purée with a handheld immersion blender. Season with pepper to taste. Swirl in the butter if using.

5. Serve the soup garnished with a dash of cinnamon and a sprinkle of parsley.

YIELD: 4 TO 6 SERVINGS

Creamy Pumpkin-Chestnut Soup

Chestnuts were once a staple of the simple diets of working people living in the northern parts of Italy and the Swiss Alps. After the decline of the Roman Empire, when wheat was no longer available and the Spanish hadn't yet brought back corn from the New World, pasta, bread, and polenta were all made from chestnut flour. Sadly, a disease destroyed nearly all of the chestnut trees in the United States and the delicious nuts now have to be imported. Nothing smells more like late autumn to me than the smoky, sweet scent of roasting chestnuts on the sidewalks of New York.

1 pound fresh chestnuts
3 tablespoons light sesame oil
   or extra-virgin olive oil
2 cups diced onions
4 cups peeled and cubed pumpkin
   or butternut squash (1-inch pieces)
4 garlic cloves, peeled
Pinch hot red pepper flakes (optional)
1 cinnamon stick
1 large sprig fresh rosemary
1 bay leaf
6 cups water
1/2 teaspoon balsamic vinegar
Coarse sea salt
Freshly milled black pepper

1. In a saucepan over high heat, bring 2 quarts of water to a boil. Score the chestnuts by making an "X" with the tip of a sharp knife. Drop the chestnuts into the saucepan and boil for 30 minutes, or until they peel easily. Drain them in a colander and cool briefly under cold running water. Peel the chestnuts, reserve the meat, and discard the shells.

2. In a heavy 3- to 4-quart soup pot over medium heat, warm the oil. Add the onions and sauté for 10 minutes, until lightly browned. Add the chestnuts, squash, garlic, and red pepper flakes. Raise the heat to medium-high and sauté, stirring occasionally, for 5 minutes.

3. Make a bouquet garni by tying together with kitchen twine or wrapping in cheesecloth the cinnamon, rosemary, and bay leaf.

4. Add the water and bouquet garni and bring the mixture to a boil. Reduce the heat to low and simmer, covered, for 30 minutes, or until the squash and chestnuts are tender. Remove and discard the bouquet garni. Add the vinegar.

5. Transfer the soup, in batches, to a blender and purée until creamy. (To avoid painful splatter burns, never fill a blender more than halfway when puréeing hot foods, or purée the soup in the pot with an immersion blender.)

6. Season with salt and pepper to taste, and serve.

YIELD: 6 SERVINGS

Apple, Fennel, and Walnut Soup

This is a special-occasion soup that's worth the effort. Your guests will applaud you even more if you use freshly harvested walnuts and apples to make this the best-tasting soup of the autumn.

FOR THE SPICE BLEND:
$1/2$ teaspoon ground coriander seeds
$1/2$ teaspoon ground cinnamon
3 whole cloves, ground,
    or a pinch of ground cloves
$1/4$ teaspoon ground cumin seeds
$1/8$ teaspoon cayenne pepper
1 teaspoon ground turmeric

FOR THE SOUP:
1 large or 2 small leeks
2 fennel bulbs
4 cups cold water or
    more as needed
1 (4-inch) piece kombu
1 teaspoon whole fennel seeds
2 tablespoons unsalted butter or olive oil
Coarse sea salt
2 Granny Smith apples, peeled and diced
1 tablespoon unbleached all-purpose flour
1 cup freshly toasted walnut pieces
    (see How to Toast Walnuts, page 373), ground
Freshly milled black pepper

1. To make the spice blend, mix together the coriander, cinnamon, cloves, cumin, cayenne, and turmeric in a small bowl. Set aside.

2. To make the broth, chop the white and tender green parts of the leeks, reserving the trimmings, and set aside. Trim and chop the fennel bulbs. Combine the leek and fennel trimmings in a 3-quart saucepan with the 4 cups water, kombu, and fennel seeds. Bring the broth to a boil over high heat. Reduce the heat to low and simmer, partially covered, for 30 minutes.

3. While the broth simmers, warm the butter in a 4-quart soup kettle over medium heat. Add the leeks and a pinch of salt and sauté gently for 7 to 8 minutes. Be careful to adjust the heat to prevent browning.

4. Stir in the fennel, apples, flour, spice mixture, and ground walnuts, and continue to simmer for another 8 to 10 minutes, stirring occasionally.

5. Strain the broth into the leek mixture. Raise the heat and bring the soup to a boil. Reduce the heat to low and simmer, partially covered, for 25 to 30 minutes, until the fennel pieces crush easily with the back of a wooden spoon.

6. Pass the soup through the medium holes of a hand-cranked food mill into a bowl, or purée it with a handheld immersion blender. Wash out the soup pot and pass the soup through a sieve back into the pot. Add more water to thin the soup to desired consistency.

7. Season with salt and pepper to taste, and serve.

YIELD: 4 TO 6 SERVINGS

Broccoli-Mushroom Soup

Most people in America think that broccoli is only good when it's cooked just until it's bright green and still crispy. But the Italians know that if you overcook broccoli, another characteristic of the vegetable comes through—it becomes meltingly tender and delicious. I use the stalks too because they are the sweetest, most flavorful part of the vegetable. The potatoes and mushrooms give the soup a great body and flavor.

6 tablespoons olive oil
1 large onion, diced
1 whole garlic bulb, separated into cloves (unpeeled)
2 shallots, peeled and halved
Coarse sea salt
1 pound cremini mushrooms,
    thinly sliced
2 tablespoons mirin or dry sherry
Cold water
2 sprigs fresh thyme
1 teaspoon freshly ground caraway seeds
1 pound russet potatoes,
    peeled and diced
1 head broccoli, stalks peeled and sliced,
    florets chopped
2 quarts All-Season Vegetable Stock
    (page 29) or water
2 tablespoons naturally brewed soy sauce
Freshly squeezed lemon juice
Freshly milled black pepper
1 small bunch flat-leaf parsley,
    stems removed, leaves minced (about $1/3$ cup)

1. In a heavy 4- to 6-quart soup kettle over high heat, combine 4 tablespoons of the oil, the onion, garlic, and shallots and bring to a simmer. Reduce the heat to as low as possible and stir in 1 teaspoon salt with a wooden spoon. Cover the kettle and cook for 40 to 50 minutes, until the vegetables are meltingly tender.

2. In a separate pan over high heat, brown the mushrooms in the remaining 2 tablespoons oil until well caramelized, 8 to 10 minutes. Deglaze the pan with the mirin and several tablespoons of cold water. Add the mushrooms and their juices to the onion mixture.

3. Add the thyme, caraway, potatoes, broccoli, and the stock to the kettle. Raise the heat and bring the soup to a boil. Reduce the heat to low and simmer, uncovered, for 30 minutes.

4. Remove and discard the thyme. Stir in the soy sauce.

5. Pass the soup through the fine holes of a food mill or purée with a handheld immersion blender.

6. Season with lemon juice, salt, and pepper to taste. Stir in the parsley and serve.

YIELD: 6 SERVINGS

DEGLAZING

Often after foods have been sautéed in some form of fat, a glaze of concentrated flavor and caramelized bits of food forms at the bottom of the pan. Deglazing is done by heating a small amount of liquid such as wine, water, or stock in the pan and stirring to dissolve the glaze and loosen the stuck bits of food. The liquid is then added back into the dish.

Kamut Berry, Kidney Bean, and "Wild" Mushroom Soup

Kamut is an ancient nonhybrid variety of wheat that was rediscovered in Egyptian tombs and imported recently to the United States. It is one of the largest whole grains, with a beautiful golden-brown color, chewy texture, and nutty taste. A welcome addition to soups, salads, and pilafs, it is widely available in whole berry and ground form at health and gourmet food stores.

I like to eat mushrooms in the springtime because I associate them with the earth's energy and quick upward growth at the end of the winter. Of course, wild mushrooms can be foraged in the summer and fall and are in markets year-round. In general, mushrooms are very light and have a cleansing effect on your system. If you have foraged for fresh wild mushrooms yourself, this soup will be all the better. However, any domesticated exotic mushrooms will do.

$1/2$ cup dried red kidney beans, sorted

$1/2$ cup whole-grain kamut

1 sprig fresh thyme

1 sprig fresh sage

4 cups All-Season Vegetable Stock (page 29) or water

2 tablespoons unsalted butter or extra-virgin olive oil

1 onion, finely diced

1 carrot, finely diced

1 celery rib with leaves, finely chopped

1 cup finely sliced savoy cabbage

8 ounces mushrooms, thinly sliced

2 garlic cloves, chopped

Coarse sea salt

2 tablespoons naturally brewed soy sauce

1 teaspoon cider or brown rice vinegar

Freshly milled black pepper

Chopped fresh parsley for garnish

1. Combine the beans and kamut in a strainer and rinse briefly under cold running water. Place them in a bowl with 4 cups cold water and soak for 6 to 8 hours at room temperature (or for up to 24 hours in the refrigerator).

2. Make a bouquet garni by tying together with kitchen twine or wrapping in cheesecloth the thyme and sage.

3. Drain the beans and kamut. Combine with the stock and the bouquet garni in a pressure cooker and cook under full pressure (15 pounds) for 30 minutes (see The Pressure Cooker Method, page 229). Alternatively, simmer the mixture in a pot for 1 to $1^1/_2$ hours, until tender.

4. While the beans cook, warm the butter in a skillet over medium heat. Add the onion, carrot, celery, cabbage, mushrooms, garlic, and salt and sauté for 5 to 7 minutes until softened. Reduce the heat to low, cover, and cook gently for 10 to 15 minutes more.

5. With a rubber spatula, scrape the vegetables and their juices into the beans. Add the soy sauce and vinegar and simmer for 15 minutes to meld the flavors. Discard the bouquet garni.

6. Season with salt and pepper to taste. Garnish with parsley and serve.

YIELD: 4 TO 6 SERVINGS

Rutabaga Soup with Sizzling Spice Oil

This soup is the very essence of rutabaga and really shows off all of its best characteristics. A base of slowly sautéed onions and toasted flour tames the rutabaga's more assertive qualities and brings out its natural sweetness. The soup is finished with an intense, fragrant spice oil, which adds richness to the soup and accentuates the inherent spiciness of the rutabaga itself.

To serve, pass around bowls of the steaming soup and then a dish of the spice oil separately. This allows each person to flavor and enrich his own bowl of soup to taste.

1 large onion, diced
4 tablespoons unsalted butter, sunflower oil, or olive oil
Coarse sea salt
1 teaspoon freshly ground caraway seeds
2 garlic cloves, peeled and left whole
1 large rutabaga, peeled and cut into 1-inch chunks
1 1/2 tablespoons unbleached all-purpose flour
Cold water
Freshly milled black pepper
Sizzling Spice Oil (page 365)

1. In a heavy 3- to 4-quart saucepan over medium heat, sauté the onion in the butter and 1/2 teaspoon salt. Reduce the heat, cover, and cook gently for 20 minutes.

2. Stir in the caraway, garlic, rutabaga, and flour. Raise the heat and sauté for 5 more minutes.

3. Add enough cold water to cover the vegetables by 1 inch, and bring to a boil. Reduce the heat to low, cover, and simmer for 30 to 40 minutes, until the rutabaga crushes easily against the side of the pan with the back of a spoon.

4. Pass the soup through the fine holes of a food mill or purée with a handheld immersion blender.

5. Add salt and pepper to taste. Serve with the spice oil on the side.

YIELD: 4 TO 6 SERVINGS

Winter Minestrone with Parsley Pesto

A steaming pot of this soup, a fresh warm loaf of wild-yeasted bread, and a bottle of Rhône wine: This is the stuff of dreams made real by loving hands. Shared with friends and enemies alike, it could be the beginning of peace on earth.

If you choose to make this soup a day ahead, wait until the last minute to cook and add the pasta.

1 tablespoon extra-virgin olive oil

2 leeks, white and tender green parts chopped

1 celery rib with leaves, sliced

1 cup sliced savoy cabbage

2 carrots, sliced

2 cups peeled and cubed winter squash

4 to 5 fresh sage leaves, chopped

6 cups Roasted Root Vegetable Stock (page 34) or water

3 cups cooked beans (half Great Northern and half pinto
    is my favorite combination), from 1 cup dried beans
    (see page 226), drained

Coarse sea salt

3/4 cup small-shaped pasta or broken spaghetti

Freshly milled black pepper

Parsley Pesto (page 378) for garnish

1. In a heavy 3- to 4-quart soup kettle over medium heat, warm the oil. Add the leeks, celery, cabbage, carrots, and squash. Sauté for 5 to 7 minutes, until softened.

2. Add the sage and stock, raise the heat, and bring to a boil.

3. Add the beans, reduce the heat to low, and simmer, covered, for 20 to 30 minutes, until the vegetables are tender.

4. While the soup cooks, bring 4 cups water to a boil in a separate pot over high heat. Add 1 teaspoon salt. When the water returns to a boil, stir in the pasta and cook for 6 to 8 minutes until al dente. Drain the pasta and add it to the soup.

5. Season the soup with salt and pepper to taste and serve garnished with the pesto.

YIELD: 4 TO 6 SERVINGS

Creamy White Bean–Garlic Soup with Rosemary

This is a very simple, very classic soup—there isn't much you have to do to get a lot of flavor out of it. You don't need to make a stock because the slowly cooked vegetables and the herbs will create the flavor. If you have some vegetable stock on hand, by all means use it, but it's not necessary.

2 cups dried Great Northern beans, sorted, soaked,
    and rinsed (see page 226)
6 cups cold water or more as needed
1 celery rib with leaves, halved
1 (3-inch) piece kombu
1 bay leaf
4 tablespoons extra-virgin olive oil
2 onions, thinly sliced
6 to 8 plump garlic cloves,
    peeled and left whole
1 tablespoon finely chopped fresh rosemary
2 tablespoons (or to taste) freshly
    squeezed lemon juice
Coarse sea salt
Freshly milled black pepper

1. In a heavy-bottomed 3-quart pot over high heat, combine the beans and water and bring to a boil. Skim off and discard any foam that rises to the top. Add the celery, kombu, and bay leaf. Reduce the heat to low and simmer, covered, for 30 minutes.

2. In a sauté pan over medium heat, warm the oil. Add the onions, garlic, rosemary, and a pinch of salt. With a wooden spoon, turn the vegetables several times to coat them with oil. Cover, reduce the heat to low, and cook gently for 30 minutes, or until the onions and garlic are meltingly tender.

3. Remove the celery, kombu, and bay leaf from the beans and discard. Scoop out 1 cup of the bean water. Add the onion mixture to the beans, then deglaze (see page 53) the sauté pan with the bean water. Return this to the soup and continue simmering until the beans are tender and crush easily when pressed against the side of the pot with the back of a spoon, 45 minutes to an hour.

4. Pass the soup through the fine holes of a food mill or purée with a handheld immersion blender.

5. Add additional water to thin the soup to desired consistency. Add the lemon juice, salt, and pepper to taste. Serve piping hot.

YIELD: 4 TO 6 SERVINGS

Preparing Garlic

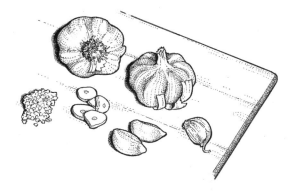

Garlic keeps best in a dry, ventilated place (a small covered basket works well) and will remain crisp and easy to peel. To peel garlic, dislodge a clove from the head and squeeze it between your thumb and index finger. The skin will snap and easily peel off the flesh.

Use garlic in different ways to provide different flavors and aromas. Whole heads can be wrapped in foil and baked. Use unpeeled cloves for broths. Peeled, whole cloves are good for flavoring oils and slow-cooked stews, casseroles, and bean dishes. Sliced garlic enlivens and decorates sautéed greens and other vegetables. Finely chopped garlic gives good flavor to quickly sautéed mushrooms as well as pungency to chopped fresh herbs and garnishes, savory spreads, and dips.

THE SWEETEST GARLIC

In some recipes, I leave my peeled garlic cloves whole because I want them sweet and subtle. If I chop them up, they will throw off too much flavor, which can be overpowering. If you don't want to peel a lot of garlic cloves, you can cut a couple of garlic bulbs on the diagonal, wrap them in cheesecloth, and just throw them in with the beans. Retrieve the garlic before puréeing the soup.

Curried Red Lentil Soup

The freshly made curry powder I use in this soup really enlivens both its fragrance and flavor. When you taste it, you'll undoubtedly see why homemade curry is so much better than store-bought.

1½ cups split red lentils, sorted and rinsed
1 (3-inch) piece kombu
2 quarts cold water
1 large onion, finely diced
1 carrot, sliced
1 celery rib with leaves, halved lengthwise and chopped
2 tablespoons unsalted butter or light sesame oil
1 tablespoon Mellow Curry Powder (page 358)
Coarse sea salt
Chopped fresh cilantro and plain yogurt for garnish

1. In a medium saucepan over high heat, combine the lentils with the kombu and water and bring to a boil.

2. Skim off and discard any foam that rises to the surface, reduce the heat to low, and simmer, partially covered, until the lentils are tender, 30 to 45 minutes, depending on the age of the lentils.

3. While the lentils simmer, combine the onion, carrot, celery, butter, curry powder, and ½ teaspoon salt in a heavy skillet. Sauté over high heat, 2 to 3 minutes, until vegetables are lightly browned. Reduce the heat to low, cover, and cook for 15 minutes.

4. Remove and discard the kombu.

5. Using a rubber spatula, scrape the vegetables and their juices into the lentils. Simmer the soup for 5 to 10 minutes to meld the flavors.

6. Season with additional salt to taste and serve garnished with cilantro and yogurt.

YIELD: 4 TO 6 SERVINGS

Hearty Stews

Wild Mushroom Stew
with Panfried Tofu

Mushrooms are one of my favorite vegetables for roasting. Since they have a very high water content, their essence is best brought out when they caramelize under high heat. In the oven, you can spread them out over a large surface (the baking pan) and reduce them very conveniently. If you sauté the mushrooms instead, you will have to cook them in batches because they won't all fit in one pan.

1 pound portobello mushrooms, stems removed and caps sliced thick
$1/2$ pound white button mushrooms, stems removed and caps sliced thick
$1/4$ pound shiitake mushrooms, stems removed and caps sliced thick
$1/4$ pound oyster mushrooms, stems removed and caps sliced thick
3 tablespoons extra-virgin olive oil
3 leeks, white and tender green parts, coarsely chopped
1 whole garlic bulb, cloves sliced
1 teaspoon chopped fresh thyme
1 tablespoon chopped fresh tarragon
1 tablespoon chopped fresh rosemary
Coarse sea salt
Olive oil for frying
1 pound firm tofu, rinsed, patted dry,
    and cut into $1/2$-inch cubes
$1 1/2$ cups All-Season Vegetable Stock (page 29), Roasted Root Vegetable Stock
    (page 34), or water
3 tablespoons naturally brewed soy sauce
2 tablespoons mirin
1 tablespoon arrowroot powder dissolved in 2 tablespoons cold water
Freshly milled black pepper
Freshly chopped parsley for garnish
3 tablespoons lightly toasted pine nuts for garnish

1. Preheat the oven to 450°F. Toss the mushrooms in a bowl with 2 tablespoons of the extra-virgin olive oil. Spread them evenly over a jelly-roll pan or cookie sheet and roast in the middle of the oven for 30 minutes, stirring occasionally to maintain even browning.

2. While the mushrooms roast, warm the remaining 1 tablespoon extra-virgin olive oil in a heavy 3-quart saucepan over medium heat. Add the leeks, garlic, thyme, tarragon, rosemary, and salt; stir to coat with the oil. Reduce the heat to low, cover, and cook gently for 15 minutes, until meltingly tender.

3. In a heavy sauté pan, pour in the olive oil to a depth of $^1/_2$ inch and heat over medium heat. Add the tofu cubes and fry until golden and crisp. Remove the tofu and drain on paper towels.

4. With a rubber spatula, scrape the roasted mushrooms and their juices into the leek mixture. Add the fried tofu, stock, soy sauce, and mirin. Raise the heat and bring to a boil. Reduce the heat to low and (cook gently) for 5 to 7 minutes to meld the flavors.

5. Add the dissolved arrowroot powder to the pan and stir until the stew thickens. Cook gently for another 5 minutes.

6. Season with salt and pepper to taste and serve garnished with chopped parsley and toasted pine nuts.

YIELD: 4 TO 6 SERVINGS

REUSING OIL

If there is a significant amount of oil left over from panfrying, it can be saved for one more use, provided it did not reach the point at which it began to smoke. To save the oil, turn off the heat and pour it through a fine-mesh sieve into a bowl. Let the oil cool to room temperature. Any leftover food particles will settle to the bottom. Slowly pour the oil into a clean glass jar. The oil should keep, well sealed and in the refrigerator, for up to 2 weeks.

Seitan Bourguignon

This is a vegetarian version of a typical French peasant stew that is usually made with the cheapest cuts of beef possible. It is a long-simmered, home-style stew with a deep, robust flavor. Since the recipe calls for only 2 cups of wine—roughly half a bottle—make sure to choose a good one, since you will probably be drinking the rest!

2 whole garlic bulbs, cloves peeled and left whole
1 cup extra-virgin olive oil
3 sprigs fresh thyme
1 sprig fresh sage
2 sprigs fresh parsley
2 cups medium-bodied, dry red wine,
    preferably from Burgundy
4 tablespoons naturally brewed soy sauce
2 tablespoons mirin
3/4 teaspoon freshly milled black pepper
1 teaspoon coarse sea salt
2 bay leaves
2 strips fresh orange zest
1 1/2 pounds seitan, preferably homemade (page 289),
    drained and cut into 1-inch cubes
1 large onion, roughly chopped
1 carrot, sliced into bite-sized chunks
1 large celery rib with leaves,
    cut into 1-inch pieces
2 tablespoons tomato paste
1 1/2 tablespoons unbleached all-purpose flour
1 pound cremini or white button mushrooms,
    left whole if small, halved or quartered if large
Chopped fresh parsley for garnish

1. In a small pan over medium heat, combine the garlic and oil and bring to a simmer. Reduce the heat to low and poach the garlic until it turns pale gold, about 20 minutes. Strain the oil into a clean glass jar. Reserve the garlic.

2. Make a bouquet garni by tying together with kitchen twine or wrapping in cheesecloth the thyme, sage, and parsley.

3. In a large bowl, whisk together the wine, soy sauce, mirin, $1/4$ cup of the garlic oil, pepper, and $1/2$ teaspoon of the salt. Add the bouquet garni, bay leaves, and orange zest. Add the seitan, cover the bowl with a plate, and set aside to marinate for 1 hour at room temperature, or for up to 8 hours in the refrigerator.

4. In a heavy 4-quart flameproof casserole over medium heat, warm 2 tablespoons of the garlic oil. Add the onion and remaining $1/2$ teaspoon salt and sauté until the onion softens, about 5 minutes. Add the carrot, celery, tomato paste, and flour. Cook for 5 more minutes, stirring with a wooden spoon to prevent sticking.

5. Pour all but $1/4$ cup of the seitan marinade over the casserole. With a wooden spoon, scrape up any browned flour stuck to the bottom of the casserole. Raise the heat and bring to a boil. Reduce the heat to low and simmer, covered, for 40 to 50 minutes.

6. Preheat the oven to 375°F.

7. While the vegetables simmer, toss the mushrooms with the seitan, leftover marinade, and 1 tablespoon of the garlic oil. Spread the seitan-mushroom mixture in a baking dish large enough to hold it in a single layer. Roast in the oven for about 30 minutes, stirring occasionally, until the mushrooms are well browned.

8. Remove the bouquet garni, orange zest, and bay leaves from the vegetables. Add the seitan-mushroom mixture to the pot and stir to combine. Add the reserved poached garlic and a bit more water if the stew is too thick. Simmer gently for 10 minutes to meld the flavors.

9. Serve garnished with chopped parsley.

YIELD: 4 TO 6 SERVINGS

Three Sisters Stew
with Corn Dumplings

In Iroquois folklore, the Three Sisters—corn, squash, and beans—are respected as deities that protect the garden. The cornerstone of most Native American cuisines, these vegetables also have a unique three-way relationship when growing. The beans add nitrogen to the soil, the sturdy cornstalks provide poles for the beans to climb, and the squash spreads out over the ground, preventing weeds from growing and keeping the soil from drying out. This sisterly bond made Native American gardens beautiful with glorious earthy shades and provided sustenance for the farmers who tended the fields.

FOR THE DUMPLINGS:

1 cup masa harina

3/4 cup water

1/2 teaspoon sea salt

1 tablespoon sunflower oil or olive oil or
softened unsalted butter

FOR THE STEW:

1 cup dried pinto beans,
sorted and soaked (see page 226)

2 tablespoons light sesame oil, sunflower oil,
or olive oil

1 large leek, white and tender green parts sliced

1 carrot, sliced

1 pound winter squash, peeled, seeded, and
cut into bite-sized pieces

1 small jalapeño pepper (optional)

1 (14-ounce) can tomatoes with their juice

2 sprigs fresh thyme or 1/2 teaspoon dried thyme

1 sprig fresh sage

Coarse sea salt

Freshly milled black pepper

2 cups thinly sliced Swiss chard, tough ribs removed

Toasted Pumpkin Seeds (page 383) for garnish

Chopped fresh cilantro for garnish

1. To make the dumplings, put the masa harina in a medium bowl. In a small saucepan over high heat, bring the water to a boil. Whisk in the salt and oil and pour over the masa. Stir with a wooden spoon to form a soft dough. Cover the bowl with a plate and set aside.

2. Combine the beans with 2 cups water in a pressure cooker and cook at full pressure (15 pounds) for 30 minutes (see The Pressure Cooker Method, page 229).

3. In a heavy 3-quart saucepan over medium heat, warm the oil. Add the leek, carrot, squash, and jalapeño pepper. Sauté for 10 minutes, stirring occasionally to prevent browning.

4. Pass the tomatoes through the smallest holes of a food mill directly into the saucepan. Add the thyme and sage. Bring the beans down from pressure and pour them, with their juice, into the saucepan. Raise the heat and bring to a boil. Reduce the heat to low and simmer, uncovered, until the vegetables and beans are tender, 20 to 30 minutes.

5. While the stew simmers, add $1/2$ inch of water to a pot fitted with a steamer and bring to a boil. Form the masa dough into bite-size oblong dumplings. Steam the dumplings, covered, for 8 to 10 minutes, or until cooked through.

6. Add the steamed dumplings to the stew and season to taste with salt and pepper. Stir in the Swiss chard. Continue to simmer, uncovered, for 5 minutes until the chard is cooked through.

7. Serve garnished with the pumpkin seeds and chopped cilantro.

YIELD: 4 TO 6 SERVINGS

Black Bean and Bell Pepper Chili with Seitan

This is a medium-hot chili, with distinctive layers of flavor and texture. Pure chipotle powder gives it its special flavor.

1 1/2 cups dried black beans,
    sorted and rinsed (see page 226)
3 cups water
4 tablespoons olive oil or light sesame oil
1 large red onion, diced
1 pound seitan, preferably homemade
    (page 289), finely chopped
1 red bell pepper, finely diced
1 green bell pepper, finely diced
1 yellow bell pepper, finely diced
3 garlic cloves, chopped
2 teaspoons freshly ground cumin
2 bay leaves
2 teaspoons chipotle powder
    (see page 68)
2 (2-inch) cinnamon sticks
1 (28-ounce) can diced tomatoes
Kernels from 2 ears sweet corn
    (reserve the cobs for a summer broth)
1 tablespoon finely chopped fresh oregano
1 teaspoon cider vinegar
1 teaspoon pure maple syrup
Coarse sea salt

1. Combine the beans with the water and 1 tablespoon olive oil in a pressure cooker and cook at full pressure (15 pounds) for 30 minutes (see The Pressure Cooker Method, page 229).

2. In a heavy 3-quart saucepan over medium heat, warm the remaining oil. Add the onion and sauté for 8 to 10 minutes until lightly browned. Add the seitan, bell peppers, garlic, cumin, bay leaves, chipotle powder, and cinnamon sticks. Sauté for 10 more minutes. Reduce the heat and stir occasionally to prevent sticking, until the vegetables soften.

3. Bring the beans down from pressure and add them to the pan with their cooking liquid. Pass the tomatoes through the medium holes of a food mill directly into the pan. Raise the heat and bring to a boil. Lower the heat and stir in the corn kernels, oregano, vinegar, and maple syrup. Simmer, uncovered, for 30 minutes, or until the chili has thickened and you can't wait any longer.

4. Add salt to taste and continue to cook for 5 to 10 minutes. Remove the bay leaves and cinnamon sticks before serving.

YIELD: 4 TO 6 SERVINGS

CHIPOTLE POWDER

Unlike chili powder, which often has garlic powder, cumin, and other spices added to it, chipotle powder is simply pure ground chipotle chilies. I've included a mail-order source for it on page 434, but you can also make it yourself. Toast one large chipotle chili in a hot, dry pan for a minute or two on each side, then grind it in a spice mill. Measure out the correct amount for the recipe and use as directed.

Moroccan-Style Vegetable Tagine with Charmoula-Baked Tempeh

Charmoula is a classic Moroccan marinade that is generally used for fish but can also be used for vegetables. The traditional ingredients are lemon juice, olive oil, cilantro or parsley, garlic, cumin, and paprika, but, as with tomato sauce in Italy, every Moroccan town has a different charmoula; there is no one way to make it. What will ultimately determine the quality of the charmoula is the freshly ground spices, good-quality olive oil, and freshly squeezed lemon juice. Serve this lively stew with basmati rice or Three-Grain Pilaf (page 198).

FOR THE TEMPEH:
$1/2$ cup extra-virgin olive oil
$1/2$ cup water
$1/3$ cup finely chopped fresh parsley
6 tablespoons freshly squeezed lemon juice
4 garlic cloves, crushed
$2 1/2$ teaspoons coarse sea salt
2 teaspoons ground cumin
2 teaspoons sweet paprika
$1/2$ teaspoon cayenne pepper
1 pound tempeh, cut into 1-inch cubes

FOR THE TAGINE:
2 tablespoons extra-virgin olive oil
2 onions, diced
2 carrots, diced
2 celery ribs, diced
1 sweet potato, peeled and diced
2 garlic cloves, peeled and left whole
Coarse sea salt
1 teaspoon cumin seeds
1 teaspoon caraway seeds
1 teaspoon coriander seeds
$1/2$ cinnamon stick
$1/2$ teaspoon sweet paprika

¹/₂ teaspoon whole black peppercorns
2 cups chopped green cabbage
1¹/₂ cups water
1 cup peeled and diced tomatoes, with their juice
1 summer squash, diced
1 zucchini, diced
Freshly squeezed lemon juice (optional)
Chopped fresh cilantro, parsley, or chives for garnish

1. Preheat the oven to 350°F.

2. To prepare the tempeh, whisk together the oil, water, parsley, lemon juice, garlic, salt, cumin, paprika, and cayenne pepper in a bowl.

3. Arrange the tempeh cubes in a single layer in a baking dish. Pour on the marinade and cover securely with foil. Bake for 35 to 40 minutes, until the tempeh has absorbed the marinade. Uncover and bake for several minutes longer to brown.

4. To prepare the tagine, warm the oil in a 3-quart heavy-bottomed saucepan over medium heat. Add the onions, carrots, celery, sweet potato, garlic, and 2 teaspoons salt. Turn the vegetables over in the oil with a wooden spoon, raise the heat, and bring to a simmer. Cover, reduce the heat to low, and cook for 20 minutes.

5. Grind the cumin seeds, caraway seeds, coriander seeds, cinnamon, paprika, and peppercorns in a mortar or coffee mill. Add them to the vegetables along with the cabbage, water, tomatoes, squash, and zucchini. Raise the heat and bring the tagine to a boil. Reduce the heat to low and simmer, uncovered, for 20 to 30 minutes, until the vegetables are tender and the tagine has thickened.

6. Adjust the seasonings with salt or a squeeze of lemon juice to taste. Serve sprinkled with cilantro, parsley, or chives.

YIELD: 4 TO 6 SERVINGS

Posole

This is a vegetarian version of posole, which refers not only to hominy itself, but to a spicy Mexican stew made with the grain. The long-simmering stew is traditionally served at Christmas and New Year's. Serve with Tomatillo Salsa (page 383).

$2/3$ cup dried whole hominy, sorted, soaked for 8 hours and drained
4 cups water
Coarse sea salt
1 cup dried Anasazi or pinto beans, sorted, and soaked (see page 226)
4 tablespoons light sesame oil, sunflower oil, or olive oil
1 large onion, diced
1 large carrot, chopped
1 celery rib, stem and leaves chopped
1 bell pepper, seeded and chopped
1 (14-ounce) can chopped tomatoes, with their juice
2 teaspoons cumin seeds, freshly ground
3 to 4 leaves fresh sage, finely chopped
4 large portobello mushrooms, stems removed
Freshly milled black pepper

1. Drain the hominy. Combine with 4 cups water and $1/4$ teaspoon salt in a pressure cooker and cook under full pressure (15 pounds) for 30 minutes (see The Pressure Cooker Method, page 229). Release the pressure and remove the lid. Drain and rinse the beans, add them to the hominy, and return to full pressure. Cook for 30 minutes.

2. In a heavy 3-quart saucepan over medium heat, warm 2 tablespoons of the oil. Add the onion and sauté for 5 minutes. Stir in the carrot, celery, bell pepper, tomatoes, cumin, and sage. Add $1/2$ teaspoon salt, cover, reduce the heat to low, and cook for 15 minutes.

3. Bring the hominy and beans down from pressure. Add them to the vegetables along with their cooking liquid. Raise the heat and bring to a boil. Reduce the heat and simmer gently, uncovered, until the vegetables are tender and the stew has thickened, 20 to 30 minutes.

4. While stew simmers, preheat the oven to 400°F. Lay the mushrooms, stem side down, in a single layer on a baking sheet. Brush the mushrooms with the remaining 2 tablespoons of oil, and roast for 30 minutes. Transfer the mushrooms to a plate to cool, then slice them into $1/2$-inch squares and add to the stew.

5. Season the stew with salt and pepper.   YIELD: 4 TO 6 SERVINGS

Seasonal

Salads

More so than any other dish, salads really should reflect the seasons. After all, they give us the chance to highlight fruits and vegetables at their peak, allowing us to capture and savor their vibrancy, flavor, and freshness. And, since the nature of the vegetable doesn't change drastically in a salad—as it does in a soup, for example—freshness is key. So, even though some people's concept of salads includes cooked foods, I prefer to keep them raw. In my mind, salads should be light, cleansing, and refreshing—a casual way of presenting produce at its best.

They are also a great jumping-off point for the beginner cook. Preparing and serving raw foods doesn't involve a lot of work or cleanup. And, as soon as you have been introduced to just a few simple techniques, such as handling delicate lettuces and mixing a well-balanced dressing, you can make a fantastic salad in no time.

In this chapter, I take you on a tour of salads through the year, showing off each season by giving you just a taste of some of my favorites.

It's amazing how much variety of produce is available, even in late fall, winter, and early spring, when finding ingredients for salads can be challenging. Every month of the year, I can find delicious fruits and vegetables at my grocer's or the farmers' market. During those colder months I use ingredients such as refreshing celery, sweet fennel, and a variety of leafy greens. You can enhance winter salads by adding complementary textural elements, such as soft, juicy orange slices or crisp, toasty homemade croutons. Most important, try to keep your vegetables seasonal and local. By now you may have noticed that I haven't been using many tropical fruits and vegetables in my recipes. That's because my background doesn't include regions where those kinds of foods grow. This book is written for the temperate zone, the place where I live and work—mangoes just aren't local for me.

If you are ever at a loss, remember that salads can be extremely minimalist and feature a single vegetable, letting it revel in the spotlight all on its own. A tumble of fresh leafy greens piled up nice and high on the plate gives a sense of simplicity, buoyancy, and lightness. And at the peak of the season, what could be simpler than a large platter of tomato slices drizzled with olive oil and sprinkled with salt and freshly milled black pepper?

Or, you can create a more involved salad, composed of many different ingredients, whose distinctive tastes, textures, shapes, and colors beg to be played with. Why not create a salad in two parts? The dressed mushrooms in the salad on page 87 are really set off by the bed of dry greens beneath them. Each component stands out, yet they harmonize and compliment one another. There are even more layers and complexity in the sea vegetable salad on page 88, where peppers, jalapeño, and arame are tossed together in an intense dressing, then served over a bed of crunchy, bitter radicchio or endive. Another way to create an interesting salad is to augment it with a simple garnish. Often I like to add textural accents, such as croutons or the tempeh that tops the warm dandelion salad on page 78. Just remember that the point of a salad is that it is the lightest part of a meal. No matter what ingredients you feature in your salad, the salad needs to feel and appear light.

So, now that you've chosen your vegetables, you need a suitable dressing. For an easy, fail-safe vinaigrette I like to use the following proportions: 1 teaspoon

Dijon-style mustard, 1 tablespoon red wine vinegar, 4 tablespoons olive oil, and salt and pepper to taste.

If you really know your dressing, you can mix it right in the salad bowl and then toss in the raw ingredients. If you're not totally comfortable with that, it's better to make a dressing on the side in a small bowl. When I mix up a dressing, I like to use either a fork or a whisk and first combine the acid ingredients with the seasonings. Acidic ingredients coax the nature and flavor out of the herbs, spices, and pungent foods, such as hot peppers, garlic, and shallots, whereas raw oil would coat these foods and lock in their flavor, smothering the taste. Whisking in the oil afterward preserves the flavors already drawn out by the vinegar or citrus juice.

Tossing is the best way to combine the salad with the dressing. It incorporates air into the salad, making it appear fluffy and light. I like to toss with my hands, but you can use a pair of wooden spoons. Never use a sharp utensil to toss, since it can tear delicate vegetables.

For the most part, I use extra-virgin olive oil because it is the best-quality basic oil around. I don't encourage the use of nut oils in this book for a couple of reasons. Even though they make an excellently flavored dressing, they are extremely expensive and have a short shelf life. Unless you have a very high-quality nut oil, it's better not to use it at all. I'd much rather toast some roughly chopped fresh nuts and add flavor that way. For the acid component, I use either lemon juice, red wine vinegar, white wine vinegar, cider vinegar, balsamic vinegar, or sherry vinegar, which is a dark and slightly smoky sweet red wine vinegar. Since different vinegars have different acidities—wine vinegar is almost twice as acidic as rice vinegar—you'll need to make adjustments to the basic vinaigrette if you substitute one vinegar for another. For example, if you replace a strong vinegar with a mild one, you may need to use a touch more. Conversely, using a strong vinegar in place of a mild one could require more olive oil and salt to balance it. Make sure to taste the dressing as you go.

If you want a dressing that's a little more specialized than my basic red wine vinaigrette, you will need to consider what exactly it is that you are dressing, and match the dressing to the salad. Assertive, dark, hearty greens, such as dandelion, endive, and romaine lettuce, need a flavorful dressing with some richness or sweetness to offset their bitter flavor. A light lemon citronnette would be totally lost on a salad made with intense greens like these, but they would be perfectly enhanced by a zesty balsamic vinaigrette. Another consideration is color. Balsamic vinegar has become so popular and has a very nice flavor, but it doesn't work with every single vegetable. For example, I'd rather dress pale, crispy cucumber slices in a lemon citronnette or light vinaigrette that uses either rice vinegar or cider vinegar. If I need some sweetness I can always add a touch of brown sugar or honey. Here's where you really need to use and trust your aesthetic sense.

Also, keep in mind that the correct proportion of fat to acid will change, depending on what the dressing is intended to accompany. For delicate leafy greens, which contain very little starch and have a high water content, you generally need a high ratio of oil to vinegar, about 3 to 1, because these vegetables cannot absorb the acid. Oil is heavy, so it balances light vegetables. On the flip side, vegetables with more density and more starch require more or less equal amounts of oil and vinegar. The greater proportion of acid will cut the proteins and starches and lighten up heavier vegetables, and adding any more oil would make the salad greasy.

Spring

Baby Spinach Salad with Lemon Citronnette and Shaved Parmesan

During the years I was executive chef of Angelica Kitchen, I often stopped in after work to visit with my friend Chris Trilivas, proprietor and host of the charming little trattoria on East Ninth Street, Col Legno. I would sit back with a glass of wine and gaze into the warm glow of his earthen, wood-burning pizza oven, as one of the kindest people in the restaurant business would talk to me of his love of gardening and his father's ancient overgrown olive groves in Greece, where he hoped to someday move to press oil and make cheese. On any given night you could have found me tucking into this salad feeling immensely well taken care of. Here is my rendition of it—thank you, Chris!

> 1 tablespoon freshly squeezed lemon juice
> 2$\frac{1}{2}$ tablespoons extra-virgin olive oil
> 1 small garlic clove, halved
> 4 ounces baby spinach
> 1 (3-inch) chunk Parmigiano-Reggiano
> Coarse sea salt
> Freshly milled black pepper

1. Put the lemon juice in a small bowl. Slowly whisk in the olive oil until creamy and emulsified. Set aside.

2. Thoroughly rub the inside of a large salad bowl with half of the garlic (save the remaining half for another use).

3. Add the spinach, then toss with the lemon citronnette and divide among 4 salad plates.

4. Using a swivel peeler, shave the Parmesan in wide sheets over the individual salads. Serve with salt and pepper on the side so that everyone can season his or her own salad to taste.

YIELD: 4 SERVINGS

Warm Dandelion Salad with Spicy Tempeh and Sage Vinaigrette

This warm salad is perfect for those damp spring days, when the chill of winter still hangs in the air. The season for dandelions isn't long, so keep your eyes out for them at the farmers' market, where they are sure to be full of character and at their most tender.

8 ounces soy tempeh, cut into $1/2$-inch cubes
3 tablespoons extra-virgin olive oil
$2^1/_2$ tablespoons naturally brewed soy sauce
$1^1/_2$ tablespoons pure maple syrup
Pinch hot red pepper flakes
Water
3 tablespoons cider vinegar
2 teaspoons fresh sage, finely chopped
1 garlic clove, finely chopped
1 bunch dandelion greens (about 1 pound),
　　trimmed and broken into 2-inch pieces
1 cup thinly sliced shiitake mushroom caps
2 scallions, green and white parts,
　　trimmed and sliced

1. In an 8-inch sauté pan, place the tempeh slices in a single layer. In a bowl, whisk together the oil, soy sauce, maple syrup, and red pepper flakes. Pour over the tempeh. Add enough water to cover and bring to a boil over high heat. Reduce the heat and simmer for 20 minutes, until the marinade has been completely absorbed. Transfer the tempeh to a large bowl.

2. In a wide skillet over high heat, combine the vinegar, sage, and garlic and bring to a boil. Turn off the heat and add the dandelion greens, mushrooms, and scallions. Turn everything over several times with a pair of tongs until just wilted.

3. Transfer the greens mixture to the bowl with the tempeh and toss gently to combine. Serve immediately.

YIELD: 4 TO 6 SERVINGS

Chopping Herbs

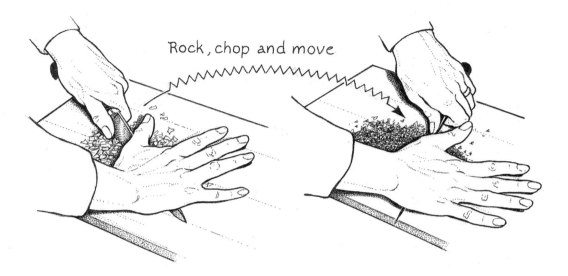

Cleaned leafy herbs such as parsley, cilantro, and dill must be thoroughly dried before chopping. Use a clean towel to blot the herbs or spin them dry in a salad spinner.

Sprout Salad with Ginger Vinaigrette and Sesame-Mint Gremolata

Spring is a time when the earth is quickening, sap is rising, and plants are sprouting. It is the perfect time for cleansing your body with this revitalizing, very light salad, alive with all sorts of sprouts. You can vary the sprouts and use parsley instead of mint.

2 cups snow pea shoots
2 cups mung bean sprouts
1 cup shredded romaine lettuce
1/2 cup clover sprouts
1/2 cup coarsely grated carrot
1/2 cup coarsely grated red radishes
1/2 cup shredded red cabbage
1/2 cup shredded green cabbage
1/4 cup apple juice
3 tablespoons rice vinegar
3 tablespoons extra-virgin olive oil
1 1/2 tablespoons mirin
1 1/2 tablespoons naturally brewed soy sauce
2 teaspoons peeled and freshly grated gingerroot
1/4 cup finely chopped mint or flat-leaf parsley
2 tablespoons lightly toasted hulled sesame seeds
1 garlic clove, finely chopped
Zest of 1/2 lemon, finely grated

1. In a large bowl, combine the pea shoots, mung bean sprouts, lettuce, clover sprouts, carrot, radishes, red cabbage, and green cabbage. Toss gently to mix.

2. In a separate bowl, combine the apple juice, vinegar, oil, mirin, soy sauce, and ginger. Whisk together well. Pour the vinaigrette over the salad and toss lightly to coat.

3. To make the gremolata, mix together the mint, sesame seeds, garlic, and lemon zest in a small bowl.

4. Mound the salad onto individual plates. Sprinkle with gremolata and serve.

YIELD: 4 TO 6 SERVINGS

Peeling Ginger

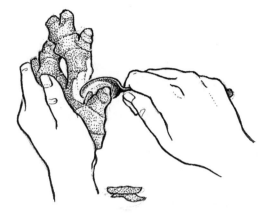

A small metal spoon will easily peel away the skin from the nooks and crannies of fresh ginger without wasting the flavorful flesh.

Summer

Crazy Chopped Salad
with Basil Vinaigrette

Summer is a time when plants are blooming and fruiting like crazy, producing a tremendous amount and variety of foods. This simple salad reflects the different colors and textures of the garden. Look for red, yellow, purple, and striped heirloom tomatoes at your local farmers' market.

3 tablespoons balsamic vinegar
2 garlic cloves, crushed
1 teaspoon whole-grain prepared mustard
Coarse sea salt
5 tablespoons extra-virgin olive oil
2 ears sweet corn
1 cup string beans (about 2 dozen), sliced into $1/2$-inch pieces
4 cups chopped romaine lettuce
2 carrots, chopped
2 fennel bulbs, trimmed and chopped
1 head radicchio, cored and chopped
2 ripe tomatoes, cored and chopped
1 yellow bell pepper, cored, seeded, and chopped
1 medium cucumber, peeled, seeded, and chopped
1 small red onion, chopped
4 or 5 red radishes, trimmed and chopped
2 tablespoons roughly chopped fresh dill
2 tablespoons roughly chopped fresh mint
2 tablespoons roughly chopped fresh cilantro
8 to 10 fresh basil leaves, torn
Fresh goat cheese, feta, or firm tofu for garnish (optional)

1. In a small bowl, combine the vinegar, garlic, mustard, and 1 teaspoon salt. Slowly whisk in the oil until creamy and emulsified. Set aside.

2. Bring a large pot of water to a boil. Add 2 tablespoons salt. When the water returns to a boil, add the corn and beans. Cook for 2 minutes, then drain and shock in a bowl of ice water. Drain again and blot dry on a towel. Slice the kernels away from the cobs. Transfer the kernels and beans to a large salad bowl.

3. Add the lettuce, carrots, fennel, radicchio, tomatoes, yellow pepper, cucumber, onion, radishes, dill, mint, cilantro, and basil to the salad bowl. Pour the dressing over the salad and toss well.

4. If desired, crumble fresh goat cheese, feta, or tofu over the salad and serve.

YIELD: 4 TO 6 SERVINGS

Seeding Cucumbers

Use a small metal spoon to seed cucumbers quickly and easily.

Cucumber, Watercress, and Red Onion Salad with Mint

Mint and cucumber, a classic match made in heaven, really shine in this cooling, juicy summertime salad. And a little salt really brings out the best in crisp, refreshing cucumbers, especially if they are a slightly bitter. If you like, you can substitute 1 tablespoon of chopped fresh dill for the mint, for another awesome taste combination.

2 tablespoons rice vinegar
2 teaspoons mirin or 1 teaspoon cane sugar
2 teaspoons extra-virgin olive oil
1 teaspoon toasted sesame oil
1 teaspoon naturally brewed soy sauce
Pinch hot red pepper flakes (optional)
6 pickling or Kirby cucumbers (about 1 1/2 pounds)
1 teaspoon coarse sea salt
1 bunch watercress
2 tablespoons thinly sliced red onion
2 tablespoons lightly toasted hulled sesame seeds
6 fresh mint leaves, torn

1. In a large bowl, combine the vinegar, mirin, oils, soy sauce, and red pepper flakes and whisk well.

2. Peel the cucumbers and slice them diagonally into $1/4$-inch pieces. Toss them with the salt and transfer them to a colander to drain.

3. Remove the tough stems from the watercress and discard or reserve to use in a soup. Pluck the leaves and roughly chop the tender stems.

4. Blot the drained cucumbers with a paper towel and add them to the bowl with the dressing. Toss to coat. Add the watercress, onion, sesame seeds, and mint and toss again.

5. Serve immediately.

YIELD: 4 SERVINGS

Hearts of Romaine
with Creamy Miso Vinaigrette

Here is my daughter Kayla's favorite way to eat salad: a highly seasoned and creamy vinaigrette in a serving bowl surrounded by crisp, crunchy romaine hearts. No knives, forks, or plates needed! And no melange of fancy tossed mesclun greens—most of which are too bitter for the average child to enjoy—just lots of scooping and munching.

This recipe makes about 2 cups of miso vinaigrette, more than enough for the salad. It is equally good as a dip for crudités or as a dressing for crisp blanched broccoli or cauliflower. You can keep the extra vinaigrette in the refrigerator for up to 2 weeks. Simply blend again before serving.

4 ounces soft tofu
3 tablespoon cider vinegar
3 tablespoons freshly squeezed lemon juice
1 tablespoon mellow white or barley miso
2 teaspoons crushed garlic
2 teaspoons peeled and finely chopped gingerroot
2 teaspoons umeboshi paste
1 teaspoon honey
1 cup extra-virgin olive oil
1 tablespoon finely chopped fresh parsley
2 heads romaine lettuce, trimmed of outer tough leaves down to their hearts

1. In a blender, combine the tofu, vinegar, lemon juice, miso, garlic, ginger, umeboshi paste, and honey. Purée until creamy. Add the oil in a slow, steady stream and blend into a thick, smooth sauce.

2. Pour the vinaigrette into a small serving bowl and garnish with parsley. Place the bowl in the center of a large platter. Separate the leaves from the lettuce hearts, arrange them around the bowl, and serve.

YIELD: 6 SERVINGS

Autumn

Spicy Kim Chee–Style
Cabbage Salad with Arame

Here I've adapted the style of the famous Korean pickled cabbage. In my version, you don't need to bury the salad in your backyard for 4 days, or use fish paste in it, either, but it still has the wonderful flavors of ginger, garlic, and hot chili pepper. The addition of arame, a mild-flavored sea vegetable, is my twist. It contains an amazing balanced source of minerals and is very convenient to use. Arame has a pleasing aesthetic, too—the thin black strands look great with the greens and white in the salad.

$1/2$ cup arame
8 cups sliced napa cabbage ($1/2$-inch strips)
6 scallions, green and white parts,
    trimmed and sliced
1 carrot, coarsely grated
2 garlic cloves, finely chopped
2 teaspoons peeled and
    finely chopped gingerroot
4 tablespoons rice vinegar
    or cider vinegar
2 tablespoons mirin
Coarse sea salt
1 teaspoon hot red pepper flakes
1 tablespoon extra-virgin olive oil
1 teaspoon toasted sesame oil

1. Combine the arame with 2 cups warm water and set aside to swell for 10 minutes.

2. In a large bowl, combine the cabbage, scallions, and carrots.

3. Drain the arame, chop it into 1-inch pieces, and add it to the bowl.

4. In a small bowl, combine the garlic, ginger, vinegar, mirin, 1 tablespoon salt, red pepper flakes, and oils. Whisk to combine and pour over the vegetables. Toss well and refrigerate for 1 hour.

5. Season with additional salt to taste, and serve.

YIELD: 4 SERVINGS

Fresh Mushroom Salad with Lemon-Thyme Vinaigrette

Many of us never think of eating raw mushrooms. Everyone knows how great they are cooked, but few realize that they have another side to them. When dressed with a simple lemon citronnette, a really different, nutty flavor is revealed. I use white button mushrooms, making sure that they are as fresh as possible. To clean mushrooms, wipe them very gently with a damp cloth. Slice and dress them immediately, or they'll turn brown.

2 tablespoons freshly squeezed lemon juice
1 tablespoon white wine vinegar
1 tablespoon finely chopped fresh thyme leaves
1 tablespoon finely chopped fresh parsley
1 teaspoon coarse sea salt
Freshly milled black pepper
6 tablespoons extra-virgin olive oil
10 ounces very fresh white button mushrooms,
    trimmed and thinly sliced
6 cups mixed baby greens, such as spinach,
    mizuna, arugula, or Bibb lettuce

1. In a large bowl, whisk together the lemon juice, vinegar, thyme, parsley, salt, and pepper to taste. Slowly pour in the oil, whisking to emulsify.

2. Add the mushrooms and toss gently to coat evenly with vinaigrette.

3. Add the greens to the mushrooms, toss gently, and serve.

YIELD: 4 SERVINGS

Sea Vegetable Salad with Roasted Peppers and Radicchio

In autumn, the very end of pepper season, I love to grab up the last of the peppers and use them wherever I can. This colorful salad is adapted from a recipe given to me by my dear friend and inspiration, Frank Arcuri, a great chef who passed away about nine years ago. The bitterness from the radicchio and endive, sweetness from the peppers, and spice from jalapeño are in perfect harmony.

1/2 cup packed dulse
1 (3-inch) piece wakame
1 red bell pepper, halved and seeded
1 yellow bell pepper, halved and seeded
1 cucumber, peeled, seeded, and sliced into thin crescents
1 small head radicchio, cored and finely sliced
1 head Belgian endive, cored and finely sliced
2 tablespoons balsamic vinegar
2 tablespoons freshly squeezed lemon or orange juice
1 tablespoon finely chopped jalapeño pepper or 1/2 teaspoon hot red pepper flakes
1 garlic clove, crushed
1 teaspoon finely grated lemon or orange zest
Coarse sea salt
Freshly milled black pepper
3 tablespoons extra-virgin olive oil
1/2 cup coarsely chopped fresh cilantro

1. Preheat the broiler. Place the dulse and wakame in separate bowls and cover each with cold water. Set aside.

2. Place the bell peppers on a baking sheet, cut side down. Broil 2 inches from the heat until black and charred. Transfer the peppers to a bowl and seal with plastic wrap. Set aside for 10 minutes or until they are cool enough to handle. The skins will easily scrape free with the back of a knife. Discard the charred skins, slice the pepper halves into thin strips, and return them to the bowl.

3. Drain the dulse and wakame. Spread out the wakame and cut away any tough veins. Coarsely chop the wakame and dulse and add them to the bowl with the peppers along with the cucumber, radicchio, and endive.

4. In a bowl, whisk together the vinegar, lemon juice, jalapeño, garlic, lemon zest, 1 teaspoon salt, and pepper. Add the oil in a steady stream, whisking to emulsify.

5. Pour the dressing over the vegetables and toss to coat. Refrigerate the salad for 30 minutes.

6. Season the salad with additional salt and pepper to taste. Sprinkle with the cilantro and serve.   YIELD: 4 SERVINGS

Sweet-and-Sour Hiziki

This is my version of a refreshing hiziki dish served in Japanese restaurants all over New York. This delicious, chewy seaweed side dish is packed with flavor and minerals and prepared without the refined white sugar that is often used.

> $1/2$ cup hiziki seaweed
> 1 tablespoon light sesame oil
> 3 tablespoons pure maple syrup
> 2 tablespoons finely sliced scallions, white and green parts
> 2 tablespoons rice vinegar
> 1 tablespoon naturally brewed soy sauce
> Pinch cayenne pepper (optional)
> 2 tablespoons lightly toasted sesame seeds

1. In a medium bowl, combine the hiziki with 3 cups water and let soak for 1 hour, until the hiziki has plumped. Pour the hiziki through a strainer, discard the soaking liquid, rinse briefly, and drain.

2. Warm the oil in a medium skillet over medium heat. Sauté the hiziki for 10 minutes, stirring occasionally. Add the maple syrup, scallions, vinegar, soy sauce, and cayenne. Pour in enough water to barely cover the hiziki.

3. Raise the heat and bring the mixture to a boil. Reduce the heat to low and cook, uncovered, until nearly all the cooking liquid has evaporated and the hiziki is tender.

4. Chill for several hours in the refrigerator.

5. Serve chilled, sprinkled with the sesame seeds.   YIELD: 4 SERVINGS

Winter

Potato, Beet, and Belgian Endive Salad with Toasted Hazelnuts

The charm of this vibrant winter salad is that the potatoes and beets are cooked and dressed separately, while still warm. This allows them to absorb their different seasonings and retain their individuality when they are finally tossed together. The balsamic vinegar in the beets softens the bitterness of the endive, while the lemon lightens up the starchy potatoes. Toasted hazelnuts round out and balance the acidity with their nutty, toasty fragrance, while the caraway and fresh dill hint of the flavors of Eastern Europe, home of my ancestors.

If you like, try garnishing this salad with a Spanish sheep's milk cheese such as manchego, or a crumbled fresh goat cheese, for added creaminess.

FOR THE BEETS:
2 medium beets, trimmed
1 1/2 tablespoons balsamic vinegar
1 1/2 tablespoons extra-virgin olive oil
1 small garlic clove, finely chopped
1/2 teaspoon ground caraway seeds
1/4 teaspoon coarse sea salt
Freshly milled black pepper

FOR THE POTATOES:
2 medium or 4 small red potatoes, peeled and cut into 1/2-inch cubes
1 1/2 tablespoons freshly squeezed lemon juice
1 1/2 tablespoons extra-virgin olive oil
Coarse sea salt
Freshly milled black pepper
3 tablespoons chopped hazelnuts
2 heads Belgian endive
2 tablespoons chopped fresh dill

1. Preheat the oven to 450°F.

2. Wrap each beet in aluminum foil, place on a baking sheet, and roast for 45 minutes, or until easily pierced with a knife. To peel the beets, hold them under cold running water as you rub off their skins. Set the beets aside to cool while you prepare the potatoes.

3. In a basket over boiling water, steam the potatoes, covered, for 8 to 10 minutes, until tender. Transfer them to a bowl and toss with lemon juice, oil, $1/2$ teaspoon salt, and pepper to taste.

4. Cut the cooled beets into $1/2$-inch cubes. Transfer them to a separate bowl and toss them with the vinegar, oil, garlic, caraway, and salt.

5. In a skillet over medium heat, toast the chopped hazelnuts, shaking the pan from time to time, for about 3 minutes, until the nuts are lightly browned and fragrant. Transfer the nuts to a bowl and set aside to cool slightly.

6. Slice $1/4$ inch off the bottom of each endive and discard any bruised outer leaves. Separate the endive into individual petals.

7. Combine the dressed beets and potatoes and toss well. Season with additional salt and pepper to taste.

8. Divide the salad among 4 plates and garnish with endive petals. Sprinkle the hazelnuts and chopped dill on top and serve.

YIELD: 4 SERVINGS

Celery Salad with Pickled Plum Vinaigrette and Toasted Walnuts

Snappy, crunchy celery gets even crisper when soaked briefly in icy water. The assertive dressing, my take on a Provençal anchovy vinaigrette, uses plum paste and balances out the wintery chill of the celery. The walnuts add a warm, complementary crunch to the salad.

> **6 large celery ribs**
> **$1/3$ cup coarsely chopped walnuts**
> **1 tablespoon umeboshi paste**
> **1 tablespoon whole-grain prepared mustard**
> **3 small garlic cloves, finely chopped**
> **2 teaspoons cane sugar or maple syrup**
> **$1^1/2$ teaspoons coarse sea salt**
> **6 tablespoons extra-virgin olive oil**

1. Peel away and discard the tough stringy fibers of the celery. Pluck enough celery leaves to pack $1/4$ cup; discard the rest. Finely chop the leaves and set aside. Slice the stalks on the diagonal into $1/2$-inch-thick pieces about 1 inch in length. Place them in a bowl of ice water and set aside.

2. In a dry skillet over medium heat, toast the walnuts for 6 to 7 minutes until fragrant, shaking the pan occasionally for even browning. Transfer the nuts to a strainer to cool slightly. When cool enough to handle, rub the nuts against the wire mesh of the strainer to remove as much of their skins as possible. Set aside.

3. In a small bowl, combine the umeboshi paste, mustard, garlic, sugar, and salt. Slowly whisk in the oil until creamy and emulsified. Set aside.

4. Drain the celery slices and spin or pat dry. Transfer them to a large bowl and toss with the toasted walnuts and dressing to taste.

5. Divide the salad among 4 plates and garnish with a sprinkling of celery leaves.

YIELD: 4 SERVINGS

Curly Endive Salad with Garlic Croutons and Mustard Vinaigrette

This satisfying winter salad is best made with small baby frisée. If large heads are all you can find, peel away the tough outer leaves and just use the tender inner ones. If you like, you can substitute Belgian endive and radicchio for the frisée.

> 1 head curly endive (frisée)
> 2 garlic cloves, peeled
> 9 tablespoons extra-virgin olive oil
> 1 teaspoon minced fresh thyme leaves
> 3 or 4 French baguette slices, cut into 1/2-inch cubes
> Coarse sea salt
> Freshly milled black pepper
> 2 tablespoons red wine vinegar
> 1 tablespoon whole-grain prepared mustard
> 1 teaspoon pure maple syrup

1. Core the endive with the tip of a sharp knife. Separate the leaves and soak in a large bowl of ice water (or refrigerate in a large bowl of cold water) for 30 minutes.

2. Meanwhile, preheat the oven to 350°F.

3. In a bowl, crush one of the garlic cloves. Add 2 tablespoons of the oil and thyme. Add the bread and toss to coat. Season with salt and pepper to taste. Spread the bread on a baking sheet and toast in the oven for 15 minutes, until crispy and golden brown. Transfer croutons to a bowl to cool.

4. In a bowl, combine the vinegar, mustard, and maple syrup. Slowly whisk in the remaining 7 tablespoons oil until creamy and emulsified. Season with salt and pepper to taste. Set aside.

5. Drain the endive and spin or pat it dry. Tear the leaves into bite-sized pieces.

6. Cut the remaining garlic clove in half and rub it all over the inside of a large salad bowl. Add the endive and toss with dressing. Toss in the croutons and season to taste with black pepper. Serve at once.

YIELD: 4 TO 6 SERVINGS

Vegetables

One of the reasons I love vegetables is their sheer variety. They have more colors, shapes, textures, and flavors than any other kind of food. Some vegetables offer up their goodness in their leaves, some in their stems or roots. We eat the bulbs of certain vegetables and the succulent fruits of others. Vegetables can be hard or soft, juicy or dry, and they all require different techniques to bring out their very best. In the course of this chapter, I hope you'll become familiar with some important methods and principles, and then apply them to vegetables that aren't featured in this book.

Another reason I love vegetables is that they are so good for our bodies. Everyone knows this, but throughout most of the country, vegetables still take a backseat to meat. When we do eat vegetables, we tend to have an aversion to cooking them. We have this idea that the most healthful way of eating vegetables is either raw or very lightly steamed. However, in cultures throughout the Mediterranean, where vegetables form the base of the diet and are eaten throughout the day, they are most often served well cooked. Cooked vegetables provide plenty of nutrients and are easier to digest than raw ones.

As a general rule of thumb, vegetables should be cooked the way they grow. Vegetables that grow in the air should be cooked in the open air. For example, dark leafy collard greens should be blanched in a pot of vigorously boiling water without a lid so that they melt in your mouth after a brief, satisfying chew. Milder greens such as tender kale, bok choy, or Swiss chard can be sautéed briefly in oil over high heat, then covered and gently steamed in their own juices until tender. Root vegetables, on the other hand, come from the ground where they are protected from the sun and wind. They are best cooked slowly, either boiled or steamed in a pot or baked in a covered casserole. Dense-fleshed winter squash, which grows slowly on the vine, is ideally baked for a long time to coax out the best of its flavor. On the flip side, delicate springtime peas, which have a high water content, should be eaten raw or lightly sautéed. Summer brings a bounty of fresh, juicy vegetables such as tomatoes, cucumbers, zucchini, eggplant, and peppers. These vegetables also have a high water content and are best eaten raw, sautéed, or fried. Who would want to boil summer squash? Some of these vegetables can be a little bitter, especially the ones in the nightshade family, such as tomatoes and eggplant, so it is nice to salt them while they're raw to draw out some of their acrid water.

ALL IN THE FAMILY

It's interesting to note which vegetables are related and compare tastes and uses in cooking. The onion family includes leeks, garlic, and chives. Artichokes—both globe and Jerusalem—burdock, and lettuce are related to daisies. The cruciferous family contains a large number of vegetables, including mustard greens, watercress, broccoli, cauliflower, cabbage, kale, kohlrabi, turnips, and radishes. Cucumbers, squash, pumpkins, and melons all belong to the same family of fruiting vines. Legumes, which are featured in the chapter on beans, include green beans, peas, and alfalfa. Some of the most delicious summer vegetables are actually members of the nightshade family and are originally from South America. They include potatoes, tomatoes, eggplant, and peppers. Spinach, Swiss chard, and beets are all related. Finally, there is the carrot family, which has been bred to produce large edible roots in carrots and parsnips, leaves in parsley, fleshy leaf stalks in celery, and a swollen base stem in fennel and celeriac.

A satisfying meal can be made from several types of vegetables cooked in different ways. Marinated steamed beets, fried potatoes, roasted asparagus, sautéed cabbage, and charred red peppers can be prepared separately and then combined in a colorful composed salad. You can also transmute the qualities of a vegetable depending on how you cut and cook it. A carrot, for example, becomes concentrated, sweet, and delicious when cut into large chunks and roasted or braised. But, if you julienne the carrot and serve it raw in a salad or use it in a quick sauté, it will taste fresh and crisp. Many root vegetables are surprisingly delicious and refreshing shredded and served raw—try it sometime with beets, Jerusalem artichokes, or kohlrabi.

Spring Vegetables

Mess o' Peas

Dive into spring with an emerald bowlful of buttery peas. This is like young love blossoming on your plate.

    1 pound green peas in the pod, shelled
    1 cup snow peas, trimmed and sliced in thirds
    1 cup sugar snap peas, trimmed and sliced in thirds
    4 scallions or small spring onions,
        whites and 1 inch of greens, thinly sliced
    1/2 cup water
    3 tablespoons unsalted butter
    1 tablespoon chopped fresh mint
    Coarse sea salt
    Freshly milled black pepper

1. In a saucepan over high heat, combine the green peas, snow peas, sugar snap peas, scallions, water, butter, and mint. Add a pinch of salt and bring to a boil. Reduce the heat to low, cover, and simmer for 4 to 5 minutes, until the peas are bright green and tender.

2. Serve immediately, sprinkled with salt and pepper to taste.

YIELD: 4 SERVINGS

Steamed New Potatoes Dressed for Spring with Lemon, Olive Oil, and Chives

What could be easier than steaming potatoes and tossing them with lemon, oil, salt, and pepper? To me this is the essence of great cuisine. All one needs is the best potatoes, brightest lemon, fruitiest green olive oil, coarse salt, and freshly milled black pepper. A flourish of snipped chives gives the dish a spark of spring.

2 pounds small red new potatoes
$1/4$ cup freshly squeezed lemon juice
$1/4$ cup extra-virgin olive oil
Coarse sea salt
Freshly milled black pepper
$1/4$ cup snipped fresh chives

1. Use a paring knife to peel away a $1/2$-inch-wide strip of skin from each potato.

2. Pour 1 inch of water into a pan and set a steamer on top. Transfer the potatoes to the steamer. Cover the pan and bring to a boil over high heat. Reduce the heat and steam for 20 minutes, or until the tip of a knife slips easily into the potatoes.

3. Transfer the potatoes to a bowl and toss with lemon juice, oil, salt, and pepper. Let the potatoes marinate and cool slightly, turning them over in the marinade every so often to absorb the seasonings.

4. Taste and add salt and pepper if necessary. Sprinkle with chives and serve.

YIELD: 4 SERVINGS

Asparagus with Vinaigrette

This recipe and the one that follows use very simple yet completely opposite cooking methods. In this one, the asparagus is cooked briefly in a large amount of boiling salted water. Serve warm or at room temperature.

4 tablespoons coarse sea salt
2 bunches asparagus (about 2 pounds)
8 tablespoons extra-virgin olive oil
4 tablespoons balsamic or red wine vinegar
Freshly milled black pepper

1. In a large pot over high heat, bring 4 quarts water to a boil. Add the salt.

2. Trim the bottom $1/2$ inch of each asparagus stalk and discard. Using a vegetable peeler, remove the tougher skin from the bottom 2 inches of the stalk.

3. Add the asparagus to the pot and boil, uncovered, for 3 to 5 minutes, until the stalks are just tender. Drain immediately and spread on a clean cloth towel to cool slightly.

4. In a bowl, whisk together the oil, vinegar, and salt and pepper to taste. Arrange the asparagus on a platter and drizzle with the vinaigrette.

YIELD: 4 SERVINGS

THICK OR THIN ASPARAGUS?

This glamorous fern is the runway model of the vegetable kingdom. Most people seem to think that thinner stalks are better, but I find the flavor and texture of the full-figured, plumper ones much more appealing. Just make sure you choose asparagus with firm, glossy stalks and tight buds.

Roasted Asparagus with Garlic

In this recipe, the asparagus is roasted briefly in a very hot oven. Serve warm or at room temperature.

2 bunches asparagus (about 2 pounds)
4 tablespoons extra-virgin olive oil
4 garlic cloves, finely chopped
1 teaspoon coarse sea salt
Freshly milled black pepper
2 lemons, cut into wedges

1. Preheat the oven to 450°F. Trim away the bottom $1/2$ inch or so of each asparagus stalk.

2. Arrange the asparagus stalks on a baking sheet in a single layer. Sprinkle with the oil, garlic, salt, and pepper and roll them to coat.

3. Roast for 8 to 10 minutes until crisp-tender.

4. Serve with the lemon wedges.

YIELD: 4 SERVINGS

Baby Artichokes à la Grecque

If you love marinated artichoke hearts, you'll be in heaven with these. They work well as part of an antipasto, in a pasta salad, or on top of pizza.

> **1 cup dry white wine**
> **1/2 cup white wine vinegar**
> **Juice of 1 lemon**
> **5 garlic cloves, sliced**
> **2 sprigs fresh thyme**
> **3 bay leaves**
> **3 tablespoons extra-virgin olive oil**
> **2 teaspoons coarse sea salt**
> **1 teaspoon black peppercorns**
> **1 teaspoon coriander seeds**
> **1/4 teaspoon hot red pepper flakes**
> **24 baby artichokes, trimmed and halved**

1. In a small saucepan over high heat, combine the wine, vinegar, lemon juice, garlic, thyme, bay leaves, 1 tablespoon of the oil, salt, peppercorns, coriander, and red pepper flakes. Whisk well. Boil the marinade, uncovered, until it is reduced to about 1 cup.

2. Place the artichokes in a wide pan and add enough water to barely cover them. Bring to a boil, reduce the heat, and simmer, covered, for 15 to 20 minutes, until the artichokes are tender.

3. Transfer the artichokes to a bowl with a slotted spoon. Remove and discard the thyme sprigs and bay leaves from the marinade. Whisk in the remaining 2 tablespoons of oil, and pour the marinade over the artichokes.

4. Let them cool at room temperature until warm, then cover and refrigerate until well chilled.

5. Serve chilled.

YIELD: 6 SERVINGS

Preparing Artichokes

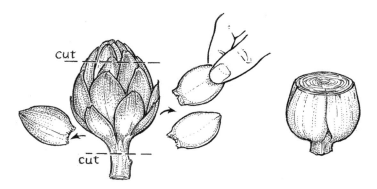

For baby artichokes
Trim the top portion of leaves and stem. Peel away the tough outer leaves to expose the tender, pale yellow inner leaves.

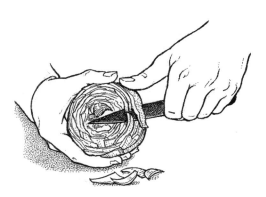

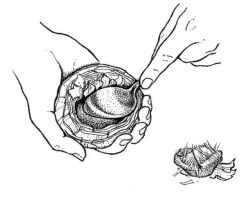

For mature artichokes
Slice off the upper third of the leaves. Trim the bottom half off the stem. Trim the leaves surrounding the choke.

Scoop out the hairy choke with a small metal spoon.

Sautéed Artichokes, Leeks, and Fennel with Olives and Gremolata

The brightness of gremolata adds extra sparkle to the quintessential flavors of the Mediterranean that come together in this vibrant sauté. Take care not to overcook the vegetables, or the dish will lose some of its charm.

12 baby artichokes, trimmed
2 tablespoons white wine vinegar or cider vinegar
$1/3$ cup extra-virgin olive oil
3 leeks, trimmed and sliced into 2-inch pieces
2 fennel bulbs, base cut into $1/2$-inch strips, fronds chopped
1 teaspoon chopped fresh thyme
$1/4$ cup dry white wine
$1/4$ cup water
1 tablespoon freshly squeezed lemon juice
$1/3$ cup roughly chopped pitted black olives, such as kalamata
Coarse sea salt
Freshly milled black pepper
Gremolata (page 378)

1. Slice each trimmed artichoke into quarters from stem to tip. Toss them into a large bowl of cold water acidulated with the vinegar. This will prevent them from discoloring.

2. In a heavy, wide sauté pan over high heat, warm the oil. Add the leeks and sauté, stirring, for 2 minutes. Add the fennel bulb strips (reserving the fronds for garnish) and thyme and sauté for 5 more minutes. Add the artichokes, white wine, water, and lemon juice and bring to a boil.

3. Reduce the heat to low, cover, and simmer until the vegetables are tender but still firm, 15 to 20 minutes.

4. Stir in the olives and season with salt and pepper to taste. Transfer the vegetables to a platter. Sprinkle with the gremolata and chopped fennel fronds and serve.

YIELD: 4 TO 6 SERVINGS

Summer Vegetables

Roasted Peppers with Red Wine Vinegar, Thyme, and Olive Oil

Charring peppers gives them a smoky edge, and removing the peels makes them more digestible. These are so much better than the roasted peppers you can buy in the store, and they'll keep for about a week. Have them on hand to use as a topping for bruschetta or pizza, in pasta salad, or tossed with blanched green vegetables.

> 4 red bell peppers, halved and seeded
> 4 yellow bell peppers, halved and seeded
> 2 tablespoons extra-virgin olive oil
> 1 tablespoon red wine vinegar
> 1 teaspoon finely minced thyme leaves
> 1 teaspoon coarse sea salt
> Freshly milled black pepper

1. Roast the bell peppers as indicated below.

2. Transfer the peppers to a cutting board. Save any juices that have collected in the bowl. With your fingers or the back of a knife, carefully peel away and discard the skins. Cut the peppers into $1/2$-inch-wide strips and return them to the bowl.

3. Add the oil, vinegar, thyme, salt, and pepper to taste, and serve.

YIELD: 4 SERVINGS

HOW TO ROAST A PEPPER

Slice the pepper in half lengthwise. Discard the core and seeds. Broil 3 inches from the flame, cut side down, until charred. Put the pepper in a bowl and cover with a plate or plastic wrap. Set aside for 10 to 15 minutes, or until the skin easily peels away. Remove the pepper from the bowl. Place the pepper, charred side up, on a board and gently scrape away the blackened skin with the back of the knife. Throw away the skin. Slice the pepper as directed.

Pan-Seared Summer Squash

This method produces results just as good as grilling. Lightly charred, somewhat bland summer squash becomes sweet and intense. Cooking with dry heat also improves the texture of soft summer squashes.

> 1½ pounds summer squash, such as pattypan, yellow,
>   crookneck, or zucchini, sliced into 1-inch pieces
> 2 large red onions, sliced into ½-inch-thick rings
> 2 tablespoons extra-virgin olive oil
> 2 tablespoons balsamic vinegar
> 2 tablespoons finely chopped fresh mint or basil
> 1 garlic clove, finely chopped
> 1 teaspoon finely chopped fresh thyme leaves
> ¼ teaspoon hot red pepper flakes
> Coarse sea salt

1. Heat a cast-iron pan over high heat until very hot. Reduce the heat to medium and lay down as many pieces of squash and onion rings as the pan will comfortably hold in a single layer. You will probably need to cook the squash and onion rings in several batches. Cook for 6 to 8 minutes on one side, until the squash is speckled with brown and beginning to blacken, but do not let it char too much. Turn the squash and onion rings over and cook for 5 more minutes. Transfer to a bowl and repeat with the remaining squash and onion rings.

2. In a small bowl, combine the oil, vinegar, mint, garlic, thyme, and red pepper flakes and whisk well. Pour the dressing over the vegetables while they are still hot and toss to coat. Savor the explosion of herbal perfume.

3. Cover the bowl and let the vegetables marinate for 10 minutes. Turn the vegetables over in the marinade and add salt to taste before serving.

YIELD: 4 TO 6 SERVINGS

Eggplant with Olives, Capers, and Fresh Basil

When I was a kid the two foods I hated most were eggplant and liver. I still dislike liver, but I am now quite fond of certain eggplant dishes. This is perfect as part of an antipasto selection and makes a great topping for grilled or toasted sourdough bruschetta.

2 eggplants (about 1 pound each)
Coarse sea salt
$^1/_3$ cup extra-virgin olive oil
1 cup finely diced sweet onion, such as Vidalia or Walla Walla
3 garlic cloves, finely chopped
1 tablespoon capers
$^1/_4$ teaspoon hot red pepper flakes
$^1/_2$ cup oil-cured black olives, pitted and finely chopped
$^1/_4$ cup freshly squeezed lemon juice
8 to 10 basil leaves, chopped
Freshly milled black pepper

1. Preheat the oven to 450°F.

2. Trim the stems from the eggplants and slice them in half lengthwise. Score the flesh in a crisscross pattern $^1/_2$-inch deep using the tip of a sharp knife. Rub the incisions with 1 teaspoon salt, put the halves back together, and wrap in aluminum foil. Bake the two eggplant packages for 1 hour, or until soft. Unwrap and transfer to a plate to cool.

3. In a pan over medium heat, warm the oil. Add the onion and sauté for 5 minutes. Add the garlic, capers, and red pepper flakes and sauté for 5 more minutes, stirring occasionally to prevent browning.

4. With a rubber spatula, transfer the onions to a mixing bowl and stir in the olives, lemon juice, and basil.

5. When the eggplant is cool enough to handle, scrape out the flesh and discard the skin. Chop the flesh and stir it into the onion mixture.

6. Season with salt and pepper to taste. Serve warm or chilled.

YIELD: 4 TO 6 SERVINGS

String Beans in Honey-Lemon-Mustard Vinaigrette

I was messing around with some string beans one day when I came up with this recipe. I gave my daughter Emma a taste and before I knew it, she had devoured the whole plate!

FOR THE STRING BEANS:
$3^1/_2$ tablespoons coarse sea salt
1 small red onion, thinly sliced
$1^1/_2$ pounds string beans,
    trimmed
1 tablespoon cider vinegar
Pinch freshly milled black pepper

FOR THE VINAIGRETTE:
2 tablespoons freshly squeezed
    lemon juice
1 tablespoon Dijon-style mustard
1 small garlic clove, crushed
1 teaspoon mild honey
$1/_2$ teaspoon coarse sea salt
$1/_8$ teaspoon cayenne pepper
3 tablespoons extra-virgin olive oil

1. Spread a clean kitchen towel on a baking sheet and set aside.

2. In a large pot, bring 3 quarts water to a boil. Add 3 tablespoons salt.

3. Place the sliced onion in a bowl and cover with 2 cups of the boiling water. Cover the bowl with a plate and set aside for 10 to 15 minutes.

4. Drop the beans into the remaining boiling water and cook, uncovered, for 4 to 6 minutes, until crisp-tender. Drain the beans and spread them on the cloth-lined pan.

5. Drain the onions and toss them with the vinegar, the remaining $1/_2$ teaspoon salt, and pepper. Set aside.

6. To make the vinaigrette, combine the lemon juice, mustard, garlic, honey, salt, and cayenne in a large mixing bowl. Whisk until smooth. Slowly whisk in the oil until creamy.

7. Drain the onions once again and squeeze dry. Add the onions and the string beans to the vinaigrette and toss well.

8. Let marinate for 15 minutes at room temperature before serving.

YIELD: 4 TO 6 SERVINGS

Caramelized Fennel

This is one of my favorite ways to eat fennel. Caramelizing really brings out the essence of this delicious bulb vegetable.

2 fennel bulbs, trimmed and halved, fronds chopped
1 whole garlic bulb, cloves separated (unpeeled)
2 tablespoons extra-virgin olive oil
$1/2$ teaspoon fennel seeds
$1/2$ cup water
1 teaspoon fresh thyme leaves
Coarse sea salt
Freshly milled black pepper

1. In a heavy 8- or 10-inch sauté pan that will hold all the fennel in a single snug layer over medium-low heat, arrange the fennel bulbs cut side up. Add the garlic cloves, oil, and fennel seeds and cook gently for 15 minutes, until well caramelized. Turn the fennel pieces over.

2. Add the water and thyme. Raise the heat and bring to a boil. Cover, reduce the heat, and simmer for 15 minutes, until the fennel does not resist the tip of a knife.

3. Uncover, and continue to cook until the juices have thickened into a rich glaze.

4. Season with salt and pepper to taste and serve sprinkled with the reserved fennel fronds.

YIELD: 4 SERVINGS

Preparing Fennel

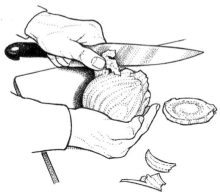

Slice off the tough stalks and reserve them for broth.

Slice off the tough base of the bulb and peel away the stringy outer layer of the bulb. Reserve the trimmings for broth.

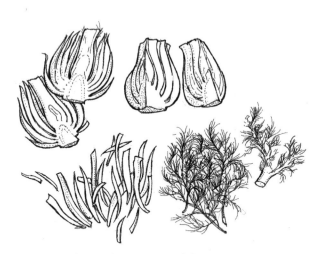

Use vertical slices for crudités; the quartered bulb for braising, roasting, and caramelizing; julienne for salads and quick sautés; and leaves for garnish.

Mushrooms

Fricassee of Mushrooms

In this fricassee, mushrooms are sautéed in butter and oil, then sprinkled with flour to create a thick, velvety sauce. A persillade, a mixture of chopped parsley and garlic, is added to this dish just before it has finished cooking.

2 tablespoons unsalted butter
1 tablespoon extra-virgin olive oil
1 onion, thinly sliced
1 1/2 pounds mixed mushrooms, such as shiitake, chanterelle, cremini, or oyster,
    sliced into 1-inch pieces
2 teaspoons unbleached all-purpose flour
1/2 cup dry red wine
1/2 cup water
2 tablespoons finely chopped fresh thyme leaves
2 teaspoons finely chopped rosemary
Coarse sea salt
2 tablespoons finely chopped flat-leaf parsley
1 large garlic clove, finely chopped
Freshly milled black pepper

1. In a wide heavy saucepan over medium heat, warm the butter and oil and heat until the butter melts. Add the onion and sauté for 8 minutes until soft and lightly browned. Add the mushrooms and flour, and sauté, stirring for 4 to 5 minutes, until the flour browns and begins to stick to the bottom of the pan.

2. Add the wine, water, thyme, rosemary, and 1 teaspoon salt. Scrape up the brown bits from the bottom of the pan with a wooden spoon and bring liquid to a boil. Reduce the heat to low, cover, and simmer for 10 minutes.

3. While the mushrooms simmer, make the persillade by combining the parsley and garlic. Add the persillade to the pan and simmer for 1 minute.

4. Season with salt and pepper to taste, and serve.   YIELD: 4 SERVINGS

Roasted Portobello Mushrooms with Balsamic Vinegar

Cooking balsamic vinegar until it reduces yields a rich, concentrated syrup that balances the dark, earthy mushrooms with a little bit of tart sweetness.

> 4 large portobello mushrooms
> 2$\frac{1}{2}$ tablespoons extra-virgin olive oil
> 1 large garlic clove, minced
> 2$\frac{1}{2}$ tablespoons balsamic vinegar
> Coarse sea salt
> Freshly milled black pepper
> 2 teaspoons finely chopped fresh parsley

1. Preheat the oven to 400°F.

2. Cut away the thick stalks of the mushrooms and discard or reserve them for making a broth. Lay the mushrooms on a baking sheet, cut side down. Brush the tops with 1 tablespoon of the oil.

3. Roast for 30 minutes or until the mushrooms are very soft and tender.

4. Transfer the mushrooms to a cutting board and set them aside until they are cool enough to handle. Slice them and transfer them to a bowl.

5. In a small saucepan over medium heat, warm the remaining 1$\frac{1}{2}$ tablespoons of oil. Add the garlic and sauté for 1 minute. Add the vinegar, raise the heat, and bring to a boil. Cook for 2 to 3 minutes, until the vinegar has reduced and the sauce has thickened.

4. Toss the vinaigrette with mushrooms and season with salt and pepper to taste. Sprinkle with chopped parsley and serve.

YIELD: 4 SERVINGS

Root Vegetables and Winter Squash

Glazed Turnips

Glazing is a simple method of tenderizing vegetables while adding to their natural sweetness and concentrating their flavors. It is also a great way to highlight a single vegetable and give it richness without much fat.

> 1 1/2 pounds turnips (baby turnips left whole,
>   mature turnips peeled and halved or quartered)
> 1 1/2 tablespoons unsalted butter
> 1 1/2 tablespoons pure maple syrup
> 3/4 teaspoon coarse sea salt
> Freshly milled black pepper
> Chopped fresh parsley for garnish

1. Place the turnips in a sauté pan large enough to hold them comfortably in a single layer. Add the butter, maple syrup, salt, pepper to taste, and enough water to cover the turnips halfway. Turn the heat on high and bring to a boil. Reduce the heat to low, cover, and simmer for 10 minutes.

2. Uncover, raise the heat, and bring to a boil. Boil until the liquid has reduced to a shiny glaze and the turnips are tender. Serve sprinkled with chopped parsley.

YIELD: 4 SERVINGS

Balsamic Glazed Beets and Greens

Whenever possible I love to cook root vegetables along with their fresh, bright green tops. The leafy portion of root vegetables such as beets and turnips has a delicate, slightly bitter and acidic flavor that harmonizes perfectly with the rich, earthy flavor of the roots.

Here, the roots simmer until they are tender and have absorbed the flavor of the vinegar and herbs. The greens are placed on top of the roots, the manner in which they grew, and steamed for a few minutes until they wilt. For me, this technique is an altogether soulful and satisfying way to enjoy the complete nature of the vegetable.

> 1 medium red onion, cut into $1/4$-inch crescents
> 4 to 5 fresh beets with tops, roots trimmed
>   and cut into 4 to 6 wedges, greens chopped
> 3 tablespoons balsamic vinegar
> 2 tablespoons unsalted butter or extra-virgin olive oil
> 2 sprigs fresh tarragon, leaves finely chopped
> Coarse sea salt
> Freshly milled black pepper

1. In a heavy pan wide enough to hold the vegetables in a snug single layer, combine the onion, beet roots, vinegar, butter, tarragon, and $1/2$ teaspoon salt. Pour in enough water to barely cover the vegetables, and bring to a boil over high heat. Reduce the heat to low and simmer, covered, for 25 minutes, or until the beets are nearly, but not quite, tender.

2. Raise the heat and boil, uncovered, until the liquid has reduced to a syrup and the beets are fork-tender.

3. Add the beet greens, reduce the heat, and simmer, covered, for 5 minutes.

4. Uncover and turn the greens over so they mix with the roots and onions. Add pepper and additional salt to taste. Simmer for 2 minutes more and serve.

YIELD: 4 SERVINGS

Teriyaki-Style Burdock and Carrots

I developed this recipe while I was at Angelica Kitchen, and it became an instant classic. The characteristic sweet, salty, and sour flavors of teriyaki are all here, in a dish that is equally delicious served hot or cold.

1 tablespoon fresh gingerroot, peeled and finely chopped
$2/3$ cup brown rice syrup (available from health food stores)
$1/3$ cup naturally brewed soy sauce
$1/3$ cup mirin
$1/3$ cup apple cider or apple juice
2 tablespoons toasted sesame oil
1 pound burdock, cut into matchsticks
$1/2$ pound carrots, cut into matchsticks
2 tablespoons lightly toasted, hulled sesame seeds
2 scallions, green and white parts chopped, for garnish (optional)
Watercress for garnish (optional)
Lemon wedges for garnish (optional)

1. In a wide heavy saucepan over medium-high heat, combine the ginger, rice syrup, soy sauce, mirin, apple cider, and oil and bring to a boil. Add the burdock, reduce the heat to low, and simmer, covered, for 10 minutes. Add the carrots and continue cooking for 20 minutes until the vegetables are tender. Remove the pan from the heat and stir in the sesame seeds.

2. Serve hot, garnished with scallions, or chill and serve as a salad over watercress with lemon wedges on the side.

YIELD: 4 SERVINGS

HOW TO WASH BURDOCK

Burdock has a very thin and tender black skin that is not at all bitter or tough. I like to cook burdock in its skin because it provides a good color contrast and is rich in minerals. To prepare burdock, scrub the root with a stiff, natural bristle vegetable brush in a basin of cold water. If you don't have a brush, use a clean kitchen towel to rub off the dirt.

Slicing Root Vegetables Such as Carrots, Burdock, and Parsnips

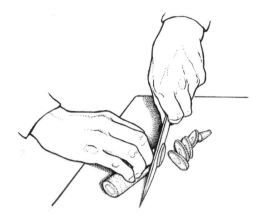

Slice the root crosswise.

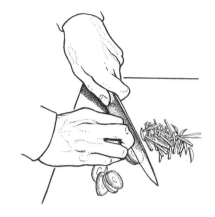

Stack the slices and cut into matchsticks.

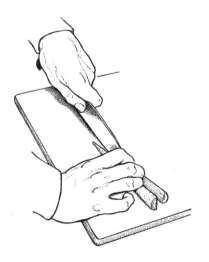

Slice the root in half lengthwise for half-moon and quarter-moon slices.

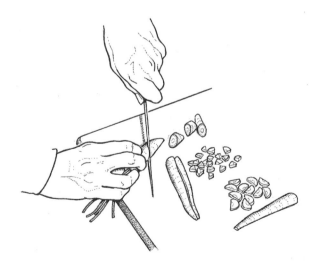

Slice the root into chunks.

Potato-Leek Gratin

This is a wholly satisfying gratin in its own right. If you are in the mood for something a bit richer to go with a light red or dry white wine, try replacing half of the olive oil with butter and add $1/2$ cup grated Gruyère cheese to the bread crumbs.

2 leeks (white and pale green parts only),
    thinly sliced
8 tablespoons extra-virgin olive oil
$1 1/4$ teaspoons coarse sea salt
2 pounds yellow potatoes, peeled and
    thinly sliced
3 garlic cloves, thinly sliced
2 teaspoons minced thyme leaves
Freshly milled black pepper
$1 1/2$ cups fresh sourdough bread crumbs
1 cup All-Season Vegetable Stock (page 29)
    or water

1. Preheat the oven to 350°F. Wash the sliced leeks in a large bowl of water. Transfer them to a steamer and steam, covered, for 5 minutes. Transfer them to a bowl and toss with 1 tablespoon of the oil and $1/4$ teaspoon of the salt.

2. In a separate bowl, toss the potato slices with 4 tablespoons of the oil, garlic, thyme, the remaining 1 teaspoon of the salt, and pepper to taste.

3. In a third bowl, toss the bread crumbs with the remaining 3 tablespoons of oil.

4. In a small saucepan over high heat, bring the broth to a boil. Turn off the heat.

5. In a 2-quart baking dish or 10-inch cast-iron skillet, arrange half of the potato mixture. Spread half of the leek mixture over the potatoes. Repeat the layers once more. Pour the stock over the gratin. Spread the bread crumbs evenly on top and bake for 1 hour until the potatoes are tender and the bread crumbs are golden brown.

6. Serve hot.

YIELD: 4 TO 6 SERVINGS

Preparing Leeks

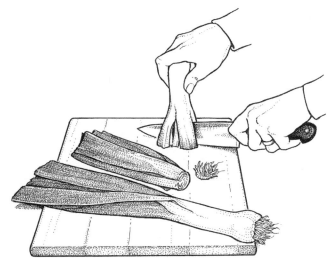

Slice off and discard the root end. Save the tough green top leaves for broth. Make several slices through the pale green upper portion of the fleshy white bottom. Do not cut through the base. Swish the cut end of the leek in a bowl of water. The grit will settle on the bottom of the bowl.

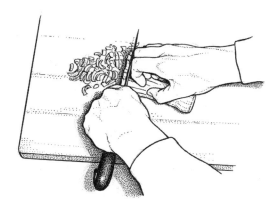

Slice the leek across into pieces.

Garlic Mashed Potatoes

Here's a great, dairy-free recipe for mashed potatoes. If you like butter, you can substitute it for the oil, but it's equally good either way. For tasty potato croquettes that will use up any leftovers (if there are any), shape them into patties, dredge them in bread crumbs, and panfry them in oil until crisp. They go really well with the All-Purpose Savory Gravy on page 381.

> 2 pounds yellow-fleshed potatoes,
>   such as Yukon Gold or Yellowfin,
>   peeled and quartered
> 8 garlic cloves, peeled and left whole
> 1 sprig fresh rosemary (optional)
> Coarse sea salt
> 5 tablespoons extra-virgin olive oil
> Freshly milled black pepper

1. In a large pot over high heat, combine the potatoes with enough cold water to cover by 2 inches, and bring to a boil. Reduce the heat to medium-low and add the garlic, rosemary, and 1 teaspoon salt. Simmer, covered, for 20 to 30 minutes, until the potatoes are tender. Drain, reserving $1/2$ cup of the cooking water. Remove and discard the rosemary.

2. Mash the potatoes well. Slowly add the oil and beat in with a stiff wire whisk or wooden spoon until fluffy and creamy. Adjust the consistency with a bit of the reserved water, if necessary.

3. Add salt and pepper to taste, and serve.

YIELD: 4 TO 6 SERVINGS

Pot-Roasted Potatoes and Shallots with Rosemary and Thyme

I love to pot-roast hardy winter vegetables. Covering them as they bake in the oven ensures delicious, intense flavor and moist, juicy vegetables. You can also use carrots, turnips, parsnips, whole small onions, and chunks of rutabaga if you like.

3/4 pound tiny red potatoes
3/4 pound tiny white potatoes
3/4 pound shallots
2 tablespoons extra-virgin olive oil
1 sprig rosemary
1 sprig thyme
2 bay leaves
1 1/2 teaspoons coarse sea salt
Freshly milled black pepper
Finely chopped fresh parsley for garnish

1. Preheat the oven to 450°F.

2. Combine the potatoes in a heavy 3-quart casserole or enameled cast-iron pot with a lid. Slice off the tops of the shallots. Scrub the roots but leave intact. Make a vertical slit on the side of each shallot with the tip of a sharp knife and peel off the skins. Add them to the pot with the potatoes. Add the oil, rosemary, thyme, bay leaves, salt, and pepper to taste. Toss lightly to coat with the oil.

3. Cover the pot and roast for 45 minutes, shaking the pot occasionally for even browning. It is done when the potatoes are creamy on the inside but still hold their shape, and the shallots are well caramelized.

4. Serve sprinkled with chopped parsley.

YIELD: 4 SERVINGS

Pumpkin-Walnut Pâté

This spreadable pâté is great smeared on top of crispy Pita Toasts or used as a dip for raw celery or fennel sticks.

> 1 pound winter squash, such as red kuri,
>   pumpkin, butternut, or buttercup,
>   peeled and cut into 2-inch chunks
> $\frac{1}{2}$ cup water
> Coarse sea salt
> $\frac{1}{2}$ cup dry-pack sun-dried tomatoes
> 4 tablespoons extra-virgin olive oil
> 1 large onion, diced
> $\frac{2}{3}$ cup walnuts, coarsely chopped
> 3 garlic cloves, chopped
> 2 tablespoons chopped fresh sage
> $\frac{1}{8}$ teaspoon hot red pepper flakes
> Freshly milled black pepper

1. Preheat the oven to 350°F.

2. In a large pot over high heat, combine the squash, water, and a pinch of salt. Bring to a boil, then reduce the heat, cover, and simmer for 15 minutes, or until tender. Drain the squash and reserve the cooking liquid.

3. In a small saucepan over high heat, combine the tomatoes and enough water to cover. Bring to a boil, then turn off the heat and set aside for 10 minutes to soften.

PITA TOASTS

Preheat the oven to 350° F. Quarter 4 pita pockets and split in half. Arrange the pita quarters on a baking sheet. In a small bowl, mix together 4 tablespoons olive oil and 1 crushed garlic clove. Brush the oil over the top of each pita. Sprinkle the pita wedges with sea salt and freshly milled black pepper. Bake for 20 minutes or until crisp. MAKES 32 PITA TOASTS

4. In a sauté pan over medium heat, warm the oil. Add the onion and sauté for 4 to 5 minutes, until it softens and begins to brown. Add the walnuts, garlic, sage, and red pepper flakes and sauté gently for 5 to 7 minutes, until the walnuts are fragrant.

5. Drain the plumped tomatoes and transfer them to the bowl of a food processor fitted with a metal blade. Add the sautéed vegetables and winter squash. Purée until creamy, adding the reserved squash water if needed, until the desired consistency is reached.

6. Season with salt and pepper to taste, and serve warm.

YIELD: 3 CUPS (4 TO 6 SERVINGS)

Roasted Vegetable Pâté

Everyone seems to love the concentrated, earthy sweetness of roasted vegetables—so why not make a pâté out of them? This spreadable pâté is wonderfully savory, due in large part to the deep-aged flavor of barley miso. Try serving it on thinly sliced toasted rounds of sourdough baguette or use it as a dip for crisp fennel, celery, or radishes. The pâté will keep for 3 to 4 days tightly wrapped in the refrigerator and should be brought to room temperature before serving.

> **2 cups diced onions**
> **2 cups sliced carrots**
> **6 ounces white button mushrooms, sliced**
> **6 plump garlic cloves, peeled and left whole**
> **3 tablespoons extra-virgin olive oil**
> **1 teaspoon finely chopped fresh herbs,**
>   **such as rosemary, thyme, or sage**
> **Coarse sea salt**
> **2 tablespoons barley miso**
> **2 teaspoons freshly squeezed lemon juice**
> **Freshly milled black pepper**
> **1 tablespoon water (optional)**
> **Finely chopped fresh parsley for garnish**

1. Preheat the oven to 425°F.

2. In a bowl, toss together the onions, carrots, mushrooms, garlic, oil, herbs, and a pinch of salt.

3. Spread the mixture on a baking sheet and roast for 20 to 30 minutes, stirring every 5 minutes or so for even browning.

4. When the vegetables are tender, transfer them to a food processor fitted with a metal blade. Add the miso, lemon juice, and pepper to taste, and purée. Add the water if the pâté is too thick.

5. Allow the pâté to rest for 5 minutes to marry the flavors before serving. Sprinkle with chopped parsley and serve.

YIELD: 4 SERVINGS

Maple-Roasted Buttercup Squash

This is the quintessential autumn dish—simple, satisfying, and yummy. I love buttercup squash because the rind roasts up so tender that it practically melts in your mouth. However, feel free to substitute any variety of winter squash.

> 1 (3- to 4-pound) buttercup squash, halved and seeded,
> sliced into wedges or 2-inch chunks
> 3 to 4 tablespoons pure maple syrup
> 1 to 2 tablespoons olive oil or unsalted butter
> $^1/_2$ to 1 teaspoon coarse sea salt, to taste

1. Preheat the oven to 450°F.

2. In a large bowl, combine the squash, maple syrup, oil, and salt and toss well.

3. Transfer the squash to a baking dish and roast, uncovered, for 35 to 40 minutes until fork-tender. Stir the squash every 10 minutes for even browning.

4. Serve hot.

YIELD: 4 SERVINGS

Candied Yams

This recipe was created for my ten-year-old friend and cooking student, Evan Chender, who used it for his Thanksgiving feast one year. Fresh ginger really spices up the sweet, meltingly tender yams.

    2 pounds garnet yams or sweet potatoes
    3 (2-inch) strips orange zest,
        white, spongy pith removed
    2 cinnamon sticks, broken in half
    1/2 cup freshly squeezed orange juice
    1/3 cup pure maple syrup
    2 tablespoons pure olive oil, light sesame oil,
        or unsalted butter
    1 tablespoon freshly squeezed lemon juice
    2 teaspoons peeled and finely chopped gingerroot
    1/2 teaspoon coarse sea salt

1. Preheat the oven to 375°F.

2. Peel and halve the yams crosswise. Cut each half lengthwise into 4 wedges. Place the yams in a baking dish that will hold them in a snug single layer. Tuck the orange zest and cinnamon sticks among the yams.

3. In a bowl, whisk together the orange juice, maple syrup, oil, lemon juice, ginger, and salt. (Note: If you're using butter, omit it in this step, but dot the assembled casserole with small pieces of it before it goes into the oven.) Pour the mixture over the yams.

4. Bake for 1 1/4 hours, basting every 15 minutes, until the yams are tender and glazed and the pan juices are syrupy.

5. Remove the orange zest and cinnamon sticks before serving.

YIELD: 4 SERVINGS

Roasted Root Vegetables

This tried-and-true method of open-pan roasting has become the premier wintertime way of cooking vegetables.

9 to 12 carrots (1 1/2 pounds),
   peeled and cut into large chunks
2 turnips (about 1/2 pound),
   peeled and cut into large chunks
2 parsnips (about 1/2 pound),
   peeled and cut into large chunks
2 red onions (about 1/2 pound),
   peeled and cut into thirds lengthwise,
   leaving root end intact
2 1/2 tablespoons extra-virgin olive oil
   or unsalted butter
1 teaspoon brown sugar
1/2 teaspoon coarse sea salt
8 garlic cloves, peeled but left whole
1 tablespoon balsamic vinegar plus
   additional to taste
Freshly milled black pepper
2 tablespoons finely chopped fresh parsley

1. Preheat the oven to 450°F.

2. In a large bowl, toss the vegetables with the oil, brown sugar, and salt.

3. Spread the vegetables in a large roasting pan and roast for 30 minutes, stirring halfway through for even browning.

4. Stir the garlic into the vegetables and roast for another 30 minutes, or until the vegetables are tender and caramelized, stirring halfway through for even browning.

5. Season the vegetables with vinegar and pepper to taste. Sprinkle with chopped parsley and serve.

YIELD: 4 SERVINGS

Cruciferous Vegetables and Greens

Sautéed Broccoli with Garlic

This is the traditional Italian treatment of cruciferous vegetables—perfect in every way. Try it with cauliflower, turnips, kale, and cabbage.

> Coarse sea salt
> 1 large head broccoli (about 1 1/2 pounds),
>   stem peeled and sliced 1/2-inch thick,
>   florets separated
> 2 tablespoons extra-virgin olive oil
> 4 plump garlic cloves, peeled and sliced
> Pinch hot red pepper flakes (optional)
> 1 to 2 tablespoons water
> 1 lemon, cut into wedges

1. In a large pot over high heat, bring 3 quarts water to a boil. Add 2 teaspoons salt.

2. Add the broccoli to the water and cook, uncovered, for 2 to 3 minutes until crisp-tender. Drain and immediately plunge the broccoli into a bowl of ice water to arrest the cooking. Drain and set aside.

3. In a wide heavy saucepan over medium heat, warm the oil. Add the garlic and sauté for 1 minute, or until pale gold. Do not let the garlic brown. Stir in the red pepper flakes, cooked broccoli, and a tablespoon or two of water. Season with salt to taste, cover, and cook for 3 to 4 minutes.

4. Serve with lemon wedges on the side.

YIELD: 4 SERVINGS

Preparing Broccoli

Slice the stalks from the crown. Peel and slice the stalks.

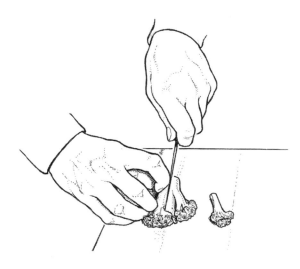

Cut through the base of the crown to form florets.

Braised Red Cabbage with Apples

Served hot, this satisfying German-style dish is perfect for a warming autumn or winter meal. At room temperature, it also makes a colorful topping for bruschetta.

2 tablespoons unsalted butter or olive oil
2 red onions (about $1/2$ pound),
    sliced into thin crescents
2 teaspoons brown sugar
1 teaspoon caraway seeds
1 teaspoon coarse sea salt
$3/4$ cup water
$2^1/2$ tablespoons cider vinegar
1 head red cabbage ($1^1/2$ to 2 pounds),
    sliced into $1/2$-inch strips
1 large firm apple, such as Rome, Crispin,
    or Granny Smith, peeled and sliced
    $1/4$ inch thick
Freshly milled black pepper

1. In a wide heavy sauté pan over medium heat, melt the butter. Add the onions, brown sugar, caraway seeds, and salt and sauté, stirring occasionally, for 5 to 7 minutes, until softened.

2. Add the water, vinegar, cabbage, and apple. Raise the heat and bring to a boil. Cover, reduce the heat to low, and braise for 25 to 30 minutes.

3. Uncover and cook over high heat for a few minutes until the juices have reduced.

4. Season with additional salt and pepper to taste, and serve.

YIELD: 4 SERVINGS

Preparing Cabbage

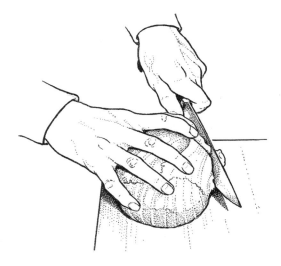

Trim and discard the base.

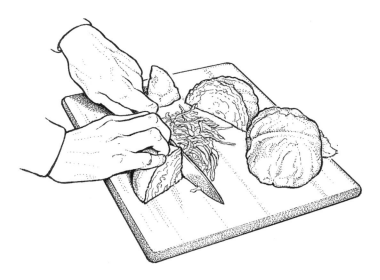

Cut the cabbage in half vertically and in half again to form wedges. Slice the wedges crosswise into strips.

Brussels Sprouts with Fennel Seed

Here's an incredibly fast-cooking method that results in mild and flavorful brussels sprouts. The fennel seeds perfume the dish and function as a digestive. You may substitute caraway seeds if you like.

> **2 tablespoons extra-virgin olive oil**
> **1 teaspoon fennel seeds**
> **1 pound brussels sprouts, trimmed, halved lengthwise,**
>   **and thinly sliced**
> **2 to 3 tablespoons water**
> **1 teaspoon coarse sea salt**
> **Cider vinegar**
> **Freshly milled black pepper**

1. In a wide sauté pan over medium heat, warm the oil. Add the fennel seeds and toast for 1 minute.

2. Add the brussels sprouts, water, and salt. Raise the heat and bring to a boil. Cover and remove from the heat. After 5 minutes, uncover and toss with cider vinegar and pepper to taste.

3. Serve hot.

YIELD: 4 SERVINGS

Spicy Roasted Cauliflower with Sweet Peppers and Cumin

Cauliflower is completely transformed from stodgy and boring to vibrant and spicy in this Indian-style dish. Serve with basmati rice and curried chick-peas or toss with penne pasta.

> 3 tablespoons freshly squeezed lemon juice
> 3 tablespoons extra-virgin olive oil
> 1 1/2 teaspoons coarse sea salt
> 1 teaspoon ground cumin
> 1 teaspoon ground coriander
> 1/2 teaspoon cumin seeds
> 1/2 teaspoon hot red pepper flakes
> 1 cauliflower (about 2 pounds), cored
>   and separated into florets
> 1 large red bell pepper, halved, seeded,
>   and sliced into 1-inch-wide strips
> 1 large yellow bell pepper, halved, seeded,
>   and sliced into 1-inch-wide strips
> 1/2 cup fresh cilantro leaves

1. Preheat the oven to 450°F.

2. In a large bowl, combine the lemon juice, oil, salt, ground cumin, coriander, cumin seeds, and red pepper flakes. Whisk to combine.

3. Add the cauliflower and bell peppers and toss well.

4. Spread the vegetables in a baking dish and roast for 45 minutes. Stir every 15 minutes for even browning.

5. Transfer the vegetables to a serving dish, garnish with fresh cilantro leaves, and serve.

YIELD: 4 SERVINGS

Broccoli Rabe with Pine Nuts and Raisins

This typical Southern Italian dish mixes sweet, dried fruit with bitter greens, clearly a North African influence.

> **8 garlic cloves, peeled and left whole**
> **2 bunches broccoli rabe (about 2 pounds), trimmed**
>   **and chopped into 2-inch pieces**
> **6 tablespoons extra-virgin olive oil**
> **6 tablespoons pine nuts**
> **6 tablespoons raisins**
> **$1/2$ teaspoon hot red pepper flakes**
> **Coarse sea salt**
> **2 lemons, cut into wedges**

1. In a large pot, bring 5 quarts water to a boil. Add the garlic and cook for 3 minutes. Remove the garlic with a spider or slotted spoon and set aside. Return the water to a boil.

2. Add the broccoli rabe to the pot and cook, uncovered, for 3 minutes, until bright green and crisp-tender. Drain.

3. In a heavy wide sauté pan over medium heat, warm the oil. Holding the handle, tip the pan so the oil pools to one side. Add the garlic and sauté until pale gold, about 2 minutes. Level the pan and stir in the pine nuts, raisins, and red pepper flakes. Sauté until the pine nuts are light gold and the raisins swell, about 2 minutes.

4. Add the broccoli rabe, season with salt to taste, and sauté until tender, about 5 to 7 minutes.

5. Serve hot with lemon wedges on the side.

YIELD: 4 SERVINGS

HOW TO CLEAN LEAFY GREEN VEGETABLES

Pull away and discard any bruised and wilted outer leaves. Fill a large basin or sink with cold water. Immerse the greens, swish them around, and lift them out with your hands or a strainer. As the sand and dirt is dislodged, it will sink to the bottom. Swish the greens around a second or third time, then drain in a colander.

Garlicky Braised Greens with Toasted Pumpkin Seeds

You can use this as a basic, all-purpose method for cooking greens. A platter of cooked greens is also a perfect occasion for using a drizzle of homemade Herbal or Chili Vinegar (pages 360 and 361).

Coarse sea salt
1 large bunch kale, collard greens,
    or mustard greens (about 2 pounds),
    trimmed; stems sliced into bite-size pieces
2 tablespoons extra-virgin olive or
    light sesame oil
2 large garlic cloves, thinly sliced
4 to 6 ounces white button mushrooms,
    thinly sliced
2 teaspoons naturally brewed soy sauce
Toasted Pumpkin Seeds (page 383)
1 lemon, cut into wedges

1. In a large pot over high heat, bring 4 quarts water to a boil. Add 2 teaspoons salt.

2. Drop the greens into the boiling water and cook, uncovered, for 2 to 3 minutes, until tender and bright green. Drain in a colander.

3. In a heavy wide sauté pan over medium heat, warm the oil. Add the garlic and sauté for 30 seconds, or until pale gold. Do not let the garlic brown. Add the mushrooms and soy sauce and sauté, stirring occasionally, for 2 to 3 minutes, until the mushrooms soften.

4. Chop the cooked greens and add them to the pan. Sauté for 3 to 5 minutes, until tender.

5. Season to taste with salt. Serve sprinkled with the pumpkin seeds and pass the lemon wedges on the side.

YIELD: 4 SERVINGS

Asian-Style Greens with Sesame, Ginger, and Soy Sauce

These tender greens cook very quickly. Make sure you add the vinegar just prior to serving or the greens will lose their fantastic emerald sheen.

   4 tablespoons light sesame oil or olive oil
   2 tablespoons white hulled sesame seeds
   2 teaspoons black sesame seeds (optional)
   4 teaspoons peeled, minced gingerroot
   2 garlic cloves, minced
   2 pounds tender Asian greens, such as baby bok choy,
      watercress, tatsoi, or mizuna, coarsely chopped
   2 tablespoons naturally brewed soy sauce
   4 teaspoons rice vinegar

1. In a wide heavy sauté pan or wok over medium heat, warm the oil. Add the sesame seeds and stir until they pop and become fragrant. Add the ginger and garlic and sauté for 1 more minute.

2. Add the greens and 1 tablespoon soy sauce, raise the heat, and cook, covered, for 1 minute. Uncover and sauté for 1 to 2 minutes more, until the greens are tender but still bright green.

3. Stir in more soy sauce and vinegar to taste, and serve immediately.

YIELD: 4 SERVINGS

Spicy Mustard Greens with Cumin

This is a true culinary jewel. I am always stunned by the effect that these slow-cooked, mouth-watering tender greens have on my guests.

2 tablespoons extra-virgin olive oil
1 onion, roughly chopped (about 1 cup)
3 garlic cloves, chopped
1 red jalapeño pepper, seeded and finely chopped, or $1/2$ teaspoon hot red pepper flakes
$1^1/_2$ teaspoons cumin seeds
1 large bunch mustard greens (about 2 pounds), chopped into bite-size pieces
Cider vinegar
Coarse sea salt
Freshly milled black pepper

1. In a large pot over medium heat, warm the oil. Add the onion and sauté until softened, about 5 minutes. Add the garlic, jalapeño, and cumin and sauté for 2 to 3 minutes more. Add the mustard greens and raise the heat. Stir until the greens wilt. Reduce the heat to low and simmer, covered, for 25 to 30 minutes, until the greens are meltingly tender.

2. Season with vinegar, salt, and pepper to taste. Serve hot or at room temperature.

YIELD: 4 SERVINGS

ON COOKING LEAFY GREENS

Kale, collards, and other bitter greens are all members of the mustard family and can have a bitter, strongly sulfurous taste. Boiling these greens briefly in salted water without a lid allows the sulfur to escape. Immediately after cooking, drain and sauté in a small amount of oil to further tenderize the greens and deepen their flavor. And, a final last-minute addition of vinegar or citrus will unlock minerals beneficial for human digestion.

Stuffed Collards Baked in Zesty Tomato Sauce

This is one of those great dishes to prepare when you are in the mood for something special—maybe on a rainy weekend. Of course this is only a sample technique for resurrecting whatever leftover grains and bread you might have. If you like cheese, try adding $1/2$ cup freshly grated Parmesan to the stuffing, but it is equally good without.

FOR THE SAUCE:
2 tablespoons extra-virgin olive oil
3 onions or leeks (white and tender green parts only), chopped
3 garlic cloves, minced
4 pounds fresh tomatoes or 2 (28-ounce) cans plum tomatoes, quartered
2 tablespoons chopped fresh herbs,
    such as tarragon, basil, or flat-leaf parsley
2 or 3 strips orange zest, white spongy pith removed
$1/4$ teaspoon hot red pepper flakes
Coarse sea salt
Freshly milled black pepper

FOR THE COLLARDS:
$1/2$ cup wild rice or 2 cups cooked brown rice
2 cups water (optional)
Coarse sea salt
2 tablespoons extra-virgin olive oil
$1/2$ cup finely diced onion
$1/2$ cup grated carrot
$1/2$ cup dried currants
$1/2$ cup finely chopped white mushrooms
$1/3$ cup pine nuts
1 tablespoon finely chopped sage or rosemary
2 cups fresh bread crumbs
    (homemade sourdough is recommended)
2 teaspoons freshly squeezed lemon juice
Freshly milled black pepper
8 large, unblemished collard leaves

1. To make the sauce, warm the oil in a 3-quart saucepan over medium heat. Add the onions and sauté for 5 minutes, or until softened. Add the garlic and sauté for 2 minutes. Raise the heat to high and stir in the tomatoes, herbs, orange zest, and red pepper flakes. Bring to a boil, then reduce the heat to low and simmer, uncovered, stirring occasionally, for 35 to 40 minutes, until thick.

2. Pass the sauce through the medium holes of a hand-cranked food mill into a bowl, discard the solids, and season the sauce with salt and pepper to taste. Set aside.

3. Rinse the wild rice in a strainer under cold running water. Drain and transfer to a small saucepan over high heat. Add the water and $1/4$ teaspoon salt and bring to a boil. Reduce the heat to low, cover, and simmer for 45 to 50 minutes, until all the water has been absorbed. (Skip this step if using cooked brown rice.)

4. Preheat the oven to 375°F.

5. Meanwhile, in a sauté pan over medium heat, warm the oil. Add the diced onion and sauté for 5 minutes. Add the carrots, currants, mushrooms, pine nuts, and herbs. Sauté for 6 to 8 minutes, until the vegetables are tender.

6. In a large mixing bowl, combine the bread crumbs with the cooked rice and vegetables. Season with lemon juice and salt and pepper to taste.

7. Bring a large pot of water to a boil. Add 2 tablespoons salt and the collard greens and cook, uncovered, for 3 to 4 minutes, until tender but still bright green. Drain and blot dry on a clean kitchen towel.

8. Place 3 tablespoons of stuffing in the center of a collard leaf. Fold the sides toward the center and roll to form neat packages. Repeat until all the collards have been stuffed.

9. Select a baking dish large enough to comfortably hold the collard rolls in a snug single layer. Pour in 3 cups of tomato sauce and place the collard rolls on top. Spoon another cup of sauce over the rolls and cover with foil, shiny side down.

10. Bake for 20 to 30 minutes, until the sauce is bubbling.

YIELD: 4 MAIN-COURSE SERVINGS; 8 APPETIZER SERVINGS

Pasta

When most Americans think of pasta, they think of Italy. For centuries, the Italians have popularized pasta as the epitome of their cuisine, devising and naming countless shapes and styles. In Italian, *pasta* translates as "paste" and literally refers to any dough made from flour and water, regardless of whether it is used to make porridge, bread, or noodles. As a matter of national pride, most Italians are loath to believe the story that Marco Polo brought pasta back from China in the thirteenth century. And they are probably right—it is more likely that he brought back some type of grain paste or dried grain cake from his visits to Asia. In Asia, it is the Koreans who claim to be the inventors of pasta. Buckwheat flour soba noodles, now widely popular in Japan, are said to have been introduced by Korea to Japan in the eighth century. Whatever the case may be, the predecessors of modern-day pasta were probably flattened unleavened cakes that could be dried to be eaten later, sometimes after being reconstituted in water or oil.

Today, it's the rare pantry that doesn't contain a package or two of spaghetti or elbow macaroni. Pasta has become a great American staple, largely because it is so quick and easy to prepare. It's the perfect choice for a fast dinner on a busy weeknight. You can sit down to a filling, nutritious meal in minutes by just cooking some noodles and tossing them with olive oil, garlic, and some grated cheese. Even slightly more involved pasta sauces are usually finished in the time it takes for the pasta water to come to a boil.

Not only is pasta easy to prepare and a good staple, it's also a food for every season. All you really need is one good pasta recipe and you can vary the sauce as the seasons change. In the summer I like to get the freshest vegetables, such as summer squash, tomatoes, eggplant, and peppers, and make a quick ragout. Autumn and winter, with their chilly temperatures, demand something heartier and more robust, such as my Creamy Walnut-Portobello Sauce (page 162). And in the spring you can serve pasta with a light and simple dashi or herb broth, both of which are intensely flavored but cleansing and without fat.

Pasta sauce is as important as the pasta itself, and, as with wine-food pairing, the two must complement each other. Just as spicy and assertive food warrants a bold wine, rigatoni, a big, hearty pasta, needs a robust, chunky sauce. Conversely, a thin, delicate noodle is best served with a light broth, a simple olive oil and herb dressing, or a light cream sauce. A basic aesthetic should lead you to choose thicker sauces for chunky pastas and lighter sauces for thinner pastas. Think about the shape of the pasta: tubular pastas call for rich, textured sauces loaded with cut-up vegetables to fill the crevices. Also, consider the flavor of the pasta itself. A fresh summer ragout is good with a lighter-tasting egg noodle. Chestnut pasta, on the other hand, is relatively intense and needs a sauce that can stand up to it. Here, I pair chestnut pasta with a rich sauce made with pumpkins and porcini mushrooms (page 152). Pizzoccheri (page 150), a traditional thin, buckwheat noodle from Northern Italy and Switzerland, has a delicate texture, but its heavy flavor would fight with a basic tomato sauce. I find that this classic home-style pasta is at its best cooked with lots of vegetables, cheese, and wine.

If you have the time and inclination, I really recommend making your own pasta. It's a lot easier than you might think, and you don't even need any special equipment. In a pinch, I once rolled out my pasta dough with a wine bottle! Pasta-making is an engaging way to get involved in the kitchen even if you've never had any cooking experience, and you get a fantastic meal in return. Like baking bread, making pasta by hand is a ritual that has its own special rhythm. Developing the dough and transforming it into pasta requires mixing, kneading, resting, rolling, drying, and finally cooking. And the more you put your whole body into the cooking experience, the more pleasure you will ultimately get out of your food. Of course, store-bought dried pasta is perfectly fine to use; you just don't get the same holistic experience from opening a package. Fresh homemade pasta is incomparable to the "fresh" pastas you can find in specialty stores, since the taste and texture of fresh pasta change dramatically in as little as 6 to 8 hours. And, when you make your own pasta, you have control over the quality of your ingredients. Using the freshest organic flour, eggs, and filtered water will yield the best results.

There are a few basic cooking techniques that will help ensure delicious, tender pasta, whether you use your own or store-bought. First, always make sure to boil the pasta in a full pot of water. Second, add the salt only after the water comes to a boil, otherwise it will take longer. Optimally, the water should return to a boil relatively soon after the pasta is thrown in. You can cover the pot partially to achieve this, but if you cover it completely, it might boil over. Once you've dropped the pasta into the water, pay attention; there's nothing worse than soggy, overcooked pasta. Fresh pasta, which really should be cooked immediately after it is cut, takes only 1 to 2 minutes; store-bought dried pasta takes longer—up to 12 minutes, depending on the type. Test the pasta about a minute before the cooking time is up to make sure you have achieved a good al dente (firm-cooked) bite. Keep in mind that the hardness of your water will affect the cooking time. I once cooked pasta in West Virginia, where the water is very hard and full of minerals. It took a long time for the water to return to a boil after the pasta was added, but it ultimately turned out just fine.

The types of pasta that I have included in this book can be categorized in several different ways: fresh or dried and with or without eggs. All my recipes are wheat-based, but if you cannot eat wheat, you may certainly substitute packaged rice pasta or soba noodles made from 100 percent buckwheat flour. Wheat-based egg pastas are the easiest to make by hand because the gluten in the wheat and the binding power of the egg hold the dough together well. I don't generally include eggs in my cooking, but here they play a major role in creating light-textured pastas with excellent resiliency and a rich flavor. Pastas made from 100 percent wheat flour can work well without eggs, especially if you add a little oil, which gives the noodles a slightly richer, more luxurious flavor and prevents them from drying out too much. Bread crumb pasta is another egg-free version—the crumbs really improve the texture.

The type of pasta everyone is most familiar with is dried semolina pasta, the kind you buy in the supermarket. Semolina is derived from very hard durum wheat and makes a strong, toothsome pasta. Since semolina flour is so hard, it is very difficult to make this pasta at home. Here is one case where it is better to leave it to powerful factory machines to produce a good, pliable dough. Semolina pasta is made without eggs and is perfect for vegan diets. I do give a recipe for pasta that uses some semolina flour in addition to whole wheat and white flour, which soften the dough up enough to knead by hand.

Mixed-flour pasta is a fun way to introduce subtle flavors and textures into the base of your dishes. I have included recipes for pasta made with a combination of wheat and chickpea flour, wheat and buckwheat flour, and wheat and chestnut flour. In general, when you are mixing in a nonwheat flour, either use a very small amount, such as 10 percent, or add an egg to help bind the dough. However, for chickpea pasta, I use 25 percent chickpea flour and leave out the egg. Chickpea flour is unique in that it has a protein similar to eggs, which gives it excellent binding capabilities even though it lacks gluten. Chestnut pasta has no natural binders and really benefits from the addition of an egg, which lends the noodles a light, smooth texture and rich flavor.

I have also included several of my favorite pasta salad recipes in this chapter. Pasta salads, though they may be heresy to traditional Italian cooks, are a unique part of traditional American fare. What would a picnic or potluck be without pasta salad? There are several keys to making a good pasta salad. First, cook the noodles until just a little firmer than *al dente.* This is because the pasta will need to be rinsed in cold water to arrest the cooking and to wash off the excess starch that would otherwise make the salad gummy. As you rinse the pasta, it will absorb some of the water and continue to soften and swell, achieving that perfect toothsome bite. Second, it is crucial that the vegetables be thoroughly drained and blotted dry before they are tossed with the remaining ingredients or they will dilute the dressing. And finally, do not add all of the dressing at once—save some for adjusting the flavor. After dressing, the salad will need to rest for 15 minutes to marry the flavors. Then you can taste to see if salt, pepper, or a bit more dressing is required for balance.

Steps for Fresh,
Handmade Pasta

Put the flour into a large heavy bowl. Make a well and add the liquid ingredients. Scramble the eggs or mix the oil and water with a fork.

Slowly incorporate the liquid into the flour until it has all been absorbed, forming a ragged mass of dough.

Shape the dough into a ball.

The dough is ready for kneading when a finger inserted into the center of the dough comes out clean.

Wash your hands and transfer the dough to a clean, lightly floured work surface. Stretch and flatten the ball of dough with the heel of your hand.

Pull the dough back onto itself, push down, and knead. Turn the dough and continue stretching, folding back, and pushing until the dough is shiny, smooth, and elastic.

Wrap the dough in wax paper or plastic wrap and set aside at room temperature to relax for at least 30 minutes and up to 1 hour.

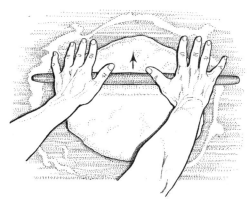

Unwrap the dough and transfer it to a lightly floured work surface. Lightly flour the surface of the dough and press it into a disk. Roll the disk in the same direction from the center to the edge. Rotate the dough after each roll.

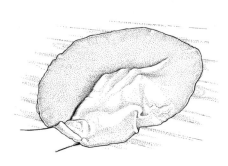

Thin the dough until you can see the outline of your hand through it.

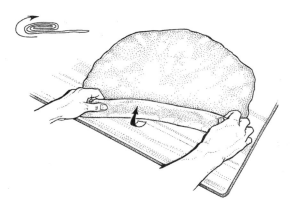

Lightly dust the surface of the dough with flour and gently fold it into a loose cylinder.

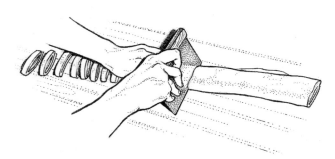

Cut the roll into desired widths.

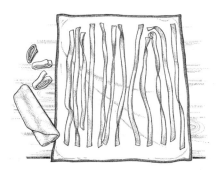

Uncurl the pasta and lay it on a clean cotton towel until you are ready to cook it.

Hot Pasta Dishes

Nabe Mono with Fresh Whole Wheat Noodles

Traditional Nabe cooking is done over a charcoal brazier at the table instead of in the kitchen. This hearkens back to a time before there was such a thing as central heating, when friends and family gathered around the table for warmth, comfort, and conviviality. Nabe-style cooking is a rich social tradition that offers diners a chance to personally select, cook, and season their own food right at the table. Traditionally the morsels would be dipped into a central colorful earthenware casserole filled with a simmering savory broth. However, modern Nabe food is often precooked, then rewarmed at the table in a light tamari or miso broth.

FOR THE NOODLES:

1 1/2 cups unbleached all-purpose or white bread flour

1 cup whole wheat bread flour

1/2 cup semolina flour plus additional flour for dusting

1 teaspoon sea salt

1 cup plus extra warm water

FOR THE VEGETABLES AND TOFU:

2 tablespoons coarse sea salt

1 head broccoli, separated into small florets,
    stalk peeled and sliced

3 medium or 2 large carrots, thinly sliced

1 daikon radish, peeled and thinly sliced

1 pound firm tofu, sliced into 1-inch cubes

2 cups snow peas, trimmed

1 head napa cabbage, outer leaves removed,
    sliced into 2-inch pieces

1 or 2 bunches watercress, trimmed and tied with twine

6 cups Seasoned Dashi (page 31)

1. To make the noodles, in a large bowl, stir together the white flour, whole wheat flour, $1/2$ cup semolina, and salt. Make a well in the center of the bowl and add 1 cup of the water. Using a wooden spoon or your fingers, slowly incorporate the water into the flour until most of it has been absorbed. The dough will seem very dry, but it will become soft and pliable when you knead it.

2. Place the dough on a clean surface. Wash off any bits of flour stuck to your hands. Cover the dough with plastic wrap and let it rest for 5 minutes. Sift the bits of flour left in the bowl through a fine mesh strainer onto the counter and put it aside to use later. Discard the dried clumps of dough left in the strainer.

3. Knead the dough vigorously for 10 minutes. The dough must be stiff, but if it is too dry to knead, add water a teaspoon at a time. When the dough is smooth and resilient, wrap it in plastic and set it aside to relax for 30 minutes. The dough will soften considerably.

4. Divide the dough into two equal pieces. Work with one piece at a time, keeping the remaining dough covered with the plastic wrap. Roll each piece into a circle about $1/16$-inch thick. Lightly dust the sheet of dough with the reserved flour and roll it into a loose cylinder. Cut the cylinder crosswise into $1/4$-inch-wide pieces and uncurl the noodles onto a clean dry towel. Repeat with the remaining piece of dough.

TIPS ON MAKING, COOKING, AND STORING PASTA

- **Always start with the best-quality ingredients. Use filtered or nonchlorinated water, organic flour, and fresh organic eggs.**
- **Knead well so that the gluten can develop, then let the dough rest for at least 20 minutes to relax the gluten so that it will be supple enough to roll out.**
- **If your dough feels too wet, flour it on both sides, fold it over, and reroll.**
- **After rolling out the dough, let it sit for 5 to 8 minutes to dry a little, so that the strips don't stick together. But don't let it get too dry, or it will become brittle and break when you try to cut it.**
- **Although I think it's best to eat freshly made pasta right away, you can also let it dry out completely, and it will keep for about 3 months. Long noodles can be hung over broomsticks or drying racks for clothes. You can dry shaped pieces on a cooling rack or on a clean towel. You need to turn the pasta over a few times each day to ensure thorough drying. When you store it, put a few paper towels in the container to absorb any lingering moisture.**

5. For the vegetables, bring a large pot of water to a boil. Add the salt. When the water returns to a boil, add the broccoli, carrots, and daikon. Cook at a brisk boil, uncovered, for 2 minutes. Add the tofu, snow peas, and cabbage. Reduce the heat and simmer for 1 to 2 minutes. Add the watercress and cook for 30 seconds. Using a slotted spoon, transfer the vegetables and tofu to a bowl of ice water to arrest their cooking and set their color. Drain in a colander and set aside. Cover the pot and allow the water to return to a boil.

6. Uncover the pot and add the noodles. Cook for 2 to 3 minutes, until al dente. Transfer the noodles to a colander, rinse under cold running water until chilled, then drain well.

7. Arrange the vegetables and tofu in a ring inside a large heavy sauté pan or flameproof casserole. Place the noodles in the middle and set the pan over medium heat.

8. In a separate pot, bring the dashi to a boil. Gently pour the hot dashi down the side of the pan until it submerges the vegetables. Once the mixture comes to a boil, transfer it to the table and let everybody serve themselves.

YIELD: 6 SERVINGS

Pizzoccheri

This is a traditional pasta from Switzerland and northern Italy. I spent a couple of summers in Switzerland, and I sampled this dish all over the place. It is hearty, homey peasant food, and the dish quickly became one of my favorites. It is a good thing I like it so much, because the woman I stayed with would make it almost every night! She would gather dandelion greens, arugula, cabbage, potatoes, string beans, and sage from her garden and make a big vegetable soup, with a good quantity of red wine. Then, she boiled the noodles in the soup and finished it with cheese. Delicious!

FOR THE PASTA:

3/4 cup buckwheat flour

3/4 cup unbleached all-purpose or white bread flour plus additional flour for dusting

1/4 teaspoon sea salt

3 large eggs

FOR THE SAUCE:

4 tablespoons unsalted butter or oil

1 red onion, sliced

Coarse sea salt

2 cups chopped green cabbage

1 russet potato, peeled and sliced

1 carrot, sliced

1 large handful string beans, trimmed and sliced

2 to 3 garlic cloves, sliced

6 sage leaves, chopped

1/4 teaspoon hot red pepper flakes

3/4 cup red wine

1/4 cup water

1 bunch Swiss chard, chopped

1/2 cup grated Gruyère or Asiago cheese, plus additional cheese for garnish

Freshly milled black pepper

Chopped fresh parsley for garnish

1. To prepare the pasta, mix the flours and salt in a bowl. Make a well in the center and crack the eggs into it. Beat the eggs with a fork and incorporate the flour from the sides of the bowl until a soft dough forms. Scoop out the dough and place it on a lightly floured surface. Rinse off any flour stuck to your hands. There will probably be some flour clumps left in the bowl. Sift them through a fine strainer onto the dough and discard the scraps. Wash out the bowl. Knead the dough for 15 minutes, adding additional flour if necessary, to form a smooth, firm elastic dough. Wrap the dough in plastic and set aside to relax for 30 minutes at room temperature. (It can also be refrigerated for up to 24 hours.)

2. Divide the dough into four equal pieces. Work with one piece at a time, keeping the remaining dough covered with a damp cloth. Flatten each piece of dough into a disk and dust lightly with flour. Roll it into a sheet about $1/16$ inch thick. Dust lightly with flour and roll into a loose cylinder. Place the dough on a cutting board and slice into $1/2$-inch-wide pieces. Uncoil the noodles and set them on a clean towel to dry for 10 minutes before boiling.

3. To make the sauce, melt the butter in a heavy saucepan over medium heat. Add the onion and a pinch of salt and sauté for 5 to 7 minutes, until softened. Stir in the cabbage, potato, carrot, string beans, garlic, sage, and red pepper flakes. Add the wine and water, raise the heat, and bring to a boil. Reduce the heat and simmer for 20 minutes, until all the vegetables are tender.

4. Bring a large pot of water to a boil. Add 2 tablespoons salt. When the water returns to a boil, add the noodles. Cook for 1 to 2 minutes, until al dente. Drain the noodles, reserving 2 cups of the cooking water, and add them to the vegetables. Add the chard and reserved noodle water. Cover the pan and simmer until the greens are tender and the noodles are cooked through, 4 to 5 minutes.

5. Stir in the grated cheese and season with salt and pepper to taste. Serve garnished with parsley and additional cheese.

YIELD: 4 SERVINGS

Chestnut Pasta with Porcini Mushrooms, Pumpkin, and Leeks

Solio is a town high in the Swiss Alps that is the nearest thing to heaven that I have ever seen. Locally harvested porcini mushrooms and chestnuts dry in the rafters of the ancient barns that line the winding narrow backstreets of this rustic little village. That was my inspiration for this autumnal dish. The dark, musky aroma and flavor of the dried mushrooms goes particularly well with the sweetness of the pumpkin and leeks. I also add red tomatoes to brighten the color and cut through the intense earthiness of this ragout.

Chestnut flour is perishable, so make sure yours is fresh. It should smell and taste pleasingly sweet and nutty without any trace of bitterness. Store the flour tightly wrapped in the freezer.

FOR THE PASTA:

$^2/_3$ cup chestnut flour (see page 434 for a mail-order source)

$1^1/_3$ cups unbleached all-purpose or white bread flour,
  plus more for dusting

$^1/_4$ teaspoon sea salt

3 large eggs

FOR THE RAGOUT:

1 ounce dried porcini mushrooms

$1^1/_2$ cups warm water

4 tablespoons unsalted butter or extra-virgin olive oil

1 cup chopped leeks, white and tender green parts

2 tablespoons chopped garlic

4 cups peeled and roughly chopped winter squash or pumpkin

1 tablespoon chopped fresh sage

1 (28-ounce) can peeled tomatoes

Coarse sea salt

Freshly milled black pepper

1 tablespoon butter

Freshly grated Parmesan cheese for garnish

2 tablespoons chopped fresh parsley for garnish

1. To make the pasta, mix the chestnut flour, $1^1/_3$ cups white flour, and salt in a bowl. Make a well in the center and crack the eggs into it. Beat the eggs with a fork and incorporate the flour from the sides of the bowl until a soft dough forms.

2. Scoop out the dough and place it on a lightly floured surface. Rinse off any flour stuck to your hands. There will probably be some flour clumps left in the bowl. Sift them through a fine strainer onto the dough and discard the scraps. Wash out the bowl.

3. Knead the dough for 15 minutes, adding additional flour if necessary, to form a smooth, firm, elastic dough. Wrap the dough in plastic and set aside to relax for 30 minutes at room temperature. (At this point it can be refrigerated for up to 24 hours.)

4. Divide the dough into four equal pieces. Work with one piece at a time, keeping the remaining dough covered with plastic wrap. Roll the dough on the counter with outstretched palms into a loose 2-foot-long cylinder the width of a thin cigar. You may need to mist the rolling surface with a spray bottle if you don't have enough friction to roll the dough. Cut off 1-inch-long pieces of dough and roll them back and forth between your palms until they are approximately 3 inches long. Place the pasta on clean towels and continue to cut and roll until all the dough is used up.

5. While the pasta dries, make the ragout. Place the mushrooms in a bowl and cover with 1 1/2 cups warm water. Set them aside to soften.

6. In a heavy 3-quart saucepan or flameproof casserole over medium heat, melt the butter. Add the leeks and sauté for 5 to 7 minutes, until they begin to color. Add the garlic, squash, and sage. Sauté, stirring occasionally, for 5 minutes.

7. Gently massage the mushrooms between your fingers. Allow the grit to settle on the bottom of the bowl. Remove the mushrooms and chop them up. Strain off and reserve 1 cup of the soaking liquid. Be careful to stop before you reach the grit.

8. Place a food mill fitted with medium disk over the vegetables and pass the tomatoes with their juice directly into the pan. Add the chopped porcini and the reserved soaking liquid, raise the heat, and bring to a boil. Reduce the heat to low and simmer for 30 to 40 minutes, until the squash is tender and the sauce has thickened. Season with salt and pepper to taste. Keep warm.

9. Bring a large pot of water to a boil and add 1 tablespoon salt. When the water returns to a boil, add the pasta and stir to prevent sticking. Cook for 6 to 8 minutes, until the pasta is al dente. Drain.

10. Transfer the pasta to a warm bowl and toss with 1 tablespoon butter. Toss again with the sauce. Serve with grated cheese and chopped parsley.

YIELD: 4 TO 6 SERVINGS

Chickpea Flour Pasta with Zesty Leek and Tomato Sauce

I've often made pasta salad with chickpeas and tomatoes and marveled at how well all the flavors go together. And I've always loved foods made with chickpea flour, such as farinata and panisse, which are traditional Mediterranean polenta-like chickpea mixtures. So one day I thought, why not make pasta using chickpea flour? *Voilà*! Nutty, golden chickpea flour gives the pasta a terrific flavor, which is further enhanced by the addition of Rosemary-Garlic oil.

Making chickpea pasta is a vegan sleight-of-hand. The pasta can be eggless because of the binding quality of the chickpeas, which have a protein similar to that of egg whites.

FOR THE PASTA:
3/4 cup chickpea flour
1 1/4 cups unbleached all-purpose or white bread flour
1/4 teaspoon sea salt
1/2 cup warm water
2 tablespoons Rosemary-Garlic Oil (page 364) plus extra for garnish
Semolina flour for dusting

FOR THE SAUCE:
2 tablespoons butter or extra-virgin olive oil
3 leeks, white parts only, thinly sliced
2 garlic cloves, chopped
4 pounds red ripe tomatoes or 1 (28-ounce) can whole tomatoes
1 bay leaf
1 sprig fresh tarragon or 6 basil leaves
1/4 teaspoon hot red pepper flakes (optional)
Finely grated zest of 1 lemon
Coarse sea salt
Freshly milled black pepper
2 tablespoons snipped chives for garnish

1. In a large bowl, stir together the chickpea flour, white flour, and salt. Make a well in the center and add the water and Rosemary-Garlic Oil. Using a wooden spoon or your fingers, slowly incorporate the water into the flour until most of it has been absorbed. The dough will seem very dry but it will become soft and pliable when you knead it.

2. Place the dough on a clean surface. Wash off any bits of flour stuck to your hands. Cover the dough with plastic wrap and let it rest for 5 minutes. Sift the remaining bits of flour left in the bowl through a fine mesh strainer onto the counter and push it to the side to use when the dough is rolled out. Discard the dried clumps of dough left in the strainer. Knead the dough vigorously for 10 minutes. The dough must be stiff, but if it is too dry to knead, add 1 or 2 tablespoons water. When the dough is smooth and resilient, wrap it in plastic and set it aside to relax for 30 minutes. The dough will soften considerably.

3. To make the sauce, warm the butter in a wide sauté pan over medium heat. Add the leeks and garlic and sauté for 6 to 8 minutes, until wilted; do not brown. Increase the heat to high, add the tomatoes, bay leaf, tarragon, red pepper flakes, and lemon zest. Bring to a boil. Reduce the heat to low and simmer for 30 to 40 minutes, until thick.

4. Meanwhile, divide the pasta dough into two equal pieces. Work with one piece at a time, keeping the remaining dough covered with the plastic wrap. Roll each piece into a circle about $1/16$-inch thick. Let the pasta rest for just 5 to 7 minutes to dry slightly. Lightly dust the sheet of dough with reserved flour and roll into a loose cylinder. Cut the cylinder crosswise into $1/4$-inch-wide strips and uncurl the noodles onto a clean dry towel. Repeat with the remaining piece of dough.

5. Bring a large pot of water to a boil. Add 2 tablespoons salt. When the water returns to a boil, add the noodles and cook for 3 to 4 minutes, until cooked through. Drain and divide among 4 to 6 plates. Drizzle the pasta with Rosemary-Garlic Oil and sprinkle with some of the chives.

6. Season the sauce to taste with salt and pepper and strain through the medium holes of a hand-cranked food mill into a serving bowl. Or press it through a sieve, pressing down with a rubber spatula.

7. Serve the pasta and pass the sauce separately, garnished with the remaining chives.

YIELD: 4 TO 6 SERVINGS

Golden Egg Noodles with Crème Fraîche and Fresh Herbs

The delicious, velvety sauce for this recipe is extremely fast to make, yet totally luxurious. If you don't have crème fraîche, you can use heavy cream, but I think that cultured cream is much better for you and brings more character to the sauce. If you have the time and inclination, you can make your own crème fraîche.

This recipe calls for a hand-cranked pasta machine. If you don't own one, you can make the pasta by hand following the instructions for any of the other recipes.

FOR THE NOODLES:
2 cups unbleached white bread flour plus additional flour for dusting
1/4 teaspoon fine sea salt
3 large eggs

FOR THE SAUCE:
2 tablespoons extra-virgin olive oil or unsalted butter
1 garlic clove, finely chopped
2 tablespoons finely chopped fresh parsley
2 tablespoons finely chopped fresh basil or cilantro
1 tablespoon snipped fresh chives
1 teaspoon finely grated lemon zest
1 cup Crème Fraîche, preferably homemade (page 390)
Coarse sea salt
Freshly milled black pepper
1/4 cup freshly grated Parmesan cheese

1. To make the noodles, add the flour to a large bowl. Stir in the salt and make a well in the flour. Crack the eggs into the well and scramble lightly with a fork. Slowly draw the flour into the eggs with the fork until you have a ragged mass of dough. Mix the dough with your hands and form it into a ball. It should not feel too sticky or too dry. Add more flour if the dough is sticky, or water if the dough is too dry. The dough is ready for kneading when a finger inserted into the center of the dough comes out clean.

2. Place the dough on a clean work surface and knead rhythmically for 8 to 10 minutes, until the dough is shiny and supple. Wrap the dough in plastic and set it aside to relax at room temperature for 30 minutes.

3. Lay several clean cloth towels on a countertop or table. Unwrap the dough and divide it into six equal pieces. Work with one piece of dough at a time, keeping the remainder covered in plastic wrap. Adjust the rollers on the pasta machine to the widest setting. Flatten a piece of dough and run it through the machine. Fold the dough in thirds, insert the narrower end into the machine, and roll it through again. Lay the rolled dough flat on a towel. Repeat the process until all of the pieces of dough have been rolled twice. Make sure the flat pieces of dough do not touch each other when you lay them on the towels or they may stick together.

4. Close the rollers one notch. Insert the narrower end of the first piece of dough into the machine and roll it through. Repeat with the remaining pieces of dough. Always roll the pieces of dough in order to prevent uneven drying and ensure consistent texture and color of the finished pasta. Continue rolling the pieces in order and narrowing the rollers one notch at a time, until the sheets of dough have all passed through the sixth setting.

5. Let the pasta sheets dry for 8 to 10 minutes, turning them over once in a while until they are pliable, with a leathery feel, but are not so dry that they will crack when cut.

6. To make fettuccine, roll each sheet through the wider of the two cutters. Lay the noodles on the towels.

7. Bring a large pot of water to a boil and add 2 tablespoons salt. When the water returns to a vigorous boil, add the pasta. Stir with a long wooden spoon to prevent sticking. Cook for 2 to 3 minutes until al dente. Drain in a colander.

8. To make the sauce, warm the oil in a wide sauté pan over medium heat. Add the garlic and sauté for 1 minute. Before the garlic browns, add the parsley, basil, chives, and lemon zest. Sauté for 30 seconds, then stir in the crème fraîche. Add salt and pepper to taste. Bring to a boil and remove the pan from the heat.

9. Add the pasta to the pan and toss to coat. Add the Parmesan, toss again, and serve immediately. YIELD: 4 TO 6 SERVINGS

PASTA MACHINES VS. HAND-ROLLED PASTA

If you are like me, you'll want to be physically involved in the pasta-making process every step of the way. While I much prefer the experience of rolling out my pasta by hand, using a hand-cranked pasta machine works just as well. And the directions for machine-rolling pasta can be applied to any of the recipes in this chapter. Conversely, if you don't own a pasta machine, you can simply follow the instructions I give for rolling pasta by hand on pages 145 and 146.

White Bean Ravioli in Herbed Vegetable and Saffron Broth

Making your own ravioli is an incredibly satisfying culinary experience. Besides getting to choose what type of pasta dough you want to make, you get to select a filling, matching its style to the character of the dough.

One of the great secrets of making ravioli is that they freeze incredibly well. Then they can be tossed directly from the freezer into a pot of boiling water and are ready to eat in just minutes. The recipe can be doubled if you want to freeze a larger batch.

FOR THE PASTA:
1/2 cup semolina flour
1/2 cup unbleached all-purpose or white bread flour
1/4 teaspoon sea salt
1 large egg
2 tablespoons warm water plus more if needed

FOR THE FILLING:
2 tablespoons extra-virgin olive oil
1/4 cup finely chopped onion
2 teaspoons minced garlic
2 tablespoons finely chopped fresh flat-leaf parsley
1 tablespoon finely chopped fresh sage
Pinch hot red pepper flakes
1 cup cooked Great Northern or cannellini beans (from 1/3 cup dried beans, see page 226), drained
1 teaspoon red wine vinegar
Coarse sea salt
Freshly milled black pepper

FOR THE BROTH:
6 cups water
1 cup diced onion
1 small celery rib with leaves, chopped
4 garlic cloves, peeled
6 leaves fresh sage
2 teaspoons fennel seeds
Pinch saffron threads (about 1/2 teaspoon)

1 (3-inch) strip orange zest
1 bay leaf
1 ripe tomato, peeled, seeded, and chopped
1/2 cup finely diced carrot
1/2 cup finely chopped fennel
Coarse sea salt
Freshly milled black pepper

FOR THE GARNISH:
2 tablespoons snipped chives
3 or 4 basil leaves or flat-leaf parsley, torn
Parmesan cheese

1. To make the pasta, stir together the semolina flour, white flour, and salt in a large bowl. Make a well in the center of the bowl and add the egg and the water. Beat the liquids lightly with a fork to break up the eggs. Using a wooden spoon or your fingers, slowly incorporate the water into the flour until most of it has been absorbed. The dough will seem very dry.

2. Transfer the dough to a clean surface. Wash off any bits of flour stuck to your hands. Cover the dough with plastic wrap and let it rest for 5 minutes. Sift the remaining bits of flour left in the bowl through a fine mesh strainer onto the countertop and set aside to use later. Discard the dried clumps of dough left in the strainer. Knead the dough vigorously for 10 minutes. The dough should be stiff, but if it is too dry to knead, add 1 to 2 teaspoons water. When the dough is smooth and resilient, wrap it in plastic and set it aside to relax for 30 minutes.

3. Meanwhile, in a sauté pan over medium-high heat, warm the oil. Add the onion and sauté for 2 to 3 minutes, until softened. Add the garlic and sauté for 2 minutes. Stir in the parsley, sage, and red pepper flakes and sauté for 1 minute. Transfer the sautéed vegetables to a bowl, add the beans and vinegar, and mash well. Season with salt and pepper to taste.

4. Divide the dough into four equal pieces and form each piece into a circle. Work with one piece at a time, keeping the remaining dough under plastic wrap. Fold the circle into thirds and roll the narrow end through the widest setting on your pasta roller. Repeat this 4 to 5 times. Dust the pasta with reserved flour if it feels sticky. Now thin the dough by tightening the rollers, one notch at a time, passing the dough once through each setting up to the sixth setting.

5. Place the dough on a work surface. Spoon rounded teaspoons of the bean filling every 2 inches lengthwise along one half of the dough, leaving a 1/2-inch border. With a damp pastry brush, moisten the area between each mound of filling. Fold the other half of the dough over

to meet the edge and gently press around each mound of filling to seal. Cut the ravioli into squares with the filling in the center of each piece. Set aside on a clean towel to dry. Do not let them touch or they could stick together. Continue to roll, fill, seal, and cut the remaining pieces of dough.

6. While the ravioli dry, make the broth. In a pot over high heat, combine the water, onion, celery, garlic, sage, fennel seeds, saffron, orange zest, and bay leaf and bring to a boil. Reduce the heat to medium-low and simmer, uncovered, for 45 minutes, or until the broth is reduced to 4 cups. Strain the broth and discard the solids. Add the tomato, carrot, and fennel and simmer gently for 10 minutes, until the vegetables are cooked through. Season with salt and pepper to taste. Keep warm.

7. In a large pot of boiling salted water, cook the ravioli for 2 to 4 minutes. Drain well.

8. Divide the ravioli among 4 to 6 warm soup plates or pasta bowls. Pour the hot broth over the ravioli and garnish with the fresh herbs and Parmesan cheese.

YIELD: 4 TO 6 SERVINGS

SAFFRON

Extracted from the stigmas of crocus flowers, saffron is the most expensive spice there is. You only need a little pinch to give dishes a bright yellow color and slightly spicy, bitter taste. You can use turmeric in its place, if you are just concerned about the color. Saffron is sold in threads and in powdered form. Some people like to crush the threads, but I like how they look left whole.

FREEZING RAVIOLI

Spread the fresh, uncooked ravioli on a cookie sheet, making sure they do not touch. Freeze until solid, then store in a sealed plastic bag for up to 3 months.

Fresh Sourdough Bread Crumb Pasta

Here is an unusual eggless pasta inspired by the great author and teacher Giuliano Bugialli. It is made with bread crumbs, which help to provide a resiliency and delicate texture to the dough. I have had particularly good results using day-old naturally leavened sourdough bread. The tang from the lactic acid in the bread subtly enriches the flavor. Serve it with your favorite pasta sauce or use the Tomato Sauce on page 138.

1 ($1/2$-inch-thick) slice day-old bread, preferably homemade sourdough
  (pages 328 and 332–340)
$1 1/4$ cups unbleached all-purpose or white bread flour
$1/4$ cup whole wheat bread flour
$1/4$ teaspoon sea salt
$2/3$ cup plus 2 tablespoons warm water
2 tablespoons extra-virgin olive oil

1. Remove the crust from the bread and grind into crumbs in a food processor. Empty the processor and measure out a firmly packed $1/2$ cup crumbs. Combine crumbs, white flour, whole wheat flour, salt, $2/3$ cup of water, and oil in the food processor. Pulse a few times to form a ball of dough. Add the remaining water, a teaspoon at a time, if the dough is too dry.

2. Place the dough on a clean work surface and knead vigorously for 10 minutes. The dough should be fairly stiff. When the dough is smooth and resilient, wrap it in the damp cloth and set aside to relax for 30 minutes. The dough will soften considerably. (It can also be refrigerated for up to 24 hours.)

3. Divide the dough into six equal pieces. Work with one piece at a time, keeping the remaining dough covered with the damp cloth. Roll the dough on the counter with outstretched palms into a 2-foot-long loose cylinder the width of a thin cigar. You may need to mist the rolling surface with a spray bottle if you don't have enough friction to roll the dough.

4. Slice off marble-sized pieces of dough. Press each piece firmly into the counter with the thumb of one hand to form an indented saucer-shaped disk. Immediately roll the disk with the index and middle fingers of your opposite hand to form a cavatelli shape. At first this may feel awkward, but, as you practice, a rhythm will develop that will take over and become almost a Zen-like exercise.

5. Spread the pasta on clean kitchen towels and dry for at least 45 minutes before cooking.

6. Cook in a large pot of boiling, salted water until al dente.   YIELD: 4 TO 6 SERVINGS

Whole Wheat Pasta with Creamy Walnut-Portobello Sauce

A must for cold weather, this velvety-rich dish is supremely elegant. The sauce is built on the foundation of a rich, earthy mushroom broth, which is thickened and enriched by walnuts. I usually serve it with whole wheat pasta, which goes nicely with the mushrooms, but egg noodles, especially homemade, are another stellar match.

This was originally a vegan recipe; to make it one again, simply substitute additional oil for the butter.

FOR THE MUSHROOM BROTH:

2 portobello mushrooms

4 cups water

4 dried shiitake mushrooms

1 small celery rib with leaves, chopped

1 small carrot, thinly sliced

2 bay leaves

1 sprig fresh thyme

1 small sprig fresh rosemary

1 teaspoon whole coriander seeds

$^1/_2$ teaspoon whole black peppercorns

FOR THE SAUCE:

2 tablespoons extra-virgin olive oil

2 tablespoons unsalted butter

1 cup diced onion

4 plump garlic cloves, chopped

2 tablespoons water

$1^1/_2$ cups freshly shelled walnuts,
    toasted (see page 373)

2 tablespoons mirin

2 tablespoons naturally brewed soy sauce

Coarse sea salt

1 pound whole wheat spaghetti or linguine or
    1 recipe Golden Egg Noodles (page 156)

1 tablespoon extra-virgin olive oil or butter for garnish

Chopped fresh parsley for garnish

1. To make the broth, snap off the stems from the portobellos and chop them. Set aside the caps for the sauce. In a 2-quart saucepan over high heat, combine the chopped stems, water, dried shiitakes, celery, carrot, bay leaves, thyme, rosemary, coriander seeds, and peppercorns. Bring to a boil, then reduce the heat to low and simmer, covered, for 30 minutes. Strain the broth and discard the solids.

2. To make the sauce, warm the oil and butter in a heavy wide sauté pan over medium heat. Add the onion and sauté for 5 to 7 minutes, until golden. Add the garlic and sauté for 2 minutes. Dice the reserved mushroom caps and add them to the pan. Raise the heat and stir until the mushrooms release their juices and begin to caramelize. Reduce the heat, add the water, and simmer, covered, for 10 to 15 minutes, until tender.

3. In a blender, combine half of the walnuts with 2 cups of broth and purée until creamy smooth. Stir the walnut cream into the sauce. Pour the remaining broth into the blender, blend for 5 seconds to clean out the remaining walnut cream, and pour into the sauce.

4. Add the mirin and soy sauce and bring to a boil. Reduce the heat to low and simmer gently until the sauce thickens to the desired consistency.

5. In a large pot over high heat, bring 6 quarts water to a boil. Add 2 tablespoons salt. When the water returns to a boil, add the pasta and stir with a long-handled wooden spoon. Cook the pasta for 10 to 12 minutes for store-bought whole wheat, or 2 to 3 minutes for homemade Golden Egg Noodles. Drain in a colander, then transfer to a serving bowl.

6. Toss the pasta with oil. Pour on the sauce, and garnish with the remaining walnuts and parsley.

YIELD: 6 SERVINGS

Penne with Chickpeas, Artichokes, Fennel, and Shiitake Mushrooms

If you plan on cooking the chickpeas for this scrumptious sauce, make sure to start soaking them at least 8 hours ahead of time.

Refer to page 229 in the bean chapter for tips on pressure-cooking chickpeas.

3 large globe artichokes

1 lemon

1 large fennel bulb,
   trimmed and chopped

2 sprigs thyme

1 bay leaf

2 sprigs parsley or a handful
   of celery leaves

5 tablespoons extra-virgin olive oil

1 onion, diced

Coarse sea salt

4 garlic cloves, sliced

2 teaspoons freshly ground fennel seeds

8 to 10 fresh shiitake mushrooms,
   caps diced and stems reserved for broth

$1/4$ cup dry white wine

1 (14-ounce) can whole peeled tomatoes

$1 1/2$ cups cooked chickpeas (from $1/2$ cup dried beans, see page 226)
   plus 1 cup cooking liquid (or water if using canned chickpeas)

$1/2$ pound whole wheat or regular penne pasta

$1/3$ cup kalamata olives, pitted and roughly chopped

Freshly milled black pepper

Chopped fresh parsley for garnish

Parmesan cheese for garnish

1. Trim the artichokes down to the hearts and scoop out the hairy chokes. Put the hearts in a bowl of cold water acidulated with the juice of half a lemon. Add the chopped fennel to the bowl.

2. Make a bouquet garni by tying together with kitchen twine or wrapping in cheesecloth the thyme, bay leaf, and parsley sprigs. Set aside.

3. In a wide heavy sauté pan over medium heat, warm 4 tablespoons of the oil. Add the onion and a pinch of salt and sauté for 5 to 7 minutes. Do not let the onion brown. Add the garlic and sauté for 2 minutes.

4. Drain the artichokes and fennel. Slice each heart into 4 to 6 wedges. Add them to the pan along with the fennel seeds and mushrooms. Sauté for 5 minutes, then add the white wine and bouquet garni.

5. Pass the tomatoes and their juice through the medium holes of a food mill directly into the pan. Add the chickpeas and their juice and stir well. Raise the heat and bring to a boil. Reduce the heat to low and simmer for 25 minutes, or until the vegetables are tender and the sauce thickens.

6. Bring a large pot of water to a boil for the pasta. Add 2 tablespoons salt. When the water returns to a boil, stir in the pasta and cook until al dente. Drain the pasta, tip it into a warm serving bowl or platter and toss with the remaining tablespoon of oil.

7. Remove the bouquet garni from the sauce and discard. Stir in the olives and simmer for 1 minute. Season the sauce with additional lemon juice, salt, and pepper to taste. Pour the sauce over the penne and sprinkle with chopped parsley and grated Parmesan.

YIELD: 4 SERVINGS

Rigatoni with Cauliflower, Pine Nuts, and Raisins

In this robust, sweet-and-sour dish, the pasta is partially cooked in boiling water and finished in the sauce. It's a great method for infusing the pasta with flavor and unifying the dish.

Coarse sea salt
1 small cauliflower, cored and separated into about 4 cups small florets
4 tablespoons extra-virgin olive oil
1 large onion, diced
1/4 cup pine nuts
3 garlic cloves, chopped
2 large bay leaves
1 pinch saffron (about 1/2 teaspoon)
1/2 teaspoon hot red pepper flakes or to taste
3 tablespoons tomato paste
1/2 cup raisins
1/2 cup water
1/3 cup dry white wine
3/4 pound rigatoni
1/4 cup finely chopped fresh parsley
Freshly milled black pepper
1/2 cup grated Parmesan cheese for garnish

1. Bring a large pot of water to a boil. Add 2 tablespoons salt. When the water returns to a boil, add the cauliflower and blanch for 2 minutes. Remove the cauliflower to a plate. Reserve the water for cooking the pasta.

2. In a wide heavy sauté pan over medium heat, warm the oil. Add the onion and a pinch of salt. Sauté for 5 to 7 minutes, until softened. Add the pine nuts, garlic, bay leaves, saffron, and red pepper flakes and sauté for 2 minutes.

3. Stir in the tomato paste, raisins, water, and wine. Raise the heat and bring the sauce to a boil. Reduce the heat to low, add the cauliflower, and simmer, covered, for 15 minutes.

4. Return the cauliflower water to a boil. Add the rigatoni and cook for 10 minutes. Drain the pasta and add it to the pot with the sauce. Simmer for 3 to 5 minutes, or until the pasta is tender.

5. Add the parsley and salt and pepper to taste. Serve with Parmesan.   YIELD: 4 SERVINGS

Whole Wheat Fusilli with Swiss Chard and Balsamic-Roasted Onions

This comforting winter pasta is a great example of how you can coax intense flavors out of your foods without using animal products. Balsamic vinegar both brightens the color of the red onions and brings out their sweetness as it helps to caramelize them.

Also, the roasted onions and wilted greens alone make an unusual crostini topping.

2 red onions, sliced lengthwise into thin wedges
1 tablespoon balsamic vinegar plus more to taste
Coarse sea salt
4 tablespoons extra-virgin olive oil
2 sprigs fresh thyme, leaves stripped
1 pound Swiss chard, trimmed
3/4 pound whole wheat fusilli
2 plump garlic cloves, peeled and sliced
1/8 teaspoon hot red pepper flakes

1. Preheat the oven to 350°F.

2. Toss the onions in a bowl with vinegar, 1/4 teaspoon salt, 1 tablespoon of the oil, and the thyme.

3. Spread the onions in a baking pan and roast for 30 to 40 minutes, until soft and caramelized. Stir the onions after 20 minutes for even roasting.

4. Bring a large pot of water to a boil. Add 2 tablespoons salt. When the water returns to a boil, add the chard and cook for 2 minutes, or until wilted and tender. Remove the chard (tongs work best) to a colander to drain. Cover the pot and return the water to a boil. Add the pasta and cook until al dente.

5. While the pasta cooks, warm the remaining 3 tablespoons oil in a heavy, wide sauté pan over medium heat. Add the garlic and tip the pan so the garlic can sizzle in a depth of oil on the side of the pan. Cook for 1 minute, or until the garlic begins to color around the edges, but do not let it brown. Add the chard, 1/4 cup of the pasta cooking water, and the red pepper flakes and simmer for 5 minutes. Remove the onions from the oven and add them to the mixture.

6. Drain the pasta and transfer to a warm serving platter or bowl. Toss the vegetables with the pasta and season with vinegar to taste. Serve at once.   YIELD: 4 SERVINGS

Farfalle with Fresh Summer Ragout

The charm of this garden sauce lies in its freshness. Don't make it unless you have perfectly ripe, farm-fresh vegetables on hand.

    2 to 3 sprigs fresh thyme
    Several sprigs fresh parsley
    1/3 cup extra-virgin olive oil
    2 red onions, chopped
    Coarse sea salt
    4 to 5 garlic cloves, chopped
    2 zucchini, diced
    1 large eggplant, peeled and diced
    3 pounds ripe tomatoes,
        peeled, seeded, and chopped
    1 pound farfalle (bow-tie pasta)
    1 tablespoon unsalted butter or olive oil
    Freshly milled black pepper
    1/2 cup fresh basil leaves, torn

1. Make a bouquet garni by tying together with kitchen twine or wrapping in cheesecloth the thyme and parsley. Set aside.

2. In a heavy 3-quart saucepan over medium heat, combine the oil, onions, and 1/2 teaspoon salt and sauté until lightly browned, 8 to 10 minutes. Stir in the garlic and sauté for 2 minutes. Add the zucchini, eggplant, tomatoes, bouquet garni, and additional salt to taste. Raise the heat and bring the sauce to a boil. Reduce the heat to low and simmer gently, uncovered, until the vegetables are tender and the sauce has thickened, 35 to 40 minutes.

3. Bring a large pot of water to a boil. Add 2 tablespoons salt. When the water returns to a boil, stir in the farfalle and cook until al dente. Drain the pasta and transfer to a warm serving platter or bowl. Toss with the butter.

4. Season the sauce with additional salt and pepper to taste. Remove and discard the bouquet garni. Stir in the basil and simmer for 1 minute longer.

5. Toss the pasta with the sauce and serve.

YIELD: 6 SERVINGS

Preparing Fresh Tomatoes

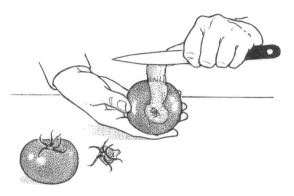

Core the tomato and blanch briefly in boiling water. Cool the tomatoes under cold running water. The skins will peel off easily.

Slice the tomatoes in half crosswise. Push out and discard the seeds.

Dice the flesh.

Cold Pasta Dishes

Cold Sesame Noodles with Radish and Cucumber

The sesame sauce for this classic Asian-style noodle dish is equally suited for steamed vegetables, rice, and tofu. Here the crispy radish and cucumber supply a refreshing relief from the smooth texture of noodles bathed in a creamy, rich sauce.

1 medium daikon radish, peeled and julienned, or
    1 small bunch red radishes,
    unpeeled and julienned (about 1 cup)
Coarse sea salt (optional)
1/2 pound udon noodles
1 cup tahini (sesame paste)
1/3 cup chopped cilantro (optional)
1/4 cup honey or pure maple syrup
3 tablespoons naturally brewed soy sauce
3 tablespoons rice vinegar
2 garlic cloves, peeled
1 tablespoon finely chopped, peeled gingerroot
1 tablespoon toasted sesame oil
1/4 teaspoon cayenne pepper plus
    additional to taste
1/2 cup water plus additional as needed
1 cucumber, halved, seeded,
    and thinly sliced
1 scallion, white and green parts,
    thinly sliced

1. Place the daikon in a bowl of cold water and refrigerate while you prepare the noodles and sauce.

2. Bring a large pot of water to a boil. Do not add salt if the noodles are salted (check ingredients on the package). Add the noodles and cook until al dente, stirring to prevent sticking. Drain the noodles in a colander and rinse under cold running water until thoroughly chilled.

3. In a blender, combine the tahini, cilantro, honey, soy sauce, vinegar, garlic, ginger, oil, cayenne, and water, and purée. Add additional water, 1 tablespoon at a time, until you have a creamy, smooth, pourable sauce. Add more cayenne to taste, if desired.

4. To serve, sauce the noodles to taste and top with the daikon, cucumber, and scallion.

YIELD: 4 SERVINGS

Chilled Soba in Asian Broth with Crunchy Vegetable Garnish

This is one of the best dishes to pick me up during hot, sultry New York City summers. A cool noodle salad and soup all in one, it's a great way to replenish the minerals lost to the heat and humidity. The broth will keep for up to a week in the refrigerator.

4 cups water
1 (3- to 4-inch) piece kombu
4 dried shiitake mushrooms
6 tablespoons naturally brewed soy sauce
4 tablespoons mirin
3 tablespoons rice vinegar
1 (1-inch) piece gingerroot, sliced into thin rounds
$1/2$ pound soba noodles
2 teaspoons toasted sesame oil
2 cups shredded romaine lettuce
1 cup julienned carrot
1 cup julienned daikon radish
1 scallion, white and green parts, thinly sliced
1 sheet sushi nori, toasted, quartered lengthwise,
    and cut crosswise into thin strips

1. Combine the water and kombu in a pot and bring to a boil. Remove the kombu and reserve for making a soup.

2. Add the mushrooms, soy sauce, mirin, vinegar, and ginger and simmer gently, uncovered, for 45 minutes. Strain the broth and discard the mushrooms and ginger. You should end up with 4 cups broth. Add water if the broth has reduced too much or continue to simmer if the broth needs further reduction. Refrigerate the broth until it is well chilled.

3. Bring a second large pot of water to a boil for the noodles and cook them until al dente. Drain the noodles, rinse them under cold running water, drain again, and toss them in a bowl with the oil.

4. Divide the noodles evenly among 4 deep bowls. Pour the cold broth over the noodles and top with fresh lettuce, carrot, daikon, and scallion. Sprinkle the nori strips over the vegetables and serve immediately. YIELD: 4 SERVINGS

Pasta Salad with Basil-Almond Pesto

Freshly peeled almonds make all the difference in the mouth-watering pesto that accompanies this pasta salad. This one is great for a late-summer picnic.

Coarse sea salt
6 cups chopped vegetables,
    such as summer squash, cauliflower,
    string beans, carrots, fennel, sugar snap peas,
    broccoli, or red onions (cut into pieces about the size of the pasta)
1/2 pound pasta, such as fusilli, chioccioli, or farfalle
2/3 cup Basil-Almond Pesto (page 377)
1/4 cup red wine vinegar
2 tablespoons extra-virgin olive oil

1. Preheat the oven to 350°F.

2. Bring 6 quarts water to a boil. Add 2 tablespoons salt. When the water returns to a boil, cook the vegetables, uncovered, for 2 to 3 minutes or until they are crisp-tender. Remove them from the water with a spider or slotted spoon and shock them under cold running water. Drain and set aside.

3. Cover the pot and return the water to boil. Stir in the pasta and cook just short of al dente. Drain the pasta in a colander and chill under cold running water. Drain thoroughly.

4. In a large serving bowl, combine the vegetables and pasta and set aside.

5. In a small bowl, whisk together the pesto, vinegar, and oil. Pour the vinaigrette over the pasta and vegetables and toss well. Cover the salad and let it rest at room temperature for 15 minutes.

6. Before serving, taste the salad and add salt if necessary.

YIELD: 4 TO 6 SERVINGS

Soba Salad

This refreshing, zesty salad is a complete meal that is perfect for picnics. Arame, a type of seaweed, is very delicate and tasty—it is not one of those rubbery seaweeds that taste like low tide! It adds a dramatic black color and slightly chewy texture to this piquant dish.

½ pound soba noodles
½ cup arame
1 pound firm tofu
2 cups trimmed and sliced snow peas
(sliced lengthwise)
3 cups sliced napa cabbage
1 large cucumber, peeled, seeded, and thinly sliced
6 tablespoons rice vinegar
3 tablespoons naturally brewed soy sauce
2 tablespoons mirin
2 tablespoons olive oil or
light sesame oil
1 tablespoon toasted sesame oil
1 tablespoon peeled and minced ginger
1 teaspoon coarse sea salt
2 teaspoons minced garlic
½ teaspoon cayenne pepper
1 cup chopped fresh cilantro
3 scallions, white and green parts,
chopped into thin rounds
1 cup unsalted dry-roasted peanuts,
roughly chopped

1. Bring 3 quarts water to a boil. Add the noodles and cook for 8 to 10 minutes, until al dente. Drain the noodles in a colander and cool under cold running water. Drain thoroughly and set aside in a large mixing bowl.

2. In a small bowl, cover the arame with lukewarm water until it is softened, 10 to 15 minutes. Drain.

3. Rinse the tofu under cold running water and pat dry. Place the tofu in a bowl and coarsely mash with a fork.

4. Pour 1 inch water into a pan and fit it with a steamer. Add the tofu and steam over high heat for 5 minutes. Remove the tofu to a plate and refrigerate.

5. Fill a bowl with ice water. Steam the snow peas for 1 minute, then immediately plunge them into the ice water until well chilled. Drain in a colander and add to the soba, along with the cabbage, cucumber, and arame.

6. In a separate bowl, combine the vinegar, soy sauce, mirin, oils, ginger, salt, garlic, and cayenne and whisk well. Add the tofu to the bowl, stir, and let marinate for 5 minutes.

7. Combine the marinated tofu, cilantro, and scallions and mix well.

8. Transfer the tofu and its marinade to the bowl containing the soba and toss well. Add the chopped peanuts just prior to serving and toss again.

YIELD: 6 SERVINGS

Pasta Salad with Tangy Sesame-Yogurt Sauce

The zesty, golden sauce makes a perfect dip for a platter full of crisp seasonal crudités if you don't feel like making the pasta salad.

> **2 tablespoons extra-virgin olive oil**
> **1 teaspoon minced garlic**
> **$1/2$ teaspoon ground cumin**
> **$1/2$ teaspoon ground coriander**
> **$1/4$ teaspoon cayenne pepper**
> **$1/2$ teaspoon turmeric**
> **$1/2$ cup water**
> **$1/2$ cup tahini (sesame paste)**
> **$1/2$ cup plain yogurt**
> **3 tablespoons freshly squeezed lemon juice**
> **Coarse sea salt**
> **1 head broccoli, cut into small florets,**
> **stalks reserved for another use**
> **2 cups string beans, trimmed and sliced**
> **into $1 1/2$-inch lengths**
> **$1/2$ pound medium shell, penne,**
> **or fusilli pasta**
> **4 to 6 plum tomatoes or**
> **2 cups cherry tomatoes**
> **2 tablespoons chopped cilantro,**
> **mint, or parsley for garnish**
> **Freshly milled black pepper**

1. In a saucepan over high heat, warm the oil. Add the garlic, cumin, coriander, cayenne, and turmeric and sauté for 30 seconds. Using a rubber spatula, transfer the mixture to a mixing bowl. Whisk in the water, tahini, yogurt, lemon juice, and $1/2$ teaspoon salt. Cover and refrigerate until you are ready to serve.

2. Bring a large pot of water to a boil. Add 2 tablespoons salt. When the water returns to a boil, add the broccoli and string beans and blanch for 2 to 3 minutes, until crisp-tender.

Transfer the vegetables with a slotted spoon to a colander and chill under cold running water. Drain thoroughly, blot with a clean towel, and reserve in a mixing bowl.

3. Return the water to a boil and add the pasta. Cook until al dente. Drain in a colander and chill under cold running water. Drain well.

4. Combine the pasta with the vegetables. Add the dressing and toss well.

5. If you are using plum tomatoes, slice them in half lengthwise and scoop out their seeds. Slice each half into thirds and add them to the salad along with the cilantro. If you have cherry tomatoes, add them whole. Toss again with additional salt and pepper to taste, and serve.

YIELD: 4 TO 6 SERVINGS

Pasta Salad with Sun-Dried Tomato Vinaigrette

Although pasta salads are definitely best the day they are made, you can prepare them a day in advance if you refrigerate the vegetables and pasta separately. Toss with dressing not more than an hour or so before serving, otherwise the vibrant colors of green vegetables will darken and turn muddy.

> **Coarse sea salt**
> **6 cups chopped vegetables, such as summer squash,**
> **cauliflower, string beans, carrots, fennel,**
> **sugar snap peas, broccoli, or red onions**
> **(cut into pieces about the size of the pasta)**
> **1/2 pound pasta, such as fusilli or farfalle**
> **1 cup dry-pack sun-dried tomatoes**
> **1/3 cup extra-virgin olive oil**
> **1/3 cup balsamic vinegar**
> **1/4 cup water**
> **12 fresh basil leaves**
> **2 garlic cloves, peeled**
> **1/2 teaspoon hot red pepper flakes**
> **Freshly chopped parsley for garnish**

1. Bring 6 quarts water to a boil. Add 2 tablespoons salt. When the water returns to a boil, cook the vegetables, uncovered, for 2 to 3 minutes, until they are crisp-tender. Remove them from the water with a spider or slotted spoon and shock them under cold running water. Drain and set aside.

2. Return the water to a boil and add the pasta. Cook until al dente. Drain and chill under cold running water. Drain well.

3. Boil the tomatoes for 2 minutes in water to cover and set aside for 5 to 8 minutes to soften. Drain and discard the liquid.

4. In a blender, purée the tomatoes along with the oil, vinegar, water, basil, garlic, 2 teaspoons salt, and red pepper flakes until creamy.

5. Toss the pasta and blanched vegetables with dressing to taste. Let the salad rest, covered, at room temperature for 15 minutes. Taste for seasoning and add more dressing or salt if necessary.

6. Toss with chopped parsley and serve.

YIELD: 4 TO 6 SERVINGS

Whole Grains,

Polenta, Risotto,
and Porridge

Ever since the health food movement began in America in the latter part of the nineteenth century, its proponents and converts have been fervent worshipers at the Altar of Whole Grains. More than any other foods, whole-grain bread and brown rice have defined a dietary and culinary movement founded on the belief that foods in their whole and unrefined state are more valuable to humans than those that are adulterated by various methods of polishing or cleaning. Along with this belief has evolved an attitude that one should eat to live rather than live to eat. This concept of food as fuel for the body alone soon translated into the catchy phrase "You are what you eat." However, these conclusions are based on an analysis of foods that have been taken out of context—extracted from time and place, tradition and culture, ritual and intuition.

I began eating whole grains more than twenty-five years ago, and it took me ten years before I realized that (a) I had become a slave to a purely theoretical way of eating; (b) I was not absorbing enough nutrients from eating whole grains exclusively; and (c) I was not enjoying my food as much as I knew I could. When I paused and took a look back in history, I saw that grain-eating cultures around the world have been cleaning their grains in one way or another since the dawn of agriculture more than ten thousand years ago: Asians polished their rice; Northern Europeans sifted their wheat and polished their barley; and Native Americans cleaned their dried corn. In the era before industrialization, these were time-consuming and sometimes arduous tasks, so why did these practices develop?

Although our ancestors probably couldn't explain their actions in scientific terms, they must have noticed that cleaned grains were easier to digest, easier to chew, faster to cook, and provided more energy than raw whole grains. Now, we know that many of the whole grains that have a distinct cleft, such as rye, barley wheat, and spelt, contain phytic acid compounds in their outer bran layer, which prevent the body from absorbing vital amino acids, calcium, and magnesium phosphate. Cleaning and polishing grains is one way of freeing up nutrients for our bodies to absorb effectively.

So, for the past fifteen years, I have expanded my diet to include a variety of whole and polished grains, as well as fermented flour products that use sourdough culture. This is what feels best to me. See what feels right for you.

Today, supermarkets and health food stores stock almost every type of grain imaginable, making it easy to eat a rich and varied diet. But, historically, grain availability was more localized. Regional geography and climate meant cuisines were based on native grains. Eventually, three distinct kinds of cookery evolved—namely, cloven grain cookery, which includes bread and beer making; corn cookery; and round or smooth grain cookery, which includes grains such as quinoa, millet, and rice.

In northern Europe, the predominant grains were barley, rye, and oats. These are very tough, cloven grains that are tricky to work with and require relatively long cooking times. Barley is probably best suited for soups. Slow cooking allows it to release some of its starch, creating a full-bodied, rich, and creamy soup. Rye is a very hearty grain with a distinct flavor. As with barley, it is often fermented into alcohol or ground and combined with wheat flour for delicious pumpernickel and rye breads. Oats, which are predominantly available as rolled flakes, can also be purchased whole and cracked fresh at home. They make a wonderful, creamy porridge and are a nice, chewy addition to multi-grain breads.

Southern Europeans included wheat in their diet. Although wheat is a cloven grain, it is far more flexible and versatile than barley, oats, or rye. You really can't make bread, as we know it, without wheat. Wheat is also the foundation of pasta, couscous, dumplings, phyllo, cookies, and tarts. Cooked on its own, as bulgur or wheat berries, it has a light, sweet, nutty taste, making it the most appealing of any of these cloven whole grains.

Corn is different from the other grains in that you can eat it either fresh or dried. The Mayans and Aztecs, who depended greatly on corn, knew that simply harvesting a grain, boiling it, and eating it would not provide the full potential of its nutrients. Instead, they boiled the kernels with ashes, lime, or other naturally occurring alkaline substances. This treatment makes the removal of the hull easier, balances the amino acids, and releases the bound niacin, which can then be absorbed effectively by the body. A diet based on too much uncleaned corn and cornmeal can lead to protein and niacin deficiencies and eventually cause pellagra, a potentially lethal degenerative disease. Though native to the Americas, corn was brought to Europe by the returning explorers, and cornmeal polenta quickly became popular among the lower classes, replacing traditional gruels and loaves made from rye, spelt, and barley. Unfortunately, the age-old methods of preparing corn did not accompany its introduction to the Old World, and subsequently, many people suffered from this mysterious ailment. It would take more than two hundred years before Dr. Joseph Goldberger discovered that what was previously believed to have been an infectious disease was actually no more than the horrible, painful, and disfiguring symptoms of a niacin deficiency caused by a diet based on whole-grain corn. In the meantime, the pellagra epidemic had spread throughout Italy, France, Africa, and the southern United States.

Warmer climates host the round or smooth grains, which, in general, are easily digestible and do not require much preparation or cooking time. Quinoa and amaranth derive from South America, and teff, a poppy seed–sized grain, originated in Ethiopia. Millet, which is used mostly as a feed crop in the United States, is an important dietary component in Africa, its native habitat, and in Asia. Rice, a grain that can be eaten whole or polished, originated in the Indian subcontinent. I really enjoy combining these quick-cooking round grains with polished grains such as white basmati, red bhutanese, arborio, or fragrant jasmine rice. I like playing with different combinations to get a variety of tastes, shapes, and textures.

There are a few things to consider when combining grains. First of all, you need to make sure that the grains have the same cooking times. Second, if you want to end up with something that is moldable, like a croquette, you must combine a quick-cooking whole grain, such quinoa, with a polished grain that will readily exude its starch, such as white rice. The starch will surround the other grains and hold them together. However, if you want to make a pilaf or a salad, you might avoid starchy polished grains because you are aiming for grains that are light, fluffy, and separate. Another thing to consider when mixing grains is aesthetics and texture. I find that it's pleasing to mix, for example, kamut, spelt, and barley, all similar-sized grains with contrasting shapes, colors, and textures. The last thing to take into consideration is flavor. Certain grains are very strong and overpowering, such as kasha, rye, and quinoa. I like to tone down these assertive flavors with a bland grain such as rice, or a sweet, nutty bulgur that balances the earthy, dark flavors.

PARCHING GRAINS

There are several incentives to parching grains. Whole grains will cook more quickly and have a fluffier consistency because the dry heat begins the cooking process by cracking the outer bran layer. Parching also brings out the hidden sweetness and flavor of grains. Millet, which is rather bland and boring on its own, benefits greatly from a little toasting. When parching grains it is important to heat them gently and evenly. Use a heavy pan on the stovetop, stirring and shaking over medium heat for about 8 minutes, or until the grains begin to emit a fragrant, nutty aroma. The grain may then be cooked using any method.

Cooking Methods

STOVETOP SIMMERING

This is a good method if you desire fluffy, separate grains. If you are cooking grains for a salad, they will be even fluffier if you bring a lightly salted cooking liquid to a boil before adding the grains. If you start cooking grains in cold liquid, they will release more starch and cook up stickier, perfect for a croquette or loaf.

The ratio of water to grain varies with the type of grain but in general, polished grains require less water than whole grains. The grain is done when it has absorbed the cooking liquid and steam holes appear on the surface.

PRESSURE COOKING

Pressure cookers are great for cooking grains that have very tough hulls, such as spelt and kamut. Another great use for your pressure cooker is cooking dense, sticky whole-grain rice for sushi rolls. Because polished grains cook faster than whole grains, they tend to overcook and become sticky and dense in the pressure cooker. Start timing the cooking when the pressure cooker has achieved full pressure.

BAKING

As with beans, baking is a very convenient way to cook grains, and it is perfect for making large quantities. The all-around heat intensifies the flavor of the grains and makes burning them next to impossible—if anything, you'll end up with grains that are a little toasted and crunchy around the sides, which can be a nice effect. Cooking grains in the oven also frees up the stovetop for other dishes. You can cook any grain in the oven, as long as you have a flameproof, ovenproof pot that is at least 3 inches deep and has a heavy lid; otherwise you can cover the pot tightly with foil.

To bake grains, first bring the cooking water to a boil. If you start with cold water, it will take forever to bake, and the grains will end up being mushy and soggy. Add the grains, cover tightly, and put the pot in a preheated 325°F oven. The grains should cook in about the same amount of time as they would on the stovetop.

PILAF METHOD

The purpose of this technique is to yield a grain that is flavorful, fluffy, dry, and separate. Start by sautéing the grains in some fat and, if you wish, with aromatics, such as onions, garlic, or leeks. Toasting the grains like this tightens up the starch so that the grains don't become creamy. The heat prevents the grains from bursting. After they have toasted for 7 to 10 minutes (and light-colored grains such as white rice have turned golden), add boiling broth or water to the pan, cover, and cook (either in the oven or on the stovetop) undisturbed, until all the liquid has been absorbed by the grain.

RISOTTO METHOD

The technique for making risotto starts out similarly to the pilaf method—sautéing the grains in fat. This time we want the starches to contract somewhat so that the resulting dish will have an al dente texture. As you gradually add simmering liquid to the grains while stirring constantly, a lot of the starches are released, creating a suave, creamy sauce. Short, plump arborio rice is one of the best grains to use for risotto. It contains two types of starches—one is easily released into the cooking liquid, creating the velvety creaminess; the other remains inside the grain, making the risotto al dente.

Grain Salads

Millet Salad Mexicano

Millet doesn't have much personality on its own, so, after toasting the grains to bring out their hidden sweetness, I've dressed them up with avocado and sweet corn.

1 cup millet, rinsed and drained
2 cups water
Coarse sea salt
Kernels from 6 ears sweet corn
$1/2$ cup freshly squeezed lime juice (from approximately 3 limes)
4 medium jalapeño peppers, seeded and minced
1 tablespoon ground cumin
$1/4$ cup extra-virgin olive oil
$1/4$ cup packed minced fresh cilantro
2 tablespoons thinly sliced scallions, white and green parts
2 ripe avocados, diced
4 tomatoes, chopped
Freshly milled black pepper

1. Place a heavy skillet (such as cast-iron) over medium heat for several minutes. When the pan is hot, add the millet and roast, stirring the grains and shaking the pan, until the moisture has cooked off and the millet is dry and very fragrant, about 5 to 7 minutes.

2. In a 2-quart saucepan over high heat, combine the millet and water and bring to a boil. Add a pinch of salt, reduce the heat to low, and simmer for 30 minutes, or until all the water has been absorbed. Spread the millet onto a baking sheet to cool.

3. Steam the corn kernels in a covered steamer over boiling water for 3 to 5 minutes, until tender. Chill in a sieve under cold running water and drain.

4. In a large mixing bowl, combine the lime juice, jalapeño peppers, cumin, and 1 tablespoon salt. Whisk in the oil. Stir in the millet, corn, cilantro, and scallions. Fold in the avocado and tomatoes and season with black pepper to taste.

5. If desired, chill before serving.   YIELD: 6 TO 8 SERVINGS

Barley Salad

Make this festive salad when you are in the mood to party. It is so pretty it could induce a profound sense of loneliness if your friends and family are not around to enjoy it. The umeboshi vinegar (a by-product of pickling plums) casts a delicate pink hue over the barley and coaxes the color out of the red onions as they marinate.

$^2/_3$ cup pearl barley
1$^1/_2$ teaspoons coarse sea salt
1 yellow squash, seeded and diced
1 zucchini, seeded and diced
$^1/_3$ cup diced red onion
1 cucumber, peeled, seeded,
   and diced
1 red bell pepper, peeled, seeded,
   and diced
2 tablespoons thinly sliced scallions,
   white and green parts
2 tablespoons minced fresh dill
   or parsley
3 tablespoons extra-virgin olive oil
2 tablespoons umeboshi vinegar
2 tablespoons freshly squeezed lemon juice
$^1/_2$ teaspoon freshly milled black pepper
1 bunch watercress leaves
   and tender stems only for garnish

1. In a 3-quart saucepan over high heat, bring 6 cups water to a boil. Add the barley and $^1/_2$ teaspoon salt and simmer for 30 minutes, or until tender. Drain the barley in a sieve and rinse under cold running water until cool. Place the sieve over a bowl to drain.

2. In a pan fitted with a steamer, combine the squash, zucchini, and red onion. Steam, covered, for 3 to 4 minutes. Shock the vegetables in a large bowl of cold water to arrest the cooking. Drain thoroughly.

3. In a large bowl, combine the steamed vegetables, barley, cucumber, red pepper, scallions, and dill.

4. In a separate bowl, whisk together the oil, vinegar, lemon juice, remaining teaspoon of salt, and black pepper to taste. Pour the dressing over the salad and mix well.

5. Mound the salad on a platter and garnish liberally with watercress.

YIELD: 6 SERVINGS

GRAIN SALADS

My favorite method of cooking grains for salads is to add them to a large volume of boiling water, as you would pasta. This way, each grain maintains its structure and is free to release its excess starch into the water. Some of the more starchy grains, like barley, wheat berries, rye, or rice, can be shocked in cold water after cooking. This gets rid of even more outside starch and cools the grain. Millet, kasha, and quinoa should not be shocked because they have such a low starch content to begin with and will only become soggy. Instead, you can spread the cooked grains on a baking sheet to let them cool.

Quinoa Salad

This crunchy, super-delicious salad is full of sunflower, pumpkin, and toasted black sesame seeds. Everyone who has tried it has loved it. I first made it at Angelica Kitchen, and it became an instant favorite. The cilantro and jalapeño make it a very zesty summertime salad, great for picnics since it keeps its crunch. It has all the goodness of delicate, halo-shaped quinoa, which is one of the most high-protein, digestible grains there is.

FOR THE SALAD:

$1/3$ cup hulled sesame seeds

$1/3$ cup hulled sunflower seeds

$1/3$ cup hulled pumpkin seeds

$1/2$ cup arame

$1 1/2$ cups water

$1/2$ teaspoon coarse sea salt

1 cup quinoa, rinsed and drained

Kernels from 2 ears sweet corn

1 red onion, diced

1 red bell pepper, diced

1 bunch red radishes (8 to 10),
    trimmed and cut into matchsticks

1 large carrot, grated

FOR THE MARINADE:

$1/2$ cup cider vinegar

$1/3$ cup extra-virgin olive oil

1 small bunch cilantro (about 1 cup), trimmed,
    leaves and tender stems chopped

2 scallions, white and green parts,
    trimmed and sliced

1 jalapeño pepper, seeded and minced

1 garlic clove, minced

Coarse sea salt

Freshly milled black pepper

1. Preheat the oven to 375°F.

2. Spread the seeds on a baking sheet and toast in the oven for 12 minutes, or until golden brown. Pour them into a bowl and set aside to cool.

3. Combine the arame with 2 cups warm water and set aside to swell for 10 minutes, until soft. Drain and set aside.

4. In a small saucepan over high heat, bring the $1^{1}/_{2}$ cups water and salt to a boil. Add the quinoa. When the water returns to a boil, reduce the heat to low, cover, and simmer for 20 minutes, or until all of the water has been absorbed. Spread the quinoa on a baking sheet to cool.

5. In a pot fitted with a steamer, combine the corn kernels with the red onion. Steam for 3 to 5 minutes, until crisp-tender. Remove to a colander and chill under cold running water. Drain thoroughly.

6. To make the marinade, in a large mixing bowl, combine the vinegar, oil, cilantro, scallions, jalapeño pepper, garlic, 2 teaspoons salt, and black pepper to taste. Whisk well.

7. Add the toasted seeds, quinoa, steamed vegetables, red pepper, radishes, carrot, and arame to the marinade. Mix well and refrigerate for 20 minutes to marry the flavors.

8. Taste for seasoning, add more salt and black pepper, if desired, and serve.

YIELD: 4 TO 6 SERVINGS

Wild Rice Salad Amandine

A rather luxurious salad, perfect for a late summer picnic or buffet when bell peppers have ripened to a lovely sun-gold. Bold colors and vibrant flavors make this one stand out in a crowd. If fresh peppers aren't available, try using lightly steamed yellow summer squash or halved seedless grapes. And, at the peak of the harvest, fresh cherry tomatoes make a fine substitute for the dried.

FOR THE SALAD:

1 cup wild rice
$1/2$ teaspoon coarse sea salt
$1/4$ cup dry-pack sun-dried tomatoes
$2/3$ cup sliced almonds
1 carrot, thinly sliced
1 small red onion, thinly sliced
1 yellow bell pepper, thinly sliced
$1/2$ cup dried currants

FOR THE VINAIGRETTE:

$1/4$ cup balsamic or sherry vinegar
$1/4$ cup extra-virgin olive oil
2 tablespoons freshly squeezed lemon juice
2 tablespoons freshly squeezed lime juice
2 tablespoons finely chopped fresh dill
Coarse sea salt
Freshly milled black pepper

1. Preheat the oven to 350°F.

2. In a medium saucepan, bring 2 quarts lightly salted water to a boil. Add the wild rice and cook at a lively simmer for 40 minutes, or until it is tender but not mushy. Transfer the wild rice to a sieve and cool under cold running water. Set the sieve over a bowl to thoroughly drain.

3. In a separate saucepan over high heat, combine the tomatoes with water to cover and bring to a boil. Boil for 2 minutes, then remove the pan from the heat. Set the pan aside and allow the tomatoes to swell for 15 minutes, or until soft.

4. Spread the almonds on a baking sheet and toast them in the oven for 12 minutes, or until lightly browned. Transfer to a bowl and set aside to cool.

5. In a pot fitted with a steamer, combine the carrot and onion. Steam for 3 to 4 minutes, then shock them in a bowl of cold water to arrest the cooking process and drain well.

6. To prepare the vinaigrette, whisk together the vinegar, oil, lemon juice, lime juice, dill, and salt and pepper to taste in a large bowl. Add the wild rice, carrot and onion, and bell pepper and toss to combine. Drain the tomatoes and cool under cold running water. Drain well and slice into bite-size pieces. Toss them with the salad.

7. Stir in the currants and toasted almonds and serve.

YIELD: 4 TO 6 SERVINGS

WILD RICE

Wild rice isn't a rice at all, although it is in the same family. It is a long-grain marsh grass native to the northern United States and southern Canada. Wild rice contains more protein than regular rice and is also rich in lysine, the amino acid most grains lack. Like brown rice, it takes about 35 to 40 minutes to cook and should be boiled only to the point where it is tender, but still chewy.

Pilafs and Grain Side Dishes

Basmati Rice Pilaf

I think of basmati as my house white. It has a toasty aroma and is very light and fluffy, which makes it perfect for a pilaf. The tradition in India is to rinse the rice seven times, until the water is crystal clear and the rice is cleaned of all excess surface starch. There's something very sensual about putting your hand in the water and swishing it around with the rice; it's part of the ritual of cooking.

An initial browning of the grains in some form of fat helps seal in the starches and results in a light and fragrant dish.

> 2 cups white basmati rice
> 1 tablespoon light sesame oil, unsalted butter, or olive oil
> 1 small leek or 1 bunch of scallions, white parts thinly sliced (about 1 cup)
> 1 bay leaf
> 1 teaspoon coarse sea salt
> 2¹/₂ cups water or unsalted vegetable broth

1. In a medium bowl, rinse the rice in several changes of cold water until the water is clear and free of excess starch. This can take up to 6 or 7 rinsings. Cover the rice by 1 inch with cold water and set aside to soak for 30 minutes. Drain the rice in a sieve and set aside.

2. In a medium saucepan over medium heat, warm the oil. Add the leek and sauté for several minutes. Add the rice, bay leaf, and salt and sauté for 2 minutes more, gently stirring with a wooden spoon, until the rice smells toasty and fragrant.

3. Add the water and bring to a boil over high heat. Reduce the heat to low, cover, and simmer until the water is absorbed, about 20 minutes.

4. Remove the rice from the heat and fluff with a fork or chopsticks. Remove and discard the bay leaf before serving. YIELD: 4 TO 6 SERVINGS

BASIC BROWN RICE

Brown rice is heartier and more substantial than white rice. You will feel fuller and more satisfied after eating brown rice, especially if you are a vegetarian. Brown rice can be parched by toasting it in a dry skillet and then cooked in boiling water for a fluffy, pilaf-style result. Toasting brown rice breaks down the bran and gives the grain another layer of flavor. Brown rice can also be pressure-cooked, which makes it stickier and more digestible. Sometimes I like to mix short-grain brown rice with white rice and cook them in the same pot. The result is an attractive and filling dish that's not too heavy.

If you want to soak your brown rice before cooking, for the best texture and flavor and the most nutrition, combine 1^1/$_2$ cups brown rice with 2^1/$_4$ cups water and ^{1}/$_2$ teaspoon sea salt; let it soak for a minimum of 4 hours at room temperature, or up to 2 days in the refrigerator. Eight hours at room temperature is ideal. Prepare as usual, though the rice might require 10 or so minutes less cooking time.

Kamut Berries, Spelt Berries, and Wild Rice

This stunning dish is one of my favorite whole-grain medleys. The golden kamut berries, which remind me of glistening sea pebbles, contrast nicely with the smaller, dark brown kernels of spelt and the long, dark, nutty-tasting grains of wild rice, which split open when cooked and curl back to reveal a beautiful tan interior. This combination of grains is great for a cold salad, because each holds its shape well, or for stuffing a squash.

^{1}/$_2$ **cup kamut berries**
^{1}/$_2$ **cup spelt berries**
^{1}/$_2$ **cup wild rice**
2 quarts water
^{1}/$_2$ **teaspoon coarse sea salt**

1. Hot soak the grains for 1 hour (see page 227).

2. In a pressure cooker, combine the soaked grains, water, and salt. Cook for 30 minutes under full pressure. (See The Pressure Cooker Method, page 229.) Alternatively, simmer the grains in a large amount of lightly salted water for 1^1/$_2$ hours, or until tender.

YIELD: 5 CUPS, OR 6 SERVINGS

Kamut Berry, Spelt Berry, and Wild Rice Stuffing

Chewy whole grains, crunchy pecans, and aromatic vegetables—one bowl of this stuffing is a meal in itself. It also makes an excellent stuffing for baked winter squash or whole onions. For a richer variation, welcome on a blustery cold night, try making it into a gratin. Spread the stuffing in a casserole pan, moisten with a little water or broth, top with fresh bread crumbs mixed with a bit of grated Parmesan or Gruyère, and dot with butter. Bake in a preheated 350°F oven for 30 minutes or until crispy and golden brown. Yum!

1/2 cup wild rice
1/2 cup kamut berries
1/2 cup spelt berries
1 cup pecan halves and pieces
2 tablespoons extra-virgin olive oil
1 cup diced onion
1 cup diced carrot
1 cup diced fennel bulb
1/2 cup diced celery
2 garlic cloves, finely chopped
1 tablespoon chopped fresh sage
Coarse sea salt
2 tablespoons water
1/2 cup firmly packed finely
    chopped fresh parsley
Freshly milled black pepper

1. Soak and cook the grains as described in the preceding recipe. Preheat the oven to 325°F.

2. Spread the pecans on a baking sheet and toast for 8 to 10 minutes. Remove them from the oven and set them aside in a bowl to cool and crisp.

3. In a wide heavy skillet over medium heat, warm the oil. Add the onion and sauté for 5 minutes, stirring occasionally to prevent sticking. Add the carrot, fennel, celery, garlic, sage, salt to taste, and water. Cover and cook for 8 to 10 minutes, until the vegetables are tender.

4. Drain the grains and add them to the vegetables. Stir in the toasted pecans, parsley, and pepper to taste, and serve.   YIELD: ENOUGH STUFFING FOR 6 TO 8 SERVINGS

Cleaning and polishing whole grains isn't the only way to get their nutrients to your body. There are ways of fermenting the grain, as in the case of African soured millet and South American fermented amaranth. The Huron Indians developed the practice of burying fresh corn in the mud and allowing it to ferment for several months before boiling or roasting it. During fermentation, beneficial bacteria begin to break down the grains and produce lactic acid. This makes the grain more digestible, preserves it, and may even raise the level of amino acids and vitamins in the grain itself.

In the same vein, some grain-eating cultures discovered that combining unfermented grains with some form of lactic acid made them more digestible. In India, people eat yogurt with rice; in Japan, all sorts of pickled vegetables are eaten with rice, not to mention miso, which is eaten with rice and noodles. The early Europeans discovered that wheat became more digestible when it was eaten in the form of sourdough bread, which is rich in lactic acid. And, in areas where people were traditionally nomads, grains were often made into flatbreads which would be dipped in yogurt and eaten.

Three-Grain Pilaf

A trio of grains gives this pilaf its tantalizing texture. It is delicate, light, and easy to digest. Mild and savory from the scallion and the butter, this is one of the most pleasant ways to consume your grains.

2 tablespoons olive oil or unsalted butter
$^1/_2$ cup scallions, white and tender green parts,
    minced
1 cup white basmati or jasmine rice
$^1/_2$ cup millet
$^1/_2$ cup quinoa
3 cups All-Season Vegetable Stock
    (page 29) or water
$^3/_4$ teaspoon coarse sea salt

1. Preheat the oven to 350°F.

2. In a 2- to 3-quart ovenproof saucepan over medium heat, warm the oil. Add the scallions and sauté for 2 to 3 minutes. Add the rice, millet, and quinoa and continue to sauté, stirring, for 3 more minutes, or until the grains are fragrant.

3. Add the stock and salt. Raise the heat and bring to a boil. Cover the pan and bake in the oven for 30 minutes.

4. Remove the pilaf from the oven and allow it to rest for 5 minutes. Fluff with a fork and serve.

YIELD: 4 TO 6 SERVINGS

Millet and Vegetable Pilaf

Millet, unlike rice, is a fairly austere, dry grain. It reminds me of a curmudgeonly, tight-lipped old uncle who needs a good deal of buttering up to come forth with one of his famous tall tales. Toasted, cooked with a bit of fat, and propped up by judiciously seasoned aromatic vegetables, millet reveals its hidden charms.

1 tablespoon olive oil
1 tablespoon unsalted butter
1 red onion, finely diced
1 carrot, finely diced
1 celery rib, finely diced
2 garlic cloves, minced
1 cup millet, rinsed and drained
2 cups water
Coarse sea salt
1/4 cup firmly packed minced fresh parsley
2 tablespoons freshly squeezed lemon juice
Freshly milled black pepper

1. In a 2- to 3-quart saucepan over medium heat, warm the oil and butter. Add the onion, carrot, and celery and sauté for 6 minutes, or until the vegetables are softened, stirring occasionally to prevent browning. Add the garlic and sauté for 2 minutes.

2. While the vegetables are cooking, toast the millet in a heavy cast-iron or stainless-steel skillet for 8 minutes, stirring and shaking the pan from time to time. Begin toasting over high heat, then reduce the heat to medium once the moisture clinging to the millet has been cooked off.

3. Stir the toasted millet into the vegetables. Add the water and 1/2 teaspoon salt and bring to a boil. Reduce the heat to low, cover, and simmer for 25 minutes.

4. Remove the millet from the heat and allow it to steam, covered, for an additional 5 minutes.

5. Stir in the parsley, lemon juice, and pepper to taste. Season with additional salt, if needed, and serve.

YIELD: 2 TO 4 SERVINGS

Polentas

Triple-Corn Polenta
with Seaweed and Carrots

This versatile dish can be served hot, at room temperature, or cold. My recipe for polenta has a higher nutritional profile than those made just from plain cornmeal due to the minerals from the hiziki seaweed and the addition of corn grits. An added benefit of blending grits with the cornmeal is that grits won't clump when stirred into boiling water. If you combine the grits with cornmeal before adding them to boiling water, you will end up with a deliciously smooth polenta with minimal effort.

> 1 to 2 tablespoons hiziki seaweed
> $4^1/_2$ cups water
> 2 tablespoons extra-virgin olive oil
> 1 teaspoon coarse sea salt
> $^1/_2$ cup cornmeal
> $^1/_2$ cup fine yellow corn grits
> 1 cup corn kernels scraped from
>   2 ears fresh sweet corn,
>   preferably white
> 1 carrot, grated

1. In a small bowl, cover the hiziki with 1 cup warm water. Set aside until the hiziki is soft, about 20 minutes. (This can also be done several hours ahead or overnight, if left in the refrigerator.)

2. Meanwhile, in a heavy 2-quart saucepan over high heat, bring the remaining $3^1/_2$ cups water to a boil. Add the oil and salt. In a bowl, combine the cornmeal and grits and mix well. Slowly whisk the cornmeal and grits into the water until no lumps remain.

3. Reduce the heat to low and simmer for 15 to 20 minutes, stirring occasionally with a wooden spoon.

4. Drain the hiziki and add it to the pot along with the corn kernels and carrot. Continue to cook for 15 to 20 minutes, stirring vigorously from time to time, until the polenta pulls away from the sides of the pot.

5. Pour the polenta into a mold and allow it to rest until firm.

6. Slice the polenta into desired shapes. The polenta can be served as is, panfried until crisp in a bit of olive oil, or baked on a lightly greased baking sheet at 350°F for 15 to 20 minutes, until crisp. It is also great brushed with oil and grilled.

YIELD: 6 TO 8 SERVINGS

FRESHLY GROUND CORNMEAL

Freshly ground cornmeal has a sweet nuttiness that you won't find in packaged cornmeal. When dried corn kernels are ground, the oils in the bran and germ are released and can go rancid, spoiling the flavor of the meal. The same happens with whole wheat when it is ground—I suggest storing all whole ground meals in the freezer.

When possible, I recommend using fine yellow grits instead of cornmeal. When a recipe does call for cornmeal (as here, or in the case of corn bread) you should make every effort to use freshly ground cornmeal. If you don't own a mill, the best thing to do is buy fresh cornmeal from a health food store where they keep it refrigerated in packages.

Soft Polenta with White Bean, Squash, and Sage Ragout

My idea of comfort is epitomized in this polenta. It demands very little effort yet gives back so much in soothing, soulful ways. As a time-saver, the ragout can even be made up to 3 days before the polenta.

So invite some friends over and enjoy this dish with sautéed greens and a sturdy *vin de pays* from the Rhône or a light Chianti. And if you like cheese, now is the perfect time for a nutty shaving of Parmesan or Gruyère.

FOR THE RAGOUT:

3 tablespoons extra-virgin olive oil

1 large onion, diced

Coarse sea salt

1 pound winter squash, such as red kuri,
    butternut, buttercup, or Hokkaido pumpkin,
    peeled and roughly chopped (about 3 cups)

2 to 3 garlic cloves, chopped

1 (1-inch) piece gingerroot, peeled and minced

1 (28-ounce) can diced tomatoes

3 cups cooked Great Northern beans
    (from 1 cup dried beans, see page 226), drained

1 tablespoon minced fresh sage

1 (2-inch) cinnamon stick

Freshly milled black pepper

FOR THE POLENTA:

6 cups water

2 tablespoons extra-virgin olive oil
    or unsalted butter

1 teaspoon coarse sea salt

3/4 cup fine yellow grits

3/4 cup yellow cornmeal

Shaved Parmesan or Gruyère for garnish

1. To prepare the ragout, warm the oil in a heavy 3-quart saucepan over medium heat. Add the onion and a pinch of salt and sauté for 5 minutes, or until the onion is softened. Add the squash, garlic, and ginger and sauté for 5 minutes. Regulate the heat to prevent browning.

2. Stir in the tomatoes with their juice. Raise the heat and bring to a boil. Add the beans, sage, and cinnamon. Reduce the heat to low, cover, and simmer gently for 25 to 30 minutes, until the squash is tender. Add water if the ragout becomes too thick. Remove the cinnamon stick and season with salt and pepper to taste.

3. While the ragout simmers, prepare the polenta. In a second heavy saucepan over high heat, bring the water and oil to a boil. Add the salt. In a bowl, combine the grits and cornmeal and mix well. Slowly add the mixture to the water, whisking until smooth. Reduce the heat to low and cook, uncovered, for 25 to 30 minutes, stirring from time to time with a wooden spoon, until the polenta pulls away from the sides of the pan.

4. To serve, pour the polenta onto a wide shallow dish and top with the ragout and some cheese, if you like.

YIELD: 4 TO 6 SERVINGS

POLENTA HISTORY

Before wheat became cheap enough for the lower classes, most "breads" were really just loaves of barley (and later, corn) gruel that were baked in the sun. In some homes in Italy, where there is a strong polenta tradition, the finished polenta was poured directly onto the dining table. Once it set, the family would gather round and help themselves. Polenta was also treasured as a portable, convenient food since it is quick to make, can be chilled or baked and sliced, and can serve as the base for so many excellent and filling dishes.

Savory Millet and Sweet Potato "Polenta" with Smothered Peppers and Onions

A nice change of pace from the usual corn polenta, millet breaks down when cooked slowly in a lot of liquid and then firms up beautifully for slicing and frying, baking, or grilling. The peppers and onions lift this dish way up into that realm of pleasure that I always seek in my cooking. If you don't plan on making the polenta, try just making the smothered peppers and onions. They are great in a sandwich, tossed with pasta, or baked atop focaccia or pizza.

FOR THE POLENTA:

2 tablespoons extra-virgin olive oil
   or unsalted butter

1 cup peeled and chopped sweet potato

1 small onion, finely diced

4 garlic cloves, minced

2 sprigs fresh thyme

1 bay leaf

4 cups water

1 cup millet, rinsed and drained

1 teaspoon coarse sea salt

2 tablespoons olive oil

Chopped fresh parsley for garnish

FOR THE SMOTHERED PEPPERS AND ONIONS:

$1/4$ cup extra-virgin olive oil

2 large onions, thinly sliced

3 yellow bell peppers, cored and
   sliced into $1/2$-inch strips

$1 1/2$ red bell peppers, cored and
   sliced into $1/2$-inch strips

Coarse sea salt

$1/4$ teaspoon hot red pepper flakes

1 teaspoon dried thyme or 2 teaspoons chopped fresh thyme leaves

$3/4$ cup drinkable red wine, such as Merlot or Chianti

1 tablespoon red wine vinegar
Freshly milled black pepper

1. To make the polenta, warm the oil in a heavy 2- to 3-quart saucepan over medium heat. Add the sweet potato and onion and sauté for 5 minutes, stirring frequently with a wooden spoon to prevent browning. Add the garlic, thyme, and bay leaf and sauté for 3 to 4 more minutes.

2. Add the water, millet, and salt and bring to a boil. Reduce the heat to low, cover the pan, and cook for 45 to 50 minutes, stirring vigorously several times during the course of cooking to help release the starch from the millet and to prevent sticking. Remove the millet from the heat when it is soft and creamy. Discard the thyme sprigs and bay leaf. Set the millet aside to rest, covered, for 5 minutes.

3. Lightly oil a 6- to 8-cup baking dish. Pour the polenta into the baking dish, smoothing the top with a moistened spatula. Set aside to cool at room temperature, then refrigerate, uncovered, until fully set, about 40 minutes.

4. Meanwhile, prepare the peppers and onions. In a wide heavy sauté pan over medium heat, warm the oil. Add the onions, bell peppers, and $1/2$ teaspoon salt. Raise the heat and sauté for 5 to 7 minutes, stirring to prevent browning. Add the red pepper flakes, thyme, wine, and vinegar and bring to a boil. Reduce the heat to low, cover, and simmer for 45 to 60 minutes, until the peppers are meltingly tender. Uncover, raise the heat, and reduce the pan juices until they form a syrup that covers the vegetables. Season with salt and black pepper to taste.

5. Unmold the polenta onto a cutting board and slice into $1/2$-inch-thick pieces. In a heavy skillet, heat 2 tablespoons oil over medium heat. Fry the slices for 5 to 7 minutes per side, until crisp (you may have to do this in several batches).

6. Serve the polenta topped with the smothered peppers and onions and a sprinkle of parsley.

YIELD: 4 TO 6 SERVINGS

Seasonal Risottos

Making risotto is a great way to reflect the seasons—once you know the basic technique you can include your favorite vegetables, beans, and seasonings in endless variations. I've supplied one recipe for each of the four seasons, but you can feel free to alter them using whatever ingredient is at its peak.

Spring White Wheat and Black Soybean Risotto with Spinach

One of the best things about risotto is that it is like a blueprint for which there are endless variations. I like to improvise on the risotto formula by choosing seasonal ingredients to sauté with my aromatic vegetables. Here, I've combined plump grains of rice, nutty soybeans, and chewy, white wheat berries and serve them together under a cloak of satiny greens.

$1/4$ cup dried black soybeans,
    sorted and soaked (see page 226)
$1/3$ cup soft white wheat berries
    (spelt berries may be substituted),
    sorted and soaked as for beans (see page 226)
4 cups water
Coarse sea salt
5 cups All-Season Vegetable Stock (page 29)
4 tablespoons extra-virgin olive oil
1 cup finely chopped onion
2 garlic cloves, finely chopped
1 tablespoon finely chopped fresh sage
1 cup arborio rice
$1/8$ teaspoon hot red pepper flakes
1 pound spinach leaves, roughly chopped

1. In a pressure cooker, combine the beans, wheat berries, water, and $1/2$ teaspoon salt. Cook under full pressure (15 pounds) for 25 minutes (see The Pressure Cooker Method, page 229). Release from pressure and test for doneness. Both the beans and grains should be perfectly tender with their shape intact. If they are not tender enough, simmer them, uncovered, for 5 to 10 minutes longer. Drain and set aside.

2. In a 2-quart saucepan over high heat, bring the stock to a boil. Reduce the heat to maintain a steady simmer.

3. Meanwhile, in a heavy 2- to 3-quart saucepan over medium heat, warm 3 tablespoons of the oil. Add the onion and sauté for 5 minutes. Add the garlic and sage and sauté for 2 minutes more. Add the rice and cook for 2 to 3 minutes, until the grains become translucent.

4. Add the red pepper flakes, $1/2$ teaspoon salt, and $1/2$ cup of the simmering stock. Regulate the heat to maintain a steady simmer. When the stock has been absorbed, add subsequent ladlefuls of stock, stirring all the while in a steady circular motion. When half of the stock has been absorbed, add the wheat and beans. Continue cooking and stirring, adding more stock until the risotto is creamy, but the grains gently resist the tooth, about 20 to 25 minutes.

5. Stir in the spinach in handfuls until it wilts and gives the rice a brilliant emerald gloss.

6. Remove the pan from the heat and stir in the remaining tablespoon of oil. Adjust the salt to taste and serve immediately.

YIELD: 4 TO 6 SERVINGS

NEW WAVE RISOTTO

I like to call this method my new wave risotto technique. Begin making the risotto as usual—sauté your aromatic vegetables, add the raw arborio rice, toasting it in the fat until it becomes translucent, then start adding the liquid. Midway through the cooking process, add some leftover cooked or canned beans, cooked brown rice, or cooked whole-grain arborio rice, millet, or quinoa and you'll end up with a delicious, uniquely multihued risotto.

Summer Risotto with Tomatoes, Leeks, and Fresh Corn

A quick and flavorful broth can be made from corn cobs and leek tops. Simply wash the leek tops well, place them in a pot with the corn cobs, cover with 6 cups water, and simmer, uncovered, for 30 minutes. Strain off and discard the trimmings and proceed with the risotto, using this corn cob broth in place of the vegetable broth.

5 cups All-Season Vegetable Stock (page 29), or water
2 tablespoons extra-virgin olive oil
2 cups thinly sliced leeks,
    white and tender green parts only
1 cup arborio rice
$1/4$ cup dry white wine, such as a Sauvignon blanc
2 cups kernels scraped from 2 ears sweet corn
1 pound ripe, juicy tomatoes, peeled, seeded, and diced
2 teaspoons minced garlic
$1/2$ teaspoon fresh thyme leaves
1 cup torn basil leaves
1 teaspoon unsalted butter (optional)
$1/4$ cup Parmesan cheese (optional)
Coarse sea salt
Freshly milled black pepper

1. In a 2-quart saucepan over high heat, bring the stock to a boil. Reduce the heat so the stock maintains a steady simmer.

2. In a heavy 3-quart pan over medium heat, warm the oil. Add the leeks and sauté for 2 minutes, or until softened. Stir in the rice and sauté for 2 minutes, until the grains are translucent. Pour in the wine and let simmer until absorbed.

3. Add the corn, tomatoes, garlic, and thyme. Add the stock, $1/2$ cup at a time, stirring constantly until the liquid has been absorbed before adding each subsequent $1/2$ cup stock. Continue stirring and adding stock, until the grains are tender and creamy, about 20 to 25 minutes. Add the basil during the last 5 minutes.

4. Stir in the butter and cheese if using, and add salt and pepper to taste. Serve immediately.

YIELD: 4 SERVINGS

Autumn Quinoa Risotto with Pumpkin and Sage

Protein-rich quinoa is one of my favorite grains. It is very energizing, and its flavor is other-worldly. It never gets gummy and it seems to lighten whatever it is cooked with. Here, it creates a nice balance with the heavily starched arborio rice and hearty chunks of pumpkin.

> 4 cups water or broth made from squash and
>   leek trimmings (see page 36)
> 2 tablespoons extra-virgin olive oil
> $1/2$ cup finely chopped leek (white part only)
> 2 cups peeled, cubed pumpkin or
>   butternut squash ($1/2$-inch pieces)
> $1/2$ cup arborio rice
> $1/3$ cup quinoa
> 2 tablespoons mirin
> 4 sage leaves, finely chopped
> Coarse sea salt
> Freshly milled black pepper
> 1 tablespoon finely chopped fresh parsley for garnish
> Toasted Pumpkin Seeds (page 383) for garnish

1. In a 2-quart saucepan over high heat, bring the water to a boil. Reduce the heat to maintain a steady simmer.

2. In a heavy 3-quart pan over medium heat, warm 1 tablespoon oil, add the leek, and sauté for 2 minutes. Add the pumpkin and cook for 2 to 3 more minutes. Add the rice and quinoa and sauté, stirring, for 2 minutes, or until the grains are fragrant.

3. Add the mirin and sage and cook until dry. Ladle in the water, $1/2$ cup at a time, stirring constantly until the liquid has been absorbed before adding each subsequent $1/2$ cup of water. Continue stirring until the grains are tender and creamy, 20 to 25 minutes.

4. Stir in the remaining 1 tablespoon oil. Add salt and pepper to taste. Serve garnished with parsley and the pumpkin seeds.

YIELD: 2 MAIN-COURSE SERVINGS, OR 4 APPETIZER SERVINGS

Wintry Root Vegetable Risotto with Red Beans

To me, making risotto is also one of the most dramatic and engaging ways of cooking—it involves all of the senses and requires your undivided attention, since you are constantly stirring. Making risotto is relaxing; I like listening to music as I stir, and I find myself becoming completely involved in the rhythm of cooking.

> **5 cups All-Season Vegetable Stock (page 29)**
> **1 cup finely chopped onion**
> **2 tablespoons extra-virgin olive oil**
> **or light sesame oil**
> **1 teaspoon coarse sea salt**
> **1/2 cup shredded burdock**
> **1/2 cup peeled and shredded turnip**
> **1/2 cup peeled and shredded parsnip**
> **1/2 cup shredded carrot**
> **1 cup arborio rice**
> **1 tablespoon tomato paste**
> **2 teaspoons peeled and minced gingerroot**
> **1 teaspoon minced garlic**
> **1 cup cooked kidney beans**
> **(from 1/3 cup dried beans, see page 226), drained**
> **2 tablespoons unsalted butter**
> **Freshly milled black pepper**
> **Chopped fresh parsley for garnish**

1. Pour the stock into a saucepan and bring it to a simmer.

2. In a heavy saucepan over medium heat, combine the onion, oil, and salt and heat until the onion sizzles. Stirring with a wooden spoon, sauté for 4 to 5 minutes, until softened. Add the burdock, turnip, parsnip, and carrot and continue to cook for 2 to 3 minutes. Add the rice, tomato paste, ginger, and garlic and cook, stirring, for 1 minute, until rice is evenly coated with tomato paste, and ginger and garlic are fragrant.

3. Add 1 cup simmering stock and adjust the heat so that the risotto maintains a lively simmer. Cook, stirring constantly, until most of the stock has been absorbed. Continue to add ladles of stock, about 1/2 cup at a time, as the liquid gets absorbed.

4. When two-thirds of the stock has been added and absorbed, stir in the beans. Continue stirring and adding stock until the rice is tender but firm to the bite, about 25 minutes.

5. Swirl in the butter, season liberally with pepper, and serve immediately, sprinkled with parsley.

YIELD: 4 SERVINGS

KEEPING GRAINS

The germ of every grain contains vital fats that are necessary to nourish new growth when the grain is planted. These fats are very unstable and will spoil quickly when exposed to light and oxygen, but as long as the grain is kept dry and intact, it will last almost indefinitely. I find it miraculous that grains found in ancient Egyptian tombs more than 7,000 years old are still viable seeds and can be sprouted to produce new plants.

Croquettes and Hearty Grain Dishes

Vegetable and Grain Croquettes with Tangy Yogurt Sauce

The tangy, spicy yogurt sauce adds some zing to these bean and grain croquettes, and it provides the lactic acid helpful in aiding digestion. Serve them with steamed vegetables of your choice, such as broccoli, summer squash, or asparagus.

1/4 cup millet
1/4 cup quinoa
1/4 cup red lentils
1/2 cup white basmati or jasmine rice
1 tablespoon white hulled sesame seeds
3 cups plus 2 tablespoons water
1 teaspoon coarse sea salt
2 tablespoons extra-virgin olive oil
1 cup peeled and finely chopped sweet potato
2 celery ribs, finely diced
4 scallions, white and green parts,
    trimmed and thinly sliced
1 garlic clove, minced
1 (1-inch) piece gingerroot,
    peeled and minced
2 tablespoons water
1/4 cup finely chopped parsley
Freshly milled black pepper
1/2 cup arrowroot powder for dredging
Pure olive oil or light sesame oil for panfrying
Tangy Yogurt Sauce (page 387)

1. Combine the millet, quinoa, lentils, rice, and sesame seeds. Rinse briefly in a strainer under cold running water. Drain thoroughly. In a 2-quart saucepan over high heat, combine them with 3 cups of water and $1/2$ teaspoon of the salt and bring to a boil. Reduce the heat to low, cover, and simmer for 35 minutes.

2. Meanwhile, warm the oil in a medium sauté pan over medium heat. Add the sweet potato, celery, scallions, garlic, and ginger. Sauté for 5 to 7 minutes, until lightly browned. Add the remaining $1/2$ teaspoon of salt and the 2 tablespoons water. Cover, reduce the heat to low, and simmer until the vegetables are tender, about 5 to 7 minutes. Transfer the vegetables to a mixing bowl.

3. When the grains are done, add them to the vegetables. Mix thoroughly and set aside to cool. Stir in the parsley and pepper to taste.

4. Spread the arrowroot powder on a plate. With moist hands, form each croquette from $1/2$ cup of the mixture. Dredge the croquettes in the arrowroot and transfer to a platter.

5. Line a baking sheet with paper towels. In a wide heavy skillet over medium-high heat, add the oil to a depth of about $1/3$ inch. When the oil is hot, panfry the croquettes for 2 to 3 minutes per side, until they are golden brown and crispy. You may have to do this in several batches to avoid overcrowding the pan. Transfer the croquettes from the pan to the baking sheet to drain.

6. Serve immediately or keep warm in a 200°F oven. Serve with the yogurt sauce on the side.

YIELD: ABOUT 4 SERVINGS (14 CROQUETTES)

BEANS AND GRAINS

It is amazing to me that for thousands of years almost every culture in the world has known to combine grains with beans to make a complete protein. Native Americans complemented the natural lack of certain amino acids in corn by accompanying the grain with beans, the Japanese combined rice with tofu and miso, and North Africans ate their couscous alongside traditional tagines (bean and vegetable stews).

Beans and grains have a natural partnership that doesn't end with their complementary nutrients. Because you treat the two in much the same way, beans and grains can often be cooked together, as long as you know the cooking times of each.

Five-Grain Croquettes
with Carrot Sauce

Here is another way to make grains the centerpiece of a meal. I like taking the time to make these tasty croquettes for a special dinner or party buffet. The colorful carrot sauce really dresses up the grains and adds a sweet-and-tart piquancy. And since these croquettes are baked, not fried, not only are they tasty, they are good for you, too.

$1/2$ cup white sushi or jasmine rice
2 tablespoons amaranth
2 tablespoons teff
2 tablespoons quinoa
2 tablespoons millet
$2^1/2$ cups water
2 teaspoons coarse sea salt
2 tablespoons extra-virgin olive oil
1 cup minced onion
$1/2$ cup finely diced red bell pepper
$1/4$ cup finely diced celery
$1/4$ teaspoon freshly milled black pepper
2 cups Carrot Sauce (page 379)
2 tablespoons finely chopped chives
    or parsley for garnish

1. Preheat the oven to 350°F. Lightly oil a baking sheet.

2. Combine the rice, amaranth, teff, quinoa, and millet in a strainer. Rinse briefly under cold running water. Drain thoroughly. In a 2-quart saucepan over high heat, combine the grains, water, and $1/2$ teaspoon of the salt and bring to a boil. Reduce the heat, cover, and simmer for 30 minutes, or until all the water is absorbed.

3. Meanwhile, in a sauté pan over medium heat, warm the oil. Add the onion, bell pepper, celery, the remaining $1^1/2$ teaspoons of the salt, and black pepper. Cook for 8 to 10 minutes, stirring occasionally to prevent sticking.

4. Reduce the heat to low, cover, and continue cooking for 10 to 15 minutes, until the vegetables are very tender. Do not brown. You may need to add a tablespoon or two of water.

5. Spoon the cooked grains into a medium bowl. Add the vegetables and mix thoroughly. Set the grain and vegetable mixture aside and allow to cool enough to handle.

6. Wet your hands and form the mixture into the croquettes the size of golf balls. Place them 1 inch apart on the baking sheet and flatten slightly with the palm of your hand. Bake for 20 minutes.

7. Serve with the Carrot Sauce, garnished with the chives.

YIELD: ABOUT 4 SERVINGS (12 TO 14 CROQUETTES)

Spelt, Black Soybean, and Vegetable Casserole

Richly textured and satisfying in a balanced, savory way, this recipe makes a great centerpiece to a late-summer meal. The vegetables are browned and slightly caramelized, forming an intensely flavored base from which the entire dish grows. If you make this casserole in the winter, omit the basil and add 1 teaspoon dried oregano or thyme. And, if you like cheese, this dish becomes even more delicious served topped with shaved Romano, Parmesan, or Monterey Jack.

**1 cup spelt berries, sorted and soaked
    as for beans (see page 226)
1 cup black soybeans, sorted and soaked
    (see page 226)
6 cups water plus more if necessary
Coarse sea salt
1/4 cup extra-virgin olive oil
1 large onion, diced
2 carrots, diced
8 ounces white button, cremini, or
    fresh shiitake mushrooms,
    trimmed and sliced
1 celery rib with leaves, diced
1 tablespoon finely chopped fresh rosemary or basil
1 (14-ounce) can plum tomatoes
2 cups chopped savoy cabbage
Freshly milled black pepper
2 tablespoons finely chopped fresh flat-leaf parsley**

1. In a pressure cooker, combine the spelt, beans, 6 cups water, and $1/2$ teaspoon salt. Cook under full pressure (15 pounds) for 30 minutes (see The Pressure Cooker Method, page 229). Drain and reserve the cooking liquid.

2. In a heavy 2- to 3-quart flameproof casserole with a lid, warm the oil over medium heat. Add the onion and sauté for 5 minutes, until softened. Add the carrots, mushrooms, celery, and rosemary. Raise the heat and cook, stirring and shaking the pan, until the vegetables release their juices and begin to caramelize, about 7 to 10 minutes.

3. Pass the tomatoes and their juice through the medium disk of a hand-cranked food mill directly into the casserole.

4. Add $1^1/_2$ cups of the spelt and bean cooking liquid and bring to a boil. Add the cabbage and salt and pepper to taste. Reduce the heat to low, cover, and simmer for 20 to 30 minutes, until the vegetables are tender.

5. Remove the lid and raise the heat. Cook for 10 minutes, or until the liquid has reduced to form a rich gravy around the grains, beans, and vegetables.

6. Adjust the seasonings to taste, stir in the parsley, and serve.

YIELD: 6 SERVINGS

Kasha Varnishkas with Savory Gravy

Made from toasted buckwheat groats, kasha isn't technically a grain. Kasha varnishkas (kasha with noodles) is a traditional Ashkenazi dish—a peasant food for the Jews of Eastern Europe. In America, kasha varnishkas are made with light, bow-tie-shaped farfalle noodles, which contrast with the rich, heavy kasha and symbolize the freedom that the impoverished and persecuted Jews of Eastern Europe sought when they fled to the New World.

Kasha varnishkas were a memorable part of my childhood—my grandma Esther cooked a lot of kasha! In the first few years that I gave up meat, I would seek out delicatessens where I could find it. So this is my interpretation of an age-old dish. In this version, I update traditional kasha varnishkas with hearty portobello mushrooms and flavorful leeks. I also like to serve it with a gravy to enhance the richness of the kasha.

FOR THE KASHA:
1 cup water
1/2 cup whole toasted buckwheat groats
 (kasha)
1/4 teaspoon coarse sea salt

FOR THE VEGETABLES AND NOODLES:
2 tablespoons light sesame oil or unsalted butter
1 large or 2 small leeks,
 white and tender green parts only,
 sliced into thin rings
1 large portobello mushroom, cap only, diced
1/2 teaspoon ground caraway seeds (optional)
Coarse sea salt
1 1/2 cups farfalle (bow-tie pasta)
Freshly milled black pepper
2 cups All-Purpose Savory Gravy (page 381)

1. To prepare the kasha, bring the water to a boil in a small saucepan over high heat. Stir in the kasha and salt, reduce the heat to low, cover, and cook for 20 minutes, or until the water is absorbed and the kasha is fully cooked. Remove from the heat and set aside.

2. To prepare the vegetables, warm the oil in a wide sauté pan over medium heat. Add the leek, mushroom, and caraway seeds. Raise the heat to high and sauté, stirring and shaking the pan from time to time, for 5 to 7 minutes, until the vegetables begin to caramelize. Reduce the heat to low, cover, and simmer for 10 to 15 minutes more, stirring occasionally to prevent sticking.

3. While the vegetables simmer, bring 2 quarts water to a boil in a large saucepan. Add the pasta and salt and boil for 8 to 10 minutes. Drain in a colander and toss with the vegetables. Stir in the kasha and add additional salt and pepper to taste.

4. Serve with hot Savory Gravy on the side.

YIELD: 2 TO 4 SERVINGS

SAVE THOSE MUSHROOM STEMS

Mushroom stems are one of the most flavorful vegetable trimmings I can think of. Wrap them in cheesecloth and add them to a pot of simmering beans or vegetable soup. The stems will release their flavor in 20 to 30 minutes, and then the cheesecloth package can be discarded.

Porridges

Mass-produced, cracked, flaked, rolled whole-grain or dry breakfast cereals that profess to be healthful and nutritious are insufficiently processed, making them poor substitutes for old-fashioned, gentle, and soothing porridge, which is wholly digestible and truly nourishing. And the taste of commercial bran cereals is no match for the naturally sweet, nutty flavor of whole-grain porridge. Once you've experienced freshly crushed whole-grain porridge, it is very hard to accept any substitute. And the practice of crushing and cooking your own grains can easily become a highly personal ritual that connects you to an age-old ancestral tradition.

Real porridge provides a powerful slow-burning energy, making it much more satisfying than flakes or rolled grains that have had their germ oxidized and their energy dissipated. The coarsely cracked and crushed bran and germ give real porridge an al dente texture, while the floury endosperm, or starch, cooks up creamy smooth. The glutinous structure that develops as the porridge is stirred allows it to be sliced when it cools and sets. This is how a tradition of primitive, protein-rich hearth breads based on sliced leftover porridge was developed.

Since there was no refrigeration in ancient times, grains that were crushed and set aside to soak in water would begin to ferment and develop lactic acid from airborne wild yeasts. This phenomenon sparked the beginning of sourdough bread-baking and beer-making. I like to encourage lactic acid formation, so I soak crushed grains for my daily porridge overnight. I often add a souring agent, such as a dollop of organic plain yogurt or a tablespoon or two of sourdough starter to the soaking water. The lactic acid and live microorganisms in the souring agent will ultimately make the cereal more nutritious and digestible.

Here are three of my favorite porridge recipes.

Creamy Crushed Oatmeal Porridge

1 cup fresh, coarsely crushed whole oat berries
3 cups filtered or well water
2 tablespoons plain yogurt, whey, or sourdough starter
    (white or whole wheat) (pages 326 and 334)
1/2 teaspoon coarse sea salt
Yogurt for topping
Fresh or cooked fruit, sliced, for topping
Pure maple syrup, honey, or evaporated cane juice crystals

1. In a heavy 2-quart saucepan, combine the oats, water, yogurt, and salt. Cover the pan and set aside overnight for 8 to 10 hours. (If your kitchen is above 70°F, or if you plan to let the grains soak for a longer period of time, it is best to refrigerate them.)

2. In the morning, put the pan over medium heat and bring to a boil, stirring constantly until the porridge thickens, about 2 to 3 minutes. Reduce the heat to low, cover, and simmer gently for 8 to 10 minutes.

3. Serve topped with fresh yogurt, fresh or cooked fruit, Pralines (page 425), Toasted Pumpkin Seeds (page 383), or Dry-Roasted Seeds with Soy Sauce (page 384). Sweeten with maple syrup, honey, or naturally evaporated cane juice crystals.

YIELD: 4 SERVINGS

TOOLS AND TECHNIQUES FOR GOOD PORRIDGE

To experience real porridge in your home kitchen, it is necessary to:

1. Begin with whole grains such as barley, wheat, or spelt.
2. Use a crushing tool, such as a large marble mortar, hand mill, or electric stone mill.
3. Season with real sea salt, which controls the rate of fermentation and prevents the porridge from becoming too sour.
4. Use only filtered or well water.
5. Stir your porridge well to develop protein and texture.

Toasted Five-Grain Porridge

Here, whole grains are parched before they are crushed. This makes for a richer flavor and a chewier texture.

FOR THE FIVE-GRAIN CEREAL:
1 cup whole oat berries
$1/4$ cup whole rye berries
$1/4$ cup whole spelt berries
$1/4$ cup whole kamut berries
$1/4$ cup whole or pearl barley

FOR THE PORRIDGE:
3 cups filtered or well water
1 cup Five-Grain Cereal (see recipe above)
2 tablespoons plain yogurt, whey, and either white
    or whole wheat sourdough starter (pages 326 and 334)
$1/2$ teaspoon coarse sea salt
Yogurt for topping
Fresh or cooked fruit, sliced for topping
Pure maple syrup, honey, or evaporated cane juice crystals

1. To make the cereal, combine the oat, rye, spelt, kamut, and barley in a large heavy skillet over medium heat. Toast, stirring, for about 8 minutes, until the grains have become slightly browned and fragrant. Transfer them to a bowl and let cool.

2. Crush the cooled grains coarsely and transfer to an airtight container or use to make porridge. The cereal will stay fresh for up to a month.

3. In a 2-quart heavy saucepan, combine the water, 1 cup of the cereal, yogurt, and salt. Cover and set aside overnight for 8 to 10 hours.

4. In the morning, place the pan over medium heat and bring to a boil, stirring constantly until the porridge thickens. Reduce the heat to low, cover, and simmer gently for 8 to 10 minutes.

5. Serve topped with fresh yogurt, fresh fruit, Pralines (page 425), Toasted Pumpkin Seeds (page 383), or Dry-Roasted Seeds with Soy Sauce (page 384). Sweeten with maple syrup, honey, or naturally evaporated cane juice crystals if desired.

YIELD: 4 SERVINGS

STIRRING FOR HARMONY

The next time you drain water from a sink, notice the direction it flows—this will tell you what the natural force of the water is where you live. Water spirals in a counterclockwise direction in the Northern Hemisphere and clockwise in the Southern Hemisphere. I like to maintain this harmony by stirring foods steadily in the natural direction.

Swiss Muesli

Muesli is another style of porridge, this one uncooked. It was developed in the Swiss Alps, and recently, when my family and I vacationed there, we all fell in love with this breakfast tradition. The popular Familia brand muesli cereal is widely available in supermarkets and health food stores. It is composed of steamed, rolled, and dried whole-grain wheat, rye, and oats; dried fruits; and chopped nuts. I learned this recipe from an innkeeper in the tiny hamlet of Fex near Saint Moritz.

As you can see, the lactic acid in the yogurt plus the live enzymes in the grated apple ensures that the phytates will break down and transform the nutritional qualities of the whole grains.

> 1 cup Familia muesli
> 1 cup water
> $1/2$ cup whole milk yogurt
> 1 tart apple, grated
> 2 tablespoons natural fruit preserves
> Fresh fruit, sliced
> Honey or pure maple syrup

1. Combine the muesli, water, yogurt, apple, and fruit preserves and mix well. Cover with a plate and refrigerate overnight.

2. Top with fresh fruit and drizzle with honey or maple syrup to taste.

YIELD: 2 TO 4 SERVINGS

Beans

and Pulses

Beans are truly one of the staffs of life and are a crucial component in the human diet. They are filling—sustaining and fortifying the body—as well as good for the heart because they lower cholesterol. They are nutritious—all beans are terrific sources of protein, iron, B vitamins, and high-quality fiber—and, with the exception of soybeans, they are also low in fat. What's more, they taste great—both on their own and when they absorb the savory flavors of the other ingredients they are cooked with. Hands down, beans are the ultimate vegetarian food. They are also the most universal: In just about every cuisine around the world, you will find traditional dishes featuring beans in their seemingly endless variety of colors and shapes.

Beans have been grown and eaten for many thousands of years. Most beans—except for chickpeas, lentils, soybeans, mung beans, and favas—are native to the New World and were not introduced to Europe until the return of the explorers in the early sixteenth century. The ancestor of the common kidney bean has been cultivated in southwestern Mexico for at least 7,000 years, and during that time hundreds of varieties have been bred, including black, navy, and pinto beans.

The Old World's native beans also date back to ancient times. The Neolithic peoples of India, Europe, and the Middle East grew and consumed great quantities of nourishing lentils, dried peas, and broad beans (favas). Soybeans have been cultivated in Asia since around the fifteenth century B.C. and remain an essential part of Asian cuisine, both in their whole natural form and as soy sauce and tofu. Adzuki and mung beans also originated in Asia, although they have never been as important to Asian diets as soybeans.

As ingredients go, beans are some of the most versatile. In recipes that use cooked beans, most are interchangeable, so you can vary the dish according to what you have on hand or can find in the market. This makes them the perfect food for a whimsical cook. Sometimes I like to put a pot of beans up, and then decide at the last minute what to do with them. By simply leaving them in the pot with their cooking liquid, adding some seasonings and a little bit of fat (which carries the flavor of the seasonings to the beans), and continuing to simmer until the starch seeps out of the beans (to thicken the mixture), I've got a terrific, flavorful bean stew that is perfect for spooning over grains or pasta. If I add more liquid, such as water, broth, or wine, and just a few chopped vegetables, I have an instant soup. Draining the beans and mashing them with seasonings and a spoonful of fat turns them into a thick, tasty dip. Or, I might leave the drained beans whole, and dress them with some oil and vinegar or lemon juice, adding whatever vegetables (or cooked grains) I've got around to make a fresh, crunchy bean salad. The best part is that the variations within each of these basic recipes (soup, sauce, dip, salad) are nearly endless. So you could eat a different bean dish every single day of your life, if you wanted to.

SORTING AND SOAKING

Before cooking, all beans require sorting. The easiest way to sort beans is to spread them on a countertop or plate and discard any that are broken, split, malformed, or shriveled. And keep an eye out for little pebbles, which often hide among dried beans and lentils. Most beans also require soaking, except for black beans (also called turtle beans), adzukis, mung beans, peas, lentils, and split peas. However, they still need to be sorted and thoroughly rinsed under cold running water before cooking.

Soaking beans before cooking both reduces the cooking time and helps to break down the indigestible oligosaccharides, which are complex sugars found in beans. Since humans have difficulty digesting these sugars, the task falls to our intestinal bacteria, which, in the process, can cause painful bloating and flatulence. Soaking reduces the amount of oligosaccharides by leaching them out of the beans. The complex sugars dissolve in the soaking water, so you can see why draining and rinsing beans after soaking is also important.

There are two basic ways to soak beans. For the hot soak method (quick soak), put the beans in a large pot with enough water to cover the beans by 3 inches. Bring the pot to a boil over medium heat. Skim off and discard any beans that rise to the surface—if the beans are of good quality and from a recent harvest, very few of them will float to the top. Then reduce the heat to low and simmer for 2 minutes. Turn off the heat, cover the pan, and allow the beans to soften and swell for 1 hour. Drain the beans in a colander and rinse well under cold running water.

Alternatively, you can use the cold (or long soak) method that is common throughout the Mediterranean. Simply cover the beans by 3 inches with cold water and let them soak in the refrigerator for 6 to 8 hours. After the beans have soaked, rinse them under cold running water and drain well.

Once soaked, there are three basic ways to cook beans: on the stovetop, in the oven, or in a pressure cooker. Uncooked starch is indigestible to humans, so the thorough cooking of all beans and pulses is important. Cooked beans are tender, never chewy. Once cooked, beans will keep for up to 5 days in the refrigerator.

You can, by the way, also use canned beans in most of these recipes. Canned beans are a great staple to keep on hand; they are very convenient and allow you to whip up a nutritious, filling meal almost instantly. Look for an organic brand and for beans that are processed without salt; they will have the best flavor. Also, since canned beans often have a much softer texture than home-cooked beans, they are really a last resort for salads (where they'll get squashed as you toss). Instead, use them in creamy dips, soups, or sauces where their mushy texture is a benefit rather than a drawback.

Cooking Methods

THE STOVETOP SIMMER METHOD

This is a good method to use when you're cooking pulses and beans for salads, since it's easy to keep an eye on them to make sure they don't overcook. If beans fall apart, some of their starch and protein will leach into the water, along with their flavor. I get the best results from cooking my beans very gently, either on the stovetop or in the oven, so that the skin stays intact and the shape and flavor of the bean is retained.

After the beans or pulses have been sorted and soaked, return them to a saucepan along with enough water to cover by 3 inches. If you are preparing slower-cooking beans, you may want to add a 3-inch strip of kombu, a type of sea vegetable, to the pot as you slowly bring it to a boil over medium heat (the kombu helps the beans cook faster). As the beans approach the boiling point, they may throw off some foam. Skim the foam off the top and discard. Reduce the heat to low and simmer, covered, for 1 hour. At this point you can add 1 teaspoon coarse sea salt to the pan and continue to simmer the beans until they are cooked through—this can take $1/2$ to $1 1/2$ hours, or even longer, depending on the type and age of the beans.

It is important not to add any acidic or salty ingredients until the beans are at least halfway to two-thirds cooked, otherwise the cooking process will be retarded. The simplest way to add flavor to beans is to season the cooking water. Adding a bay leaf, a sprig of fresh herb, some olive oil, or a few unpeeled garlic cloves will all lend flavor to the beans. And, adding about a tablespoon of oil to a pot of beans makes them cook faster and helps them become tender and creamy on the inside.

THE OVEN METHOD

Although it is time consuming, baking beans in the oven, where they can cook at a very slow, gentle simmer, can yield terrific results. Cooking this way preserves the shape and texture of the beans, which means that their flavor will not leach out into the cooking liquid. And the long cooking time means that the indigestible complex sugars in the beans have a chance to break down further.

In the oven, the entire cooking vessel is surrounded by heat, mimicking a traditional cooking method of burying a cast-iron or clay pot in the hot ashes of a wood- or coal-burning stove. Early American cast-iron and clay pots were actually made with raised rims on top of the lids, so you could put hot coals on top of the pot. In South America and the Middle East, people would make a fire in a dug-out hole, place the pot in the hole, surround it with coals, cover the hole with earth and let the beans cook for a day or two, which resulted in very tender, very tasty beans.

After you have sorted, soaked, and rinsed the beans, put them in a pot made from either cast iron, enamel-coated cast iron, or earthenware. Add enough cold water to cover by 1 to 2 inches and a 3- to 4-inch piece of kombu. Slowly bring to a boil on the stovetop. After the beans have been boiled and skimmed, cover the pot, and bake in a preheated 275°F oven. If you cook beans in a hotter oven, they will break up and fall apart. Let the beans simmer gently for an hour, then salt them and continue to bake until they are tender, which can take 30 minutes to an hour, depending upon the type and age of the bean.

THE PRESSURE COOKER METHOD

Pressure cooking is my standard method of preparing beans because it is so fast. Beans that take 2 to 3 hours to cook on a stovetop can be cooked in a pressure cooker in just 30 to 45 minutes. Also, pressure cooking requires less liquid than stovetop cooking because very little steam is released. You can cover the beans by just 1 inch of water, whereas in a saucepan you should cover them by 3 inches. I especially like cooking chickpeas in a pressure cooker because they can take as long as 4 hours to cook on the stovetop. However, if you're trying to maintain the beans' texture for a salad, it is a little trickier using a pressure cooker than a pot on the stove because you don't have as much control, making it easy to overcook the beans.

To cook beans in a pressure cooker, sort, soak, and rinse the beans as described on pages 226–227. Put them in the pressure cooker with water to cover by 1 inch and any spices or kombu you may be using. (Do not fill the pressure cooker more than two-thirds full.) Bring the beans to a boil over medium heat and skim off any foam. This is a crucial step, because the foam not only contains the bitter, indigestible complex sugars from the beans but can also clog the valve on your pressure cooker. If you add a teaspoon or two of oil to the pressure cooker, this foam will not form, and you can skip the skimming step. Add salt at this point and attach the lid. Raise the heat, bring to full pressure (15 pounds), reduce the heat to as low as possible to maintain full pressure, then begin timing. In general, it is a good idea to bring down the pressure and check the beans after 20 minutes. The easiest and safest way to do this is to place the cooker under cold running water in the sink. It will take about 15 to 20 seconds to release the pressure, after which you can uncover the pot safely. Taste a bean. If it is not tender, return the cooker to the stove and simmer the beans, uncovered, until they finish cooking. If the beans need a lot more cooking, cover the cooker and bring them back up to pressure. Reduce the heat to low and cook for another 10 minutes before checking again.

BEANS, PULSES, AND KOMBU: A GREAT COMBO

When kombu (a member of the kelp family) is cooked with beans, it takes less time for both the kombu and the beans to soften. The minerals in the kombu help to break down the proteins, fat, and complex carbohydrates in the beans. If you simmer kombu on its own, it will stay tough for an hour, but in the presence of beans, it will melt and the beans will become tender quite quickly. I use kombu throughout the book because I find that it's both a convenient way of getting high-quality trace minerals in a diet and a great flavor-enhancer.

Dips and Spreads

Spiced Hummus with Roasted Garlic

What was once an exotic Middle Eastern spread has quickly become an American staple. In this recipe I wanted to come up with something more exciting than the average hummus. I love the surprising flavor of this spicy dip and its beautiful, bright yellow color.

When serving a bean dip, I find it is nice to make a shallow depression in the center and drizzle in a little spice or herb oil to create another level of flavor. (See the recipes on pages 362 to 365). Or, you can just sprinkle some plain extra-virgin olive oil on top.

> 1 whole garlic bulb, cloves separated (unpeeled)
> 1/4 cup plus 1 teaspoon olive oil
> 1 onion, finely chopped
> 1 teaspoon ground coriander
> 1/2 teaspoon ground cumin
> 1/4 teaspoon freshly milled black pepper
> 1/8 teaspoon turmeric
> Pinch cayenne pepper
> 2 cups cooked chickpeas (from 2/3 cup dried chickpeas,
>   see page 226), drained, with cooking liquid reserved
> 3 tablespoons freshly squeezed lemon juice
> 2 1/2 teaspoons coarse sea salt

1. Preheat the oven to 350°F. Toss the garlic with 1 teaspoon of the oil, wrap in a piece of foil, and roast for 1 hour.

2. While the garlic roasts, combine the remaining 1/4 cup oil with the onion in a small pan and cook over medium heat for 3 to 4 minutes, stirring until the onion softens. Reduce the heat to low and add the coriander, cumin, black pepper, turmeric, and cayenne. Cook gently for 3 to 4 minutes. Remove from the heat.

3. When the garlic is done, remove it to a plate to cool. Squeeze the pulp from the skin directly into the onion mixture.

4. In the bowl of a food processor fitted with a metal blade, combine the onion mixture, chickpeas, lemon juice, and salt. Purée until smooth, adding a bit of the chickpea cooking liquid or water, if necessary, to achieve a desired consistency.

5. Serve chilled or at room temperature.

YIELD: 2 CUPS

BUYING DRIED BEANS

In general, dried beans vary greatly, since they continue to dry sitting on the shelf. Older beans are tougher and take longer to cook; so when you are buying beans, it is important to look for ones that are whole, uniform, plump, and shiny. If you see a lot of split or shriveled beans, you are looking at an old batch.

DIFFERENT TYPES OF LENTILS

Whole, unpeeled lentils come in three basic varieties: green are the largest, then brown, and then tiny gray French lentils (also called *lentilles de Puy*). Peeled lentils include large red lentils (also called Egyptian lentils), small red lentils, and peeled brown lentils, which range in color from pink to yellow. Peeled lentils cook faster than whole lentils and are best for dhal (a spicy Indian dish) and soup, since they don't hold their shape well. Whole lentils are better for salads.

Red Lentil Pâté

In this recipe, I've used red lentils to form the base of a Moroccan-inspired pâté. The spicy flavors are similar to my harissa, with the addition of the lentils and toasted pine nuts. This pâté is firmer than a dip and is great served either warm or chilled, accompanied by Pita Toasts (page 122) or crudités.

> 1 cup large or small red lentils, sorted and rinsed (see page 226)
> 1 bay leaf
> 3 tablespoons extra-virgin olive oil
> 1 small onion, finely diced
> $1/3$ cup pine nuts
> 3 garlic cloves, finely chopped
> 1 tablespoon tomato paste
> 1 teaspoon ground coriander
> $1/2$ teaspoon ground caraway seeds
> $1/2$ teaspoon ground cumin
> $1/8$ teaspoon cayenne pepper
> 1 teaspoon coarse sea salt
> Freshly squeezed juice of $1/2$ lemon

1. In a 3-quart saucepan over medium heat, combine the lentils and 4 cups water and bring to a boil. Skim and discard any foam and add the bay leaf. Reduce the heat to low, cover, and simmer for 30 minutes, or until the lentils are tender. Drain.

2. While the lentils simmer, in a small sauté pan, warm the oil over medium heat. Add the onion and pine nuts and sauté for 5 to 7 minutes, until the onion softens and the pine nuts begin to color. Stir in the garlic, tomato paste, coriander, caraway seeds, cumin, cayenne, and salt. Continue to sauté for 5 minutes. Stir in the lemon juice to deglaze the pan (see page 53).

3. In a food processor fitted with a metal blade, combine the cooked lentils and the onion mixture and purée until smooth.

4. Transfer to a serving bowl and serve at once or chill in the refrigerator and serve cold.

YIELD: 3 CUPS

Porcini Mushroom, Red Wine, and Walnut Terrine

This is a rough-textured terrine with a rich, hearty flavor. Top it with a few sprigs of fresh parsley or the garnish of your choice and serve it as the centerpiece to a buffet. It slices beautifully and can be served alongside a small tossed salad and slices of fresh home-made bread.

    3 cups water
    1 cup full-bodied red wine
    2 ounces dried porcini mushrooms
    2 tablespoons unsalted butter
    2 tablespoons extra-virgin olive oil
    1 carrot, finely diced
    1 onion, finely diced
    2 bay leaves
    3 garlic cloves, chopped
    2 tablespoons naturally brewed soy sauce
    $1^1/_2$ tablespoons tomato paste
    3 to 4 sprigs fresh thyme
    1 sprig fresh rosemary
    $3^3/_4$ cups cooked cranberry, Anasazi, or
        red kidney beans (from $1^1/_4$ cups dried beans,
        see page 226), drained
    $1^1/_2$ cups firmly packed fresh sourdough bread crumbs
    $^3/_4$ cup walnuts, toasted
        (see How to Toast Walnuts, page 373)
        and coarsely chopped
    2 tablespoons chopped fresh flat-leaf parsley
    2 teaspoons coarse sea salt
    2 teaspoons coarsely crushed black peppercorns

1. Preheat the oven to 350°F.

2. In a saucepan over medium heat, combine $2^1/_2$ cups water, wine, and mushrooms and bring to a simmer. Cook for 2 minutes, then turn off the heat and let stand for 20 minutes. With a slotted spoon, transfer the mushrooms to a strainer. Place the strainer with the mushrooms in

a bowl of cold water and remove any grit clinging to the crevices of the mushrooms. Drain and coarsely chop the mushrooms; set aside. Pass the mushroom liquid through a fine sieve, stopping just short of the grit, and reserve.

3. In a wide pan over medium heat, warm the butter and oil. Add the carrot, onion, bay leaves, and garlic and sauté for 5 minutes. Add the mushrooms and their liquid, soy sauce, tomato paste, thyme, and rosemary. Raise the heat and bring to a boil. Reduce the heat to medium and simmer, uncovered, until nearly dry. Remove the bay leaves.

4. In a food processor fitted with a metal blade, purée the beans with the remaining $1/2$ cup water until smooth. Scrape the beans into a large mixing bowl. Add the mushroom mixture, bread crumbs, walnuts, parsley, salt, and peppercorns. Stir well to combine.

5. Spoon the pâté into a lightly greased 8- by 4-inch loaf pan. Smooth the top with a moistened rubber spatula and bake for 1 hour.

6. Remove the pan to a rack to cool for 30 minutes, then refrigerate until firm.

7. To serve: Run a thin knife or spatula around the sides of the terrine. Place an inverted plate on top and unmold. Serve as part of a buffet with crudités and yogurt dip or Soy Sour Cream (see page 391).

YIELD: 1 LOAF

White Bean Dip with Dill, Lemon, and Garlic

White beans are Italian favorites, especially among the Tuscans, who are jokingly called *mangiafagioli* (bean eaters) by their countrymen. Although in recent history beans have widely been considered peasant fare, when they first came to Italy in the sixteenth century, the reigning Duke of Florence declared beans very fashionable.

In this zesty springtime dip, creamy textured white beans are enlivened with plenty of fresh dill and lemon. Serve with Pita Toasts (page 122).

> 3 cups cooked white beans (from 1 cup dried beans, see page 226), drained
> 3 tablespoons freshly squeezed lemon juice
> 3 tablespoons plus 1 teaspoon extra-virgin olive oil
> 2 tablespoons chopped dill
> 2 garlic cloves, crushed
> Finely grated zest of 1 lemon
> Coarse sea salt
> Freshly milled black pepper
> Paprika for garnish

1. To prepare the dip, purée the beans in a food mill or mash by hand in a medium bowl. Add the lemon juice, 3 tablespoons of the oil, dill, garlic cloves, lemon zest, $1^{1}/_{4}$ teaspoons salt, and pepper to taste. Transfer to a serving bowl and refrigerate until you are ready to serve.

2. Just before serving, season with additional salt to taste, dust with paprika, and drizzle with the remaining teaspoon of oil. YIELD: 6 TO 8 SERVINGS

THE PARTNERSHIP OF BEANS AND GRAINS

Grains and legumes make up an astounding two-thirds of the world's dietary protein. Although grains are deficient in the amino acid lysine, and beans lack sulfur-containing amino acids, when the two are combined, they form a complete protein. Native Americans traditionally planted bean vines trained right onto growing corn stalks. Legumes act as a sort of green manure. The nitrogen-fixing bacterial nodules found on the roots form a unique symbiotic relationship with certain soil bacteria. When planted together, or in rotation, legumes enrich the soil, providing nourishment for nitrogen-hungry grains.

Black Bean Salsa

I use this salsa in several ways. It is definitely great scooped up with tortilla chips, but it is more than just a dip. It can transform plain rice or panfried tofu into a delicious, simple summer dish. You can also turn it into a salad by adding more corn, diced avocado, and some leftover rice. Or, try serving it with the polenta on page 200 or the corn dumplings from the Three Sisters Stew on page 65.

> 1 ear sweet corn, shucked and silks removed
> 1 (14-ounce) can diced tomatoes
>   or 1 pound (3 or 4 medium) fresh tomatoes,
>   peeled, seeded, and diced
> 3³/₄ cups cooked black beans (from 1¹/₄ cups dried beans,
>   see page 226; note that black beans do not require soaking)
> Freshly squeezed juice of 2 limes
> 1 tablespoon extra-virgin olive oil or light sesame oil
> 1 jalapeño pepper, seeded and minced
> 1 cup cilantro, loosely packed,
>   tender stems and leaves chopped
> 1 scallion, white and green parts,
>   finely sliced
> 1 garlic clove, minced
> 2 teaspoons freshly ground cumin
> Coarse sea salt

1. Steam the corn for about 5 minutes. Rinse under cold running water to cool. Slice off the kernels.

2. Toss the corn kernels in a bowl with the tomatoes, beans, lime juice, oil, jalapeño pepper, cilantro, scallion, garlic, cumin, and 1¹/₂ teaspoons salt. Let the salsa marinate for 10 minutes before serving.

3. Taste and add salt if needed. Serve at room temperature.

YIELD: 4 CUPS

Bean Salads

French Lentil Salad
with Creamy Yogurt Dressing

French lentils have a beautiful, slate gray color. They remind me of the pebbles you find by the sea. They also have a very nutty, sweet flavor and, since they are a whole, unpeeled lentil, they hold their shape well and are perfect for salads.

FOR THE SALAD:
1 1/3 cups French lentils, sorted and rinsed (see page 226)
2 teaspoons coarse sea salt
2 carrots, finely diced
    (to the size of the lentils)
1 celery rib, finely diced
    (to the size of the lentils)
1/2 red bell pepper, finely diced
    (to the size of the lentils)
1/2 yellow bell pepper, finely diced
    (to the size of the lentils)
2 tablespoons chopped fresh dill
2 tablespoons snipped fresh chives
2 tablespoons chopped fresh tarragon
2 tablespoons chopped fresh parsley

FOR THE DRESSING:
1 cup plain yogurt
2 tablespoons freshly squeezed lemon juice
2 teaspoons white wine vinegar
3 tablespoons extra-virgin olive oil
Coarse sea salt
Freshly milled black pepper

1. To prepare the salad, bring 6 cups water to a boil in a medium saucepan. Add the lentils and boil for 10 minutes. Add 2 teaspoons salt and boil for 10 to 15 minutes, until the lentils are cooked through but are still firm enough to hold their shape. Drain them in a sieve and rinse under cold running water until cool. Drain thoroughly and transfer to a serving bowl.

2. Add the carrots, celery, bell peppers, dill, chives, tarragon, and parsley. Stir to combine.

3. In a bowl, combine the yogurt, lemon juice, vinegar, oil, 2 teaspoons salt, and $1/2$ teaspoon black pepper. Whisk until smooth. Pour the dressing over the salad and mix well. Let the salad rest for 10 to 15 minutes.

4. Adjust seasonings to taste, and serve.

YIELD: 4 TO 6 SERVINGS

Black Soybean Salad

Black soybeans are one of my favorite beans. They have a nutty sweetness unlike any other bean, are not mealy, and hold their shape beautifully. Black soybeans are much easier to digest than their yellow cousins (which are almost always consumed in a fermented form). These beans are perfect tossed into salads or stirred into a risotto. You can also substitute them for the black beans in my Black Bean Salsa on page 237.

FOR THE SALAD:

2 cups dried black soybeans,
    sorted, soaked, and rinsed
    (see page 226)
1 tablespoon olive oil
1 cup thinly sliced celery
1 cup thinly sliced red onion
1 cup thinly sliced carrot
1 cup thinly sliced yellow bell pepper

FOR THE VINAIGRETTE:

$1/2$ cup freshly squeezed lime juice
$1/2$ cup extra-virgin olive oil
$1/4$ cup chopped fresh cilantro
$1 1/2$ tablespoons minced jalapeño pepper
2 garlic cloves, minced
$2 1/2$ teaspoons coarse sea salt

1. To prepare the salad, combine the beans with water to cover by 1 inch in a pressure cooker. Bring to a boil over high heat. Skim the foam and add the oil. Attach the lid and bring to full pressure (15 pounds; see The Pressure Cooker Method, page 229). Reduce the heat to low and cook for 25 minutes. Place the cooker under cold running water to bring down the pressure.

2. Drain the beans in a colander. Spread a clean kitchen towel over a baking sheet, arrange the beans in a single layer on the towel, and let cool.

3. Meanwhile, combine the celery, red onion, and carrot in a steamer and steam for 2 to 3 minutes, until crisp-tender. Chill the steamed vegetables in a bowl of cold water. Drain and set aside.

4. To prepare the dressing, combine the lime juice, oil, cilantro, jalapeño pepper, garlic, and salt in a medium mixing bowl. Whisk until creamy.

5. In a large serving bowl, combine the steamed vegetables, soybeans, and the yellow pepper. Add dressing to taste, and toss to combine.

YIELD: 6 TO 8 SERVINGS

BEANS OR PULSES?

Legumes (from the Latin *legere,* meaning "to gather") are a family of plants that produce somewhat fleshy pods that contain several seeds that can be eaten as a vegetable before they dry. Technically, beans are any seed, or pod, whether fresh or dried, in the legume family. But, in culinary terms, the word refers especially to those that are oval and kidney-shaped, such as lima, black, kidney, and cannellini. Pulses are also from the legume family, specifically dried legumes, and refer especially to lentils and peas.

Warm Lentil Salad with Sun-Dried Tomatoes

Lentils have been grown since 7000 B.C., making them one of the oldest cultivated legumes. They are indigenous to the southwestern region of Asia and southeastern Europe and are now an integral part of the cuisines of India, Eastern Europe, the Middle East, and the Mediterranean. Here, the addition of sun-dried tomatoes gives this dish a decidedly Mediterranean flavor.

6 to 8 dry-pack sun-dried tomatoes
1 cup green lentils, sorted and rinsed
Coarse sea salt
$1/3$ cup extra-virgin olive oil
1 large red onion, finely diced
1 carrot, finely diced
$1/2$ celery rib, finely diced
1 garlic clove, minced
Freshly squeezed juice of 1 lemon or 3 to 4 tablespoons red wine vinegar
Freshly milled black pepper
Chopped fresh parsley or cilantro for garnish

1. In a small saucepan, combine the tomatoes with water to cover. Bring to a boil, remove the pan from the heat, and set aside.

2. In a medium saucepan, bring 2 quarts water to a boil. Add the lentils and boil, uncovered, for 15 minutes. Add $1/2$ teaspoon salt and continue to boil for 10 to 15 minutes, until the lentils are tender but still hold their shape. Drain, transfer the lentils to a mixing bowl, and toss them with 1 tablespoon of the oil.

3. In a heavy skillet over medium heat, warm the remaining oil. Add the onion, carrot, and celery, and cook, stirring often, until tender, 8 to 10 minutes. Add the garlic and cook 2 minutes longer. Stir the vegetables into the lentils.

4. Drain the tomatoes, slice them into quarters, and add them to the lentil mixture.

5. Season the salad with lemon juice or vinegar, add salt and pepper to taste, and garnish with chopped parsley. Serve.

YIELD: 4 SERVINGS

Hearty Bean Dishes

White Beans with Sugar Snap Peas and Mint

If picked while still young and tender, sugar snap peas can be eaten whole, both the peas and the pods. They add a sweet, juicy burst of freshness to this bright springtime dish.

1¼ cups dried Great Northern beans, sorted,
    soaked, and rinsed (see page 226)
Coarse sea salt
3 tablespoons extra-virgin olive oil
1 small onion, diced
1 small yellow bell pepper, peeled, seeded, and diced
1 garlic clove, finely chopped
Finely grated zest of 1 lemon
¼ cup dry white wine
¾ pound sugar snap peas, strings removed, sliced crosswise into thirds
2 tablespoons finely chopped fresh mint
Freshly milled black pepper

1. In a medium saucepan over medium heat, combine the beans and 4 cups cold water and bring to a simmer. Skim and discard any foam that rises to the surface, reduce the heat to low, and simmer, covered, for 45 minutes. Add 1 teaspoon salt and continue to cook gently until the beans are tender, 30 minutes to 1 hour, depending on age of beans.

2. While the beans simmer, warm the oil in a wide saucepan over medium heat. Add the onion and a pinch of salt and sauté for 5 minutes. Add the yellow pepper, garlic, and lemon zest and sauté for 5 minutes. Add the wine, raise the heat, and simmer until reduced by half, 5 to 7 minutes. Add the cooked beans and 1 cup of their cooking liquid and bring to a simmer. Add the peas, cover, and cook for 5 to 7 minutes, until the peas are bright green and crisp-tender.

3. Stir in the mint and season with salt and pepper to taste. Simmer for another minute or so to meld the flavors, and serve.   YIELD: 4 TO 6 SERVINGS

Smothered Beans

I like to imagine that up in heaven the saints all order this dish at a club where Louis Armstrong is leading the band. It is that delicious.

This version of smothered beans is best suited to fall and winter. In the spring try using fresh favas (briefly blanched and peeled) and fresh, crisp lettuce along with the canned tomatoes. In the summer, use fresh cranberry beans, Swiss chard, and juicy ripe tomatoes that have been peeled, seeded, and coarsely chopped.

> 1 cup dried Great Northern beans, sorted,
>   soaked, and rinsed (see page 226)
> 1/4 cup dried pinto beans, sorted, soaked,
>   and rinsed (see page 226)
> 3 tablespoons extra-virgin olive oil
> 2 leeks, white and tender green parts, thinly sliced
> 3 garlic cloves, thinly sliced
> 1 tablespoon chopped fresh oregano or
>   1 teaspoon dried oregano
> 1 1/2 teaspoons coarse sea salt
> 3/4 pound collard greens, sliced into
>   1/2-inch-wide strips
> 1 (14-ounce) can chopped tomatoes
> Freshly milled black pepper

1. Preheat the oven to 275°F.

2. In a saucepan over medium heat, combine the beans with 4 cups water and bring to a boil. Skim the foam, reduce the heat, and simmer, partially covered, for 30 minutes.

3. While the beans cook, warm the oil in a heavy flameproof casserole over medium heat. Add the leeks, garlic, oregano, and 1 teaspoon of the salt. Sauté for 5 minutes, until the leeks begin to soften. Cover the casserole, reduce the heat to low, and simmer gently for 10 minutes.

4. Place the collard greens in a bowl, add the cooked leeks, and stir to combine.

5. Place a strainer or colander over a bowl and pour in the beans. Measure out the cooking liquid and add enough fresh water to equal 2 cups.

6. Place half of the greens mixture in the casserole. Add the strained beans. Spread the remaining greens over the beans and top with the tomatoes. Sprinkle the remaining $1/2$ teaspoon salt over the tomatoes and add a few grinds of pepper. Without disturbing the layers, gently pour enough of the bean water down the side of the casserole to barely cover the tomatoes.

7. Place the casserole over high heat and bring to a boil. Remove from the stovetop, cover, and bake for 1 hour. Remove the cover and check the casserole, adding a little more water if it is drying out. The casserole should be just slightly juicy when pressed gently with the back of a wooden spoon. Replace the cover and continue to braise for 20 to 30 more minutes, until the beans are tender and the greens and leeks have melted.

8. Serve hot.

YIELD: 4 TO 6 SERVINGS

APHRODISIAC LEGUMES?

In some parts of Europe, beans were thought of as a dangerously erotic foodstuff for many centuries. In his book *On Food and Cooking,* Harold McGee writes that Saint Jerome actually forbade his nuns to eat offensive legumes because, he said, *"in partibus genitalibus titillationes producunt,"* or "they tickle the genitals." And centuries later, the English author Henry Buttes wrote that beans produce "flatulencie, whereby they provoke to lechery."

Kidney Beans Stewed in Red Wine with Tomatoes and Herbs

The kidney bean is probably the best known and appreciated of all beans. In fact, hundreds of bean varieties have been bred from this single species.

In this slow-baked dish, hearty kidney beans will satisfy your craving for a rich, deeply seasoned ragout that you can serve over pasta or rice.

1 1/2 cups dried dark red kidney beans,
    sorted, soaked, and rinsed (see page 226)
Water
3 tablespoons olive oil or 2 tablespoons unsalted butter
    and 1 tablespoon olive oil
1 small red onion, chopped
1 small carrot, finely diced
1 small celery rib, preferably with leaves,
    finely diced
Coarse sea salt
4 tablespoons tomato paste
3 garlic cloves, coarsely chopped
1/4 teaspoon hot red pepper flakes
1/2 cup full-bodied red wine, such as rioja,
    Rhône, or chianti
1 teaspoon balsamic vinegar
1 bay leaf
2 sprigs fresh flat-leaf parsley
1 sprig fresh thyme
1 sprig fresh sage
1 sprig fresh rosemary
Freshly milled black pepper
Minced parsley or Gremolata
    (page 378) for garnish

1. Preheat the oven to 275°F.

2. In a saucepan over medium heat, combine the beans with 4 cups water and bring to a boil. Skim the foam, reduce the heat to low, and simmer, partially covered, for 1 hour.

3. In a 3- or 4-quart flameproof casserole over medium heat, warm the oil. Add the onion, carrot, celery, and a pinch of salt. Sauté for 5 minutes. Add the tomato paste, garlic, and red pepper flakes and continue to cook for another 5 minutes, stirring occasionally to prevent sticking.

4. Pour in the wine and bring to a boil. Add the vinegar and bay leaf. Add the beans with their cooking liquid. Make a bouquet garni by tying with kitchen twine or wrapping in cheesecloth the sprigs of parsley, thyme, sage, and rosemary. Toss in the bouquet garni and enough additional water to barely cover the beans.

5. When the beans return to a boil, cover the casserole and bake for 1 to 2 hours, until the beans are creamy smooth on the inside but still retain their shape and the liquid has thickened into a rich sauce. Remove the bouquet garni.

6. Season to taste with salt and pepper and serve garnished with minced parsley or gremolata.

YIELD: 4 SERVINGS

Chickpea Bouillabaisse

Bouillabaisse is a simple fish stew made along the coastal regions of France. Here, I have preserved the traditional Mediterranean flavors of fennel, artichokes, and potatoes, and simply substituted delicious chickpeas for the fish. French bouillabaisse is often served with rouille, a spicy pepper sauce that has its origins in northern Africa. As with all spicy condiments, the rouille should be served on the side so that everyone can flavor their own bowl of soup to taste.

2 leeks, white parts sliced,
    green tops reserved for stock
2 fennel bulbs, bulbs sliced,
    outer tough leaves and stalks reserved for stock
Cold water
$1/2$ cup dry white wine
2 teaspoons whole fennel seeds
Freshly squeezed juice of 1 lemon
4 to 6 baby artichokes,
    depending on size
2 tablespoons olive oil
Coarse sea salt
3 garlic cloves, thinly sliced
$3/4$ pound potatoes (about 2),
    peeled and chopped into $1/4$-inch pieces
1 (14-ounce) can chopped tomatoes
    or 1 pound tomatoes, peeled, seeded, and diced
2 cups cooked chickpeas
    (from $2/3$ cup dried, see page 226)
$1/4$ teaspoon saffron threads
Rouille (page 380)

1. In a saucepan over high heat, combine the leek tops, fennel stalks, 4 cups water, wine, and fennel seeds. Bring to a boil. Reduce the heat to low and simmer, uncovered, for 25 to 30 minutes. Strain, reserving the liquid and discarding the solids.

2. While the stock simmers, fill a medium bowl with cold water and add the lemon juice. Trim the top third of each artichoke and pull away the tough outer leaves until the tender pale

leaves are exposed. With a paring knife, trim away the tough portions of the stem, being careful not to cut into the heart. Slice the artichokes in half lengthwise and scoop out the feathery chokes with a spoon. Cut lengthwise into quarters and place in the lemon water.

3. In a 3- to 4-quart soup kettle over medium heat, warm the oil. Add the white part of the leeks and $1/2$ teaspoon salt. Sauté for about 5 minutes, or until the leeks soften. Add the garlic and sauté about 2 minutes. Add the sliced fennel, potatoes, tomatoes, chickpeas, and saffron. Pour enough stock over the vegetables to cover by 1 inch. Raise the heat and bring to a boil, then reduce heat to low and simmer, partially covered, for 35 minutes, or until the potatoes are tender.

4. Drain the artichokes and add them to the soup kettle. Simmer for 10 minutes longer, or until the artichokes are tender.

5. Adjust the seasoning to taste. Serve with the rouille passed on the side.

YIELD: 4 TO 6 SERVINGS

Boston-Style "Baked Beans"

In the days when people heated their homes with potbellied stoves, they would prepare a pot of beans in the morning and leave them to simmer on the top of the stove all day long. Here, the process is magically speeded up with the help of a pressure cooker.

You can use barley malt syrup, rice malt, or molasses in place of the maple syrup.

2 cups dried pinto or Great Northern beans,
     sorted, soaked, and rinsed (see page 226)
1 onion, peeled and stuck with 3 cloves
1 celery rib with leaves, cut in half crosswise
1 carrot, quartered
3 garlic cloves (unpeeled)
1 (3-inch) piece kombu (optional)
2 (¹/₄-inch-thick) slices gingerroot
1 bay leaf
Cold water
¹/₄ cup pure maple syrup
3 tablespoons naturally brewed soy sauce
2 tablespoons olive oil or unsalted butter
2 teaspoons Dijon-style mustard
Coarse sea salt
Freshly milled black pepper

1. In a pressure cooker, combine the beans, onion, celery, carrot, garlic, kombu, ginger, and bay leaf. Add enough water to cover by 1 inch. Bring to a boil over high heat. Skim off and discard the foam that rises to the top. Attach the lid and bring to full pressure (15 pounds). Reduce the heat to low and cook for 40 minutes (see The Pressure Cooker Method, page 229).

2. Transfer the pressure cooker to the sink and release the pressure under cold running water. Remove and discard the vegetables and seasonings. Add the maple syrup, soy sauce, oil, and mustard. Return the cooker to the stove over medium heat and simmer the beans, uncovered, for 15 to 20 minutes, until they are meltingly tender and the liquid has thickened into a rich sauce. Add salt and pepper to taste.

3. Serve hot.   YIELD: 6 SERVINGS

Italian-Style Baked Beans
with Garlic and Sage

In this simple recipe, garlic and sage add their pungent, earthy qualities to tender white beans, resulting in an exquisitely flavored dish.

> **2 cups dried Great Northern, pinto, or cannellini beans,**
> **sorted, soaked, and rinsed (see page 226)**
> **2 tablespoons extra-virgin olive oil**
> **2 garlic cloves (unpeeled)**
> **1 sprig fresh sage**
> **Coarse sea salt**
> **Freshly milled black pepper**

1. Preheat the oven to 300°F.

2. In a large, flameproof casserole over medium heat, combine the beans, oil, garlic, and sage. Add water to cover by 1 inch, bring to a simmer, then cover and place in the oven.

3. Bake for 1 to 1$\frac{1}{2}$ hours, until the beans are tender. Add salt and pepper to taste, and continue to cook for just 5 more minutes.

4. Serve hot.

YIELD: 4 TO 6 SERVINGS

Savory Adzuki Beans

Adzukis are native to China and are immensely popular there as well as in Korea and Japan, where they are most often made into a sweet paste and used in desserts and confectionery. However, this is a savory creation that is flavored with tangy ginger and sweet rice wine. This is a perfect example of how easy it is to transform beans into delicious sauces to accompany a grain or serve as a hearty soup. And this one is especially simple to make because adzukis do not require soaking.

 1 cup dried adzukis, sorted and rinsed
    (see page 226)
 5 cups water
 1 small onion, peeled, left whole,
    and stuck with 3 cloves
 6 quarter-sized slices gingerroot
 3 garlic cloves (unpeeled)
 2 tablespoons mirin
 2 tablespoons light sesame oil or olive oil
 1 bay leaf
 Coarse sea salt

1. In a heavy 3-quart saucepan over high heat, combine the beans with the water, onion, ginger, garlic, mirin, oil, and bay leaf. Bring to a boil. Reduce the heat to low, cover, and simmer for $1^{1}/_{2}$ to 2 hours, or until the beans are completely tender.

2. Remove and discard the onion, bay leaf, ginger, and garlic. Add salt to taste and simmer for 2 to 3 minutes longer until the flavors meld.

YIELD: 4 CUPS (6 TO 8 SERVINGS)

Refried Beans

There are many ways to season refried beans. If you are preparing the beans from scratch, cook them with a dried chili pepper, such as chipotle. They will soak up the flavor as they cook. Then simply drain them and discard the pepper. If you're starting with unseasoned cooked beans, sauté them with chopped fresh jalapeño pepper or dried chili powder.

1 1/4 cups dried beans, such as pinto, Anasazi, cranberry, or
    Great Northern, sorted, soaked, and rinsed (see page 226)
1/4 cup olive oil or light sesame oil
1 onion, diced
3 garlic cloves, chopped
2 teaspoons cumin seeds, freshly ground
1 teaspoon dried oregano (Mexican, if possible)
1 teaspoon chipotle chili powder or 1 small jalapeño pepper, seeded and chopped
Coarse sea salt
Freshly milled black pepper

1. In a pressure cover, cover the beans in water by 1 inch. Pressure cook at full pressure (15 pounds) for 30 minutes (see The Pressure Cooker Method, page 229). Drain, reserving the cooking liquid.

2. In a wide, heavy skillet over medium heat, warm the oil. Add the onion and sauté for 5 minutes. Add the garlic, cumin seeds, oregano, chipotle powder, 1 teaspoon salt, and black pepper to taste. Sauté for 5 to 10 minutes, until lightly browned.

3. Add the beans and 1 cup of their cooking liquid. Raise the heat and bring to a boil. Reduce the heat to low and simmer 10 to 15 minutes, partially mashing the beans with the back of a wooden spoon or potato masher.

4. Season with salt and pepper to taste, and serve hot.

YIELD: 4 TO 6 SERVINGS

VARIATION: SIMMERED WITH TOMATOES

Add 1 (14-ounce) can chopped tomatoes to the sautéed onions and reduce the bean liquid in step 3 to 1/4 cup.

Baby Lima Bean
and Spinach Gratin

Don't be deceived! Baby lima beans are not young lima beans at all; they are a distinct variety of lima, with a more subtle, delicate flavor than their larger cousin. Try making your own sourdough bread (see pages 322 to 348) to use for the toasted bread crumbs.

1 garlic clove, peeled and cut in half
5 tablespoons extra-virgin olive oil
    plus more for brushing
1$\frac{1}{4}$ cups dried baby lima beans, sorted,
    soaked, and rinsed (see page 226)
2 pounds fresh spinach, thick stems removed
1 onion, diced
2 teaspoons fresh thyme leaves, chopped
Coarse sea salt
Freshly milled black pepper
1 slice sourdough bread
Freshly grated Parmesan cheese (optional)
1 to 2 teaspoons red wine vinegar

1. Preheat the oven to 375°F. Rub the bottom and sides of a 6-cup gratin dish with the cut garlic clove. Brush the dish lightly with oil.

2. In a pressure cooker, combine the beans with water to cover by 1 inch. Cook at full pressure (15 pounds) for 25 minutes (see The Pressure Cooker Method, page 229). Drain the beans and reserve their cooking liquid for soup if desired. Transfer the beans to a medium mixing bowl.

3. Wash and drain the spinach and place it in a large pot with any water that clings to it. Cover the pot and steam the spinach over high heat for 1 to 2 minutes, until wilted. Drain the spinach and chill under cold running water. Using your hands, squeeze the spinach until it is almost dry, then transfer it to a cutting board and chop. Add the chopped spinach to the beans and set aside.

4. In a medium sauté pan over medium heat, warm 4 tablespoons of the oil. Add the onion, thyme, and salt and pepper to taste. Sauté for 5 minutes. Reduce the heat to low, cover, and

continue to cook for 10 minutes, or until the onion is lightly caramelized. Remove from the heat and stir into the bean mixture.

5. Toast the bread until lightly browned. Remove the crust and pound the bread into crumbs in a mortar or grind in a food processor. Combine the bread crumbs with the remaining tablespoon of oil and some grated cheese to taste.

6. Season the bean and spinach mixture with the vinegar and additional salt and pepper to taste. Spread the bean mixture in the gratin dish and top with an even layer of bread crumbs. Bake for 30 minutes, or until golden brown.

7. Serve hot.

YIELD: 4 SERVINGS

Chickpea
Vegetable Curry

My dear friend Diane Carlson, director of the Natural Gourmet Institute for Food and Health in New York City, asked me to develop a cooking class based on quick, satisfying meals from the pressure cooker. If canned chickpeas are used, a hot, hearty meal can be on your table in under 20 minutes. If you put on a pot of white basmati rice or quinoa while you prepare the curry, it will finish in perfect time.

1 cup chopped onion
2 tablespoons unsalted butter or
    extra-virgin olive oil
2 garlic cloves, chopped
1 tablespoon curry powder,
    preferably homemade
    (see pages 358–359)
2 cups cooked chickpeas
    from $2/3$ cup dried beans (see page 226)
$1/2$ cup diced carrots
$1/2$ cup peeled and diced turnips
1 cup peeled and diced potatoes
1 cup peeled and diced winter squash
1 cup water
Coarse sea salt
$1/2$ pound spinach, leaves only
Freshly chopped cilantro for garnish
Plain yogurt for garnish

1. In a pressure cooker over medium heat, combine the onion, butter, garlic, and curry powder and sauté for 5 minutes (see The Pressure Cooker Method, page 229).

2. Raise the heat to high and add the chickpeas, carrots, turnips, potatoes, squash, water, and 1 teaspoon salt. Bring to a boil.

3. Attach the lid and bring to full pressure (15 pounds). Reduce the heat to low and cook for 8 minutes.

4. Transfer the pressure cooker to the sink and hold under cold running water to bring down from pressure.

5. Remove the lid, add the spinach, and return to the stove. Simmer over medium heat for 2 to 3 minutes, until the spinach wilts.

6. Add salt to taste, and serve topped with cilantro and yogurt.

YIELD: 4 SERVINGS

Tofu, Tempeh,

and Seitan
Protein-Rich Canvases

Although I usually try to avoid comparing vegetarian ingredients to meat, in this case I think it is fitting. Tofu, tempeh, and seitan all play a role in vegetarian cooking similar to that of chicken in the meat-eating world. Like chicken, they are culinary chameleons, able to take on the characteristics of any dish, adopting flavors at the whim of the cook. As the nineteenth-century French gastronome Brillat-Savarin said, "Poultry is for the cook what canvas is for a painter." I like to think of tofu, tempeh, and seitan as being blank canvases as well, ready to be painted with as many flavors as your palate desires.

This means that with a little creativity on the part of the cook, tofu, tempeh, and seitan can be transformed into a veritable buffet of shapes, textures, and flavors, including crispy fried cutlets, sautéed juicy morsels, spicy grilled patties, and even sweet, creamy tofu desserts. With these versatile foods, the possibilities seem infinite.

In this chapter, I want to share with you some of my favorite ways of using tofu, tempeh, and seitan. I also want to encourage you to trust your burgeoning culinary creativity and to experiment with your own favorite flavor combinations and cooking styles.

Of the three, tofu is the most bland on its own, which makes it the most versatile. It is also smooth-textured and relatively high in fat compared to tempeh and seitan, making it a natural choice for blending into creamy sauces and desserts. I tend to focus on developing the flavors of my tofu dishes with herbs and spices, rather than with butter and oil, which aren't as readily absorbed because tofu has enough fat on its own. For example, I use chilis, sage, and cumin for a southwestern-style tofu; curry for an Indian flavor; lemongrass, ginger, and soy sauce for an Asian dish; and garlic, basil, olive oil, and lemon for a taste of the Mediterranean.

Tempeh has the most pronounced flavor and texture of the three. It is firm and chunky with a mysteriously nutty flavor and aroma due to the fermentation it undergoes. Panfried, tempeh becomes quite chewy and meaty; simmered in a bath of spices, vinegar, and oil, it becomes juicy and succulent. As with tofu, tempeh also caramelizes well in the oven, turning nicely burnished and brown. It can be served in a vegetarian wrap or a traditional sandwich or incorporated into nori maki. And tempeh is a great finger food. Simply cut the tempeh into cubes, bake it in any one of the marinade recipes in this chapter, brush it with oil, broil it for a few minutes, then serve it with toothpicks.

The last of the three canvases, dark and chewy seitan, is a great substitute for ingredients like ground beef because it has a firm texture and gets juicier as it cooks. And, unlike delicate tofu and crumbly tempeh, it will hold its shape when thinly sliced. Seitan is extremely rich in protein and has almost no fat content, making it a naturally healthful choice.

TOFU

In Asia, people discovered early on that uncooked soybeans were indigestible, so they eventually came to produce tofu, an ingenious way of accessing the nutrition of the soybean. Making tofu is an intensive process that begins by boiling the beans and extracting the soy milk, then curdling the milk and separating the curds from the whey, much like making cheese. The curds can then be pressed into blocks of a soft, medium, firm, or extra-firm density. Fresh, lightly pressed tofu is still in a curd form and looks a bit like cottage cheese. The longer you press the curds, the more water is extracted, and the firmer the tofu becomes. In some of my recipes, I direct you to squeeze the tofu in a clean towel in order to extract any extra water, because less water means more room for the flavor to be absorbed.

If you want tofu that's really chewy to use as a stuffing or in a chili, try freezing it. Freezing tofu changes its texture dramatically. When ice crystals form, the protein in the tofu expands into a sponge-like structure. After defrosting, the water recedes from the tofu and you are left with a block full of those little pockets. It is a little dry, but at the same time it absorbs marinades very well and crumbles readily. To freeze tofu, first drain it thoroughly, pat it dry, and wrap it tightly in plastic wrap. Frozen tofu will turn from creamy white to dark beige.

I recommend buying prepackaged tofu, because unless its water is changed frequently and it is kept properly refrigerated, tofu can develop toxic bacteria. You will know your tofu is spoiled if it feels slimy and smells offensive. After opening the package and draining the tofu, you should soak the tofu in fresh water for about 5 minutes to get rid of the slightly sour flavor caused by a toxin naturally present in soybeans. An opened package of tofu can be stored in a sealable container filled with clean water for up to 2 weeks, if you change the water every other day.

TEMPEH

Tempeh is thought to have originated in Java, Indonesia, where the soybean is very much a staple of the diet, both for meat-eaters and vegetarians. Tempeh results from a method of inoculating soybeans with certain spores to make them more digestible. Whole cooked soybeans are mixed with *Rhizopus oligosporus,* a mold culture, and allowed to incubate for 18 to 24 hours. Often, grains or seeds will be mixed in as well, providing extra texture and complementary protein. The cakes are then packed into bags and incubated on trays at 90°F for 18 to 24 hours. The result is a white, chunky-textured, nutty-smelling slab of tempeh (about ³/₄ inch thick) that is held together by a complex web of white mold.

Pasteurized tempeh will keep for up to 3 months in the freezer and for about 3 weeks in the refrigerator, tightly wrapped. Any white or black spots are perfectly harmless, but orange or green spots are a sign that it has gone off. Marinated and baked, tempeh can keep in the refrigerator for up to 10 days.

SEITAN

Said to have been discovered by the Chinese Buddhists, seitan is the cooked gluten (a type of protein) that has been extracted from wheat flour. And although you've probably never seen raw gluten, if you have ever eaten mock duck, you have eaten seitan. Transforming gluten into seitan involves simmering it in a flavorful broth, such as the traditional Japanese mixture of soy sauce, ginger, and kombu (a seaweed). Raw gluten will spoil in a matter of days, but cooked in a salty medium, it can last for up to a week. In Asia, raw gluten is sometimes rolled into sheets called *fu* and dried to preserve it. Then, as needed, the sheets are reconstituted in water and either simmered in seasoned broth, deep-fried, stir-fried, or wrapped around rice and vegetable stuffings.

Tofu

Sweet Ginger Tofu

This Asian-style dish is great served with soba noodles. Or after it is cooked, cut it up and simmer it in simple dashi broth or miso soup (see pages 30 and 37–41). You can also julienne the cooked tofu and use it as a protein-rich filling for the Nori Maki on page 286.

1/4 cup naturally brewed soy sauce
1/4 cup mirin
1/4 cup rice vinegar
2 tablespoons light honey
2 tablespoons minced gingerroot
2 tablespoons light sesame oil
1 teaspoon minced garlic
1 pound firm tofu, rinsed, patted dry,
   and sliced 1/2 inch thick

1. Preheat the oven to 350°F.

2. In a bowl, combine the soy sauce, mirin, vinegar, honey, ginger, oil, and garlic. Lay the tofu slices in a baking dish that can hold them in a single snug layer. Pour the marinade over the tofu.

3. Bake for 45 minutes, or until the tofu is nearly dry and well browned.

4. Serve hot or cold.

YIELD: 4 TO 6 SERVINGS

Chickpea Flour Crêpes with Tofu and Roasted Vegetables

Chickpea flour is a great substitute for eggs. Its high protein content works as a binder, just like egg whites. These earthy, nutty-tasting crêpes are yet another unusual way of using tofu. Because the filling has a texture like ricotta cheese, you could easily use it to make vegan manicotti. Try laying the rolled-up crêpes in a dish, spooning on some tomato sauce, and baking in a 350°F oven for about 45 minutes.

FOR THE CRÊPES:

1 cup chickpea flour

1 cup unbleached all-purpose
    or white bread flour

2 tablespoons light sesame oil

$1/2$ teaspoon sea salt

FOR THE TOFU:

$1/4$ cup extra-virgin olive oil

1 tablespoon chopped fresh herbs
    (basil, rosemary, thyme, or oregano,
    alone or in combination)

1 teaspoon minced garlic

1 pound firm tofu, rinsed and blotted dry

6 tablespoons freshly squeezed lemon juice

1 teaspoon coarse sea salt

Freshly milled black pepper

FOR THE VEGETABLES:

$1/2$ pound fresh shiitake mushrooms,
    stems reserved for another use

$1/2$ pound asparagus, trimmed and peeled

2 bunches scallions,
    white and green parts, trimmed

2 tablespoons extra-virgin olive oil

Coarse sea salt

1. Preheat the oven to 425°F.

2. To make the crêpes, whisk together 3$^1/_2$ cups cold water, flours, oil, and salt in a bowl to form a thin batter. Strain through a sieve, cover, and set aside.

3. To prepare the tofu, warm the oil in a small skillet over medium heat; sauté the herbs and garlic in the oil for 1 minute.

4. In a bowl, combine the tofu, garlic-herb oil, lemon juice, and salt and mash well. Season with pepper and set aside.

5. To prepare the vegetables, lay the mushrooms, asparagus, and scallions evenly in a single layer on 1 or 2 baking sheets, brush them with oil, and sprinkle them with salt. Roast for 15 minutes, or until lightly browned and tender.

6. Heat a crêpe pan or 8-inch nonstick skillet. Brush with oil and pour in $^1/_3$ cup batter at a time. Tilt the pan so that the batter spreads to coat evenly. Cook until the crêpe is set and the bottom begins to brown, about 1 minute. Using a spatula, flip the crêpe with a quick flick of the wrist. Cook for 30 seconds on the second side, then remove to a platter.

7. Once all the crêpes are made, spread each with 2 or 3 tablespoons of tofu filling, top with roasted vegetables, roll up, and serve.

YIELD: 6 SERVINGS

Spicy Stir-Fried Broccoli Rabe
with Lemon-Basil Tofu

This dish is perfect accompanied by pasta or any grain to make a complete meal. If you can't find broccoli rabe, you can use other tender greens, such as mustard greens, turnip greens, Swiss chard, or spinach. Just remember to adjust the cooking times accordingly.

If you don't want to make the spicy greens stir-fry, you can use the lemon-basil tofu on its own as a sandwich filler. Smear slices of whole-grain bread with some Green Olive and Onion Tapenade (page 376) or Basil-Almond Pesto (page 377). Top with the tofu. Add some sun-dried tomatoes, shredded lettuce, and cucumber, and you've got an instant gourmet sandwich.

FOR THE TOFU:

3 tablespoons freshly squeezed lemon juice

2 tablespoons naturally brewed soy sauce

2 tablespoons freshly chopped basil leaves

2 tablespoons extra-virgin olive oil

1 tablespoon balsamic vinegar

1 teaspoon finely grated lemon zest

1 pound firm tofu, rinsed, patted dry,
    and sliced $1/2$ inch thick

FOR THE BROCCOLI RABE:

2 pounds broccoli rabe,
    tough stalks trimmed

4 tablespoons extra-virgin olive oil

8 plump garlic cloves, peeled and left whole

$1/2$ teaspoon hot red pepper flakes

Coarse sea salt

Freshly milled black pepper

Lemon wedges for garnish

1. Preheat the oven to 375°F.

2. In a bowl, combine the lemon juice, soy sauce, basil, oil, vinegar, and lemon zest. Lay the tofu slices in a baking dish that can hold them in a single snug layer. Pour the marinade over the tofu.

3. Bake for 30 minutes, or until the tofu is nearly dry and well browned.

4. To make the broccoli rabe, chop the tender stalks and greens into 2-inch pieces and soak them in a large basin of cold water.

5. In a heavy, wide sauté pan over medium heat, warm the oil. Add the garlic and sauté gently for 3 to 5 minutes, until golden. Add the red pepper flakes and sauté for 1 minute.

6. Scoop the greens from the water and add them to the pan. Raise the heat and turn the greens over in the oil with a pair of tongs. When the greens begin to simmer, reduce the heat to low and cover. Cook for 8 to 10 minutes, until the greens are tender. Add the tofu and cook 1 minute longer.

7. Season with salt and pepper and serve drizzled with some of the pot liquor and garnished with the lemon wedges and garlic cloves.

YIELD: 4 TO 6 SERVINGS

MAKING EXTRA-FIRM TOFU

Tofu contains a lot of water. Because of its lower water content, extra-firm tofu absorbs marinades better and develops a meaty texture that is perfect for sautéed sandwich fillings. To make extra-firm tofu, wrap a block of tofu in a clean towel, rest a plate on top, and place a jar of water on top of the plate. Press the tofu for 20 to 30 minutes, then unwrap and slice it.

Tofu in Garlic-Thyme Vinaigrette

Here is a purely delicious Mediterranean-style marinade. The marinated tofu makes a lovely sandwich filling with sliced tomatoes, grilled summer squash, red onions, and egg-plant on a crusty baguette. Or, once it has chilled, cube the tofu and toss it with fusilli pasta, olives, and fresh cubed tomatoes.

> 3 tablespoons extra-virgin olive oil
> 3 tablespoons red wine vinegar
> 2 tablespoons freshly squeezed lemon juice
> 1 tablespoon minced garlic
> 2 teaspoons fresh thyme leaves
> 1 1/2 teaspoons coarse sea salt
> 2 bay leaves, crumbled
> Pinch hot red pepper flakes
> 1 pound firm tofu, rinsed, patted dry, and sliced 1/2 inch thick

1. Preheat the oven to 350°F.

2. In a bowl, combine the oil, vinegar, lemon juice, garlic, thyme, salt, bay leaves, and red pepper flakes. Lay the tofu slices in a baking dish that can hold them in a single snug layer. Pour the marinade over the tofu.

3. Bake for 45 minutes, or until the tofu is nearly dry and well browned.

4. Serve hot or cold.

YIELD: 4 TO 6 SERVINGS

Tofu in White Wine, Mustard, and Dill

When a friend of mine returned from Greece, I was somewhat disappointed to be presented with what turned out to be a terrible bottle of wine. However, it did manage to spark an idea for this sweet and tangy Greek-style marinade. Of course, the tofu will taste much better if you use a good white wine. Try serving it in a Greek salad tossed with dill vinaigrette, as a pizza topping, or crumbled into a pasta salad.

$1/2$ small red onion, thinly sliced

3 tablespoons extra-virgin olive oil

2 tablespoons white wine vinegar

2 tablespoons dry white wine

2 tablespoons finely chopped fresh dill

1 tablespoon whole-grain prepared mustard

2 teaspoons mild honey

$1^{1}/2$ teaspoons coarse sea salt

$1/2$ teaspoon coarsely milled black pepper

1 pound firm tofu, rinsed, patted dry, and sliced $1/2$ inch thick

1. Preheat the oven to 350°F.

2. In a bowl, combine the onion, oil, vinegar, wine, dill, mustard, honey, salt, and pepper. Lay the tofu slices in a baking dish that can hold them in a single snug layer. Pour the marinade over the tofu.

3. Bake for 45 minutes, or until the tofu is nearly dry and well browned.

4. Serve hot or cold.

YIELD: 4 TO 6 SERVINGS

Pizza Vegano

This cheeseless pizza is totally delicious and satisfying without trying to mimic cheese. The recipe below is for a very straightforward pie, and it can and should be varied to satisfy your personal appetite. You might want to strew some lightly sautéed onions, leeks, or mushrooms over the tomatoes. Or try adding some grilled or roasted eggplant, summer squash, and peppers. For a more intense flavor, scatter some chopped olives or capers on top.

It is best to bake the pizza directly on a pizza stone, but you can also use a baking sheet sprinkled with cornmeal. To be sure the oven is fully preheated, turn it on at least 30 minutes before you plan to bake the pizza.

FOR THE CRUST:
1 1/2 cups unbleached all-purpose
    or white bread flour
3/4 cup warm water
2 teaspoons active dry yeast
Sea salt
1 cup whole wheat bread flour
Olive oil

FOR THE TOPPING:
5 tablespoons Rosemary-Garlic Oil (page 364)
1 pound firm tofu,
    rinsed and patted dry
1 tablespoon red wine vinegar
3/4 teaspoon coarse sea salt
1/4 teaspoon freshly milled black pepper
2 pounds ripe tomatoes,
    sliced into 1/4-inch-thick rounds

1. In a bowl, whisk together 1/2 cup of the all-purpose flour, water, yeast, and a pinch of salt to form the sponge. Cover with a clean cloth and set aside to rise for 20 to 30 minutes.

2. Stir in the remaining 1 cup all-purpose flour, whole wheat flour, and 3/4 teaspoon salt. Turn the dough out onto a clean surface and knead for 10 to 15 minutes, until you have a smooth, elastic, and slightly sticky dough.

3. Wash and dry the mixing bowl and smear it with oil. Place the dough in the bowl and turn to coat with oil. Cover the bowl with a clean damp towel or plastic wrap and set it aside until it doubles in volume, 1 to 2 hours. Or you may refrigerate it in a tightly sealed plastic bowl or bag for up to 24 hours.

4. Place a pizza stone on the lower third of the oven and preheat oven to 450°F. After the dough has risen, remove it from the bowl and slap it a few times on the counter to deflate it. Shape it into a ball and let rest, covered with a damp towel, for 5 minutes. Roll out the dough into a 14-inch round. Place the dough on a cornmeal-dusted baker's peel or a baking sheet.

5. Brush the crust with some Rosemary-Garlic Oil.

6. Mash the tofu in a bowl with the remaining Rosemary-Garlic Oil (including some of the garlic cloves), vinegar, salt, and pepper.

7. Spread the tomato slices evenly over the pizza, leaving a $1/2$-inch border uncovered. Top with mashed tofu and sprinkle with a bit more of the oil, if desired. Slide the pizza onto the stone or baking sheet.

8. Bake for 25 minutes, or until the crust is crispy, the tomatoes are cooked, and the tofu is golden.

9. Cut into wedges and serve hot.

YIELD: 4 TO 6 SERVINGS

Spanakopita

Everyone loves this classic Greek pie. A combination of spinach and Swiss chard give the pie more body than spinach alone, and the tofu stands in for the traditional feta cheese. With layers of crunchy phyllo, this dish is a great way to introduce someone to tofu.

2 tablespoons extra-virgin olive oil,
   plus more for brushing the phyllo
4 cups thinly sliced onions
2 tablespoons chopped garlic
3 bay leaves
1 teaspoon dried oregano
Coarse sea salt
1 pound Swiss chard
1 pound spinach
1 pound extra-firm tofu, rinsed,
   squeezed to remove excess water, and patted dry
Finely grated zest of 1 large lemon
4 tablespoons freshly squeezed lemon juice
$1/3$ cup kalamata olives, pitted and chopped
Freshly milled black pepper
$1/2$ pound phyllo dough

1. Preheat the oven to 350°F.

2. In a heavy saucepan over medium heat, warm the oil. Add the onions, garlic, bay leaves, oregano, and 2 teaspoons salt. Raise the heat and stir the onion mixture until it begins to sizzle. Reduce the heat to low, cover, and cook for 25 to 30 minutes, until the onions are meltingly tender, stirring occasionally to prevent sticking.

3. While the onion mixture cooks, fill a large bowl with cold water. Remove the tough stems of the chard and spinach and reserve for making a soup or gratin. Rinse the greens in several changes of water. Transfer the greens to a large pot and cook, covered, over high heat for 3 to 5 minutes, until they wilt. Drain in a colander and chill under cold running water. Squeeze the greens until they are nearly dry, and coarsely chop.

4. In a medium bowl, mash the tofu. Add the greens, onion mixture, lemon zest, lemon juice, olives, and additional salt and pepper to taste. Mix well.

5. Lay the phyllo dough on a clean surface and cover with a clean damp towel or piece of plastic wrap. Brush the bottom and sides of a 2-quart shallow baking dish with oil and cover with a sheet of phyllo. Brush the phyllo with oil and layer another piece on top. Brush the next layer with oil and repeat until you have 5 layers. Spread the tofu-vegetable filling over the phyllo. Top with 10 more sheets of phyllo, lightly brushing each sheet with oil.

6. Score the casserole into 6 pieces by gently cutting through the top layers of phyllo with the tip of a sharp knife. Bake the spanakopita for 70 minutes, or until golden brown.

7. Slice through the score marks and serve hot.

YIELD: 6 SERVINGS

Spinach-Mushroom Quiche

I had the pleasure of serving quiches and tarts based on the savory treatment of tofu and vegetables to countless customers during the years that I was executive chef at Angelica Kitchen in New York City. This kind of dish satisfies an appetite many of us share for French-style tarts made with cream, cheese, and eggs.

FOR THE CRUST:

1/2 cup rolled oats

3 tablespoons sesame seeds

1 cup whole wheat pastry flour
    or whole spelt flour

1/2 teaspoon baking powder

3/4 teaspoon sea salt

1/4 teaspoon freshly milled black pepper

1/3 cup unflavored soy milk or water

1/3 cup light sesame oil or pure olive oil plus more for brushing the pan

FOR THE FILLING:

7 tablespoons extra-virgin olive oil

1 cup finely diced onion

10 ounces white button mushrooms,
    thinly sliced

2 tablespoons dry white wine or water

1 1/2 teaspoons coarse sea salt

3 garlic cloves, sliced crosswise into 1/8-inch rounds

10 to 12 fresh basil leaves, chopped

1/2 teaspoon finely chopped
    fresh thyme leaves

Pinch hot red pepper flakes

1 pound firm tofu, rinsed and patted dry

2 tablespoons freshly squeezed lemon juice

1 tablespoon rice vinegar

2 pounds fresh spinach

Paprika for dusting

1. Preheat the oven to 350°F.

2. To make the crust, spread the oats and sesame seeds on a baking sheet and toast in the oven for 8 minutes.

3. Transfer the toasted oats and sesame seeds to the bowl of a food processor fitted with a metal blade. Add the flour, baking powder, salt, and pepper, and process until the oats are finely ground.

4. In a medium bowl, whisk together the soy milk and oil. Using a wooden spoon, mix in the dry ingredients to form a dough.

5. Lightly brush a 9-inch or 10-inch tart pan with oil. Put the dough in the tart pan. Place a piece of plastic wrap on the dough and press down evenly, making sure to fill in the fluted sides of the pan. Trim the tart of any excess dough and refrigerate while you make the filling.

6. To make the filling, in a wide sauté pan over medium heat, warm 2 tablespoons of the oil. Add the onion and mushrooms, raise the heat to high, and sauté for 10 to 12 minutes, stirring and shaking the pan until the vegetables are caramelized. Add the wine and scrape up any brown bits from the bottom of the pan with a wooden spoon. Season with $1/2$ teaspoon of the salt and continue to cook until dry. Using a rubber spatula, scrape the vegetables into a mixing bowl and set aside.

7. In a small saucepan over medium heat, warm the remaining 5 tablespoons of oil. Add the garlic, basil, thyme, and red pepper flakes. Simmer gently for 3 to 4 minutes or until the garlic is golden. Do not let the garlic brown, or it will become bitter. With a rubber spatula, scrape the garlic oil into the bowl of a food processor.

8. Crumble the tofu into the bowl of the food processor. Add the lemon juice, vinegar, and remaining 1 teaspoon of salt and purée until smooth. With a rubber spatula, scrape the purée into the mushroom-onion mixture.

9. Remove and discard the tough stems of the spinach. Wash the leaves in a large bowl with several changes of cold water. Transfer the spinach to a pot and cook, covered, over high heat for several minutes, just until wilted. Drain in a colander and rinse under cold water to arrest the cooking. Drain well and squeeze dry. Transfer the spinach to a cutting board and chop fine. Add the spinach to the rest of the filling and stir well to combine.

10. Fill the tart shell with the tofu and vegetable mixture and smooth the top with the back of a spoon. Dust with paprika. Bake for 45 to 50 minutes, until firm.

11. Let the tart cool for 8 to 10 minutes before slicing and serving.   YIELD: 4 TO 6 SERVINGS

Tofu Scramble

The turmeric gives this classic brunch dish its yellow egg-like coloring. It is a highly seasoned, perfectly textured scramble that's a great way of bridging the vegetarian and meat-eating worlds—everyone will love it.

3 tablespoons extra-virgin olive oil
$1/2$ cup finely chopped onion
1 plump garlic clove, finely chopped
2 tablespoons pine nuts
$1/2$ teaspoon freshly ground cumin
$1/4$ teaspoon hot red pepper flakes
$1/2$ teaspoon turmeric
1 pound firm tofu, rinsed, squeezed to remove excess moisture, and patted dry
1 large ripe tomato, peeled, seeded, and chopped
Coarse sea salt
2 tablespoons freshly squeezed lime juice

1. In a wide, heavy skillet over medium heat, warm the oil. Add the onion and sauté for 2 to 3 minutes. Stir in the garlic, pine nuts, cumin, red pepper flakes, and turmeric and sauté for 2 minutes.

2. Place the tofu in a bowl and mash. Add the mashed tofu, tomato, $1^{1/2}$ teaspoons salt, and lime juice to the skillet. Raise the heat and simmer, stirring, for 5 minutes to heat through.

3. Taste and adjust seasonings. Serve hot.

YIELD: 4 SERVINGS

Tempeh

Tempeh and Mushroom Fricassee with Forty Cloves of Garlic

I really must tip my hat to the classic Provençal chicken dish that inspired this recipe. Forty cloves may seem like an awful lot of garlic, but they lose their harshness as they cook, and turn out sweet and caramelized. The tempeh also undergoes a change: as it slowly simmers, it becomes very succulent and flavorful. This dish is a wonderful centerpiece to build a meal around.

    4 tablespoons olive oil
    ³/₄ pound tempeh,
        sliced into bite-size pieces
    ¹/₄ cup dry white wine
    2 tablespoons naturally brewed soy sauce
    2 leeks, white and tender green parts, julienned
    1 pound mixed exotic mushrooms,
        such as cremini, portobello, shiitake, and oyster, sliced
    1 tablespoon unbleached all-purpose flour
    1¹/₂ cups All-Season Vegetable Stock (page 29)
    40 very fresh garlic cloves, peeled
    2 sprigs fresh thyme
    1 sprig parsley
    Small handful celery leaves
    Coarse sea salt
    Freshly milled black pepper
    Chopped fresh parsley for garnish

1. In a wide, heavy sauté pan over medium heat, warm 2 tablespoons of the oil. Add the tempeh and sauté until golden brown on all sides, 8 to 10 minutes. Add the wine and soy sauce, raise the heat, and bring to a boil. Cook until the liquid is reduced to half its original volume. Transfer the contents of the pan to a bowl and set aside.

2. Warm the remaining 2 tablespoons oil in the pan over medium-high heat. Add the leeks and mushrooms and sauté, stirring and tossing until the vegetables are lightly caramelized. Stir in the flour and continue to cook until the flour smells toasted and fragrant, 2 to 3 more minutes.

3. Add the stock and garlic. Make a bouquet garni by tying together with kitchen twine or wrapping in cheesecloth the thyme, parsley, and celery leaves. Add the bouquet garni and bring the stock to a boil. With a wooden spoon, scrape up any browned bits that cling to the bottom of the pan. Reduce the heat to low and add the tempeh with any juices that have collected in the bowl.

4. Cover and simmer gently for 30 minutes. Uncover and continue to cook for 5 minutes, until the liquid thickens into a sauce.

5. Remove the bouquet garni. Season with salt and pepper to taste, sprinkle with chopped parsley, and serve.

YIELD: 4 TO 6 SERVINGS

WHAT KIND OF TEMPEH SHOULD I USE?

If possible you should purchase unpasteurized tempeh, which is sold from the freezer case. It will have a better texture and ability to absorb marinades than pasteurized tempeh. Pasteurized tempeh is found in the refrigerator case, and while it is good, it generally lacks some of the flavor and texture of unpasteurized tempeh.

You also may have noticed that tempeh blocks are sold in a wide array of styles and flavors. Although I have based my recipes on plain blocks of tempeh, please feel free to experiment with the many different types on the market, which include such ingredients as long-grain rice, sesame seeds, and seaweed.

Barbecued Tempeh Sandwich Filling

Get ready for some intense flavor! This is everything barbecue should be: sweet, spicy, and smoky, thanks to the chipotle chilis. And once the tempeh is baked in the marinade, it's great for the grill. To make this filling into a sandwich, spread your favorite sandwich bread with some Spicy Sun-Dried Tomato Spread (page 375). Top with the tempeh, and your choice of chopped lettuce, sliced Kirby or pickling cucumber, clover sprouts, watercress, and shredded carrots.

1 pound tempeh
$1/2$ cup cider vinegar
$1/2$ cup naturally brewed soy sauce
$1/2$ cup pure olive oil
$1/3$ cup pure maple syrup
2 teaspoons ground cumin
2 teaspoons ground chipotle chili
1 teaspoon dried thyme
1 teaspoon sweet paprika

1. Preheat the oven to 350°F.

2. Slice each block of tempeh in half horizontally, then slice each piece in half. Select a baking dish that can hold the slices in a single snug layer.

3. In a bowl, whisk together the vinegar, soy sauce, oil, maple syrup, cumin, chili, thyme, and paprika. Pour half of the marinade into the baking dish. Place the tempeh on top and pour on the remaining marinade.

4. Cover the dish with foil (shiny side down), forming a tight seal. Bake for 45 to 50 minutes, until most of the marinade is absorbed. Uncover and bake for 10 minutes, or until well browned.

5. Remove the tempeh to a plate to cool, and use in a sandwich. (At this point the tempeh will stay fresh for up to 10 days tightly wrapped in the refrigerator.)

YIELD: 4 TO 6 SERVINGS

Apple-Mustard Baked Tempeh Sandwich Filling

When my wife, Meggan, was pregnant with our first daughter, Kayla, she would often crave tempeh and sauerkraut. This sandwich filling always takes me back to that golden time in our lives when life seemed simpler—well, at least sibling rivalry had not entered our lives yet!

This sandwich filling is great served on toasted whole-grain bread accompanied by tahini, sauerkraut, mustard, and some shredded lettuce or clover sprouts.

1 pound tempeh
1 1/3 cups apple juice or fresh apple cider
1/3 cup olive oil or light sesame oil
3 tablespoons naturally brewed soy sauce
3 tablespoons whole-grain prepared mustard plus more to spread
1 teaspoon ground caraway seeds
1 teaspoon ground cumin
1/4 teaspoon freshly milled black pepper
Sauerkraut, preferably homemade (page 374)

1. Preheat the oven to 350°F.

2. Slice the tempeh horizontally, then slice each piece in half. Transfer the tempeh to a steamer over boiling water and steam for 8 minutes.

3. In a bowl, whisk together the apple juice, oil, soy sauce, mustard, caraway seeds, cumin, and pepper.

4. Arrange the tempeh slices in a single snug layer in a baking dish. Pour the marinade over the tempeh and bake, uncovered, for 35 to 40 minutes, until most of the marinade has been absorbed and the tempeh is nicely browned.

5. To serve, spread your favorite sandwich bread with tahini and mustard to taste. Top with tempeh, sauerkraut, and sprouts or lettuce.

YIELD: 4 SERVINGS

Tempeh Simmered in Broth

This simple preparation is one of my favorite ways to enjoy tempeh. It is an excellent way to begin including this "other white meat" into your daily diet. Feel free to vary the herbs and add a few of your favorite chopped seasonal vegetables and some leftover grains or pasta to the broth. It will make a terrific one-pot meal!

> 1 pound tempeh, sliced into bite-sized pieces
> 4 cups water
> 3 tablespoons naturally brewed soy sauce
> 1 tablespoon extra-virgin olive oil
> 3 to 4 garlic cloves, lightly bruised with the side of a knife
> 2 to 3 quarter-sized gingerroot slices
> 1 sprig fresh rosemary
> 1 sprig fresh thyme
> Thinly sliced scallion, green and white parts, for garnish

1. In a saucepan over high heat, combine the tempeh, water, soy sauce, oil, garlic, ginger, rosemary, and thyme. Bring to a boil.

2. Reduce the heat to low and simmer, covered, for 30 minutes. Remove the herb sprigs and serve sprinkled with scallion.

YIELD: 4 TO 6 SERVINGS

Tempeh and Vegetables Braised in a Spicy Lemon-Coconut Broth

This recipe uses a technique of my friend and fellow cookbook author Lorna Sass for pan-browning, then braising tempeh. Here I used a fragrant coconut milk broth seasoned with lemon zest, coriander, ginger, and hot red pepper. Serve the tempeh with jasmine rice.

2 tablespoons light sesame oil
1/2 pound tempeh,
    sliced in half horizontally
1 cup thinly sliced onion
Coarse sea salt
1 cup sliced carrot
2 garlic cloves, thinly sliced
1 tablespoon minced gingerroot
1 teaspoon ground coriander
1 teaspoon turmeric
1 teaspoon sweet paprika
1 teaspoon sugar or maple syrup
1/2 teaspoon caraway seeds
1/2 teaspoon hot red pepper flakes
1 (14-ounce) can coconut milk
    (full fat is best)
2 tablespoons mirin
2 tablespoons naturally brewed soy sauce
2 tablespoons freshly squeezed lemon juice
Finely grated zest of 1 lemon
4 cups sliced green cabbage (1/2-inch slices)
1/4 cup chopped fresh cilantro

1. In a 8- to 10-inch sauté pan over medium heat, warm 1 tablespoon of the oil. Add the tempeh. Flip the pieces over to coat both sides with the oil. Cover and cook for 2 to 3 minutes, until the slices are flecked with brown. Turn the slices over, cover, and cook for 2 to 3 minutes more, until lightly speckled. Transfer the tempeh to a plate and set aside.

2. Add the remaining 1 tablespoon of oil to the pan along with the onion and 1/2 teaspoon salt. Sauté for 5 minutes, or until the onion softens.

3. Add the carrot, garlic, ginger, coriander, turmeric, paprika, sugar, caraway seeds, and red pepper flakes. Sauté, stirring occasionally, for 3 minutes.

4. Add the tempeh, coconut milk, mirin, soy sauce, lemon juice, and lemon zest. Raise the heat and bring to a boil. Reduce the heat to low, cover, and let simmer gently for 15 minutes.

5. Place the cabbage on top of the tempeh and sprinkle on $1/2$ teaspoon salt. Cover the pan and simmer for 10 minutes. The cabbage should exude enough of its own juices to keep the braise from drying out. If not, add 1 to 2 tablespoons water.

6. Uncover and gently turn the cabbage over several times in the pan juices to coat. Adjust the seasonings to taste, stir in the cilantro, and serve.

YIELD: 4 SERVINGS

Tempeh Provençal

This is a great dish for a casual summer buffet. In it, sliced vegetables and tempeh are layered with a scattering of fresh herbs, chopped olives, and garlic, then anointed with olive oil. The full assembly is bathed in white wine and baked until the tempeh and vegetables are meltingly tender and flavorful.

$1/3$ cup extra-virgin olive oil
1 pound tempeh,
   sliced into $1/4$-inch-by-1-inch-by-2-inch pieces
2 medium zucchini,
   sliced into $1/4$-inch-by-1-inch-by-2-inch pieces
Coarse sea salt
Freshly milled black pepper
2 tablespoons chopped fresh oregano
2 tablespoons chopped fresh basil
$1/2$ cup black olives, pitted
$1 1/2$ pounds ripe tomatoes, sliced into $1/2$-inch-thick rounds
4 cloves garlic, thinly sliced
1 large yellow bell pepper,
   cored, ribs and seeds removed, and sliced
$1/2$ cup dry white wine

1. Preheat the oven to 350°F.

2. Brush a 2-quart casserole with 1 tablespoon of the oil. Add a layer of tempeh and top with a layer of zucchini. Sprinkle on a tablespoon of oil and season with salt and pepper and $1/2$ tablespoon each of the oregano and basil. Spread half of the olives and garlic over the zucchini and top with half the sliced tomato. Season with salt and pepper, another tablespoon of the olive oil, and another $1/2$ tablespoon each of the oregano and basil. Next, make a layer of tempeh, yellow pepper, and the remaining olives. Season with salt, black pepper, oil, oregano, and basil. Layer with the remaining zucchini, and season with salt, black pepper, herbs, and oil. Top with the remaining tomatoes and season with salt, black pepper, and the remaining oil and herbs. Pour the wine over the top, cover with a sheet of parchment paper, and seal with foil.

3. Bake for 1 hour. Uncover and bake 15 minutes more. Remove the casserole from the oven and allow it to sit loosely covered for 10 to 15 minutes before serving.

YIELD: 6 TO 8 SERVINGS

Sweet-and-Sour Tempeh with Spicy Peanut Sauce

Peanuts and tempeh are a terrific combination. Here I pair them in a tangy, Thai-inspired dish that manages to achieve a perfect balance of sweet, spicy, and sour. It is great served over rice or noodles.

FOR THE TEMPEH:
1/4 cup light sesame oil
1 tablespoon toasted sesame oil
1/4 cup naturally brewed soy sauce
1/4 cup rice vinegar
1/4 cup mirin
1 tablespoon minced, peeled gingerroot
1 garlic clove, crushed
1 pound tempeh, cut into 1-inch cubes

FOR THE PEANUT SAUCE:
1 cup natural-style unsalted peanut butter
4 tablespoons pure maple syrup or honey
3 tablespoons naturally brewed soy sauce
3 tablespoons rice vinegar
1 tablespoon finely chopped, peeled gingerroot
2 garlic cloves, crushed
1/2 teaspoon cayenne pepper
1/2 to 1 cup hot water
Hot cooked white rice
Thinly sliced radish, scallions, and cilantro for garnish

1. To prepare the tempeh, in a bowl, whisk together the sesame oils, soy sauce, vinegar, mirin, ginger, and garlic.

2. Arrange the tempeh in a single layer in a wide sauté pan. Pour the marinade over the tempeh and bring to a boil over high heat. Reduce the heat to low, cover, and simmer for 20 minutes. Uncover, raise the heat, and cook until nearly dry. (At this point, the tempeh may be refrigerated, tightly wrapped, for up to a week.)

3. To prepare the peanut sauce, combine the peanut butter, maple syrup, soy sauce, vinegar, ginger, garlic, and cayenne in a blender. Purée, adding enough water to form a creamy, pourable sauce.

4. Serve the tempeh over white rice with the peanut sauce and garnish with radish, scallions, and cilantro.

YIELD: 4 TO 6 SERVINGS

Nori Maki

Everybody I have ever met seems to love nori maki. These little rolls make perfect lunch-box treats or hors d'oeuvres at a picnic or party. If you like, you can substitute strips of Sweet Ginger Tofu (page 263) in place of the tempeh.

You can keep the rolls, uncut and wrapped in plastic, in the refrigerator for 2 days.

FOR THE TEMPEH:
1/2 pound tempeh, sliced lengthwise into 1/2-inch strips
2 tablespoons naturally brewed soy sauce
2 tablespoons rice vinegar
3 tablespoons mirin
2 teaspoons toasted sesame oil
2 tablespoons light sesame oil
1 tablespoon brown rice syrup
1/4 teaspoon cayenne pepper (optional)

FOR THE RICE:
2 cups white sushi rice
1/2 teaspoon coarse sea salt
1 tablespoon mirin
2 teaspoons rice vinegar

FOR THE VEGETABLES:
1 large carrot, sliced lengthwise into 1/4-inch-wide strips
16 to 20 string beans, trimmed
4 sheets pretoasted nori (available in health
    food stores and Asian markets)

FOR THE GARNISH:

1 to 2 tablespoons umeboshi paste

2 tablespoons lightly toasted sesame seeds

2 scallions, white and green parts,
    trimmed and thinly sliced

FOR THE DIPPING SAUCE:

1/2 cup naturally brewed soy sauce

1/2 cup water

1. Preheat the oven to 375°F.

2. Arrange the tempeh in a baking dish large enough to hold it in a single snug layer. In a bowl, whisk together the soy sauce, vinegar, mirin, sesame oils, rice syrup, and cayenne and pour over the tempeh. Cover with foil and bake for 30 to 40 minutes, until most of the marinade has been absorbed and the tempeh is well browned.

3. While the tempeh bakes, make the rice. In a medium saucepan over high heat, combine $3^{1}/2$ cups water, the rice, $^{1}/2$ teaspoon salt, mirin, and vinegar. Bring to a boil. Reduce the heat to low and simmer, covered, for 20 minutes, or until the water has been absorbed and the rice is tender. Turn off the heat and keep covered for 5 minutes. Transfer the rice to a bowl to cool.

4. Steam the carrot and string beans over boiling water for 2 to 3 minutes, until crisp-tender. Then cool under cold running water. Drain thoroughly and set aside.

5. Place a sheet of nori on a nori mat, shiny side down. Moisten your hands and scoop up one-quarter of the rice into a ball. Spread the ball of rice evenly on the nori. Leave 1 inch along the top and $^{1}/2$ inch along the bottom of the nori exposed.

6. Spread approximately $^{3}/4$ teaspoon umeboshi paste evenly over the rice and sprinkle with sesame seeds. Starting 1 inch up from the bottom of the rice lay succeeding lengths of tempeh strips, carrot, and string beans. Sprinkle with a fourth of the scallions.

7. Lightly moisten the top of the nori and roll into a cylinder. Apply even pressure on the roll. Repeat with the remaining ingredients.

8. To make the dipping sauce, combine the soy sauce and water and mix well.

9. Slice the nori maki into $^{1}/2$-inch rounds with a sharp knife. Serve accompanied by the dipping sauce. YIELD: 4 NORI MAKI

Seitan

MAKING SEITAN

Since seitan can be hard to find in the market and is more expensive than tofu, I have decided to give directions for making it at home. Making it is an amazing experience, plus you will get a workout from the kneading, and the vitamin E-rich bran will cleanse the pores and soften the skin on your hands as you work the dough. If you do use purchased seitan, taste it for saltiness and either soak it in water or decrease the salt called for in the recipe accordingly.

Before the gluten is extracted from the wheat, it first needs to be developed by a vigorous kneading. As you work the dough, the strands of protein become more elastic and more toned, just like what happens to our muscles when we exercise. Bread flour contains the highest amount of gluten; in fact, 11 to 14 percent of bread flour is protein. For the best-textured gluten, you need to use a mixture of half white and half whole wheat bread flour. If you use all white flour, the gluten will be too dense and gummy. It is the wheat germ and bran that create some space in the gluten so that the dough can absorb flavors.

As you knead and wash, there will probably be a point where you will start to panic and fear that you are dissolving everything and the dough will wash away. Don't worry! The gluten will stay put, but you have to be patient and allow it to separate from the starch. About 70 percent of the dough is starch, so you will be left with a much smaller portion of the mass you began with. But when you cook the gluten, it will expand somewhat as it absorbs the broth.

If your gluten turns out too rubbery, it means you have overwashed it. As you wash, make sure you can still see a fair amount of bran specks and that the ball isn't too firm. It takes a little practice, but you'll get it! If you slice a piece of seitan after cooking it, and it is white in the middle, it was too dense (overkneaded) and couldn't absorb the soy sauce from the broth. If you drastically underknead the dough, the gluten will not have a chance to form and will wash away during the rinsings. But, if you have underkneaded only slightly, the ball will just turn out a little looser.

Seitan can be frozen in its cooking liquid for up to 6 months and will not change color or texture when thawed.

Homemade Seitan

FOR THE GLUTEN:

2 pounds unbleached all-purpose or white bread flour

2 pounds whole wheat bread flour

4 to 5 cups cold water, or enough to form a firm dough

FOR THE STOCK:

$2^1/_2$ pounds carrots, halved lengthwise

1 pound onions, quartered

2 celery ribs, including the leaves, halved lengthwise

$1^1/_2$ cups tamari or naturally brewed soy sauce

4 garlic cloves, halved

8 (1-inch) rounds gingerroot

12 whole black peppercorns

2 sprigs fresh thyme

2 bay leaves

1. To make the gluten, in a large bowl, combine the flours and 4 cups water and form into a firm ball. Add more water if the dough is dry. Transfer the dough to a counter and knead for 15 minutes, or until the dough is smooth and elastic and springs back when pulled.

2. Put the dough in a mixing bowl and cover with lukewarm water. Let the dough rest for 30 minutes so that the gluten can relax. If it is not allowed to relax, the gluten will not separate itself from the starch, bran, and germ.

3. In an 8- to 10-quart stockpot over high heat, combine 4 quarts water, carrots, onions, celery, tamari, garlic, ginger, peppercorns, thyme, and bay leaves. Bring to a boil. Reduce the heat and simmer while you prepare the seitan.

4. Meanwhile, place the dough in a colander inside a mixing bowl. Put the bowl containing the colander and dough into the sink and fill with cold tap water. Wash the dough in the cold water for 5 minutes, squishing, pulling, and squeezing the dough in your hands. Then wash it for 5 minutes in warm water. Repeat the cold-water, then warm-water, rinsings and end with a 2-minute cold-water wash for a total of 5 rinsings. With each washing, the water will become clearer and clearer, and the gluten will be more and more developed. At first it will feel like there is an amazing amount of starch coming off; then the gluten starts to break away and the dough feels and looks like a wet, ragged mass. Then it will become spongy with a lot of loose

strands. The strands should start to get tighter, and finally it will become a smooth round ball. What remains is the glutinous part of the wheat: the protein. All of the starch and 90 percent of the bran have been washed away.

5. Pinch off golf-ball size pieces of the gluten and simmer in the stock for 1 hour. The pieces of gluten will expand as they absorb the stock. Add water from time to time to keep the balls submerged.

6. Strain the stock and reserve it for use in a soup or sauce. Use the seitan in a recipe or store submerged in the stock, refrigerated, up to 1 week.

YIELD: 2½ POUNDS (6 TO 8 CUPS) SEITAN

Step-by-Step Seitan

Fully kneaded ball of dough.

Washing the dough. Warm water loosens and washes away the starch and bran. Cold water tightens and strengthens the gluten.

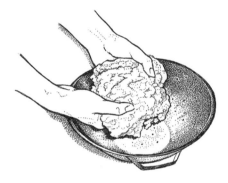

Halfway through the washing process.

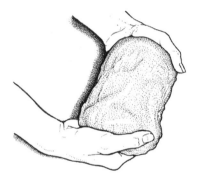

Fully washed gluten is shiny and elastic.

You will wind up with a ball of gluten about the size of a softball.

Beer-Braised Seitan
with Sauerkraut and Onions

This is inspired by the Flemish dish *carbonnades à la flamande*. In keeping with Belgium's great beer tradition, beef is braised in rich dark ale until it is very juicy, sweet, and tender, and it is often accompanied by sauerkraut. This is my vegetarian version, which retains all of the savory juiciness of the original. You can substitute a lighter ale, depending on what you like. Serve with roasted root vegetables, mashed potatoes, or smashed turnips.

$1/4$ cup olive oil
2 pounds onions, thinly sliced
2 teaspoons natural brown sugar or molasses
Coarse sea salt
3 cups sauerkraut,
 preferably homemade (page 374)
2 garlic cloves, crushed
$1/2$ teaspoon caraway seeds
Freshly milled black pepper
2 bay leaves
1 pound seitan, preferably homemade (page 289),
 sliced into bite-size pieces
1 (12-ounce) bottle dark beer
Chopped fresh parsley for garnish

1. Preheat the oven to 300°F.

2. In a heavy flameproof casserole over medium heat, warm the oil. Add the onions, brown sugar, and a pinch of salt and sauté for 8 to 10 minutes, until the onions are tender and juicy. Stir in the sauerkraut, garlic, caraway seeds, pepper, and bay leaves. Spread the seitan over the vegetables and pour in the beer. Raise the heat and bring to a boil. Cover the casserole and bake for 1 hour.

3. Sprinkle with fresh parsley and serve.

YIELD: 4 SERVINGS

Shepherd's Pie

Shepherd's pie is a hearty, traditional English dish made with leftover mutton or other meat. I've substituted seitan for the meat while retaining the overall texture of the dish.

3 tablespoons olive oil
2 cups chopped onions
Coarse sea salt
2 carrots, sliced into $1/2$-inch chunks
12 ounces mushrooms, thickly sliced
$1^1/2$ cups trimmed and sliced string beans (1-inch lengths)
2 teaspoons chopped fresh thyme
2 teaspoons chopped fresh sage
1 (14-ounce) can tomatoes
1 pound seitan, preferably homemade (page 289), sliced into $1/2$-inch chunks
$1/2$ cup water
2 tablespoons mirin
1 tablespoon naturally brewed soy sauce
Freshly milled black pepper
Garlic Mashed Potatoes (page 120)
Extra-virgin olive oil and paprika for finishing the casserole

1. Preheat the oven to 375°F.

2. In a heavy wide pan over medium heat, warm the oil. Add the onions and a pinch of salt and sauté for 7 to 8 minutes, until the onions are soft and juicy. Add the carrots, mushrooms, string beans, thyme, and sage and sauté for 5 minutes.

3. Place a hand-cranked food mill over the pan and pass the tomatoes through the medium disk directly into the vegetables. Add the seitan, water, mirin, and soy sauce. Raise the heat and bring to a boil. Reduce the heat to low and simmer, covered, for 25 minutes, or until vegetables are tender. Uncover and cook for a few minutes, if necessary, to reduce the liquid until slightly thickened.

4. Season with salt and pepper to taste and pour into an earthenware or glass casserole. Spread the mashed potatoes over the vegetables, brush with oil, and dust with paprika. Bake for 30 minutes, or until golden brown.

5. Serve hot.

YIELD: 6 SERVINGS

Savory Seitan-Stuffed
Summer Squash Provençal

Seitan proves once again its amazing ability to adapt itself to the whimsy of the cook. Here it takes on the classic flavors of Provence: olives, garlic, rosemary, and thyme. This versatile dish can be served straight from the oven or cooled to room temperature. I think it makes an especially lovely centerpiece to a casual summer buffet. Serve it with any light-bodied red wine, such as Chianti, Shiraz, or Côtes du Rhône. The seitan can be finely chopped with a sharp knife or ground in a food processor fitted with the metal blade.

2 medium zucchini, trimmed

2 medium yellow summer squash,
     such as gold bar or crookneck, trimmed

$1/2$ cup coarsely ground fresh bread crumbs,
     preferably from homemade sourdough (pages 328, 332, 336)

$1/4$ cup finely grated Parmesan or
     Gruyère cheese (optional)

3 tablespoons extra-virgin olive oil

2 red onions, finely diced

8 ounces white button mushrooms,
     finely chopped

3 garlic cloves, chopped

Coarse sea salt

$1/2$ cup red wine

1 tablespoon chopped fresh rosemary

2 teaspoons chopped fresh thyme

2 cups finely chopped seitan,
     preferably homemade (page 289)

$1/2$ cup pitted, chopped kalamata olives

Freshly milled black pepper

2 cups Zesty Tomato Sauce (page 138)

1. Preheat the oven to 375°F.

2. Halve each zucchini and yellow squash lengthwise. Scoop out and discard the seeds with a small spoon. Set the squash halves in a steamer and steam over boiling water until they

pierce easily with the tip of a sharp knife but are still firm, about 5 minutes. Transfer them to a plate and set aside.

3. Mix the bread crumbs in a bowl with the cheese, if using, and set aside.

4. In a heavy skillet over medium heat, warm 2 tablespoons of the oil. Add the onions, mushrooms, and garlic. Add a pinch of salt and sauté until the vegetables are lightly browned, about 8 to 10 minutes, stirring with a wooden spoon to prevent sticking. Add the wine, rosemary, and thyme. Cook until nearly dry. Add the seitan, olives, and salt and pepper to taste.

5. Pour the tomato sauce in either 1 or 2 baking dishes large enough to hold the squash in a single snug layer. Fill the squash halves with the vegetable stuffing and top with the bread crumb mixture. Drizzle with the remaining 1 tablespoon olive oil and bake, uncovered, for 40 minutes, or until golden brown.

6. Serve hot or room temperature.

YIELD: 4 SERVINGS

Eggplant and Seitan Falafel

Although I am a big fan of traditional chickpea falafel, I wanted to make something different. So I took the chickpea off center stage and added eggplant. Like seitan, eggplant works a lot like a sponge, readily soaking up flavor. These intense croquettes can be made smaller for spearing with toothpicks and serving as hors d'oeuvres. They are particularly delicious accompanied by one of the Yogurt Creams (pages 388–390), Soy Sour Cream (page 391), or Zesty Tomato Sauce (page 138).

1 pound eggplant,
    peeled and cut into 1-inch cubes
$1^1/_2$ teaspoons coarse sea salt
2 tablespoons extra-virgin olive oil
1 cup finely chopped onion
2 tablespoons finely chopped garlic
2 teaspoons freshly ground coriander
1 teaspoon freshly ground cumin
$^1/_2$ teaspoon cayenne pepper
$^1/_2$ teaspoon sweet paprika
$^1/_2$ pound seitan,
    preferably homemade (page 289)
1 tablespoon white hulled sesame seeds
$^1/_4$ cup finely chopped fresh cilantro
1 scallion, white and green parts,
    trimmed and thinly sliced
6 tablespoons chickpea flour
2 cups pure olive or canola oil

1. Preheat the oven to 400°F.

2. Toss the eggplant with 1 teaspoon of the salt and 1 tablespoon of the oil. Spread the cubes on a baking sheet and roast in the oven for 30 minutes, or until soft, stirring the eggplant after 15 minutes for even browning.

3. In a small skillet over medium heat, warm the remaining 1 tablespoon of oil. Add the onion, garlic, remaining $^1/_2$ teaspoon salt, coriander, cumin, cayenne, and paprika. Sauté for 5 minutes, stirring occasionally.

4. Wrap the seitan in paper towels and squeeze to extract the excess moisture.

5. In a food processor fitted with a metal blade, grind the seitan. (Alternatively, the seitan can be very finely chopped with a sharp knife.) Add the onion mixture and the eggplant and pulse a few times to combine. Scrape the mixture into a bowl and stir in the sesame seeds, cilantro, scallion, and chickpea flour. Cover with a plate and refrigerate for 1 hour.

6. Form the mixture into 16 balls and flatten slightly between the palms of your hands.

7. In a large saucepan or skillet over medium-high heat, warm the oil until hot. Add the falafel and fry until golden brown on one side, about 4 to 5 minutes per side. Turn them over and brown the other side.

8. Transfer the falafel to paper towels to drain, and serve hot.

YIELD: 4 SERVINGS

Seitan-Stuffed Tamales with Anasazi Beans and Roasted Tomatoes

Masa harina is a finely ground flour made from whole, dried, cleaned field corn. It is sold widely in ethnic food markets. For truly superior tamales with a delicate and somewhat mysterious sweetness, consider grinding your own from whole dried hominy. That is what I do.

The best texture for the filling is achieved by chopping the seitan, scallion, and bell pepper individually with a sharp, heavy knife. Alternatively, each ingredient can be pulsed briefly in a food processor. Traditional tamales are steamed in reconstituted dried corn husks. Don't be put off if you don't have any on hand—aluminum foil is a fine substitute.

FOR THE BEANS AND VEGETABLES:

1 1/2 cups dried Anasazi beans,
    sorted, soaked, and rinsed (see page 226)
1 small red onion, peeled and left whole
2 pounds plum tomatoes, cored, sliced in half, and seeded
3 jalapeño peppers, seeds and stems removed, cut into 1/2-inch rounds
1 whole garlic bulb, separated into cloves and peeled
2 tablespoons extra-virgin olive oil
Freshly squeezed juice of 1 lemon
8 to 10 fresh basil leaves, shredded
Coarse sea salt
Freshly milled black pepper

FOR THE DOUGH:

3 cups masa harina
3 cups water
4 tablespoons extra-virgin olive oil
3/4 teaspoon sea salt

FOR THE STUFFING:

2 tablespoons extra-virgin olive oil
1/4 cup firmly packed finely chopped scallions,
    white and green parts
1/3 cup finely chopped green bell pepper
1 teaspoon freshly ground cumin

¹/₂ teaspoon dried oregano
¹/₄ teaspoon ground chipotle chili or cayenne pepper
1 tablespoon tomato paste
¹/₄ pound seitan,
     preferably homemade (page 289), finely chopped
¹/₄ teaspoon brown sugar
Coarse sea salt

Chopped fresh cilantro for garnish
Plain yogurt or sour cream for garnish

1. To make the beans and vegetables, combine the beans and onion in a pressure cooker. Add water and cook at full pressure (15 pounds) for 25 minutes (see The Pressure Cooker Method on page 229). Alternatively, the beans and onion can be simmered in a pan with water to cover by 2 to 3 inches for 1 hour, or until tender.

2. Preheat the oven to 375°F.

3. Line a baking sheet or jelly-roll pan with parchment paper. Spread the tomatoes and jalapeño peppers cut-side down evenly over the pan. Add the garlic. Brush oil over all and roast for 30 minutes, or until the skin of the tomatoes is shriveled and pulls away easily from the flesh. Remove the pan from the oven and set aside for a few minutes to cool.

4. Pluck the skins off the tomatoes with your fingers. With a rubber spatula, transfer the tomatoes, peppers, and garlic to a 2- to 3-quart saucepan. Add the cooked beans and enough of their cooking juices to form a sauce around the beans. Set the onion aside until cool enough to be handle, then chop it and add to the beans. You don't want the beans to be too dry or they will lose their shape. Add the lemon juice, basil, and salt and pepper. Bring the beans to a simmer and cook gently for 10 minutes to meld the flavors.

5. To make the dough, put the masa harina in a mixing bowl. In a small saucepan over high heat, bring the water, oil, and salt to a boil. Pour over the masa harina and mix well with a wooden spoon to form a soft smooth dough. Cover the dough with a clean damp cloth or plastic wrap and set aside.

6. To make the stuffing, warm the oil in a small skillet over medium heat. Add the scallions, green pepper, cumin, oregano, and chili. Sauté for 2 minutes. Stir in the tomato paste and seitan and sauté for 2 to 3 minutes. Using a rubber spatula, scrape the stuffing into a small bowl and season with brown sugar and salt to taste. The stuffing should be well seasoned to offset the relatively bland dough.

7. Unwrap the dough and divide it into 12 equal pieces. Form each piece into a ball and gently squeeze each in the palm of one hand while you make a $^1/_2$-inch deep indentation on the long side of the dough with the index finger of your other hand. Stuff the indentation with 1 tablespoon of the filling and press the dough around it to form a neat seal. Set the tamale aside and continue rolling and stuffing until each piece of dough has been used.

8. Place an 8- or 10-inch square of aluminum foil, shiny side up, on a clean surface. Center a tamale 3 inches from the bottom edge. Fold the edge over the tamale. Fold the sides of the foil toward the center and roll the tamale up to form a tight oblong cylinder about 3 inches long and 1 inch wide. Repeat until all the tamales are wrapped.

9. Fit a large pot with a steamer basket. Add water and bring to a boil. Reduce the heat to low, place the tamales in the basket and steam, covered, for 25 minutes. Use a pair of tongs to remove the tamales from the pot and unwrap them.

10. Garnish the tamales with cilantro and plain yogurt and serve with hot beans on the side.

YIELD: 4 TO 6 SERVINGS

Crispy Seitan Chips with Sweet-and-Spicy Dipping Sauce

Asian cuisine often features a combination of sweet, salty, and spicy flavorings. In this Asian-inspired dish, I use garlic, ginger, and hot pepper for the spiciness; soy sauce for the salty taste; and either plum or apricot preserves for the sweet component. This is a great, easy-to-make appetizer—the perfect party food!

1 teaspoon light sesame oil

1 teaspoon minced, peeled gingerroot

1 teaspoon minced garlic

1/4 teaspoon hot red pepper flakes

1/3 cup natural apricot or plum preserves

2 1/2 tablespoons water

1 tablespoon naturally brewed soy sauce

2 teaspoons rice vinegar

2 cups canola oil

1 pound seitan,
     preferably homemade (page 289)

1/2 cup arrowroot powder

1. To prepare the dipping sauce, warm the oil in a small saucepan or skillet over medium heat. Add the ginger, garlic, and red pepper flakes and sauté for 1 minute. Do not let the garlic brown or it will overpower the sauce. Add the preserves, water, soy sauce, and vinegar. Whisk to dissolve the preserves and simmer gently for 1 minute. Pour the sauce into a bowl and set aside to cool. For a very smooth sauce, strain through a fine sieve.

2. In each of two frying pans over medium heat, warm 1 cup canola oil. Drain the seitan and pat dry with a clean towel. Slice it into rounds that are about 1 to 2 inches in diameter and 1/8 inch thick. Pour the arrowroot onto a plate and dredge the seitan in it. Shake off excess powder and fry the chips until crisp, about 2 minutes on each side.

3. Drain the pieces on paper towels and serve hot with the dipping sauce.

YIELD: 6 TO 8 SERVINGS

Breads

Bread baking is a huge subject and one that cannot fully be discussed in a single chapter.

However, I want to share some of the wonderful adventures I have had working and playing with flour, water, and various kinds of leavening agents.

For the most part there are four basic types of bread:

- Flatbreads, both leavened and unleavened
- Breads leavened with man-made refined strains of yeast
- Sourdough breads leavened with wild yeast
- Quick, cakelike breads made from batter and leavened with baking soda or baking powder

Many thousands of years ago, before flatbreads and long before bread as we know it today, there was gruel: whole grains mixed with water. Eventually, someone figured out how to transform these wet mixtures into dried cakes, which kept longer than raw grain and were easy to transport. Not far up on the ladder of bread evolution came unleavened flatbreads made from whole-grain flour, seasonings, and water. These are simple, small-scale breads that were made throughout the world, in every region where there is a bounteous supply of grain, from the Middle East to India to China to the pre–Columbian Americas. Flatbreads continue to be made today and are especially common in places where fuel is scarce, since they can be baked, steamed, or fried much faster than it takes to bake loaf breads. Flatbreads come in many shapes and sizes—they may be leavened, thick, and sliceable like an Italian focaccia or unleavened and very thin, like chapatis. Some are even made with potatoes or legumes, such as Indian dosas.

The first leavened loaf breads probably developed around 4000 B.C. in the region known as the Fertile Crescent, a stretch of land now encompassed by modern-day Turkey, Syria, and Iraq. Wheat was the principal agricultural grain in that part of the world and the only one that yielded a flour with the proteins necessary to create gluten and produce true bread. In all likelihood, raised bread was an accidental discovery. A flour-and-water dough was probably left out in the heat and began to ferment. Wild yeasts, naturally present in the air, were attracted to the carbohydrates in the dough and released carbon dioxide as they fed and multiplied. This gas would have escaped back into the air if it weren't for the strong, elastic sheets of gluten that developed when water was added to the wheat flour, and the dough was mixed and kneaded. Thanks to gluten's remarkable netlike structure, the air and gases produced by the yeast were trapped, forming pockets of air that were retained in the baked loaf. And so the predecessor of tender, light, and crusty modern-day bread was born. The ancient Greeks and Romans refined the process, adding different ingredients, such as fruits, nuts, spices, and oils, and combining wheat flour with other, less expensive grains to make a variety of risen loaves. In Northern Europe, yeast was derived as a by-product of beer making and was used to leaven the heavy rye and barley-based breads of the region.

Today you can buy stabilized "active" dry yeast in little packets, but I prefer the more nuanced flavor of bread that uses a starter created from the wild yeasts in the air. Also, breads made from commercial yeast don't contain any lactic acid, a natural preservative and digestive, and tend to go stale faster and are not as easily digested as breads made from a sourdough starter. People who are told that they are allergic to yeast are often only allergic to commercially produced yeast and tend not to have adverse reactions to wild yeast. This is because the strains of yeast that you buy in the store are very different genetically from wild yeasts. In fact, products labeled "yeast-free" in bakeries often contain wild yeasts. As our notions of healthy living and eating evolve, we find ourselves looking back to ancient, healthy bread-baking practices that connected humankind to the forces of the organic world. Our ancestors ground their own flour, used only pure water and unrefined sea salt, and took the time to cultivate naturally occurring complex wild yeasts. They knew that the process of true bread baking cannot be rushed.

Today, for the most part, bread is mass produced, leavened with commercially produced yeast, and made with refined flour, refined land salt, synthetic vitamins, preservatives, and chlorinated water. Humankind may have succeeded at controlling leavening time, flavor, and appearance, but we have sacrificed the robust flavor and healthfulness of true bread. With the exception of some genuinely great bakers, true bread baking has almost become extinct.

But you can bake healthful, nourishing loaves in your own kitchen. This is one of my favorite culinary pastimes. For me, bread baking is the most demanding, dynamic, and ultimately satisfying form of cooking. It requires enormous patience and awareness and involves the cook in a way that no other process does. You get to cultivate, control, and nourish the growth of living culture. Bread baking is both a science and an art and will simultaneously develop your intellect and intuition.

Flatbreads

Ancient bread-baking styles have survived in most cultures around the world, especially those that didn't have abundant fuel sources and that tended to migrate. Examples include Tibetan barley bread, Indian chapatis and naan, oat and barley cakes from the British Isles, rye crisps from Scandinavia, and buckwheat crêpes from northern France. The ancient Hebrews hastily baked unleavened wheat breads, or matzoh, to take along during their flight from slavery. In reverence to the great worldwide tradition of flatbreads, here are some of my favorite recipes.

Indian Rice and Lentil Pancakes: Dosas

This recipe was inspired by Bebian Aranka, an assistant at several of the cooking schools I teach at in New York. One night before a class, I noticed that she had a big bowl of batter that she was spooning onto a griddle to make pancakes. When I tried one I was amazed—they were light, fluffy, and absolutely delicious, yet completely wheat-free and not leavened with baking powder, baking soda, eggs, or yeast. Bebian told me that a traditional Indian bread is made with urad dhal, a special variety of peeled lentils that are sort of sticky and ferment quickly (you can buy these at Indian markets; see page 434 for mail-order sources). The lentils are mixed with rice and soaked for 12 hours. Then the mixture is drained, puréed, and fermented in a warm place for at least 8 to 12 hours, in which time the mixture thickens and doubles in volume. These pancakes are even wonderful the next day and go very well with curry. For a variation, add 1 cup chopped sautéed zucchini or bell pepper or onion to the batter before frying.

$^1/_2$ cup urad dhal lentils
1$^1/_2$ cups white basmati rice
1$^3/_4$ to 2 cups cold, nonchlorinated water
1 tablespoon fine sea salt
1 tablespoon sugar or maple syrup
Oil or unsalted butter for frying

1. Combine the urad dhal, rice, and water. Soak for 8 to 12 hours at room temperature.

2. Drain and rinse the lentils and rice. Combine them in a blender and purée with the salt, sugar, and enough water to form a pourable batter.

3. Wash out a glass or ceramic bowl with boiling water.

4. Transfer the batter to the bowl. Cover with a towel or plastic wrap and set in a warm place (I like to use my gas oven with the pilot on) for 8 to 12 hours until the batter doubles in volume.

5. In a skillet over medium heat, warm a little oil. Pour in $^1/_2$ cup of the batter to form a thin pancake. Cover and cook for 3 to 4 minutes, until set. Uncover, flip the pancake, and finish cooking, uncovered, until speckled brown and cooked through, 2 to 3 minutes.

6. Keep the dosas warm under a towel as you make them. Serve warm.

YIELD: ABOUT 6 SERVINGS

White Corn Arepas from Hominy

Since 1998, the Collective Heritage Institute has been reviving ancient strains of corn, which are organically grown on Native American reservations. I have had the honor of learning from leading historians of North American white corn, including John Mohawk, professor of Native American studies in Buffalo, New York.

These traditional unleavened corn breads from South America can be made either from cooked whole hominy or from tamale flour, also known as masa harina. I much prefer the true corn flavor of organic hominy (see Sources, page 434).

Serve these arepas with Black Bean and Bell Pepper Chili with Seitan (page 67), Anasazi Beans with Roasted Tomatoes (page 298), or Black Bean Salsa (page 237). Or eat them on their own—they are that good.

> **1 cup whole dried hominy**
> **Fine sea salt**
> **3 tablespoons canola oil**
> **1/2 teaspoon freshly milled white pepper**

1. In a medium bowl, combine the hominy and 4 cups water. Soak overnight in the refrigerator.

2. Drain and rinse the hominy and transfer it to a pressure cooker. Add 3 cups water and a pinch of salt. Pressure-cook at full pressure (15 pounds) for 1 hour (see The Pressure Cooker Method, page 229). Drain the hominy, reserving 1/4 cup of the cooking liquid.

3. Preheat the oven to 375°F. Lightly oil a baking sheet.

4. In a food processor, combine the hominy, 3/4 teaspoon salt, oil, pepper, and enough of the reserved cooking water to make a smooth dough. The hominy is now in the form of masa.

5. With wet hands, form the masa into 2-inch balls. Place them on the baking sheet about 2 inches apart. With the palm of your hand, gently flatten the balls to form 1/2-inch-thick patties. Bake for 20 minutes.

6. Serve hot or at room temperature.

YIELD: 4 SERVINGS

White Corn Arepas from Masa Harina

2 tablespoons olive oil, corn oil, or unsalted butter
1 teaspoon fine sea salt
2 cups white masa harina (see Sources, page 434)

1. In a saucepan over high heat, bring 2 cups plus 2 tablespoons water, oil, and salt to a boil. In a heavy glass or ceramic mixing bowl, add the masa harina. Pour the liquid over the masa harina and stir with a wooden spoon until well combined. Cover the bowl with a plate or plastic wrap and set aside for 15 minutes.

2. Divide the dough into 8 equal pieces. With moist hands, form the pieces into 2-inch balls. Shape the balls into patties about $1/2$ inch thick and 3 inches across.

3. Heat a dry, well-seasoned cast-iron skillet or griddle over medium heat until hot. Cook the patties until speckled and lightly browned, about 6 minutes per side. Do not crowd the pan—you may need to do this in batches.

4. Serve warm.

YIELD: 4 SERVINGS

Chapatis

These thin, pliable breads are like Indian wheat tortillas, and you can use them to wrap curries, rice, and vegetables. After they are baked, stack them on a plate and cover them with a clean, slightly damp towel so that they stay warm and soft. They're the perfect accompaniment to curries and stews. You can also try baking them a little longer, until crisp. Allow the chapatis to air-dry before breaking into crackers and serving with a dip.

Chapatis are at their best made with freshly ground flour and relatively soft, nonchlorinated water.

2 cups fresh whole wheat bread flour
1 teaspoon fine sea salt
$3/4$ cup lukewarm nonchlorinated water
2 tablespoons olive oil or melted unsalted butter (optional)

1. In a bowl, combine the flour and salt. Stir in the water and oil or butter, if using, and mix to form a thick dough.

2. Transfer the dough to a clean, lightly floured surface and knead for 15 minutes, until the dough is smooth and elastic. The dough should not be sticky. Poke a finger into the center of the dough. If it comes out clean, the dough is ready. If not, knead in a bit more flour. Cover the dough with plastic wrap or a clean, damp towel and let rest at room temperature for 1 hour.

3. Unwrap the dough and divide it into 8 equal pieces. Work with one piece at a time, keeping the remaining pieces covered. Roll a piece between your palms to form a ball. Place the ball on the counter and press it into a $1/16$-inch-thick circle. Repeat with the remaining dough.

4. Heat a dry cast-iron skillet or griddle over medium heat until hot. Cook the chapatis one at a time, until lightly browned with dark speckles, about 3 to 4 minutes per side.

5. Serve warm.

YIELD: 8 CHAPATIS

Commercial Yeasted Breads

If your schedule doesn't allow much time for baking, and you aren't allergic to commercial yeast, you might want to try making a basic yeasted dough using some commercial yeast. This is also a good place to start if you are new to bread baking because it is relatively quick and easy. There are also some instances where using a basic yeasted dough is preferable, such as making pizza (see page 312) or Whole Wheat Sandwich Bread (page 318), where you don't necessarily want the complex character of a sourdough starter. In this chapter, I have outlined three methods that you can follow to make a basic yeasted dough: the straight method, the sponge method, and the *biga* method.

The straight method lets you mix the dough one day, let it rise in the refrigerator overnight, and bake your bread the next day. The sponge method requires more time, but produces bread with a better flavor. The dough begins as a sponge, a mixture made from packaged yeast, flour, and water, which is set aside to ferment slightly before more flour and water are mixed in. The dough is kneaded, set aside to rise, and then baked, all in the same day. If you are in the mood for a more intense bread-baking experience, try making a *biga*, an Italian, slightly sour starter made with commercial yeast. This requires some planning on your part, since the sponge starter needs to ferment for a few days before using.

Regardless of which method you choose, the creation of a good loaf of bread should always be a slow, steady, and rhythmic process. It does take planning and patience, but making bread at home does not need to feel like a chore. Making your own bread allows you to control what goes into the dough and nurture it through the course of kneading, rising, and baking. You will be amazed at how relaxing and rewarding an experience bread baking can be.

The same simple, all-purpose dough can be used for pizza, focaccia, or any sort of free-form flatbread. Depending on your schedule, choose the one most convenient for you. Each will produce 1 loaf of bread or 2 (12-inch) pizzas or 1 focaccia.

Basic Yeasted Bread:
The Straight Method

The most convenient of the three bread-making methods, here the dough is mixed, kneaded, and left to rise for 12 hours, or for up to 2 days in the refrigerator. After that, just let it return to room temperature, shape, and bake. It's great for fitting into a tight schedule or unpredictable workweek.

> 1 teaspoon active dry yeast
> 1 1/3 cups lukewarm (95° to 105°F) nonchlorinated water
> 1 teaspoon sugar, barley malt syrup, or honey
> 2 tablespoons olive oil
> 2 teaspoons fine sea salt
> 3/4 cup whole wheat bread or whole rye flour
> 3 cups unbleached white bread flour
> Pizza toppings or extra-virgin olive oil,
>   coarse sea salt, and chopped fresh herbs (optional)

1. In a bowl, combine the yeast, water, and sugar. Stir to blend and let stand until foamy, about 5 minutes. Stir in the oil and salt.

2. Add all of the whole wheat flour and enough of the white flour to form a ragged mass of dough. Scoop the dough out onto a clean, lightly floured surface. Wash out the bowl and thoroughly clean and dry your hands.

3. Knead the dough for 10 minutes until it is smooth and elastic.

4. Lightly coat the inside of the bowl with oil. Turn the dough over several times in the bowl and cover tightly with plastic wrap.

5. Refrigerate the dough for at least 12, or up to 48, hours.

6. Remove the dough from the refrigerator and let it come to room temperature, about 2 hours.

7. **TO SHAPE THE DOUGH FOR A LOAF,** gently press it into a 1-inch-thick circle. Fold the top third of the dough over and press to form a seam in the middle of the circle. Fold the bottom third up to meet the seam and press firmly with your fingers to seal. Flip the dough over and tuck in the edges. Place the dough, seam side down, in a lightly greased loaf pan. Cover the dough with a damp towel and set aside for about 1 hour, or until the dough rises an inch above

the pan. Uncover the dough and gently brush the top with oil or melted butter. Bake for 45 minutes at 400°F until it sounds hollow when tapped underneath or the internal temperature reaches 200°F. Turn the bread out onto a rack to cool for at least 45 minutes before slicing.

TO MAKE PIZZA, divide the dough in half. Cover one piece with plastic wrap or a damp towel. Roll out the other into a free-form circle and transfer it to an inverted cookie sheet or peel dusted with cornmeal. Add the toppings and slide the dough onto a preheated baking stone. Bake at 500°F for 12 to 15 minutes. Repeat with the second piece of dough.

TO MAKE FOCACCIA, use your fingertips to press the dough into a lightly oiled 12-by-17$^{1}/_{2}$-inch jelly-roll pan, making small dimples all over. Brush the dough liberally with extra-virgin olive oil and scatter some coarse salt and chopped fresh herbs on top. Let the focaccia rise in the pan for 1 hour. Then bake it in a 450°F oven for about 25 to 30 minutes, until golden brown.

YIELD: 1 BREAD LOAF, 2 (12-INCH) PIZZAS, OR 1 FOCACCIA

Basic Yeasted Bread: The Sponge Method

This method uses the same ingredients as the previous recipe, but the method is a little more involved. It starts with a pre-ferment, or sponge, starter that rises for up to 2 hours in a warm spot before mixing and kneading the dough. This will produce bread with a more intense flavor, but it is ready to bake a mere 3 to 4 hours after it is mixed.

> **1 teaspoon active dry yeast**
> **1 1/3 cups lukewarm (95° to 105°F) nonchlorinated water**
> **1 teaspoon sugar, barley malt syrup, or honey**
> **2 tablespoons olive oil**
> **3 cups unbleached white bread flour**
> **2 teaspoons fine sea salt**
> **3/4 cup whole wheat bread or whole rye flour**
> **Pizza toppings or extra-virgin olive oil,**
> **   coarse sea salt, and chopped fresh herbs (optional)**

1. In a bowl, combine the yeast, water, and sugar. Stir to blend and let stand until foamy, about 5 minutes. Stir in the oil and 2 cups of the white flour. Cover the bowl with plastic wrap and set in a warm spot to ferment for 2 to 3 hours, until tripled in volume.

2. Uncover the sponge and stir in the salt, all of the whole wheat flour, and enough of the remaining white flour to form a ragged mass of dough. Scoop the dough out onto a clean, lightly floured surface. Wash out the bowl and thoroughly clean and dry your hands.

3. Knead the dough for 10 minutes, until it is smooth and elastic.

4. Lightly coat the inside of the bowl with oil. Turn the dough over several times in the bowl and cover tightly with plastic wrap.

5. Set the bowl of dough in a warm spot to ferment until doubled in volume, about 1 1/2 hours.

6. Transfer the dough to a clean, lightly floured surface and pummel it with the sides of your palms to deflate it. Let the dough rest for 5 minutes.

7. **TO SHAPE THE DOUGH FOR A LOAF,** gently press it into a 1-inch-thick circle. Fold the top third of the dough over and press to form a seam in the middle of the circle. Fold the bottom third up to meet the seam and press firmly with your fingers to seal. Flip the dough over and

tuck in the edges. Place the dough, seam side down, in a lightly greased loaf pan. Cover the dough with a damp towel and set aside for about 1 hour, or until the dough rises an inch above the pan. Uncover the dough and gently brush the top with oil or melted butter. Bake for 45 minutes at 400°F, or until it sounds hollow when tapped underneath. Turn the bread out onto a rack to cool for at least 45 minutes before slicing.

TO MAKE PIZZA, divide the dough in half. Cover one piece with plastic wrap or a damp towel. Roll out the other into a free-form circle and transfer it to an inverted cookie sheet or peel dusted with cornmeal. Add the toppings and slide the dough onto a preheated baking stone. Bake at 500°F for 12 to 15 minutes. Repeat with the second piece of dough.

TO MAKE FOCACCIA, use your fingertips to press the dough into a lightly oiled 12-by-17$\frac{1}{2}$-inch jelly-roll pan, making small dimples all over. Brush the dough liberally with extra-virgin olive oil and scatter some coarse salt and fresh chopped herbs on top. Let the focaccia rise in the pan. Then bake it in a 450°F oven for about 25 to 30 minutes, until golden brown.

YIELD: 1 BREAD LOAF, 2 (12-INCH) PIZZAS, OR 1 FOCACCIA

Caramelized Onion Tart
with Roasted Red Peppers

Here's my vegetarian version of the classic Niçoise pissaladière. I've kept the traditional caramelized onions, but substituted roasted red peppers for the anchovies.

$1/2$ recipe Basic Yeasted Bread dough (page 312)
4 tablespoons extra-virgin olive oil
3 pounds onions, thinly sliced
3 to 4 sprigs fresh thyme or rosemary
2 bay leaves
3 large garlic cloves, minced
1 teaspoon fine sea salt
3 large red bell peppers, roasted
    (see How to Roast a Pepper, page 105) and cut into $1/2$-inch strips
Coarse sea salt
Freshly milled black pepper
1 tablespoon finely chopped fresh parsley

1. Prepare the dough according to the recipe directions through step 5.

2. While the dough rises, sauté the onions in 2 tablespoons of the oil over medium heat until softened, about 7 to 8 minutes. Add the herbs, garlic, and salt. Reduce the heat to low and cook, covered, for 1 to $1^1/2$ hours, until the onions are meltingly tender and sweet. Transfer the onions to a bowl to cool. Remove and discard the thyme and bay leaves.

3. Preheat the oven to 375°F. Lightly oil a baking sheet or jelly-roll pan.

4. Deflate the dough and allow it to rest for 5 minutes covered by a clean towel.

5. Uncover the dough and roll it out into a $1/4$-inch-thick rectangle about the size of the baking pan. Loosely roll the dough onto the pin and transfer it to the baking sheet. Unroll the dough and crimp the edges to form a border. Arrange the cooled onion mixture and red pepper strips evenly over the dough.

6. Drizzle the tart with the remaining 2 tablespoons oil and sprinkle with coarse salt and black pepper to taste. Bake for 50 to 60 minutes, or until the crust is golden brown.

7. Cool slightly, sprinkle with parsley, and serve.   YIELD: 8 SERVINGS

Biga

Biga, the Italian word for starter, is a great way to become comfortable with fermenting a sponge made from commercial yeast for a few days. For most of us Americans, the idea of leaving food out of the refrigerator is a little unsavory; we are scared that it will spoil. But fermentation will give the bread more flavor and better keeping power. Because we are using commercial yeast, the fermentation process will take just 1 to 3 days; but the longer you let the sponge mature, the more flavorful the bread will be.

Use this starter to make pizza or focaccia or in the recipes on pages 318 to 321.

3 tablespoons lukewarm (95° to 105°F) nonchlorinated water
¼ teaspoon active dry yeast
½ cup cool (about 70°F) nonchlorinated water
1½ cups unbleached white bread flour

1. In a bowl, combine the lukewarm water and yeast. Set aside for 5 to 10 minutes, until the yeast dissolves and becomes creamy.

2. Add the cool water and flour. Stir vigorously with a wooden spoon to form a thick sticky batter. Cover the bowl with plastic wrap and ferment at room temperature for up to 24 hours. The biga should triple in volume and then collapse. It will loosen up and become bubbly. At this point it is ready to use. You can also cover it with plastic wrap and store it in the refrigerator for up to 2 days. After that it will have lost much of its leavening power.

YIELD: ABOUT 1½ CUPS

Whole Wheat Sandwich Bread

You are on the road to sourdough bread baking with this all-purpose bread that uses a combination of biga and yeast.

>**2 tablespoons barley malt syrup**
>**¼ cup lukewarm (95° to 105°F) nonchlorinated water**
>**1 teaspoon active dry yeast**
>**1 recipe Biga (page 317), 1 to 3 days old**
>**1¼ cups cool (about 70°F) water**
>**2 cups whole wheat bread flour**
>**1¾ cups unbleached white bread flour**
>**¼ cup wheat bran**
>**2½ teaspoon fine sea salt**
>**Oil or melted butter**

1. Dissolve the barley malt syrup in the warm water. Add the yeast and set aside for 5 to 7 minutes, until it turns creamy.

2. Add the biga and the cool water. Break up the biga with your fingers until the water turns a chalky white. Don't worry if there are some small lumps—they will smooth out when the dough is mixed and kneaded.

3. In a large mixing bowl, combine the flours, bran, and salt. Make a well in the center and pour in the biga-yeast mixture. Sprinkle several tablespoons of flour over the biga. Cover the bowl with a clean cloth and let it sit for 20 minutes. Incorporate the flour a little at a time until it forms a shaggy mass of dough.

4. Scoop the dough out onto a clean, lightly floured surface. Wash out the bowl and thoroughly wash and dry your hands. Invert the bowl over the dough and let it rest for 5 minutes.

5. Uncover the dough and knead vigorously for 10 minutes. Invert the bowl over the dough and allow it to rest for 20 minutes. Uncover the dough once more and knead for 5 minutes.

6. Lightly coat the inside of the bowl with oil. Turn the dough over several times in the bowl and cover tightly with plastic wrap or a damp cloth. Set aside until it more than doubles in volume, 2 to 3 hours.

7. Preheat the oven to 400°F. Lightly grease a loaf pan.

8. Uncover the dough and gently deflate it by pressing down with your flat outstretched fingers. Place the dough on the counter and let it rest, covered, for 5 minutes. Gently press the dough into a 1-inch-thick circle. Fold the top third of the dough over and press to form a seam in the middle of the circle. Fold the bottom third up to meet the seam and press firmly with your fingers to seal. Flip the dough over and tuck in the edges.

9. Place the dough in the loaf pan, seam side down. Cover the dough with a damp towel and set aside until the dough rises an inch above the pan, about 1 hour. Uncover the dough and gently brush the top with oil or melted butter.

10. Bake for 45 minutes, or until the bread sounds hollow when tapped underneath.

11. Turn the bread out onto a rack and let it cool for at least 45 minutes before slicing.

YIELD: 1 LOAF

MEASURING FLOUR AND WATER

Remember that in the entire bread-making process, flour and water measures can never be exact. The humidity of the environment and the subtle variations in different batches of flour mean that you need to have a sense of what the texture should be and add more water or flour accordingly. Also, you will probably need a little more water if you're using a greater proportion of whole wheat flour, since bran can absorb a lot of water.

Cracked Wheat and Sesame Wedges

I came up with this recipe one day when I was trying to develop a nice dinner roll. After my dough fermented and doubled in size, I punched it down into a nice big disk. When I looked down at it, I wondered what it would be like cut into wedges instead of formed into rolls. So I made wedges, and they were great.

1/2 cup coarsely cracked bulgur wheat
1/2 cup boiling water
2 tablespoons barley malt syrup
1 1/2 cups lukewarm (95° to 105°F) nonchlorinated water
1 teaspoon active dry yeast
2 cups whole wheat bread flour
2 cups unbleached white flour
2 tablespoons olive oil
1/2 cup Biga (page 317)
1 tablespoon fine sea salt
3/4 cup white hulled sesame seeds

1. In a small bowl, combine the cracked wheat and boiling water. Cover the bowl with a plate and set aside.

2. In another small bowl, dissolve the barley malt syrup in the lukewarm water. Sprinkle in the yeast and let stand for 5 minutes, until the mixture turns creamy.

3. In a large bowl, combine half of the whole wheat and white flours. Add the dissolved yeast, oil, and biga. Mix to form a thick batter. Cover the bowl with plastic wrap or a damp cloth and allow it to ferment at room temperature for 1 1/2 to 2 hours, until bubbling.

4. Mix in the remaining flour, the cracked wheat, and salt to form a slightly sticky dough. Let rest for 5 minutes to absorb some of the moisture.

5. Scoop the dough out onto a clean, lightly floured surface. Wash out the bowl and thoroughly wash and dry your hands. Knead the dough for 10 to 15 minutes to form an elastic, slightly sticky dough.

6. Lightly coat the inside of the bowl with oil. Turn the dough over several times in the bowl and cover tightly with plastic wrap or a damp cloth. Allow the dough to ferment in a warm place until doubled in volume, about 1 hour.

7. Gently deflate the dough by pressing down on it with your fingers. Remove it from the bowl and knead for a minute or two, then return it to the bowl. Cover with plastic wrap and refrigerate for 8 to 12 hours.

8. Remove the dough from the refrigerator and turn it out onto a clean, lightly floured surface. Press the dough into a 1-inch-thick round. Dust with flour, cover with a clean towel, and let it rise for $1^1/_2$ to 2 hours, until doubled.

9. Preheat the oven to 425°F. Lightly oil two baking sheets, or line them with parchment paper.

10. Uncover the dough and slice it into 12 equal wedges. Spread the sesame seeds on a plate. Lightly mist the wedges with a spray bottle, gently roll them in the sesame seeds to coat, and place them on the baking sheets.

11. Bake for 30 minutes, rotating the pans halfway through to ensure even browning.

12. Cool the wedges on a wire rack for 20 minutes before serving.

YIELD: 12 SERVINGS

Sourdough Breads

If you feel ready for the ultimate bread-making experience, you can create your very own sourdough starter, which relies on wild airborne yeasts and produces breads that are truly out of this world. The humble sourdough breads I bake at home in my tiny gas oven have added so much to my family's health and well-being. My daughters' friends come over and devour the thick-crusted, steamy-hot loaves with incredible gusto. Of course they don't fully understand the complexity and history of wild-crafted bread—to them the breads are a little mysterious, exotic, and "totally yummy."

Once a culture is created (that is, the flour and water have attracted some wild yeast from the air), the biggest challenge is learning how to control the rate of fermentation. As your sourdough starter matures, its metabolism speeds up and it becomes more and more active. You must pay attention to the starter as if it were a child. You are culti-vating strength and character in the culture. It is really alive. Taste it, smell it, and tend to it accordingly. For your efforts, you will be paid back royally. And once you have a fully matured starter, it will last indefinitely. I have had my starter for several years now and look forward to the day when I will hand it down to my great-grandkids.

In this book, I give directions for a wet starter, which is my preferred method; it is the easiest and most practical. There are also a few other ways of making and keeping a dry sourdough starter. One method is to form a little ball of flour and water dough and wrap it in cloth. Each day you unwrap it, peel away the crusty outer layer, mix in a bit more flour and water, and wrap it up again. After 2 weeks, you've got a powerful starter. Another method is the Belgian desem, which is made by burying a ball of dough in a sack of flour and simply storing it at a cool tem-perature for two weeks. A third method, levain, really works only if you bake at least as often as every other day. Each time you make dough, you break off a little piece and save it to start the next batch of dough.

To make a sourdough starter, you need wild yeasts, which are naturally occur-ring in the air, although the quantity and quality depend on your environment. If you use a lot of toxic cleansers and detergents in your kitchen and stock it with commercially raised produce, there will not be many wild yeasts present. But by introducing fresh, organic fruits and vegetables, such as cabbages and grapes, into your home, you will also be bringing in the wild yeasts on their surfaces. These will help create a suitable environment for creating sourdough starter.

Sourdough starter requires a lot of attention, especially in the beginning stages of its development. You must use sterile utensils when nurturing your starter during the first 4 or 5 days. The yeasts are feeding and multiplying, but the lactic acid bacteria won't have kicked in yet, and the starter is vulnerable to attacks from harmful bacteria. To sterilize your bowls and utensils, submerge them in a large pot of boiling water for 10 minutes. Let the sterilized equipment air-dry and cool to room temperature before you begin mixing the ingredients for your starter.

It is also important to set your starter in a draft-free place, making sure to leave it uncovered so that the wild yeasts can settle. Store your starter at room temperature, about 70° to 78°F. If the temperature exceeds about 85°F, the starter will overferment; it will get too sour and will quickly die. During the summer, or if you have a hot kitchen in general, take the temperature of the dough and refrigerate it for a while or turn on the air conditioner if it is getting too hot. If the temperature is too cold, the starter will take longer to ferment. So it is better to err a little on the cold side than on the hot side. I keep a little thermometer tacked to my refrigerator and I always store my starter away from the stove.

If you are still harboring reservations about keeping your starter at room temperature, remember that when people didn't have refrigeration, they made fermented foods all the time. As the healthful bacteria begin producing lactic and acetic acids, they create a natural immunity against undesirable putrefying strains of bacteria. You may notice an "off" smell and some gray liquid floating on the top at this point. This is caused by oxidation and is harmless—just stir it back in. However, if the liquid is pink, the starter has spoiled, and you need to toss it and start over. You do not need to worry about using sterilized utensils after this point.

You have to feed your starter twice a day, stirring well each time you feed it, to incorporate oxygen. It is most important that you keep to a strict feeding schedule. (Keeping a calendar on your refrigerator might be helpful.) Like a child, your starter will come to expect regular feedings. If you neglect to feed your starter, the yeasts will starve to death. Take a moment to marvel as the yeast cells multiply and grow, developing the enormous leavening power required to raise heavy, wet lumps of dough into light, airy loaves of bread with satisfyingly chewy interiors and crackling crusts.

When your starter is 2 weeks old, you can make it dormant by storing it in the refrigerator in a glass, earthenware, or hard plastic container with a lid. Once it is refrigerated, you need to feed it only once a week. When you want to bake, take it out of the refrigerator 2 or 3 days beforehand, and feed it twice a day until you use it. At 14 days, you have a very potent starter that will continue to develop and mature for a month.

Now that you have a fully developed starter, you can get to the baking! One of the most confusing and difficult humps to get over about sourdough baking is figuring out a schedule that works for you. There are at least 22 steps over a 24-hour period that take place in a well-choreographed sourdough performance. I have suggested two strategies that work well for me (see pages 346 to 348), but you can adjust them to suit your needs.

The most physically intimate step in the bread-making process is kneading, which is crucial for developing the gluten structure to trap the carbon dioxide. You have kneaded enough when the dough feels smooth and elastic. Although you can use an electric mixer fitted with a dough hook, I prefer the wholly satisfying process of kneading by hand. If you do use a mixer, take care not to overknead the dough—it is done when the sides of the bowl are clean and the dough has formed a smooth ball around the hook. I definitely encourage you to try kneading by hand. The process of rolling, folding, and turning the dough becomes a mesmerizing rhythm that involves not just your hands, but your entire body.

After kneading, cover the dough with a damp cloth, and set it aside to relax and rise. This is the time when the carbon dioxide and alcohol released by the still-growing yeast enlarge the air pockets trapped between the gluten layers. When you poke your finger into the dough and the indentation remains, you know it has risen. After this first rising, you need to press the dough down gently, so that any clumps of yeast are broken apart and spread throughout the dough. Now each yeast cell is surrounded by a new food supply, and the rising process can begin again.

Once the dough has risen for the directed number of times, you can deflate it again and form it into loaves. You will probably need to divide the dough into two or more pieces and press it into shape, but avoid kneading the dough or handling it too much at this point because you want the gluten to remain relaxed while you shape it. Gently, so as not to tear the gluten sheets, fold the dough into thirds and place the loaves, seam side down, into lightly oiled loaf pans. I find that black stainless-steel pans produce the best crusts. If you invest in a pizza stone, you will find yourself freed up to shape and slash your loaves any way you choose—you are no longer restricted to the confines of a rectangular loaf pan. And baking your breads directly on a super-hot surface results in loaves with incomparable crusts that crackle with personality! Or bake your bread in a covered cast-iron or earthenware pot. This gives loaves a gleaming, golden finish and a terrific crunchy crust.

No matter how you have chosen to shape your loaves, let them rise one last time, covered with a damp cloth, before slashing the tops and popping them into the oven.

The second key to producing artisanal breads is to bake them in a humid environment. This serves to crisp the crust and give a boost to what bakers call "oven spring," the final rise that takes place during the first 20 minutes or so of baking. A common plant mister is a convenient and effective way to inject steam into the oven.

When is sourdough bread done? Although yeasted breads can be considered done when they sound hollow when thumped, in my experience sourdough breads are only fully baked when the internal temperature reaches 210°F. Using a long-stemmed instant-read thermometer will ensure sourdough success. When you think the bread might be done, simply insert the thermometer into the center of the loaf and take its temperature.

Cool the loaves on wire racks so that air can circulate around the bread. If you are baking sourdough bread, this might be the hardest part—you must use all your willpower and let the loaves sit for at least 1 hour after they come out of the oven. They are actually still cooking and will become tough if you cut into them too soon. Once the loaves have cooled and you can't stand the suspense any longer, slice off a thick piece for yourself. Make a cup of tea, relax, and enjoy the fruits of your labor.

Tools and Ingredients for Authentic Sourdough Bread

Clockwise from upper left: organic flour, barley malt syrup, heavy mixing bowl and dough whisk, tepid chlorine-free water, unrefined sea salt, long-stemmed instant-read thermometer, measuring spoons and cups, and active live starter.

White Sourdough Starter

I first read about this method for creating a starter using organic grapes in a recipe Steve Sullivan contributed to Paul Bertolis's excellent book, *Chez Panisse Cooking.* It really grabbed my imagination, but I put it on the back burner for three or four years until I found myself at home a lot more, getting antsy for something new to try. On my way home one evening, I stopped in to a late-night bookstore and started thumbing through a stack of cookbooks. I came across Nancy Silverton's incredible opus on naturally leavened bread, *Breads from La Brea Bakery.* Never before had I encountered a bread book totally dedicated to the how and why of naturally leavened bread baking. Most baking books approached the subject superficially and provided recipes for sourdough starters made with commercial yeast—a mere shadow of the true wild-crafted sourdough that I longed to know about. Flipping through that book profoundly changed the course of my cooking—I felt as though I had just stumbled upon the holy grail of true baking.

Whole wheat starter ferments at a more rapid rate than white starter. I suspect that since white flour is the product of merely the endosperm of the wheat kernel, it has been deprived of the lactic acid–producing bacteria and wild strains of yeast that live in the outer layers of the seed coat. The addition of grapes compensates for what white flour lacks. Here, I have modified Nancy Silverton's recipe only slightly, and cut it in half since it makes a very large quantity, most of which needs to be either given away or thrown out during the various stages. Use this starter in the recipes on pages 328 to 333.

¹/₂ pound organic sweet red or green grapes
5 pounds organic unbleached white bread flour without the germ
Nonchlorinated water

1. Rinse the grapes briefly under cold running water if necessary. If the grapes appear clean, do not bother to wash them, so as not to sacrifice any of the yeasts clinging to the skins. Place the grapes in the center of a double layer of cheesecloth and tie up the corners to form a neat bundle.

2. In a 2- or 3-quart sterilized glass, plastic, or earthenware container (see page 323), combine 2 cups of the flour and slightly more than 2 cups of nonchlorinated room-temperature water and stir to form a paste. Squeeze the bundle of grapes over the batter so that most of their juice comes out. Stir well. Submerge the cheesecloth bundle in the batter and secure the container with a tight-fitting lid or several layers of plastic wrap. Set aside at room temperature, out of the way of drafts or intense heat, for 3 days.

3. Once a day, uncover the starter and, using a sterilized utensil, stir the bundle of grapes around in the batter.

4. On the fourth day, uncover the container and stir in $1/2$ cup room temperature water and $1/2$ cup of the flour. Replace the cover and set aside for another 6 days. Make sure that the starter does not get too warm. Don't worry if the starter separates and has a yellowish liquid on top. It may also have a funky or sharp alcoholic odor after 4 or 5 days, but eventually the yeasts will build up in number and begin to exude a pleasant aroma.

5. Starting on the tenth day, you will need to feed the starter 3 times per day for 4 days. Rinse out a $1^1/2$- to 2-quart glass, plastic, or earthenware container with boiling water. Let it air-dry and cool to room temperature. Uncover the starter; remove and discard the bundle of grapes. Stir the starter well and pour 2 cups of it into the prepared container. Give away or discard the remaining starter. Add $1/2$ cup room-temperature water and a heaping $1/2$ cup flour. Stir well, cover, and let the starter ferment for 4 to 6 hours. Stir in 1 cup water and 1 heaping cup flour. Stir well once more, cover, and let ferment another 4 to 6 hours. Finally, feed the starter 2 cups room-temperature water and $2^1/2$ cups flour. Stir well, cover, and let the starter ferment overnight, for up to 12 hours.

6. The next day, discard all but 2 cups of the starter and repeat the same feeding schedule for 3 more days. Remember to begin the process each day with only 2 cups of the starter.

7. About 8 to 12 hours after the final feeding on the fourteenth day, your starter is ready to be used. At this point you can store it tightly covered in the refrigerator. Feed it $1/4$ cup water and $1/4$ cup flour 2 times per week to maintain it. It is good to take the starter out of the refrigerator and refresh it with a feeding 8 to 12 hours before you plan on baking. I like to keep about 3 cups of starter in my refrigerator at all times.

8. Always replenish the remaining starter when you use it. If the recipe calls for $1^1/2$ cups of starter, add about 1 cup flour and 1 cup water to the remaining starter.

HELPFUL GUIDELINES FOR CREATING SOURDOUGH STARTER

○ **Set up a regular feeding schedule for the first 2 weeks. After that you will have more flexibility. As the parent of this newly born life-form, you will find that careful attention and nurturing in the beginning will result in a strong, resilient, and mature starter.**
○ **Feed your starter with top-quality, organically grown ingredients and fresh, nonchlorinated water.**
○ **For the first 4 or 5 days, make sure all utensils and containers that come into contact with the culture have been sterilized in boiling water.**

French Country Sourdough
White Bread

This is the most impressive bread experience you'll ever have. The mostly white flour dough makes a very light, cultured loaf with the best rise and the biggest air holes of any of the breads in this chapter. This dough works especially well for making baguettes or rolls.

1½ cups White Sourdough Starter (page 326)
3 cups lukewarm (70° to 80°F) nonchlorinated water
1 tablespoon barley malt syrup (optional)
6 cups unbleached white bread flour
1 cup whole wheat bread flour
4 teaspoons fine sea salt
Cornmeal

1. In a large mixing bowl, combine the starter, water, and barley malt syrup and stir until the starter is dissolved.

2. Add the flours and mix to form a ragged mass of dough. Cover the bowl and allow the dough to rest for 5 minutes.

3. Scoop the dough out onto a clean, lightly floured surface. Wash out the bowl and thoroughly wash and dry your hands. Knead for 10 minutes. Invert the bowl over the dough and let it rest for 15 minutes.

4. Uncover the dough, add the salt, and knead for 5 to 10 minutes, until the dough is smooth and elastic. The dough should be quite moist and sticky. Avoid adding extra flour as you knead it. Lightly flour your hands if you have trouble keeping the dough from sticking.

5. Lightly coat the inside of the bowl with oil. Turn the dough over several times in the bowl and cover tightly with plastic wrap. Set aside at room temperature until nearly tripled in volume, 4 to 6 hours.

6. Gently press on the dough to deflate it. Cover the bowl tightly with plastic wrap and refrigerate for 8 to 12 hours.

7. Remove the dough from the refrigerator. Remove the plastic wrap and sprinkle with a little flour. The dough will be very cold and stiff. Cover the bowl with a clean towel and set aside for 2 to 3 hours, or until the internal temperature of the dough is 68°F.

8. Turn the dough out onto a clean, lightly floured surface. Cut the dough in half and press each piece into a 1-inch-thick circle. Tuck the edges of each piece of dough under to form a loose round. Let the dough rest for 5 minutes. Then, with the palms of your hands, gently roll one piece of dough back and forth until it resembles a torpedo with slightly tapered ends. Pinch the seam to seal. Repeat with the second piece.

9. Place the dough seam side down on floured cloths. Sift a light veil of flour over the loaves. Cover with a clean cloth and let sit for 1 hour.

10. Preheat the oven to 500°F at least 45 minutes before the dough is ready to bake. Set a heavy pan on the floor of the oven. Set a baking stone or inverted baking sheet on the middle rack. Dust a peel or inverted baking sheet with cornmeal.

11. Press the dough with a fingertip. If the dough springs back quickly, it requires more time. If the dough springs back slowly or holds the indentation, it is ready to bake.

12. Gently transfer one piece of dough onto the peel, seam side down. Slash the dough lengthwise, making an incision $1/2$-inch deep starting and stopping 1 inch from the ends.

13. Open the oven and pour 1 cup of water into the baking pan. Close the door.

14. Open the oven and slide the dough onto the baking stone or baking sheet. Make sure to allow enough space for the second piece of dough. Close the door.

15. Load the second piece of dough onto the peel. Slash it and slide it onto the stone or sheet. Heavily mist the floor, sides, and ceiling of the oven with the spray bottle. Shut the door. Mist 2 more times during the first 5 minutes, taking care not to mist the loaves themselves.

16. Turn the oven temperature to 450°F. Do not open the oven door for 20 minutes.

17. Open the oven and rotate the loaves for even browning. Continue to bake for 15 minutes. The bread is done when the internal temperature reaches 210°F, or when a loaf sounds hollow when tapped on the bottom.

18. Cool the loaves on a wire rack for no less than 1 hour before slicing.

YIELD: 2 LOAVES, EACH WEIGHING APPROXIMATELY 2 POUNDS

Fruit and Nut Bread

This is one of my favorite breads. There used to be a bakery in New York that made an amazing fruit and nut roll. Sadly, they went out of business. So, to satisfy my craving, I had to come up with my own. Since it's based on sourdough, it's got incredible lasting power and is a supreme toasting bread. The trick with this bread is that the nuts have to be absolutely fresh—they should not have an off smell or rancid flavor.

FOR THE SPONGE:

$^1/_2$ cup White Sourdough Starter (page 326)

$^1/_2$ cup cool (about 70°F) nonchlorinated water

1 cup whole wheat bread flour

FOR THE DOUGH:

$^3/_4$ cup cool (about 70°F) nonchlorinated water

$^1/_4$ cup White Sourdough Starter

$^1/_4$ cup pure maple syrup

2 tablespoons unsalted butter, melted

1 teaspoon vanilla extract

$2^1/_2$ cups unbleached all-purpose flour

2 teaspoons fine sea salt

1 teaspoon ground cinnamon

$^1/_2$ cup raisins

$^1/_2$ cup dried cranberries

$^1/_2$ cup roughly chopped dates

$1^1/_2$ cups walnuts (preferably freshly shelled),
   lightly toasted (see How to Toast Walnuts, page 373) and roughly chopped

Cornmeal or rolled oats

1. To make the sponge, mix together the starter, water, and flour. Let ferment at room temperature for 8 to 10 hours.

2. To make the dough, combine the sponge with the water, starter, maple syrup, butter, and vanilla in a bowl. Mix well. Stir in the flour, salt, and cinnamon.

3. Scoop the dough out onto a clean, lightly floured surface and knead for 10 minutes. Wash and dry the bowl, invert it over the dough, and let it rest for 15 to 20 minutes.

4. Uncover and knead for 5 minutes. Lightly oil the bowl, place the dough in it, cover with a plate, and let it ferment at room temperature for about 3 hours, or until tripled in volume.

5. In a bowl, combine the raisins, cranberries, and dates. Add warm water to cover and let soak for 15 minutes. Drain.

6. Scoop the dough out onto a clean, lightly floured surface and press into a 1-inch-thick circle. Let rest for 5 minutes. Spread the raisins, cranberries, dates, and walnuts over the dough, fold in the sides, and knead briefly to incorporate the fruit and nuts. Don't worry if some of them protrude; the dough will rise around them later. Let the dough rest for 5 minutes, covered with a damp cloth.

7. Shape the dough into a boule, and place, seam side up, in a 3-quart bowl lined with a lightly floured cloth. Pinch the seam to seal, and cover with a plate. Let the dough proof for 3 hours, or until doubled in volume.

8. At least 1 hour before the bread is ready to bake, preheat the oven to 500°F. Set a heavy metal baking pan or cast-iron skillet on the floor of the oven, pour 1 cup of hot water into the pan, and shut the door.

9. When the dough is ready, sprinkle a peel or the underside of a baking sheet with cornmeal or rolled oats. Gently invert the dough onto the peel. Sift a light veil of white flour evenly over the dough and slash the loaf. Open the oven and mist the walls, ceiling, and stone with a spray bottle. Immediately slide the dough onto the center of the stone and shut the oven door. Mist the walls and floor of the oven two more times during the first 5 minutes of baking. This helps the bread rise in the oven and develop a crispy crust.

10. Reduce the oven temperature to 450°F. Do not open the door for the next 20 minutes, until the bread has set. After 20 minutes, rotate the bread to ensure even cooking and browning of the crust. Bake for another 20 minutes, or until the bread has reached an internal temperature of 210°F. If you don't have an instant-read thermometer, tap the bottom of the bread with your index and middle fingers. If you hear a deep thumping sound, then it is done.

11. Transfer the bread to a wire rack to cool for at least 1 hour before slicing. This may be the hardest part of baking. If you put an ear to your bread, you will hear it hissing. It is still cooking outside the oven! If the bread is cut before it finishes baking, it will toughen and never reach its full potential.

YIELD: 1 (2-POUND) LOAF

Sourdough Rye

Rye flour has a very earthy, complex flavor with a slight tang to it, even before you add the starter. Its sourness goes beautifully with sweet corn grits, so I've combined them here in this dense, hearty loaf. Don't be discouraged when you find yourself having to knead the dough more than usual. Rye flour has less gluten than wheat flour, so it takes longer to develop a strong gluten structure.

> 1 cup freshly ground dark whole rye flour
> 3 cups unbleached white bread flour
> 1/3 cup fine yellow corn grits
> 1 1/2 cups lukewarm (95° to 105°F) nonchlorinated water
> 1 tablespoon rye malt syrup or barley malt syrup
> 3/4 cup White Sourdough Starter (page 326)
> 2 1/2 teaspoons fine sea salt
> 1 tablespoon caraway seeds

1. In a bowl, mix together the flours and grits. Make a well in the center and add the water, rye malt syrup, and starter. Slowly mix in enough flour from the sides of the bowl to form a sponge. Cover the bowl with a damp towel and set aside at room temperature until the batter is bubbling, 2 to 3 hours.

2. Stir the remaining flour into the sponge to form a ragged dough. Cover the bowl and let it rest for 5 minutes.

3. Scoop the dough out onto a clean, lightly floured surface. Wash out the bowl and thoroughly wash and dry your hands. Knead for 10 minutes. The dough should be sticky and a bit hard to manage. It helps to have a dough scraper or wide spatula to scrape up the dough when it sticks. You may also want to wash your hands several times as you knead. Invert the bowl over the dough and let it rest for 15 to 20 minutes.

4. Uncover the dough and sprinkle with the salt and caraway seeds. Knead for 8 to 10 minutes, until a smooth and slightly sticky dough is formed.

5. Lightly coat the inside of the bowl with oil. Turn the dough over several times in the bowl and cover tightly with plastic wrap or a damp cloth. Set aside at room temperature until doubled in volume, 4 to 6 hours.

6. Turn the dough out onto the kneading surface, lightly dust the dough with flour, and press with your hands to deflate it. Let the dough rest for 5 minutes. Tuck the edges of the dough under to form a loose round and let it rest for 5 minutes more.

7. Sift some white flour onto a clean kitchen towel. Line a 3-quart bowl with the towel, floured side up.

8. Shape the dough into a boule and place it seam side up in the bowl. Pinch the seam to seal. Cover the bowl with several pieces of plastic wrap. Let the dough rise for 1 hour at room temperature, then age in the refrigerator for 8 to 10 hours.

9. Remove the dough from the refrigerator. Take off the plastic wrap and dust the boule with white flour. Cover with a clean cloth and set aside at room temperature for 2 to 3 hours, until the dough no longer springs back and holds an indentation when gently poked with a finger.

10. At least 1 hour before the bread is ready to bake, preheat the oven to 500°F. Place a baking stone or inverted baking sheet on the middle rack. Set a heavy pan on the floor of the oven. Dust a wooden peel or inverted baking sheet with cornmeal.

11. Pour 1 cup of hot water into the pan at the bottom of the oven and shut the oven door.

12. Gently invert the dough onto the peel, dust with white flour, and slash the top.

13. Open the oven and heavily mist the floor, walls, and ceiling. Mist the stone, if using. Quickly slide the dough onto the stone or sheet and immediately close the door.

14. Mist two more times during the first 5 minutes of baking. Do not spray the loaf itself or the flour on the crust will cake and crack, and the bread will look dappled and unappealing.

15. Reduce the oven temperature to 450°F and bake undisturbed for 20 minutes.

16. Open the oven and rotate the loaf to ensure even browning. Continue to bake for 15 to 20 minutes, until the bread reaches an internal temperature of 210°F, or sounds hollow when the bottom is tapped.

17. Set the bread on a wire rack to cool for at least 1 hour before slicing.

YIELD: 1 (2-POUND) LOAF

For optimal flavor, whole-grain flours are best freshly ground. Contrary to popular belief, freshly ground grains should be allowed to oxidize for 2 to 3 days before using. This aging mellows the flour and makes for a lighter, tastier loaf.

However, fresh whole-ground flours can be difficult to find and only last for about 1 month, so I encourage you to invest in a home mill. See page 434 for Sources. My home mill has an important place in my home kitchen—it's always there when I need to grind flour for bread, crack oats for porridge, or coarsely grind corn for polenta.

I must applaud Paul Bertoli, who has been a major inspiration to me. His restaurant, Oliveta, in Oakland, California, is the only one I know where time is taken to grind fresh corn. The result— unbelievably delicious, fresh-tasting polenta.

Whole Wheat Sourdough Starter

This starter is fairly simple to make and yields excellent results. To create a healthy, vigorous whole wheat starter, it is essential to find a supply of freshly milled flour. And I strongly recommend that you purchase a mill to grind the flour yourself. Missing the experience of the aroma and texture of freshly milled whole-grain wheat or rye is like having drunk apple juice only from concentrate and never tasting freshly pressed apple cider. The difference is that dramatic.

Use this starter in the recipes on pages 336 to 340.

13 cups freshly milled hard spring or winter wheat flour

1. In a sterilized 1-gallon glass (see page 323), hard plastic, or earthenware container, combine 2 cups of the flour with 3 cups room-temperature (75° to 78°F) nonchlorinated water. Cover the container with a plate or a piece of plastic wrap and set aside away from drafts at room temperature for 3 days. Uncover and stir with a sterilized utensil once a day.

2. On the fourth day, uncover the container and stir in 1 cup flour and 1 cup room-temperature water. Replace the cover and set aside until the next day. Repeat this for 3 more days. The container will start to fill up.

3. On the eighth day, scoop out 2 cups of the starter and place it in a clean 1-quart container. Discard or give away the remaining starter. Stir in 1/2 cup flour and 1/2 cup room-temperature

water, cover, and set aside. Repeat the same feeding 12 hours later. Continue to feed the starter twice a day for 6 more days, reducing the starter to 2 cups each day before feeding.

4. At 14 days, your starter will be strong enough to raise bread and to give it flavor and keeping power. It is very important to keep the feedings regular, or the starter may become too sour, and the yeast may begin to starve from lack of nourishment. If you skip a feeding, double the size of the next one.

5. At this point, you can store the starter tightly covered in the refrigerator. Feed it $1/4$ cup water and $1/4$ cup flour two times per week to maintain it. It is good to take the starter out of the refrigerator and refresh it with a feeding 8 to 12 hours before you plan to bake. I like to keep about 3 cups of starter in my refrigerator at all times.

6. As always, replenish the starter when you use it. If the recipe calls for $1^1/2$ cups of starter, add about 1 cup flour and 1 cup water to the remaining starter.

YIELD: 3 CUPS STARTER

WHOLE WHEAT VS. WHITE FLOUR

White flour lasts much longer than wheat flour (about 4 months compared to just 1) before going rancid, because it doesn't contain the oils found in the bran and germ of whole wheat flour. That's why it is so important to use freshly ground whole wheat flour.

When kneading whole wheat dough, try to be a bit more gentle, because the bran present in whole wheat flour has sharp edges and tends to cut the gluten sheets, breaking them up and yielding a less fabulous rise. In addition, more bran means more weight for the starter to push up. Dough with a high content of unbleached white flour will be easier to knead, will have a bigger rise, and will yield light loaves with larger air holes than dough made with a greater proportion of whole wheat flour.

Whole Wheat Boule

Boule, French for ball, is the name for this classic round loaf. This bread is similar to the French Country Sourdough White Bread on page 328. However, because it is based on whole wheat, you will have to knead it longer, since the gluten is not released as quickly as it is with white flour. And although this dough is too heavy for a baguette, it makes an excellent bread to accompany soup. I really love the superior character and nutty flavor of whole wheat bread, especially when it is made from freshly milled whole wheat flour.

I like to use whole wheat starter for this rustic and hearty loaf, but it can be made with a white starter as well. If you choose to use the white starter, reduce the white flour to 3 cups and increase the whole wheat flour to 4 cups.

> 1$^3/_4$ cups Whole Wheat Sourdough Starter (page 334)
> 3 cups lukewarm (95° to 105°F) nonchlorinated water
> 4 cups unbleached white bread flour
> 3 cups whole wheat bread flour
> 1$^1/_2$ tablespoons fine sea salt
> Cornmeal

1. In a large mixing bowl, combine the starter and water and stir until the starter is dissolved.

2. Add the flours and mix to form a ragged mass of dough. Cover the bowl and allow the dough to rest for 5 minutes.

3. Scoop the dough out onto a clean, lightly floured surface. Wash out the bowl and thoroughly wash and dry your hands. Knead for 10 minutes. Invert the bowl over the dough and let it rest for 15 minutes.

4. Uncover the dough, sprinkle on the salt, and knead for 5 to 10 minutes, until the dough is smooth and elastic. The dough should be quite moist and sticky. Avoid adding extra flour as you knead it. Lightly flour your hands if you have trouble keeping the dough from sticking.

5. Lightly coat the inside of the bowl with oil. Turn the dough over several times in the bowl and cover tightly with plastic wrap. Set aside at room temperature until nearly tripled in volume, 3 to 4 hours.

6. Lightly flour a clean work surface. Pull the dough away from the sides of the bowl, invert, and ease the dough onto the work surface. Dust the dough lightly with flour and press with your fingers to deflate. Let the dough rest for 5 minutes.

7. Divide the dough into 2 equal pieces with a dough cutter and gently tuck the edges of each piece under to form a loose ball. Cover the dough with a clean towel and let it rest for 5 minutes.

8. Line 2 (3-quart) bowls with clean kitchen towels. Dust each towel with white flour.

9. Hold a piece of dough between your open palms and rock the dough back and forth, rounding it into a ball. Cup your palms over the top of the ball and apply gentle downward pressure. Stretch the surface of the dough down and under to form a neat ball. Invert the first boule into one of the bowls and pinch the seam to seal. Repeat with the second boule. Cover with several layers of plastic wrap and refrigerate for 8 to 12 hours.

10. Remove the dough from the refrigerator. Take off the plastic wrap and dust each boule with white flour. Cover with a clean cloth and set aside at room temperature for 2 to 3 hours until the internal temperature of the dough is 68°F.

11. At least 45 minutes before the bread is ready to bake, preheat the oven to 500°F. Place a baking stone or inverted baking sheet on the middle rack. Set a heavy pan on the floor of the oven. Dust a wooden peel or the inverted baking sheet with cornmeal.

12. Pour 1 cup hot water into the pan at the bottom of the oven and shut the oven door.

13. Invert one of the dough balls onto the prepared peel. Dust lightly with white flour. Slash the dough, making a cross $1/2$ inch deep and 4 inches in length. Make 4 shallow 2-inch-long cuts in between each vertical of the cross.

14. Heavily mist the walls, floor, and ceiling of the oven.

15. Slide the boule onto the left rear of the stone or sheet and shut the oven door.

16. Repeat step 13 with the other boule. Slide it onto the right front corner of the stone or sheet. Mist the bottom and sides of the oven, taking care not to mist the loaves themselves.

17. Mist two more times in the next 5 minutes. Reduce the oven temperature to 450°F and bake for 20 minutes without opening the oven door.

18. Rotate the loaves for even browning and bake for 20 minutes longer, until they have an internal temperature of 210°F, or sound hollow when tapped on the bottom.

19. Cool on a wire rack for 1 hour before slicing.

YIELD: 2 (2-POUND) LOAVES

Bread in a Pot

Here is a great method for baking that I learned from my friend and master baker, Jim Lahey, owner of the Sullivan Street Bakery in New York City. I was complaining to him one evening over dinner about how I had inconsistent results with the color of my bread. I brought him a loaf, and he examined it carefully. While the bread was delicious, with a light crumb, irregular cell structure, and the complex flavor of aged sourdough, it lacked the rich, golden hue of a regular bakery loaf. Jim quickly made the diagnosis. An overly dry environment had caused crystallization of salts on the surface of the dough to produce the dull, unexciting finish. He suggested that I bake my next loaf in a covered cast-iron pot. Late that evening I returned home and quickly mixed up a dough, let it rise, and later baked it in a covered pot. I didn't need to spray the oven with water to create a humid environment, and I was completely amazed at what I saw when I uncovered the pot. The color was bright and golden, the slash marks in the dough tinged with a deep mahogany. The bread was everything I imagined it would be.

This recipe will yield one 2-pound loaf or two 1-pound round loaves. A 4- to 5-quart pot is large enough to accommodate a 1- to 2-pound loaf. If you plan on baking more than one loaf and have only one pot or enough room in your oven to bake only one loaf at a time, simply leave the second loaf refrigerated an hour longer than the first one. Double the recipe if you plan on baking two 2-pound boules.

> 1 cup Whole Wheat Sourdough Starter (page 334) or White Sourdough Starter (page 326)
>
> 1½ cups cool (about 70°F) nonchlorinated water
>
> 1 tablespoon barley malt syrup
>
> 2 teaspoons fine sea salt
>
> 2½ cups unbleached white bread flour plus additional for dusting
>
> 1½ cups whole wheat bread flour
>
> ¼ cup wheat bran
>
> Cornmeal, bran, or rolled oats

1. Combine the starter, water, barley malt syrup, and salt in a large mixing bowl, and stir until the starter is dissolved.

2. Add the flours and bran. Mix with your fingers or a wooden spoon to form a ragged mass of dough.

3. Scoop up the dough and transfer it to a lightly floured work surface.

4. Wash and dry the bowl and thoroughly clean your hands. Coat the inside of the bowl or a rising bucket with a tablespoon of oil.

5. Knead the dough for 15 minutes. To tell if the dough is thoroughly kneaded, stretch it—it will feel smooth, strong, and elastic. Or press your finger into the dough ball. The dough will spring back immediately.

6. Turn the dough over several times in the bowl or rising bucket and cover the bowl or bucket with plastic wrap or a damp cloth. Set aside at room temperature until nearly tripled in volume, about 4 to 6 hours.

7. Lightly flour a clean work surface. Pull the dough away from the sides of the bowl, invert, and ease the dough onto the work surface.

8. Dust the dough lightly with flour and press with your fingers to deflate. Let the dough rest for 5 minutes.

9. If you plan on baking 2 loaves, cut the dough in half. For each loaf, fold the sides into the center and press down with your fingers to seal. Invert the dough and form into a loose round. Let the dough rest for a few minutes.

10. Shape each loaf by cupping your palms over the top of the ball and applying firm but gentle downward pressure. Stretch the surface of the dough down and under to form a neat ball. Do this 4 or 5 times, but be very careful not to tear the surface of the dough. Next, hold the dough between your open palms and rock it back and forth, rounding it into a ball.

11. For each boule, sift a generous layer of white flour onto a clean kitchen towel. Lay the towel, flour side up, in a 3-quart bowl.

12. Invert the boule(s) into the bowl and pinch the seam to seal. Cover the bowl with several layers of plastic wrap and refrigerate for 8 to 12 hours.

13. Remove the dough from the refrigerator. Take off the plastic wrap and dust the boule with white flour. Cover with a clean cloth and set aside at room temperature for 2 to 3 hours, or

until the dough reaches an internal temperature of 68° to 70°F when tested with a long-stemmed instant-read thermometer. The dough will have formed a dome and will feel very soft and tender. Gently press an index finger into the dough. If the indentation hesitates before slowly springing back, the bread is fully proofed and ready for baking.

14. At least 1 hour before the bread is ready to bake, place the pot on the middle shelf of the oven and preheat the oven to 450°F.

15. Transfer the hot cast-iron pot from the oven to a heat-proof surface.

16. Uncover the dough and sprinkle the top with cornmeal, bran, or rolled oats. Run a floured hand around the rim of the dough to loosen it a bit. Tilt the bowl and flip the dough into the pot. Do not worry if the dough loses a bit of its shape; it will spring back. Make sure the dough is in the center of the pot.

17. Sift a light veil of white flour over the surface of the dough.

18. With a clean, single-edge razor, slash an X or another pattern in the dough about 2 inches long and $1/2$ inch deep.

19. Cover the pot and bake for 30 minutes. Uncover and bake for 10 more minutes or until the bread reaches an internal temperature of 210°F. Transfer the bread to a rack and let cool for 1 full hour before slicing.

YIELD: ONE 2-POUND LOAF OR TWO 1-POUND LOAVES

Step-by-Step Sourdough

Bread baking is a constantly evolving, somewhat improvised craft, and as you develop your baking skills you will discover your own favorite methods. But to help you really absorb some of the basic methods, here are some illustrations to show step by step how sourdough bread is made. These illustrations match the instructions for the Bread in a Pot recipe on page 338 specifically, but they apply to all the recipes in one way or another, with only slight variations. For instance, if you use a sponge starter as in the Sourdough Rye and Fruit and Nut Bread recipes, mix the sponge as shown in the first illustration. If you are baking a loaf on a stone instead of in a pot, simply invert the dough after it has fully proofed onto a lightly floured baker's peel before sliding it onto the stone. If you want to make the classic torpedo-shaped loaves described in the French Country Sourdough White Bread recipe, try baking the loaves on a preheated stone or cookie sheet and invert the bottom of a large, oval roasting pan over the loaves. This will imitate the covered pot and trap the humidity in the dough, forming the same beautiful, golden-brown crust.

Combine water and starter in a heavy bowl.

Dissolve the starter in the water.

Mix in the flour and salt with a wooden spoon. Form a shaggy mass of dough with your fingers.

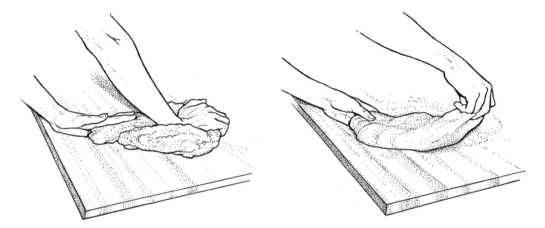

Transfer the dough to a clean, lightly floured work surface and begin kneading. Push down and away with the heel of your hand, then pull the dough back on itself.

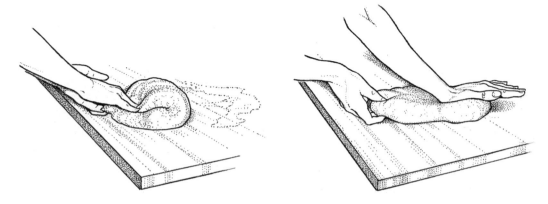

Then push down and away again. Continue kneading in a smooth rhythm for up to 15 minutes.

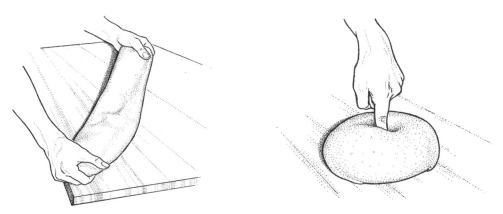

There are two ways to tell if the dough is fully kneaded. First, when you stretch the dough it will feel smooth, strong, and elastic. Second, if you press your finger into the dough ball, the dough will spring back immediately.

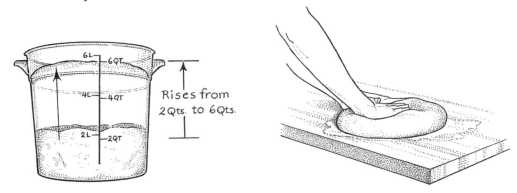

Rises from 2Qts. to 6Qts.

Transfer the dough to a lightly oiled rising bowl or bucket. Cover with a damp towel or plastic wrap and set aside in a warm, draft-free place to proof for 4 to 6 hours or until tripled in volume. Ease the risen dough out of the bowl or bucket onto a lightly floured work surface.

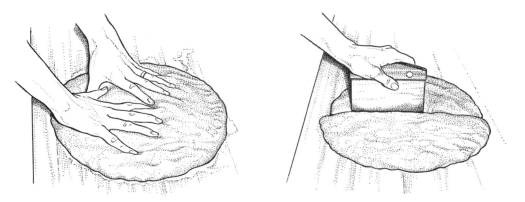

Deflate the dough by pressing down evenly with outstretched fingers. The dough will feel spongy and alive. Let the dough rest for 5 minutes. If you are making two loaves, cut the dough in half.

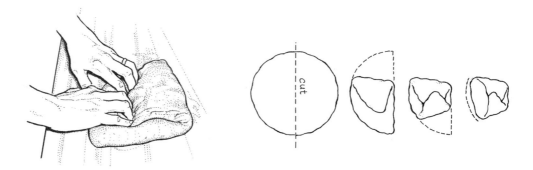

Fold the edges of the dough into the center and press down firmly with your fingertips to seal. Do not overwork the dough.

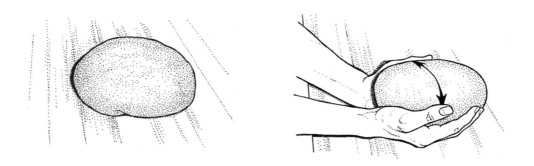

Flip the dough over and allow it to rest for 5 minutes. Shape each loaf by cupping your palms over the top of the ball and applying firm but gentle downward pressure. Stretch the surface of the dough down and under to form a neat ball. Do this 4 or 5 times, but be very careful not to tear the surface of the dough.

Next, hold the dough between your open palms and rock it back and forth, rounding it into a ball. The dough should feel as warm and tender as a baby's bottom.

Turn the dough over and transfer it to a floured rising basket or bowl lined with a floured cloth.

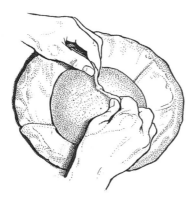

Pinch the seam to form a tight seal. Cover the dough with several layers of plastic wrap and set in the refrigerator to age for 8 to 36 hours.

Unwrap the dough and set aside at room temperature covered with a clean cloth for 2 to 3 hours, until the center of the dough is 65 to 70 degrees and the dough is fully risen. This dough is shown resting in a French banneton, a specially designed rising basket.

Carefully invert the dough into a preheated iron pot. Sift a light veil of flour over the dough.

Slash the dough, cover the pot, and bake. The loaf is finished when the internal temperature is 210 degrees.

The crisp crust and irregular, holey interior of a thoroughly aged, well formed, fully baked loaf.

Sourdough Timetables

The two timetables below are not recipes. They are your marching orders—a shorthand reference for you to follow once you become comfortable with sourdough bread baking.

TIMETABLE 1: TOTAL TIME, ABOUT 24 HOURS

This method works when I have a day off, and I want to bake the following morning before going to work. That way I will have a fresh loaf waiting for me when I return in the evening.

Starting at 7:00 A.M. I perform steps 1 through 8. Around noon, the dough is refrigerated. I go to sleep early and set my alarm clock for 5:00 A.M. When I wake up, I remove the dough from the refrigerator so it can proof, and I preheat the oven to 500°F. Meanwhile, I go back to sleep until 7:00 A.M. By then, the dough has usually finished proofing, since the oven has warmed up the room considerably. The bread is baked and on the cooling rack by 8:00 A.M.

1. Mix the starter, flour, and water.
2. Let the dough rest for 5 minutes.
3. Knead for 10 minutes for white bread; 15 minutes for whole wheat or rye.
4. Rest for 20 minutes.
5. Add salt and knead for 5 minutes.
6. Ferment in a lightly oiled bowl for up to 6 hours at room temperature.
7. Deflate and rest for 5 minutes.
8. Shape and rest for 5 minutes.
9. Cover with plastic and age in the refrigerator for 12 to 15 hours.
10. Uncover, lightly flour, and cover with a damp cloth. Let the dough sit for 2 to 3 hours at room temperature.
11. Preheat the oven to 500°F, with a baking stone on the middle rack and a cast-iron pan in the bottom of the oven.
12. Add 1 cup hot water to the cast-iron pan.
13. Invert the dough onto a peel dusted with corn grits.

14. Lightly dust the loaves with flour and slash them.
15. Mist the oven with a spray bottle and place the loaves in the oven.
16. Mist the oven walls and floor twice more during the first 5 minutes of baking.
17. Reduce the oven temperature to 450°F and bake the bread, undisturbed, for 20 minutes.
18. Rotate the loaves and bake for another 15 to 20 minutes, until they reach an internal temperature of 210°F, or sound hollow when tapped on the bottom.
19. Transfer the loaves to a wire rack and let cool, undisturbed, for 1 hour.

TIMETABLE 2: TOTAL TIME, ABOUT 21 HOURS

This method is perfect for the end of the workweek. I can start the process before retiring and celebrate the following evening with super-fresh bread for supper. I love this method because I can do it when I am really tired. The sponge can be mixed in less than 5 minutes and requires no special attention for at least 8 hours.

At 8:00 P.M., I mix a sponge and let it ferment at room temperature until 11:00 P.M. The sponge is refrigerated until the following morning. At 7:00 A.M., I mix the dough and let it ferment at room temperature. Around 2:00 P.M., I deflate and shape the dough. By 5:30 P.M., the dough is ready for baking. The bread is on the cooling rack by 6:15 P.M. At 7:15 P.M., a prayer is offered, wine is poured, bread is broken, and dinner is served.

1. Mix the starter, flour, and water.
2. Cover and ferment at room temperature (3 hours for white or wheat; 2 hours for rye).
3. Refrigerate the sponge for 8 to 12 hours.
4. Add more starter, flour, water, and malt to the sponge and mix to form a wet dough.
5. Let rest for 5 minutes to absorb water.
6. Knead the dough (10 minutes for white; 15 minutes for whole wheat or rye).
7. Let rest for 20 minutes.
8. Add salt and knead for 5 minutes.
9. Place the dough in a lightly oiled bowl for 6 to 8 hours and let it rise at room temperature until tripled in volume.
10. Gently deflate the dough and let it rest for 5 minutes.
11. Shape the dough and let it rest for 5 to 10 minutes.
12. Shape the dough and place it in a floured cloth-lined container.
13. Let the dough rise for 2 to 3 hours at room temperature.

14. Preheat the oven to 500°F. Place a baking stone or inverted baking sheet on the middle rack and a cast-iron pan on the oven floor. Dust a peel or inverted baking sheet with corn grits.
15. Add 1 cup hot water to the cast-iron pan.
16. Invert the dough onto the peel.
17. Lightly dust the dough with flour and slash it.
18. Mist the ceiling, floor, and walls of the oven.
19. Slide the dough onto the stone or sheet.
20. Mist the oven walls and floor two more times during the first 5 minutes of baking.
21. Reduce the oven temperature to 450°F and bake, undisturbed, for 20 minutes.
22. Rotate the bread for even browning and bake for 15 to 20 minutes more, until the bread reaches an internal temperature of 210°F, or sounds hollow when the bottom is tapped.
23. Cool the loaves for 1 hour on a wire rack before slicing.

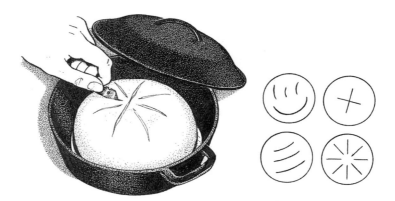

Slash the dough, cover the pot, and bake. The loaf is finished when the internal temperature is 210 degrees.

TYPES OF WHEAT FLOUR

If you are wondering what all these different types of wheat flour are all about, here is a short lesson. Pastry flour is made from soft wheat, which contains less gluten than hard wheat and results in more tender baked goods. Bread flour is made from hard wheat, which has a high gluten content (gluten enables the bread to rise). Finally, all-purpose flour is made from a combination of wheats and is suitable for most types of baking.

Quickbreads

These vegan quickbreads capture classic flavors without the use of eggs or dairy products. However, if you are inclined, any of these recipes will be even better if you reduce the liquid called for by ¹/₂ cup and replace it with 2 eggs.

Banana-Walnut Bread

This sweet vegan bread toasts very well and is ideal for breakfast.

  1 cup walnuts or pecans, roughly chopped
  1¹/₂ cups whole wheat pastry flour
  1¹/₂ cups unbleached all-purpose white bread flour
  1 tablespoon baking powder
  1¹/₂ teaspoons ground cinnamon
  1 teaspoon fine sea salt
  2 cups mashed ripe bananas
  ¹/₂ cup water
  ¹/₂ cup unrefined corn oil or melted unsalted butter
  ¹/₂ cup pure maple syrup or honey
  4 teaspoons vanilla extract

1. Preheat the oven to 350°F. Lightly oil a 4-by-8-inch loaf pan or 8-inch-square baking dish.

2. Spread the walnuts or pecans on a baking sheet and toast in the oven for 8 minutes. Transfer to a bowl to cool.

3. In a bowl, whisk together the flours, baking powder, cinnamon, and salt.

4. In a separate bowl, whisk together the bananas, water, oil, maple syrup, and vanilla.

5. Using a rubber spatula, fold the wet mixture into the dry mixture. Fold in the toasted nuts. Do not overmix—a few lumps won't matter, and you will wind up with a lighter, fluffier bread.

6. Pour the batter into the prepared pan and bake for 1 hour, or until a toothpick inserted into the middle of the loaf comes out clean.

7. Cool in the pan for 15 minutes before serving.   YIELD: 8 SERVINGS

Basic Vegan Skillet Corn Bread

This is everything a corn bread should be—light, corny-tasting, and golden yellow, all without the usual eggs, milk, and sugar. The use of masa harina in this recipe really lightens and refines the texture and flavor of this bread. If you can't find masa harina (available in most large supermarkets), you can substitute fine yellow or white corn grits.

> 1 cup unbleached white bread flour
> $1/2$ cup yellow cornmeal
> $1/2$ cup masa harina
> 2 teaspoons baking powder
> 1 cup plus 1 tablespoon water
> $1/4$ cup unrefined corn oil
> 3 tablespoons pure maple syrup
> 2 tablespoons finely chopped scallion, white and green parts
> 1 jalapeño pepper, seeded and minced (optional)
> $3/4$ teaspoon fine sea salt

1. Preheat the oven to 350°F. Grease a 9-inch cast-iron skillet, 8-inch-square baking dish or 9-inch pie pan.

2. In a bowl, whisk together the flour, cornmeal, masa harina, and baking powder.

3. In a separate bowl, whisk together the water, corn oil, maple syrup, scallion, jalapeño pepper, and salt.

4. Using a rubber spatula, fold the wet mixture into the dry mixture. Do not overmix—a few lumps won't matter, and you will wind up with a lighter, fluffier bread.

5. Pour the batter into the prepared pan and bake for 25 to 30 minutes, until a toothpick inserted into the middle of the corn bread comes out clean.

6. Cool in the pan for 15 minutes before serving.

YIELD: 4 TO 6 SERVINGS

Sweet Potato–Pecan Drop Biscuits

These colorful drop biscuits are great for Thanksgiving or any festive spread. Serve with Barbecued Tempeh Sandwich Filling (page 279) and a side of collard greens. If you don't have sweet potatoes, steamed or roasted carrots, winter squash, or parsnips will work as well.

1^1/$_2$ cup shelled pecans, roughly chopped
1 pound sweet potatoes, peeled and diced (about 3 cups)
1 cup water
^{1}/$_3$ cup cider vinegar
^{1}/$_4$ cup pure maple syrup or honey
^{2}/$_3$ cup olive oil, unrefined corn oil, or melted unsalted butter
2 cups unbleached all-purpose or white bread flour
1^1/$_2$ cups whole wheat pastry flour
^{1}/$_2$ cup cornmeal
1 tablespoon baking powder
1^1/$_2$ teaspoons baking soda
2 teaspoons fine sea salt
2 teaspoons freshly milled black pepper

1. Preheat the oven to 350°F. Lightly oil 2 baking sheets.

2. Spread the pecans on an ungreased baking sheet and toast in the oven for 8 minutes. Transfer them to a bowl to cool.

3. Steam the sweet potatoes until tender.

4. In a blender, combine the water, sweet potatoes, vinegar, and maple syrup. Purée until creamy. Alternatively, pass the potatoes through the medium disk of a food mill into a bowl, then whisk in the water, vinegar, and maple syrup.

5. In a large bowl, whisk together the flours, cornmeal, baking powder, baking soda, salt, and pepper.

6. Using a rubber spatula, fold in the sweet potato mixture and the pecans. Do not overmix— a few lumps won't matter, and you will wind up with lighter, fluffier biscuits.

7. Drop the dough ^{1}/$_2$ cup at a time 2 to 3 inches apart on the baking sheets and bake for 15 minutes. Rotate the baking sheets for even browning. Bake for another 10 to 15 minutes, until a toothpick inserted into the middle of a biscuit comes out clean.

8. Serve warm.   YIELD: 1 DOZEN BISCUITS

Five-Grain Sunflower Spelt Bread

Teff, millet, amaranth, quinoa, and spelt flour are all combined to create this nubby whole-grain loaf. For all my wheat-sensitive friends in the world, this bread's for you.

$^1/_2$ cup hulled sunflower seeds
3$^1/_2$ cups water
3 tablespoons whole-grain teff
3 tablespoons amaranth
3 tablespoons quinoa
3 tablespoons millet
1$^3/_4$ teaspoons fine sea salt
3 cups whole spelt flour
2$^1/_2$ teaspoons baking soda
$^1/_2$ teaspoon baking powder
9 tablespoons unrefined corn oil
    or melted unsalted butter
2 tablespoons cider vinegar

1. Preheat the oven to 350°F. Lightly oil an 8-by-4-inch loaf pan or 8-inch-square baking dish.

2. Spread the sunflower seeds on a baking sheet and toast in the oven for 8 minutes.

3. In a small saucepan, bring 2 cups of the water to a boil. Add the teff, amaranth, quinoa, millet, and $^1/_4$ teaspoon salt. Reduce the heat and simmer, covered, for 30 minutes, or until the water is absorbed. Transfer the grains to a bowl to cool.

4. In a large bowl, whisk together the flour, sunflower seeds, baking soda, baking powder, and remaining 1$^1/_2$ teaspoons salt.

5. Add the remaining 1$^1/_2$ cups water, oil, and vinegar to the cooked grains and whisk well.

6. Fold the grain mixture into the flour mixture to form a thick batter. Do not overmix—a few lumps won't matter, and you will wind up with lighter, fluffier bread.

7. Pour the batter into the prepared pan and smooth the top with a wet spatula. Bake for 50 minutes, or until a toothpick inserted into the middle of the loaf comes out clean.

8. Allow the bread to cool for 30 minutes before slicing. Serve warm. YIELD: 8 SERVINGS

Oat-Currant Scones

Bake these scones for friends and host a tea party. They are one of my all-time favorites—just rich enough without being too sweet. For vegan scones, substitute oil for the butter and 1 cup water mixed with 2 tablespoons lemon juice for the whey.

If you drain the whey the day before, you will have delicious thickened yogurt to spread on your warm scones.

2 cups whole wheat pastry flour
3/4 cup unbleached all-purpose
   or white bread flour
3/4 cup rolled oats
1/2 cup sunflower seeds
1 1/2 teaspoons baking powder
3/4 teaspoon baking soda
1 teaspoon ground cinnamon
1 teaspoon fine sea salt
1 cup whey (page 407) or plain yogurt
3/4 cup dried currants
1/2 cup melted unsalted butter
1/2 cup pure maple syrup
2 teaspoons vanilla extract

1. Preheat the oven to 375°F. Line 2 baking sheets with parchment paper or lightly grease them with oil or butter.

2. In a large bowl, whisk together the flours, oats, sunflower seeds, baking powder, baking soda, cinnamon, and salt.

4. In a separate bowl, whisk together the whey, currants, melted butter, maple syrup, and vanilla.

5. Using a rubber spatula, fold the wet mixture into the dry mixture. Do not overmix—a few lumps won't matter, and you will wind up with a lighter, fluffier bread.

6. Drop the dough 1/3 cup at a time 2 inches apart on the prepared baking sheets. Bake for 20 minutes, or until a toothpick inserted into the middle of a scone comes out clean.

7. Serve warm.

YIELD: ABOUT 1 DOZEN

Condiments

and Sauces

Around the world, intense, concentrated condiments have always been used to pique our interest in food. They both stimulate the appetite and make dishes more appealing and flavorful. They can be raw such as a fresh salsa, cooked like a chutney, or dry like a freshly ground spice. Condiments are generally easy to make and keep for long periods, convenient to use, and good digestives, but most of all, they ensure that food doesn't become dull or routine.

The beauty of condiments is that you can stick to one recipe for, say, a basic vegetable soup and use different accompaniments to make it unique every night of the week. A relatively bland or boring meal of plain rice and beans can be made infinitely more interesting by adding a zesty condiment, such as a red or green salsa. And exploring different condiment-food combinations can really open up your culinary world. Adding a sweet and piquant chutney to lentils gives the dish an Indian flavor, whereas using a rich, pungent tapenade hints at the Mediterranean.

In this chapter I include condiments from all over, as varied in their scope and style as the countries of their origin. Seaweed, fresh and dried, is typically used in East Asia, while sweet and sour chutney and creamy raita hearken from India. The Middle East yields spicy harissa, and Northern and Eastern Europe is home to tangy sauerkraut and crisp pickled vegetables. The vast Mediterranean region is rich with a variety of condiments, including tapenades, rouille, garlic and herb oils, and pesto. And, last, the New World is represented here with piquant tomato and tomatillo salsas, spicy pumpkin seeds, and super-hot pickled jalapeño peppers.

For centuries, condiments have also served the function of protecting foods from spoilage, while capturing their essences and enhancing their flavors. In the days before refrigeration, foods were primarily preserved in one of four ways. One method involves using salt to assist in dehydration. In Japan, a relatively humid country, foods such as seaweeds tend to be preserved this way. Some foods can be preserved through salting or lactic acid fermentation, to produce cheeses and sauerkraut. Dried herbs, spices, and sun-dried vegetables, which tend to lose their potency in the open air, can be kept fresh when submerged in oil or vinegar. Finally, there is the ancient process of storing foods in a brine solution of vinegar and salt, also known as pickling.

Pickling is a simple, effective, and almost universal practice. In many parts of the world, all sorts of freshly harvested vegetables are pickled in vinegar and salt to last through the winter. In Japan, foods are often pickled in miso, which preserves with its active enzymes and lactic acid. In recent years, pickling has been done in increasingly unhealthful ways, by using highly refined vinegars, salts, and sugars. Pickles that were once healthful and excellent digestives now contain no enzymes because they are pasteurized, making them shadows of what good pickles can be.

Vinegars, especially flavorful cider or wine varieties, are one type of condiment most people already have on hand. Vinegar has been used medicinally and as a disinfectant since Hippocrates' day and is said to ease the pain of headaches and soothe the stomach. In fact, in addition to transforming food from dull, dreary, or monotonous to vibrant, zesty, and flavorful, all condiments help to quicken the pulse, stimulate the gastric juices, and prepare the digestive system to receive food. In particular, caraway, cumin, and fennel are good for digesting fibrous legumes and sulfur-rich vegetables in the cabbage family. Yogurt and sour cream, fermented dairy products, contain lactic acid bacteria, which aids in the digestion of legumes and grains. Studies have shown that lactic acid bacteria can neutralize the phytic acids in beans and in the outer bran layer of grains, facilitating greater absorption of B vitamins and minerals. They also stimulate the pancreas, helping to regulate blood sugar and insulin levels.

After becoming familiar with some of the condiments in this chapter, you will develop even more confidence in your cooking, knowing that you will always be able to spice up casual dishes with a sweet and sour chutney, round out any rough edges with a creamy yogurt cheese, or encourage the flavors to surface to their full extent with a spicy vinegar.

I find it is nice to keep several homemade condiments in my cupboard and refrigerator. Most of the recipes in this chapter are quick and easy to make and most of them will last for quite a while, from about 1 week for the fresh salsas, pesto, and yogurt-based condiments, to 1 month for the chutney, toasted seeds, and freshly ground spice blends, to indefinitely for the spiced vinegars. And if you end up with extra on hand, they make the best kind of gifts—ones you have made with your own hands.

Mellow Curry Powder

This basic medium-hot curry powder will deliver more flavor than any ready-made curry you can buy. It will keep for about 1 month, after which the flavors will begin to fade, but continue to deliver much more flavor than average store-bought varieties.

> 2 tablespoons coriander seeds
> 1 tablespoon cumin seeds
> $1/2$ cinnamon stick
> 1 teaspoon caraway seeds
> 1 teaspoon fennel seeds
> 1 teaspoon black peppercorns
> $1^1/2$ tablespoons turmeric
> 1 teaspoon ground ginger
> $1/4$ teaspoon cayenne pepper

1. In a heavy pan over medium heat, combine the coriander, cumin, cinnamon, caraway seeds, fennel, and peppercorns. Toast until the seeds begin to pop and smell fragrant, about 2 minutes.

2. Transfer the toasted seeds and cinnamon to a clean coffee mill or heavy mortar and grind to a powder. Transfer the ground spices to a bowl, add the turmeric, ginger, and cayenne and mix well.

3. Transfer to a clean glass jar and store in a cool dark place.

YIELD: ABOUT $1/3$ CUP

Spicy-Hot Curry Powder

As outstanding in freshness and flavor as the preceding curry powder recipe, this one really packs heat.

> **2 tablespoons coriander seeds**
> **$1/2$ cinnamon stick**
> **2 teaspoons black peppercorns**
> **$1^1/2$ teaspoons cumin seeds**
> **3 cardamom pods**
> **$1/2$ teaspoon fenugreek seeds**
> **1 tablespoon ground turmeric**
> **$1^1/2$ teaspoons ground ginger**
> **$1/4$ teaspoon cayenne pepper**

1. In a heavy pan over medium heat, combine the coriander, cinnamon, peppercorns, cumin, cardamom, and fenugreek. Toast until the seeds begin to pop and smell fragrant, about 2 minutes.

2. Transfer the toasted seeds and cinnamon to a clean coffee mill or heavy mortar and grind to a powder. Transfer the ground spices to a bowl, add the turmeric, ginger, and cayenne and mix well.

3. Transfer to a clean glass jar and store in a cool dark place.

YIELD: ABOUT $1/3$ CUP

For thousands of years, vinegar has been the primary means of capturing and preserving the essence of fresh herbs. Herb vinegars are great sprinkled over salads or cooked greens. They also make wonderful additions to marinades for tempeh and tofu. And in addition to adding charm and personality to your cupboard and cuisine, they'll keep indefinitely.

For lighter, more delicate herbs, such as marjoram, oregano, mint, tarragon, lemon balm, and anise hyssop, I use white wine or rice vinegar. Stronger, earthier herbs, such as rosemary, sage, thyme, and savory, are best preserved in red wine or apple cider vinegar.

Standard Herb Vinegar

2 large bunches herbs
4 cups white wine vinegar, rice vinegar, red wine vinegar, or cider vinegar

1. In a bowl, combine the herbs with vinegar. Cover the bowl tightly with plastic wrap and set aside at room temperature for at least 1 week.

2. Begin smelling and tasting the vinegar. When it is strong enough for you, strain into a clean glass bottle and discard the herbs.

3. Label the bottle or add 1 fresh sprig of the herb to help identify it. Store at room temperature.

YIELD: 1 QUART

Quick Herb Vinegar

This method speeds up the process a bit. It will produce decent vinegar, but it will lack a certain finesse that develops with the slower method.

2 large bunches herbs
4 cups white wine vinegar, rice vinegar, red wine vinegar, or cider vinegar

1. In a saucepan over low heat, combine the herbs and vinegar in a nonreactive pan and heat gently for 1 hour. Do not let the vinegar come to a boil.

2. Remove the pan from the heat and set aside for 24 hours.

3. Strain the vinegar into a clean glass bottle and discard the herbs.

4. Label the bottle or add 1 fresh sprig of the herb to help identify it. Store at room temperature.

YIELD: 1 QUART

Chili Vinegar

This medium-hot all-purpose vinegar is great on braised greens and will keep indefinitely.

1 dried ancho chili
1 dried chipotle chili
2 cups cider vinegar or red wine vinegar

1. In a preheated cast-iron (or other heavy) skillet over medium heat, toast the chilies, turning frequently, for 2 minutes. Transfer the chilies to a plate. When cool enough to handle, break the chilies open and discard the stems and seeds.

2. In a small saucepan over medium heat, combine the vinegar and toasted chilies and let simmer for 5 minutes. Remove the pan from the heat and set aside for 20 minutes to cool.

3. Transfer the chilies and vinegar to a blender and purée until smooth.

4. Use a funnel to transfer the chili vinegar to a 16-ounce glass or heavy plastic bottle. Store at room temperature.

YIELD: 2 CUPS

Curry Oil

This beautiful bright yellow oil is wonderful for drizzling on any soup, accenting it with a savory hint of curry. You can also sauté vegetables in it.

2 tablespoons homemade curry powder (pages 358 and 359)
1 1/2 tablespoons water
1 1/2 cups mild oil, such as grapeseed, sunflower, or pure olive

1. In a medium ceramic or glass bowl, combine the curry powder and water to form a paste. Whisk in the oil and cover tightly with plastic wrap.

2. Let the oil infuse for 2 days at room temperature. Stir the oil 2 to 3 times each day.

3. On the third day, without disturbing the solids collected at the bottom of the bowl, slowly pour off the clear oil through a strainer lined with 2 layers of cheesecloth into a clean container. Discard the solids.

4. Store in the refrigerator for up to 3 months.

YIELD: ABOUT 1 1/2 CUPS

FLAVORED OILS AND VINEGARS

Fresh foods with a high water content, including garlic, can spoil when stored in oil for more than just a few days. For longer storage, these are best pickled in vinegar. On the other hand, dried foods such as spices, herbs, and tomatoes are well preserved in oil, which retains a purer flavor than vinegar. Vinegars are very strong and should be used only in small doses, whereas oils can be used more lavishly.

Flavored oils and vinegars last a long time, from 1 to 3 months for the oils to almost indefinitely for the vinegars. Both flavored oils and vinegars make wonderful gifts for fellow food enthusiasts.

Basil Oil

This is my favorite oil for dressing juicy ripe tomato salad, drizzling over grilled eggplant and zucchini, or mixing together with lemon juice and tossing with cold leftover rice and blanched broccoli florets. For something even simpler, rub grilled or toasted sourdough bread with garlic and use the oil for dipping. Heaven.

2 cups firmly packed basil leaves
1 1/3 cups extra-virgin olive oil

1. Fill a medium bowl with ice water and set aside. Bring 3 quarts of water to a boil. Add the basil and cook for 15 seconds. Remove the basil with a spider or slotted spoon and transfer immediately to the ice bath. When the basil is chilled, remove it and squeeze dry.

2. Coarsely chop the basil, transfer it to a blender with half of the oil, and purée for 3 to 4 minutes. Pour the bright green oil into a bowl and stir in the remaining oil. Cover tightly and refrigerate for 24 hours.

3. Strain the oil through a double layer of cheesecloth into a clean glass jar. Discard the solids. Return the oil to the refrigerator for another day, then strain through a coffee filter. The oil is now ready to use.

4. Store the oil for up to 6 days in the refrigerator.

YIELD: 1 1/2 CUPS

Rosemary-Garlic Oil

This flavorful oil can be used in many ways. I use it as a dip for bread, for drizzling over steamed vegetables, or in place of plain olive oil in vinaigrettes. If you make this oil for the Pizza Vegano on page 270, save the garlic to mash into the tofu topping. Otherwise, you can mash the garlic on its own and use it as a spread for crostini or blend it into a sauce or vinaigrette.

> 1 cup extra-virgin olive oil
> 8 garlic cloves, peeled
> 2 small sprigs fresh rosemary

1. In a saucepan over medium heat, combine the oil, garlic, and rosemary and bring to a simmer. Reduce the heat to as low as possible and simmer gently for 20 minutes or until the garlic turns light gold. Do not let the garlic brown or the oil will turn bitter.

2. Strain the oil into a clean glass jar and let cool.

3. Store in the refrigerator for up to 1 month.

YIELD: 1 CUP

Spicy Herb Oil

Made in minutes from ingredients you probably already have in your cabinets, an herb and spice oil can be an amazing garnish for all kinds of dishes. It is also terrific drizzled on plain steamed vegetables, used as a dipping sauce for bread, or whisked right into a sauce or salad dressing in place of regular oil. You can use almost any combination of herbs and whole spices; just keep the flavors of the original dish in mind, and choose herbs and spices that will complement rather than overwhelm them.

> 1 cup extra-virgin olive oil
> 2 garlic cloves, peeled and halved lengthwise
> 1 (4-inch) sprig fresh rosemary, sage, or thyme
> 2 bay leaves
> 1/2 teaspoon hot red pepper flakes

1. In a small heavy saucepan over medium-low heat, combine the oil, garlic, herb, bay leaves, and red pepper flakes and simmer gently for 15 to 20 minutes. Carefully regulate the heat to prevent the garlic from browning, which will turn the oil bitter. The garlic should be pale golden and fragrant.

2. Strain the oil into a clean glass jar and set aside to cool.

3. The oil will keep in the refrigerator for up to 1 month.

YIELD: 1 CUP

Sizzling Spice Oil

This oil is made from freshly ground spices that are gently heated in olive oil until they release their heady flavors. It's terrific in Rutabaga Soup (page 56) and on mashed potatoes or hummus.

> 1/4 cup extra-virgin olive oil
> 1 garlic clove, peeled and lightly bruised
> 1/4 teaspoon cayenne pepper
> 1/4 teaspoon freshly ground coriander
> 1/4 teaspoon freshly ground cumin

1. In a small skillet over high heat, combine the oil, garlic, cayenne, coriander, and cumin. Cook until the garlic turns golden and the spices are fragrant, about 2 minutes.

2. Remove the garlic and pour the oil into a small bowl. Serve immediately.

YIELD: 1/4 CUP

Marinated Sun-Dried Tomatoes

Although you can buy sun-dried tomatoes already packed in oil, they tend to be quite expensive. It is much better to make them yourself. When shopping for sun-dried tomatoes, avoid those that have been salted or preserved with sulfur dioxide (read the label).

You can add some chopped rosemary to this basic recipe, but I discourage adding garlic because it will decrease how long the tomatoes will last.

2 cups dry-pack sun-dried tomatoes
2 cups extra-virgin olive oil

1. Place the tomatoes in a large bowl. Add enough boiling water to cover the tomatoes by an inch and set aside until soft and plump, about 15 to 30 minutes.

2. Drain and discard the liquid. Blot the tomatoes dry with a clean towel. Wash out a 1-quart jar with boiling water and let air-dry. Pack the tomatoes into the jar and pour in the oil.

3. The tomatoes will keep for several months in the refrigerator, so long as they remain submerged in oil. Make sure to top off the tomatoes with fresh oil as you use them.

YIELD: ABOUT 3 CUPS

Hiziki Caviar

Hiziki is a very strong-tasting seaweed, more assertive than arame. Finely chopped and seasoned with soy and ginger, striking black hiziki is truly the poor man's caviar, especially when served over soy sour cream on a blini. Or try it on sesame seed crackers, as an accompaniment to an Asian-style rice and vegetable dish, or with any grain.

There are two different styles of hiziki available. One is gnarled, thick, wiry, and up to 4 inches in length, while the other is thinner and is sold in $1/2$-inch pieces. Either will work in this recipe. When a recipe calls for hiziki or other dried sea vegetables, such as wakame or dulse, it is best measured by weight.

1 ounce hiziki seaweed (about $1/2$ cup)
2 tablespoons light sesame oil or extra-virgin olive oil
2 tablespoons naturally brewed soy sauce
2 tablespoons mirin

**1 (2-inch) piece finely grated gingerroot, squeezed to yield 1 tablespoon ginger juice
Coarse sea salt**

1. Combine the hiziki and warm water to cover by 3 inches in a bowl. Set aside for 1 hour, or until the hiziki is swollen and tender. Drain the hiziki in a strainer and rinse well under cold running water. Transfer it to a cutting surface and finely chop.

2. In a sauté pan over medium heat, warm the oil. Add the hiziki and sauté for 5 minutes, stirring frequently.

3. Add the soy sauce, mirin, and ginger juice plus enough fresh water to cover. Bring to a boil, reduce the heat, and simmer until dry. Add salt to taste.   YIELD: 1 CUP

Cucumber and Hiziki Salsa

Condiments made with sea vegetables are a great way to incorporate these healthful, mineral-rich delicacies into your diet. Try serving this fresh, crunchy salsa with a polenta or rice dish.

**2 tablespoons hiziki seaweed
2 cups peeled, seeded, and finely chopped cucumber
1 scallion, green and white parts, trimmed and finely sliced
2 tablespoons finely diced red onion
2 teaspoons peeled and very finely chopped gingerroot
1 jalapeño pepper, seeded and very finely chopped
2 tablespoons rice vinegar
2 teaspoons cane sugar
Coarse sea salt**

1. Combine the hiziki and 2 cups of water in a pan. Bring to a boil and simmer for 30 minutes. Drain the hiziki in a strainer and cool under cold running water. Drain well, coarsely chop, and transfer to a bowl.

2. Add the cucumber, scallion, onion, ginger, jalapeño pepper, 2 tablespoons vinegar, sugar, and 2 teaspoons salt. Set the salsa aside to marinate for 30 minutes in the refrigerator.

3. Taste for seasoning and add more salt or vinegar to taste. Serve at once.

YIELD: 2½ CUPS

Crispy Pickled Vegetables

Vegetables will achieve their full marinated flavor in just 1 to 2 days using this great, all-purpose preserving method. You can use all sorts of hard vegetables, such as cauliflower, carrots, string beans, zucchini, summer squash, cabbage, turnips, kohlrabi, and red onions. Just keep these proportions: 1 quart pickling brine to 2 quarts vegetables. You can also vary the brine with different spices or fresh herbs.

4 cups water
1/2 cup cider vinegar
1/4 cup coarse sea salt
1 tablespoon finely chopped garlic
3 bay leaves
2 teaspoons mustard seeds
1/2 teaspoon turmeric (optional)
8 cups assorted hard vegetables, cut into bite-sized pieces
3 or 4 sprigs fresh dill

1. To make the pickling brine, combine the water, vinegar, salt, garlic, bay leaves, mustard seeds, and turmeric in a saucepan over high heat. Bring to a boil. Reduce the heat and simmer for 5 minutes. Remove from the heat and set aside to cool.

2. In a 3-quart glass or ceramic bowl, combine the vegetables and dill—or pack the vegetables into clean glass mason jars. Cover with the cooled brine and refrigerate for 24 hours before serving.

3. Store for up to 3 months in the refrigerator.

YIELD: 3 QUARTS

Spicy Jalapeño and Vegetable Pickles

This is based on picadillo, a popular Spanish-style dish made with ground meat and a spicy pickle. In Cuba, the requisite onions, garlic, tomatoes, and spices are paired with rice and black beans. This pickle adds a great spicy accent to greens or any bean dish.

 4 cups water
 $1/2$ cup rice vinegar or cider vinegar
 $1/4$ cup kosher salt
 6 garlic cloves, sliced
 1 teaspoon coriander seeds
 1 teaspoon cumin seeds
 6 to 8 small jalapeño peppers, seeded and sliced into $1/4$-inch rings
 2 onions, sliced
 2 carrots, thinly sliced
 1 red bell pepper, seeds and membranes removed, sliced
 $1/4$ cup packed mint leaves

1. To make the pickling brine, combine the water, vinegar, salt, garlic, coriander, and cumin in a saucepan over high heat and bring to a boil. Reduce the heat and simmer for 5 minutes. Remove from the heat and set aside to cool.

2. In a second saucepan, bring 2 quarts water to a boil. Add the sliced jalapeño peppers and onions and blanch for 2 minutes. Transfer to a colander and cool under cold running water. Drain thoroughly and transfer to a 3-quart glass or ceramic bowl.

3. Add the carrots, red pepper, and mint. Pour in the cooled brine. Cover and refrigerate for 2 days before serving. Pickles will keep for up to 6 months submerged in their brine and refrigerated.

YIELD: 1 QUART

Date Chutney with Lemon

This intense sweet-and-sour chutney is a wonderful accompaniment to stew and really spices up plain basmati rice and lentils.

> 1 tablespoon sunflower oil or light sesame oil
> 2 cups finely diced onions
> 2 tablespoons peeled and finely chopped gingerroot
> 1 small jalapeño pepper, seeded and finely diced
> Pinch coarse sea salt
> 3 cups pitted chopped dates
> 1/2 cup freshly squeezed lemon juice
> 1/4 cup honey
> 1 cinnamon stick
> Finely grated zest of 1 lemon

1. In a heavy saucepan over medium heat, warm the oil. Add the onions, ginger, jalapeño pepper, and salt. Sauté for 8 to 10 minutes, stirring frequently to prevent browning.

2. Add dates, 2 3/4 cups water, lemon juice, honey, cinnamon, and lemon zest. Raise the heat and bring to a boil. Reduce the heat to low and simmer, uncovered, for 1 hour, or until the chutney is thick.

3. Remove and discard the cinnamon stick. Let cool before serving.

4. Store in the refrigerator for 1 month.

YIELD: ABOUT 1 QUART

Apple-Ginger Chutney

This fresh fruit chutney is a little more delicate than the date chutney. For a delicious summertime variation, try substituting peaches for the apples and honey for the maple syrup. Steam the peaches whole for 2 minutes, then slip off the skins, dice them, and cook as directed.

    2 cinnamon sticks
    4 cardamom pods
    4 whole cloves
    1 tablespoon light sesame oil
        or sunflower oil
    1 cup finely diced onions
    1 tablespoon finely chopped gingerroot
    Pinch coarse sea salt
    2 cups fresh apple cider
    3 cups peeled, diced firm apples,
        such as Mutsu, Granny Smith,
        or Golden Delicious
    1/2 cup raisins
    3 tablespoons cider vinegar
    2 tablespoons maple syrup

1. Place the cinnamon, cardamom, and cloves on a square of cheesecloth, gather the corners, and tie into a neat bundle.

2. In a heavy saucepan over medium heat, warm the oil. Add the onions, ginger, and salt. Sauté for 8 to 10 minutes, stirring frequently to prevent browning.

3. Add the spice sachet, cider, apples, raisins, vinegar, and maple syrup. Raise the heat and bring to a boil. Reduce the heat to low and simmer, uncovered, for 1 hour, or until the chutney is thick.

4. Remove and discard the sachet. Let cool before serving.

5. Store in the refrigerator for 1 month.

YIELD: 1 QUART

Chunky Tomato and Walnut Tapenade

This chunky tapenade is superb spread atop a toasty bruschetta or on crispy triangles or baked or fried polenta. You can also thin it down with a little bit of pasta water and toss it with a hearty pasta, such as rigatoni.

> **2 cups Marinated Sun-Dried Tomatoes,**
>   **preferably homemade (page 366)**
> **$1/3$ cup walnut pieces, lightly toasted and skins removed**
> **3 tablespoons balsamic vinegar**
> **1 tablespoon capers, rinsed**
> **1 tablespoon chopped fresh basil**
> **2 teaspoons honey (optional)**
> **1 garlic clove, crushed**
> **Coarse sea salt**
> **$1/2$ teaspoon finely grated orange zest**
> **$1/4$ teaspoon hot red pepper flakes**
> **Freshly milled black pepper**

1. Drain the oil from the tomatoes, reserving 2 tablespoons of it. Roughly chop the tomatoes and place them in a large heavy mortar or the work bowl of a food processor.

2. Add the walnuts, vinegar, capers, basil, honey, garlic, $3/4$ teaspoon salt, orange zest, red pepper flakes, and pepper to taste. Pound or pulse to form a thick, chunky paste.

3. Season with extra salt and pepper to taste. Serve chilled or at room temperature. Store tapenade topped with a thin layer of olive oil, tightly covered and refrigerated, up to 1 month.

YIELD: ABOUT 3 CUPS

The aim of toasting nuts is to draw out the flavors contained within their oils. The best walnuts are freshly cracked from their shells, so if you want to go all out, buy whole nuts and crack them yourself. But, either way, arrange the shelled nuts on a baking sheet and toast them for about 8 minutes in a 350°F oven (stir the nuts halfway through the cooking so they will brown evenly). Because walnuts have bitter skins, I like to skin them before using. To do this, transfer the cooled, toasted nuts to a sieve and, holding the sieve over the sink, rub the nuts against the wire until the skins loosen and fall off.

Sauerkraut

This Eastern European staple is so much tastier when made at home. And because sauerkraut is loaded with lactic acid, beneficial bacteria, and enzymes, it is also good for you.

5 pounds green cabbage, cored and shredded
3 tablespoons coarse sea salt
1 tablespoon caraway seeds

1. Fill a 1-gallon ceramic pickle crock or bowl with boiling water. Drain and let air-dry.

2. In a large bowl, toss the cabbage with salt and caraway seeds.

3. Pack the mixture into the crock or bowl and cover with a clean plastic bag. Place a heavy weight (such as a couple of bricks or a large jar filled with water) on top of the plastic. Let the cabbage ferment at room temperature (68° to 78°F) for 10 days. The cabbage must always stay submerged in the brine that forms. Watch the kraut carefully and skim off any scum that forms. The kraut is ready when it no longer tastes salty, but has a pleasing sour taste.

4. Transfer the sauerkraut to a clean glass or heavy plastic container, cover, and store in the refrigerator for up to 3 weeks.

YIELD: ABOUT 2 QUARTS

Spicy Sun-Dried Tomato Spread

This is the perfect spread for a Barbecued Tempeh Sandwich (page 279) and is also great slathered on wedges of grilled or baked polenta.

2 cups dry-pack sun-dried tomatoes
2 tablespoons extra-virgin olive oil
1/2 cup finely chopped onion
2 teaspoons minced garlic
1 teaspoon ground cumin
3/4 teaspoon coarse sea salt
1/2 teaspoon dried oregano
1/2 teaspoon chipotle powder
1 tablespoon mirin
1 tablespoon cider vinegar

1. In a saucepan over high heat, bring the tomatoes and 1 quart water to a boil. Reduce the heat and simmer for 2 minutes. Remove from the heat and allow the tomatoes to swell for 10 minutes. Drain and set aside.

2. In a small skillet over medium heat, warm the oil. Add the onion, garlic, cumin, salt, oregano, and chipotle powder. Sauté for 15 minutes, stirring occasionally to prevent sticking. Add mirin and vinegar and cook for 2 minutes.

3. Combine the tomatoes and seasonings in a food processor and purée until smooth. Add several tablespoons of water to thin if the spread is too thick.

4. Store tightly covered in the refrigerator up to 1 month. Serve at room temperature.

YIELD: 3 CUPS

Green Olive and Onion Tapenade

Tapenades, which originated in Provence, are thick pastes traditionally made with olives, capers, and anchovies and served with crudités. Tapenades are also great to spread on toast. You can thin any one of the tapenades in this chapter with some water and use it as a dip or pour it over pasta.

> **2 tablespoons extra-virgin olive oil**
> **$1/2$ cup finely chopped onion**
> **Coarse sea salt**
> **3 to 4 garlic cloves, finely chopped**
> **1 teaspoon fresh thyme leaves**
> **2 tablespoons dry white wine**
> **1 tablespoon white wine vinegar**
> **1 cup pitted green olives, such as picholine**
> **Freshly milled black pepper**

1. In a saucepan over medium heat, warm the oil, then add the onion and a pinch of salt. Sauté for 7 to 8 minutes, stirring frequently to prevent browning.

2. Stir in the garlic and thyme and sauté for 2 minutes more. Add the wine and vinegar, raise the heat, and bring to a boil. Reduce the heat and simmer until nearly dry.

3. Transfer the mixture to a large mortar or food processor, add the olives, and mash or purée until smooth. Season with additional salt and pepper to taste, and serve. Store, tightly sealed, in the refrigerator for 2 to 3 weeks.

YIELD: 1 CUP

Basil-Almond Pesto

Traditionally, pesto is made with pine nuts. Here I use almonds, which are less expensive and impart a milder flavor. Feel free to experiment with different nuts, such as walnuts and cashews.

As well as using this recipe for the pasta salad on page 173, you can spread the pesto on sandwiches or use it as a dip with crudités.

> 1 1/2 cups whole almonds, peeled and lightly toasted
> 2 cups packed fresh basil leaves
> 2 plump garlic cloves, peeled and left whole
> 3 tablespoons freshly squeezed lemon juice
> 1 teaspoon finely grated lemon zest
> 3/4 cup extra-virgin olive oil
> Coarse sea salt

1. In the bowl of a food processor fitted with a metal blade, grind the blanched almonds to a meal.

2. Add the basil, garlic, lemon juice, and lemon zest and purée. Slowly add the oil and process until smooth. Blend in 1 teaspoon salt and adjust the seasoning to taste.

3. Serve at once. Cover any leftover pesto with a film of olive oil in a tightly sealed jar and refrigerate for up to 2 weeks.

YIELD: 2 CUPS

HOW TO PEEL ALMONDS

In a small saucepan over high heat, bring 3 cups water to a boil. Toss in 1 cup almonds and let them blanch for 1 to 2 minutes. Drain the almonds and rinse them in a strainer under cold running water until they are cool enough to handle. Squeeze each almond between your index finger and thumb and pop them out of their skins onto a plate. Discard the skins. Spread the almonds on a clean tea towel to dry.

Parsley Pesto

This recipe is a variation on the Basil-Almond Pesto (page 377). Other interesting variations include substituting 2 cups cilantro for the parsley, replacing the toasted walnuts with toasted pine nuts, and replacing 1 cup of the parsley with $1/2$ cup cilantro and $1/2$ cup mint.

> $1 1/2$ cups toasted walnuts
>   (see How to Toast Walnuts, page 373)
> 4 cups packed fresh flat-leaf parsley leaves
> 2 plump garlic cloves, peeled and left whole
> 3 tablespoons freshly squeezed lemon juice
> 1 teaspoon finely grated lemon zest
> $3/4$ cup extra-virgin olive oil
> Coarse sea salt

1. In the bowl of a food processor fitted with a metal blade, grind the walnuts to a meal.

2. Add the parsley, garlic, lemon juice, and lemon zest and purée. Slowly add the oil and process until smooth. Blend in 1 teaspoon salt, and adjust the seasoning to taste.

3. Serve at once. Cover any pesto with a film of olive oil in a tightly sealed jar and refrigerate for up to 2 weeks.

YIELD: 2 CUPS

Gremolata

Gremolata is a citrus-flavored Italian condiment that really sharpens the flavor of hearty dishes. Serve gremolata sprinkled over soups, stews, and pastas within 2 hours of making it, since its freshness is what makes it so delicious.

> $1/4$ cup finely chopped fresh parsley
> 1 garlic clove, finely minced
> Zest of 1 lemon, finely grated

In a bowl, combine the parsley, garlic, and lemon zest. Mix well and serve.

YIELD: ABOUT $1/4$ CUP

Carrot Sauce

I originally made this sauce to accompany grain croquettes; however, its sweet, herbal notes will brighten most cooked grains, especially millet. As a variation, try replacing the lemon juice and peel with orange. And if you are in the mood, you can punch it up with a pinch of cayenne pepper.

2 teaspoons extra-virgin olive oil
2 scallions, trimmed, white parts thinly sliced, green parts set aside
1 teaspoon finely chopped fresh thyme leaves
Coarse sea salt
2 cups fresh carrot juice
2 teaspoons freshly squeezed lemon juice
1 (2-inch) strip lemon zest
2 tablespoons arrowroot powder
2 tablespoons cold water
2 teaspoons finely chopped fresh parsley

1. In a heavy saucepan over medium heat, warm the oil. Add the scallions, thyme, and a pinch of salt. Sauté for 1 minute, cover, and cook over the lowest possible heat for 5 minutes. Do not let the scallions brown.

2. Add the carrot juice, lemon juice, and lemon zest. Raise the heat and bring to a boil. Reduce the heat to low and simmer, uncovered, for 2 minutes.

3. In a small bowl, dissolve the arrowroot in water. Add it to the pan and stir continuously until the sauce thickens. Remove and discard the lemon zest. Add the parsley and simmer for 1 minute.

4. Serve immediately or cool to room temperature and refrigerate. The sauce will keep for up to 2 days.

YIELD: 2 CUPS

Harissa

Harissa is a traditional Tunisian hot sauce that can be used to spice up plain couscous or added to soups and stews.

1 tablespoon whole cumin seeds
1 1/2 teaspoons whole caraway seeds
1/4 teaspoon coarse sea salt
4 tablespoons extra-virgin olive oil
2 tablespoons freshly squeezed lemon juice
1 tablespoon cayenne pepper

1. In a mortar or clean coffee mill, grind the cumin, caraway seeds, and salt to a powder. Transfer the ground spices to a bowl if you are using the coffee mill.

2. Stir in the oil, lemon juice, and cayenne.

3. Serve at once. Store up to 1 week, tightly sealed, in the refrigerator.

YIELD: 1/3 CUP

Rouille

This popular French spicy pepper sauce has its origins in northern Africa and is commonly served with bouillabaisse. As with all spicy condiments, it should be served on the side so that everyone can flavor his own dish to taste.

1 slice sourdough bread, crust removed
    (or enough to yield 1/4 cup when soaked
    in water and squeezed dry)
1 red bell pepper, roasted
    (see How to Roast a Pepper, page 105)
2 garlic cloves, peeled and left whole
1/2 teaspoon coarse sea salt
1/2 teaspoon cayenne pepper
1/4 cup extra-virgin olive oil
Freshly squeezed lemon juice

1. Soak the bread in 1 cup lukewarm water for 10 minutes or until soft. Squeeze dry and set aside.

2. In a food processor fitted with a metal blade, combine the bread, red pepper, garlic, salt, and cayenne and purée. While puréeing, add the oil in a thin stream until the mixture is emulsified.

3. Scrape the mixture into a bowl and stir in lemon juice to taste.   YIELD: 1 CUP

All-Purpose Savory Gravy

This rich and satisfying sauce will enhance most whole-grain pilafs, mashed potatoes, or steamed tempeh, tofu, or vegetables.

If you're making the Kasha Varnishkas on page 218, you'll have a fat portobello mushroom stem on your hands and the beginnings of a rich vegetable broth. (You can also use any one of the broths featured in the soup chapter instead.) If you don't have the time to make broth, you can use water instead. The gravy will lack some of its complexity, but it will still serve admirably.

> **2 tablespoons light sesame oil or extra-virgin olive oil**
> **3 tablespoons unbleached all-purpose wheat, spelt, or rice flour**
> **1¾ cups All-Season Vegetable Stock (page 29) or water**
> **2 tablespoons naturally brewed soy sauce**
> **Coarse sea salt**
> **Freshly milled black pepper**

1. In a medium saucepan over medium heat, warm the oil. Add the flour and stir constantly with a wooden spoon until the flour absorbs the oil, begins to brown, and releases a nutty fragrance, 5 to 8 minutes. Regulate the heat so that the flour browns gently without scorching.

2. Slowly add the broth, whisking constantly to prevent lumps. Raise the heat and bring the gravy to a boil. Reduce the heat to low and simmer gently, uncovered, for 15 to 20 minutes, until the gravy thickens to a desired consistency.

3. Add the soy sauce, season to taste with salt and pepper, and simmer for another minute before serving. The gravy freezes well for several months and will keep, tightly sealed, in the refrigerator for up to a week.   YIELD: 2 CUPS

Quick Tomato Salsa

Personally, I find most store-bought salsa to be flat and boring. Here is a basic tomato salsa with real character that you can whip up in about 5 minutes. Punch up the heat as much as you like with extra jalapeño pepper or a dose of red pepper flakes.

> 1 (14-ounce) can peeled, chopped, or whole plum tomatoes
> 2 tablespoons chopped fresh cilantro
> 1 tablespoon freshly squeezed lime or lemon juice
> 1 tablespoon finely sliced scallion, white and green parts
> 1 small jalapeño pepper, seeded and finely chopped
> 1 small garlic clove, crushed
> 1 teaspoon freshly ground cumin
> Coarse sea salt

1. Place the tomatoes with their juice in a bowl. Stir in the cilantro, lime juice, scallion, jalapeño pepper, garlic, cumin, and salt to taste.

2. Serve at once. This salsa will keep in the refrigerator for 1 week.   YIELD: 2 CUPS

Tomatillo Salsa

Tomatillos are fruits belonging to the tomato family and are available in the summer and fall. They have a thin, papery husk, which is very easy to peel away, and you don't even need to seed them. This bright green salsa tastes incredibly fresh thanks to the enlivening flavors of lime juice and cilantro. It goes great with tamales or arepas and can also serve as a dip for tortillas.

> 1 teaspoon cumin seeds
> 1 pound tomatillos, husks removed
> 2 jalapeño peppers, cored and seeded but left whole
> 2 tablespoons finely chopped sweet white onion, such as Vidalia or Walla Walla
> 1/4 cup packed chopped fresh cilantro
> 1 tablespoon freshly squeezed lime juice
> Coarse sea salt

1. Warm a cast-iron skillet over medium heat. Add the cumin and toast for 1 to 2 minutes or until fragrant. Transfer the seeds to a mortar or a clean electric coffee mill and grind to a fine powder.

2. Put the tomatillos and jalapeño peppers in the skillet and cook for 12 to 15 minutes, shaking the pan from time to time and occasionally turning the tomatillos over with a pair of tongs, until they are speckled with black marks. They will hiss and pop as they heat.

3. Transfer the contents of the pan to a food processor fitted with a metal blade and purée. Add the onion and pulse a few times to blend.

4. Transfer the mixture to a serving bowl and stir in the cilantro, lime juice, cumin, and salt to taste, and serve. The salsa will keep in the refrigerator for about 1 week.

YIELD: 2 CUPS

Toasted Pumpkin Seeds

These seeds are popular in Mexico, where they are known as *pepitas.* Be careful not to eat these in places where there are strict dietary laws forbidding excessive consumption—you might need a twelve-step recovery program to help you and your family deal with the uncontrollable urge to roast and munch on these instead of the more conventional Toll House cookies.

> **1 cup hulled pumpkin seeds**
> **1 teaspoon olive oil**
> **$^1/_2$ teaspoon cayenne pepper**
> **$^1/_2$ teaspoon fine sea salt**

1. Preheat the oven to 375°F.

2. In a bowl, toss together the pumpkin seeds, oil, cayenne, and salt.

3. Spread the seeds on a baking sheet and toast in the oven for 15 minutes.

4. Remove the seeds to a bowl to cool.

YIELD: 1 CUP

Dry-Roasted Seeds with Soy Sauce

There is something incredibly elegant about these fragrant and freshly toasted seeds. The water helps to cook the seeds slowly and draws the oil out from inside, crisping the seeds, preserving them, and making them more digestible. The soy sauce gives the finished seeds a beautiful deep mahogany color.

1 cup hulled sunflower seeds or pumpkin seeds, or a combination of both
1 tablespoon water
1 tablespoon top-quality naturally brewed soy sauce or tamari

1. Preheat the oven to 350°F.

2. Place a heavy skillet (cast iron is best) over medium-high heat. Add the sunflower seeds, water, and soy sauce. Stir the seeds around with a wooden spoon until the steam subsides and the seeds begin to dry out, about 3 to 5 minutes.

3. Transfer the skillet to the oven and roast for 10 minutes. Shake the skillet after 5 minutes to ensure even browning.

4. Scrape the seeds into a bowl and cool until crisp.

YIELD: 1 CUP

Cucumber-Apple Raita

This creamy and cooling cucumber salad can be served with any Indian-style dish, such as curried vegetables and dhal.

2 cups plain whole milk yogurt
1 cucumber, peeled, seeded, and finely diced
1 small Granny Smith or other tart, crisp apple, peeled and finely chopped
2 teaspoons cumin seeds
1/2 teaspoon coriander seeds
2 tablespoons chopped fresh cilantro
1 tablespoon chopped fresh mint
1 tablespoon extra-virgin olive oil
1 tablespoon freshly squeezed lemon juice
1 teaspoon finely grated lemon zest
1 teaspoon coarse sea salt
Small pinch cayenne pepper

1. Spoon the yogurt into a sieve lined with double layer of cheesecloth and let it drain, refrigerated, for 1 hour.

2. In a medium serving bowl, combine the yogurt, cucumber, and apple.

3. Warm a heavy skillet over medium heat. Add the cumin and coriander and toast them, shaking the pan occasionally, for 2 minutes. Transfer the seeds to a plate to cool, then grind to a fine powder in a mortar or clean electric coffee mill. Stir the ground spices into the yogurt mixture.

4. Add the cilantro, mint, oil, lemon juice, lemon zest, salt, and cayenne. Stir well.

5. Refrigerate for 30 minutes prior to serving in order to let the flavors meld.

YIELD: ABOUT 2 1/2 CUPS

Cucumber Raita with Soy

Here's a great vegan version of raita.

> 1 1/2 cups plain Soy Sour Cream (page 391)
> 1 large or 2 small cucumbers, peeled, seeded, and finely chopped
> 1/2 cup grated carrot
> 1/2 small jalapeño pepper, seeded and minced
> 2 teaspoons cumin seeds
> 1/2 teaspoon coriander seeds
> 2 tablespoons chopped fresh cilantro
> 1 tablespoon freshly squeezed lemon juice or to taste
> Coarse sea salt

1. In a medium serving bowl, combine the soy sour cream, cucumber, carrot, and jalapeño pepper.

2. Warm a heavy skillet over medium heat. Add the cumin and coriander and toast, shaking the pan occasionally, for 2 minutes. Transfer the seeds to a plate to cool, then grind them to a fine powder in a mortar or clean electric coffee mill. Stir the ground spices into the soy sour cream mixture.

3. Add the cilantro, lemon juice, and salt to taste and stir well.

4. Refrigerate for 30 minutes prior to serving to allow the flavors to meld.

YIELD: ABOUT 3 CUPS

Savory Yogurt-Cheese Spread

Drained for 12 hours or more, plain yogurt is transformed into a light and tangy cheese, perfect for spreading on toast or as a dip for crudités. It can be left plain or perfumed with the heavenly flavors of fresh herbs, garlic, and extra-virgin olive oil.

> 4 cups plain whole milk yogurt
> 1 tablespoon extra-virgin olive oil
> 2 teaspoons finely chopped fresh herbs, such as thyme, rosemary, or basil

1 small garlic clove, crushed
Coarse sea salt
Freshly milled black pepper

1. Spoon the yogurt into a sieve lined with a double layer of cheesecloth and let it drain, suspended over a bowl in the refrigerator, for 12 hours.

2. Transfer the thickened yogurt to a bowl and whisk in the oil, herbs, garlic, $1/2$ teaspoon salt, and pepper to taste.

3. Let the yogurt sit for 10 minutes to absorb the flavors, then adjust the seasoning, if necessary.

YIELD: 1 CUP

Tangy Yogurt Sauce

This is a great dip for Pita Toasts (page 122) or crudités and a super dressing for a plain cucumber, grated carrot, or chopped crisp celery.

2 teaspoons coriander seeds
1 teaspoon cumin seeds
1 teaspoon caraway seeds
1 teaspoon turmeric
1 teaspoon cayenne pepper
2 cups plain yogurt
Freshly squeezed juice of 1 lime
Coarse sea salt
$1/2$ teaspoon honey or pure maple syrup

1. In a mortar or electric coffee mill, grind the coriander, cumin, and caraway seeds.

2. Transfer the ground spices to a small skillet, and add the turmeric and cayenne. Toast over medium heat for 1 minute, or until fragrant.

3. In a bowl, whisk together the yogurt, toasted spices, lime juice, salt to taste, and honey.

4. Serve at once or store in an airtight container in the refrigerator up to 1 week.

YIELD: 2 CUPS

Basic Yogurt Cream

Lactic acid in cultured dairy products has amazing preservative power. You can substitute tofu if you like—the only thing missing will be the enzymes in yogurt that aid in digestion. Plain, thick yogurt cream is the perfect accompaniment for spicy bean dishes such as Black Bean and Bell Pepper Chili, Chickpea Vegetable Curry, or Refried Beans and Rice.

2 cups plain whole milk yogurt

1. Spoon the yogurt into a sieve lined with a double layer of cheesecloth and let it drain at room temperature, suspended over a bowl, for 2 hours.

2. Serve at once or store in an airtight container in the refrigerator for up to 2 weeks.

YIELD: 1 CUP

Yogurt Cream with Mustard, Red Wine Vinegar, and Dill

This makes a great dip for crudités or Pita Toasts (page 122).

1 cup Basic Yogurt Cream
2 teaspoons whole-grain prepared mustard
1 tablespoon chopped fresh dill
1 teaspoon red wine vinegar
1 teaspoon honey
1 teaspoon coarse sea salt
Freshly milled black pepper

1. In a bowl, whisk together the yogurt cream, mustard, dill, vinegar, honey, salt, and pepper.

2. Allow the cream to absorb the flavors for 10 minutes, then adjust the seasoning if necessary.

YIELD: ABOUT 1 CUP

Yogurt Cream with Cilantro, Cumin, and Lime

Serve this creamy condiment over black beans and rice, Three Sisters Stew with Corn Dumplings (page 65), or Moroccan-Style Vegetable Tagine with Charmoula-Baked Tempeh (page 69).

> 1 teaspoon cumin seeds
> 1 cup Basic Yogurt Cream
> 1 to 2 tablespoons chopped fresh cilantro
> 1 tablespoon extra-virgin olive oil
> 2 teaspoons freshly squeezed lime juice
> $1/2$ small jalapeño pepper, seeded and very finely chopped
> 1 teaspoon coarse sea salt
> $1/2$ teaspoon finely grated lime zest

1. Warm a heavy skillet over medium heat. Add the cumin and toast, shaking the pan occasionally, for 2 minutes. Transfer the seeds to a plate to cool, then grind to a fine powder in a mortar or clean electric coffee mill.

2. In a bowl, whisk together the yogurt cream, cumin, cilantro, oil, lime juice, jalapeño pepper, salt, and lime zest.

3. Allow the cream to absorb the flavors for 15 minutes, then adjust the seasoning if necessary.

YIELD: ABOUT 1 CUP

Yogurt Cream with Curry and Mint

Serve this delicious, refreshing yogurt cream with steamed new potatoes, cauliflower, or cooked chickpeas.

    1 cup Basic Yogurt Cream (page 388)
    1 tablespoon canola oil or light peanut oil
    2 teaspoons freshly squeezed lemon juice
    2 teaspoons finely chopped fresh mint
    1 teaspoon fresh Curry Powder (pages 358 and 359)
    1 teaspoon very finely chopped scallion
    1 teaspoon coarse sea salt
    1/2 teaspoon finely grated lemon zest

1. In a bowl, whisk together the yogurt cream, oil, lemon juice, mint, curry powder, scallion, salt, and lemon zest.

2. Allow the cream to absorb the flavors for 10 minutes, then adjust the seasoning if necessary. YIELD: ABOUT 1 CUP

Crème Fraîche

Your very own crème fraîche is a snap to make, requiring no special equipment, only time and patience. Suddenly, relatively mundane fettuccine alfredo will become an alluring adventure. It is also a classic topping for many desserts, including fruit, brownies, crisps, tarts, and pies. Start your crème fraîche at least 2 days before you plan on serving it. Once the cream is cultured, it will keep for up to a week in the refrigerator.

    1 pint heavy cream (see Note)
    2 tablespoons plain yogurt

1. Bring a large pot of water to a boil. Place 1 quart glass jar or ceramic bowl in the water and boil for 10 minutes to sterilize. Remove to a clean towel to air-dry.

2. In a small saucepan over medium-low heat, heat the cream to lukewarm. Transfer the cream to the sterilized container and stir in the yogurt.

3. Store the cream away from drafts, loosely covered with plastic wrap, for 24 to 36 hours to thicken.

4. Age the cream, tightly covered, in the refrigerator for 24 hours to develop its delicate tangy flavor. Store in the refrigerator for up to 1 week.

YIELD: 2 CUPS

NOTE: For the best result, use a high-quality organic pasteurized cream that has not been ultrapasteurized.

Soy Sour Cream

This all-purpose dairy-free sour cream is pure vegan bliss. Bright white, creamy, and delicious, it is great served over rice and beans, a curried stew, pan-fried polenta, or black bean soup, or used as a dip. As far as variations go, your imagination is the limit. Try adding a seeded roasted jalapeño, fresh tarragon, basil, toasted curry powder, or roasted garlic.

> **1 pound firm tofu, rinsed and squeezed to remove excess moisture**
> **$1/3$ cup pure olive oil or sunflower oil**
> **$1/4$ cup freshly squeezed lemon juice**
> **1 tablespoon cider vinegar**
> **$1^1/2$ teaspoons coarse sea salt**

1. In a food processor fitted with a metal blade, combine the tofu, oil, lemon juice, vinegar, and salt and purée until creamy smooth.

2. Serve immediately. Store in an airtight container in the refrigerator for up to 1 week.

YIELD: $2^1/2$ CUPS

Desserts

A good dessert is a natural extension of the meal—a light and simple conclusion to a nutritious and satisfying dinner. Desserts shouldn't be so heavy that you leave the table feeling overly full and weighed down. Nor should the dessert be over the top in terms of richness, sweetness, or presentation. I like my desserts to be unpretentious and homey rather than precious or perfect.

For the most part, my favorite desserts, in addition to being casual and low in fat, are relatively uncomplicated and easy to execute, making them perfect for the beginning cook. Desserts don't have to be time-consuming, elaborate creations in order to be enjoyed. In fact, one of the nicest desserts I know is made by spooning some drained yogurt over some sweet fresh berries with a little honey drizzled over the top. What could be simpler?

The recipes in this chapter are very forgiving—you won't have to worry about fallen egg whites, overbeaten cream, or seized chocolate. Once you have mastered a few simple techniques, such as dissolving agar, you'll have no problems getting consistent, satisfying results. Another wonderful aspect of these recipes is that they don't require any sophisticated equipment. If you have the basic utensils and a sense of adventure, you are set.

For even better flavor, you can substitute melted butter for the oil in any of these recipes. You can also use dairy, nut, rice, and soy milk interchangeably.

BINDERS

I consciously avoid using soy in desserts. Although it produces a nice, creamy consistency, I find it too heavy and beany tasting. You can achieve the same smooth texture with ingredients such as yogurt, bananas, or agar, which also act as binders and make cakes moist and light.

You will notice that most of the desserts in this chapter are vegan and none require eggs. These recipes were developed over the years in response to students who wanted really good dessert recipes without having to use eggs. The secret is using agar and arrowroot. Agar is a natural sea gelatin that works to congeal liquids. Unlike animal gelatin, which must be refrigerated to set, agar mixtures will thicken at room temperature. The more agar you use, the thicker the mixture will become, eventually gelling to a sliceable consistency.

Arrowroot is a natural vegetable starch that works like cornstarch to thicken liquids into smooth custards. I prefer arrowroot to cornstarch, a by-product of the corn sugar industry, primarily because it's less processed. Arrowroot is also a better thickener for delicate sauces and desserts. I like to use agar and arrowroot in combination because arrowroot maintains a smooth texture and prevents the agar from separating or becoming too hard.

FATS

In vegan baking, the fat issue becomes a big problem. Once you move beyond butter, you are really faced with a conundrum. There are so many different fats out there, it is hard to know which are healthful, which are most stable and will not break down, and which will give you the best results. In my experience, the best vegetable oils for baking are pure olive oil, coconut oil, and corn oil.

Pure olive oil is the most versatile of the three. It bakes well, is relatively flavorless, and is not too heavy. In baking, use extra-virgin olive oil, which is darker and more viscous than pure olive oil, only if you want a dense, pungently olive-flavored cake.

Coconut oil, which has been used for thousands of years in Southeast Asia and Hawaii, is now being produced organically, though it is still relatively expensive and hard to find. It is a good-quality oil that is high in saturated fats and is a grainy-textured solid at room temperature. It has a tropical, fruity flavor that makes it nice to use in desserts like pineapple cake or coconut custard pie. Coconut oil needs to be melted before using because it doesn't have the same creaming ability as butter. It works quite well for crunchy toppings, crispy cookies, and nut crusts, but not for pie crusts and cakes, which won't turn out as tender as you would like. Once it cools off too much, coconut oil contracts, making cakes grainy and spongy. And cakes that use coconut oil will not tenderize if you rewarm them, as butter-based cakes do. But in a warm-from-the-oven coconut cake, it's fabulous.

Good, old-fashioned unrefined corn oil is relatively rich and thick, so I often blend it with another oil. Corn oil gives baked goods a nice golden color. It also has a very pronounced corn flavor, making it a good choice for desserts such as sweet corn bread, or for pie crusts that will hold an assertive filling, such as rhubarb.

I have to admit that when it comes down to it, I most often opt for butter. It is high in saturated fat, which makes it much more stable than unsaturated vegetable oils. I find it performs better, has a better flavor, and is purer than other fats. Butter also has a good creaming ability and produces consistent, reliable results. Although it has been demonized in the health food movement, saturated fat, in moderation, is an important part of the diet. I use butter in relatively small amounts so I get the flavor without an exorbitant amount of fat. For example, my pie crusts generally have half the fat of traditional ones.

SWEETENERS

When I first became enamored of whole foods, the only sweetener I would use was barley malt syrup. On the plus side, it's quite nutritious and not too sweet. But it is also very heavy, and since it is high in maltose, it becomes brittle and hard as it dries after cooking. I found that barley malt syrup was really good for only certain kinds of sweetening, like making crunchy caramel corn or using with another sweetener in a cookie, for example. Nowadays I don't look to dessert for my nutrition—I get that from my meals. The most important thing about desserts is the pleasure you get from eating them, so while my desserts are not overly sweet, I don't get hung up on whether there's some cane sugar in them. Thankfully, today there are good sources of white sugar from companies that are using sustainable agricultural methods, raising the cane organically and doing very low-tech sugar production.

There are two basic types of sweeteners: dry and wet. Of the dry sweeteners, the most unrefined is Sucanat, which is simply pressed cane juice that is heated to the point where the sugar crystallizes. It is a high-quality sweetener, but it is very dark and has a pronounced, slightly bitter molasses flavor. Sucanat works well in dark, rich, heavily flavored desserts, such as spice cake, chocolate cookies, or a peanut butter tart.

Sifted organic cane sugar is my favorite sweetener because it is the most versatile. Cane sugar is flavorless, pale-colored pure sucrose, which doesn't overpower desserts the way Sucanat can. "Sifted" means that the raw sugar has gone through a series of washings to remove the molasses, without the use of bleaches or other chemicals normally used in processing cane sugar.

I've used maple sugar extensively in my cooking. Its texture is comparable to white sugar; however, it makes everything taste like maple. And since maple sugar is almost prohibitively expensive, I find it is best used in small quantities to supplement a blander sweetener.

Maple syrup is cheaper, more readily available than maple sugar, and milder in flavor as well. It comes in several different grades. The grade A light amber is the most expensive and is made with the very first sap of the season. It is sweet, light, and thin and has the most refined maple flavor. Grade A dark amber has a heavier mineral flavor and is less expensive. This is the best syrup for pouring on pancakes and over fruit. Slightly metallic and acidic in flavor, Grade B, the cheapest grade, is the best syrup for baking. However, if you are making something delicate, like a rice pudding, using grade A light amber will result in a lighter color and finer taste.

Honey, which, of course, is not vegan, goes extremely well with fresh fruit and nuts. However, it doesn't bake very well since levulose (the type of sugar in honey) has a propensity to melt and get dense and sticky—just think of traditional honey cakes.

Molasses, another liquid sweetener, is very heavy and strong. It is the by-product of washing cane sugar, so you get an intense mineral flavor. I don't tend to use much molasses, except as an addition to a spice cake or in savory foods, such as barbecue sauces and marinades.

Brown rice syrup and barley malt syrup are both good binders, since they thicken as they cool. They work well in wheat-free baked goods, which lack the binding power of gluten. Brown rice syrup is a little sweeter than barley malt syrup, but I find it has an unpleasant, medicinal aftertaste. Both are better when combined with another liquid sweetener, such as maple syrup, or when used in highly flavored desserts.

Cakes

Vanilla Cake with Warm Plum Sauce

This simple, low-fat cake is a good place to start if you have never baked before. If you like, the sauce can also be used as a topping for ice cream, porridge, or Thick Yogurt Cream (page 407). You really get a big bang for your buck with this recipe.

FOR THE CAKE:
1 1/3 cups unbleached all-purpose flour
2/3 cup whole wheat pastry flour
1 teaspoon baking powder
1 teaspoon baking soda
1/2 teaspoon fine sea salt
1 cup pure maple syrup
2/3 cup water
1/3 cup pure olive oil or melted unsalted butter
2 teaspoons cider vinegar
1 tablespoon vanilla extract

FOR THE SAUCE:
3 pounds Italian prune plums
    or any semiripe black, purple,
    or red plums, halved and pitted
2/3 cup pure maple syrup
2/3 cup apple juice
2 (3-inch) cinnamon sticks
1/8 teaspoon ground cloves
1/4 teaspoon fine sea salt
1 vanilla bean

1. Preheat the oven to 350°F. Lightly oil a 9-inch springform pan and dust it with unbleached white flour.

2. In a mixing bowl, sift together the flours, baking powder, baking soda, and salt.

3. In a separate bowl, whisk together the maple syrup, water, oil, vinegar, and vanilla.

4. Add the wet mixture to the dry mixture and stir just until combined, taking care not to over-mix.

5. Pour the batter into the cake pan and bake for 25 minutes, or until a toothpick inserted near the center comes out clean. Set the cake pan on a rack to cool.

6. Meanwhile, prepare the sauce. In a 3-quart saucepan, combine the plums, maple syrup, apple juice, cinnamon, cloves, and salt. Slice the vanilla bean in half lengthwise and scrape the seeds into the saucepan. Drop in the bean as well. Bring the mixture to a boil over high heat, then reduce the heat to low, cover, and simmer for 20 minutes. Uncover, raise the heat, and boil for 5 minutes, or until the sauce thickens.

7. Remove and discard the vanilla bean and cinnamon sticks. Cool slightly. To serve, unmold the cake from the pan and cut into wedges. Serve with the warm sauce spooned on top.

YIELD: 8 SERVINGS

Chocolate Cake with Raspberry Sauce

This simple cake uses one of my favorite flavor combinations: chocolate and raspberries. It's even better served with homemade Crème Fraîche (page 390) or lightly sweetened Thick Yogurt Cream (page 407).

FOR THE CAKE:

1 cup whole wheat pastry flour

1 cup unbleached all-purpose flour

$1/2$ cup unsweetened cocoa powder

2 teaspoons baking powder

1 teaspoon baking soda

1 teaspoon ground cinnamon

$1/2$ teaspoon fine sea salt

$1 1/2$ cups pure maple syrup

1 cup water

$1/2$ cup pure olive oil or melted unsalted butter

2 teaspoons vanilla extract

1 teaspoon cider vinegar
  or rice vinegar

FOR THE SAUCE:

2 cups raspberries (fresh or frozen)

2 tablespoons pure maple syrup

$1/2$ teaspoon vanilla extract

1. Preheat the oven to 350°F. Lightly oil and flour a 9-inch springform cake pan.

2. In a medium bowl, sift together the flours, cocoa, baking powder, baking soda, cinnamon, and salt. Whisk to combine.

3. In a separate bowl, combine the maple syrup, water, oil, vanilla, and vinegar. Whisk to combine.

4. Using a rubber spatula, stir together the wet and dry ingredients, taking care not to overmix.

5. Scrape the batter into the cake pan and bake for 25 minutes, or until a toothpick inserted near the center comes out clean.

6. Transfer the cake pan to a rack and cool for 30 minutes before releasing the springform.

7. Meanwhile, make the sauce. In a blender or food processor, purée the raspberries. Strain to remove the seeds. Stir in the maple syrup and vanilla.

8. To serve, cut the cake into wedges and pour the sauce over them, or serve on the side.

YIELD: 8 SERVINGS

Spice Cake

It might sound odd, but the black pepper in this recipe is a marvelous addition to a mix of sweet spices. Just a pinch helps bring out the spiciness and molasses flavor of the moist, dark cake. This cake is particularly good served with a warm sauce. Try using the sauce recipe for the Vanilla Cake (page 398) and substitute pears, apples, or figs for the plums. A dollop of sweetened Thick Yogurt Cream (page 407) is also recommended.

1/2 cup plain, unflavored soy milk
1/2 cup pure maple syrup
6 tablespoons molasses
6 tablespoons canola oil or melted unsalted butter
1 tablespoon vanilla extract
2 teaspoons cider vinegar
1 cup whole wheat pastry flour
1 cup unbleached all-purpose flour
2 tablespoons ground ginger
2 1/2 teaspoons ground cinnamon
1 1/2 teaspoons baking soda
1 1/2 teaspoons baking powder
1/2 teaspoon fine sea salt
1/4 teaspoon ground cloves
1/4 teaspoon ground nutmeg
Pinch freshly milled black pepper

1. Preheat the oven to 350°F. Lightly oil an 8-inch-square baking pan and dust it with flour.

2. In a medium bowl, whisk the soy milk, maple syrup, molasses, oil, vanilla, and vinegar.

3. In a separate bowl, sift together the flours, ginger, cinnamon, baking soda, baking powder, salt, cloves, nutmeg, and pepper.

4. Fold the dry ingredients into the wet mixture with a rubber spatula, taking care not to overmix.

5. Pour into the baking dish and bake for 30 minutes, or until toothpick inserted near the center comes out clean.

6. Allow the cake to cool, in the baking dish, to room temperature before slicing.

YIELD: 8 SERVINGS

Pies, Tarts, and Fruit Desserts

Pumpkin Pie

This pie is a great example of how agar and arrowroot work in concert to thicken the sweetened pumpkin into a sliceable, custardy pie filing. Squat, light-fleshed cheese pumpkin is my favorite variety; but if you can't find it, use creamy butternut squash.

If you don't want to use the butter crust, try the vegan crust on page 405.

FOR THE CRUST:
1/2 cup whole wheat pastry flour
1/2 cup unbleached all-purpose flour
2 teaspoons white or brown sugar
1/4 teaspoon fine sea salt
9 tablespoons cold unsalted butter, thinly sliced
1/4 cup ice cold water

FOR THE FILLING:
3 pounds cheese pumpkin or butternut squash,
    halved, seeds removed and skin left on
    (or 4 cups cooked puréed pumpkin)
1/2 cup coconut milk, soy milk, or dairy milk
1/2 cup pure maple syrup
4 1/2 teaspoons agar flakes
2 teaspoons vanilla extract
2 tablespoons arrowroot powder
2 tablespoons melted butter or canola oil
1 teaspoon ground cinnamon
1 teaspoon ground ginger
1/2 teaspoon fine sea salt
1/4 teaspoon freshly grated nutmeg

1. To make the crust, combine the flours, sugar, and salt in a bowl. Whisk to combine. Rub the butter into the flour mixture with your fingertips or cut it in with a pair of knives until the mixture resembles sand with pebbles. Add the water and mix gently just until it forms a dough. If the dough feels too dry, add more water, 1 teaspoon at a time. Gather the dough into a ball and transfer it to a clean surface. Shape the dough into a disk and wrap in plastic or wax paper. Let the dough rest in the refrigerator for at least 30 minutes or up to 2 days. (The dough can be frozen for up to 2 months and thawed in the refrigerator before using.)

2. Preheat the oven to 350°F. Lightly butter a 9- or 10-inch pie plate.

3. To make the filling, put the pumpkin cut-side down in a baking dish. Add 1 cup hot water and bake for 1 hour, or until the flesh pierces easily with a knife. Set the squash aside to cool.

4. Remove the dough from the refrigerator and allow it to warm up for 10 to 15 minutes. This will make the dough more pliable and easier to roll.

5. In a saucepan over medium heat, combine the milk and maple syrup and bring to a simmer. Add the agar flakes and cook for 5 to 7 minutes, stirring from time to time, until the agar dissolves (see How to Dissolve Agar, page 415). Stir in the vanilla and turn off the heat.

6. Peel the skin from the pumpkin. In a food processor fitted with a metal blade, combine the pumpkin flesh, agar mixture, arrowroot, butter, cinnamon, ginger, salt, and nutmeg. Purée until creamy and smooth.

7. Unwrap the dough and transfer to a lightly floured surface. With a rolling pin, roll the dough into a 12-inch circle. Roll the dough onto the pin and unroll it into the pie plate. Gently press the dough into the bottom and sides of the plate. Trim the edges with a knife. Indent the rim of the dough all the way around with the tines of a fork. Pour in the filling and smooth the top with a wet spatula.

8. Bake for 70 minutes, or until the top is lightly browned, with a few thin cracks breaking the surface.

9. Cool on a wire rack for 1 hour, or until the pie has firmed up. Serve.

YIELD: 6 TO 8 SERVINGS

For pies and tarts I use three basic crusts: butter, oil, and nut. Within each recipe you can vary the type of flour, nut, or flavoring—simply use the same proportions and techniques.

Traditional butter crusts use lots of chilled butter, which is rubbed into the flour to make flaky, French-style pastry. Butter crusts are probably the trickiest to make, since the ingredients must be chilled and it is easy to accidentally overwork the dough. Oil crusts are easier to work with (see page 411), since they are less fragile and don't have to be kept cold. But oil crusts can never be as flaky as butter crusts. Lastly, there are nut crusts, which are the easiest of all. They won't get tough, since they're made with less flour than normal crusts. And nut crusts are pressed into a pan rather than rolled out. If you are afraid of pastry, this is a good place to start.

Rolled Pie Pastry

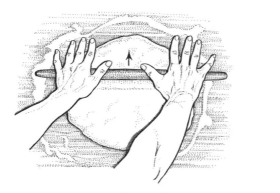 

Unwrap the dough and transfer it to a lightly floured work surface. Lightly flour the surface of the dough and press it into a disk. Roll the disk in the same direction from the center to the edge. Rotate the dough after each roll.

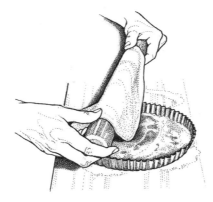

Drape the dough over the pin and transfer it to a pie or tart pan.

Strawberry-Rhubarb Pie

This is a classic springtime pie. The corn oil in the crust gives it a rich golden color, while the assertive flavor of the strawberries and rhubarb work to balance its slight corn flavor.

FOR THE FILLING:
1 pound rhubarb, sliced into 1-inch-thick pieces
3 pints strawberries, hulled, large ones halved
1 cup cane sugar
$1/2$ teaspoon fine sea salt
1 tablespoon freshly squeezed lemon juice
1 teaspoon finely grated lemon zest
$1/4$ cup arrowroot powder

FOR THE CRUST:
2 cups unbleached all-purpose flour
1 cup whole wheat pastry flour
2 tablespoons cane sugar
$1/2$ teaspoon fine sea salt
$1/2$ teaspoon baking powder
$1/2$ cup unrefined corn oil
$1/2$ cup cold water

1. To make the filling, in a bowl, combine the rhubarb, strawberries, sugar, and salt. Toss to combine and set aside for 1 hour. The rhubarb and strawberries will release their juices and form a syrup.

2. To make the crust, combine the flours, sugar, salt, and baking powder in a bowl and mix well. Drizzle in the oil and rub with your fingertips until it is evenly distributed and the mixture resembles wet sand. Stir in the water and mix briefly to form a mass. If the dough seems too dry, add additional water, 1 teaspoon at a time, until the dough is soft and marbled in appearance. Divide the dough in half and pat each piece into a disk. Wrap in plastic and let rest in the refrigerator for 1 hour.

3. Strain the strawberry/rhubarb juices into a small saucepan. Whisk in the lemon juice, lemon zest, and arrowroot. Cook over medium heat, stirring, for 1 to 2 minutes, until the syrup thickens and become clear. Stir the syrup back into the fruit.

4. Preheat the oven to 450°F.

5. Unwrap the dough and transfer it to a lightly floured work surface. Roll each piece into a 12-inch circle. Line a 9-inch pie plate with one piece of dough. Fill with the fruit and cover with the second piece of dough. Trim the edges and press with the back of a fork to seal. Cut a 2-inch X in the top to allow steam to escape.

6. Place the pie on a cookie sheet (this will prevent any spills from the bubbling fruit while the pie bakes) and bake for 15 minutes. Reduce the oven temperature to 350°F and bake for 1 hour, or until the crust is golden and the fruit is bubbling and tender.

7. Cool the pie on a rack for 1 hour before serving.

8. Serve warm or chilled.

YIELD: 6 TO 8 SERVINGS

THICK YOGURT CREAM

Drained yogurt can form the base for delicious dessert toppings. And since yogurt is rich in lactic acid, it is also a great after-dinner digestive. To make it, place a sieve lined with several layers of cheesecloth over a bowl. Pour in 1 quart of plain whole milk yogurt and gently twist the ends of the cheesecloth together. Let it drain in the refrigerator for 2 to 3 hours. At this point the yogurt will have thickened into a creamy dessert topping. Sweeten the strained yogurt to taste with brown sugar, organic sifted cane sugar, maple syrup, honey, or molasses.

To turn the drained yogurt into a spreadable cheese for bread or crackers, place a weighted plate on top of the cheesecloth bundle and drain for an additional 12 hours. The cloudy liquid that collects in the bowl is the whey, and can be used in place of buttermilk in quick breads, waffles, and muffins. I also use it to ferment my morning porridge and to make crème fraîche.

Biscuits with Seasonal Fruit and Sweet Yogurt Cream

This recipe makes a tender, not-too-sweet biscuit that goes well with lightly stewed or freshly marinated fruits. In the late fall and winter, try cooking some sliced pears and apples in a little bit of juice until they become soft and using them in place of the berries or stone fruits. Or substitute your own Crème Fraîche (page 390) for the Yogurt Cream.

FOR THE YOGURT CREAM AND WHEY:
1 quart whole milk plain yogurt
3 tablespoons honey, pure maple syrup, or cane sugar
1/2 teaspoon vanilla extract
   or finely grated lemon zest

FOR THE BISCUITS:
1 cup whole wheat pastry flour
1 cup unbleached all-purpose flour
1/4 cup cane sugar or Sucanat
2 teaspoons baking powder
1/2 teaspoon baking soda
1/2 teaspoon fine sea salt
6 tablespoons unsalted butter, cut into pieces
   (or substitute 6 tablespoons corn oil or canola oil)
3/4 cup whey or 2/3 cup water mixed with 1 tablespoon lemon juice

FOR THE FRUIT:
1 quart sliced soft summer fruits,
   such as peeled peaches, nectarines,
   strawberries, blueberries, raspberries,
   blackberries, or a mixture of several
Honey or cane sugar

1. Spoon the yogurt into a sieve lined with a double layer of cheesecloth. Place the sieve in the refrigerator and let it drain until it is nice and thick, about 8 hours or overnight (see Thick Yogurt Cream, page 407).

2. Reserve the whey that collects in the bowl. Set 3/4 cup aside for the biscuits. (Reserve the remainder for porridge, pickles, or more biscuits. It will keep for up to a week in the refrigerator.)

3. In a small bowl, combine the thickened yogurt cream, honey, and vanilla. Add additional honey to taste, if desired. Refrigerate until needed.

4. When you are ready to make the biscuits, preheat the oven to 400°F. Lightly grease a baking sheet or jellyroll pan or line with parchment paper.

5. In a mixing bowl, combine the flours, sugar, baking powder, baking soda, and salt.

6. Add the butter and rub it in with your fingertips until the mixture resembles cornmeal.

7. Add the $3/4$ cup whey and mix with a fork just until the dough comes together in a mass. Do not overmix the dough or the biscuits will be tough.

8. Scoop out dollops of the dough, $1/3$ cup at a time, and space them 2 inches apart on the baking sheet. Bake until the biscuits are lightly browned and a toothpick inserted near the center of one comes out clean, about 25 minutes.

9. Meanwhile, toss the fruits with the sweetener and set aside until they release their juices.

10. When the biscuits are done, transfer them to a wire rack to cool slightly. Slice them in half and top with the fruit and the sweetened yogurt cream. Serve at once.

YIELD: 6 SERVINGS

Walnut Tart

Intensely sweet and gooey, this tart satisfies the kid in all of us.

FOR THE CRUST:
1 cup shelled walnuts, halves and pieces
1 cup whole wheat pastry flour
1/8 teaspoon fine sea salt
1/4 cup pure maple syrup
1/4 cup melted unsalted butter or coconut oil

FOR THE FILLING:
1 1/2 cups coarsely chopped walnuts
1 cup water, plus 3 tablespoons
5 teaspoons agar flakes
3/4 cup pure maple syrup
1/2 cup brown rice syrup
1/4 cup barley malt syrup
1/8 teaspoon fine sea salt
1 tablespoon arrowroot powder
1 teaspoon vanilla extract

1. Preheat the oven to 350°F.

2. To make the crust, combine the walnuts, flour, and salt in a food processor fitted with a metal blade, and grind to a fine meal. Add the maple syrup and butter and pulse a few times to form a dough.

3. Transfer the dough to a 9-inch tart pan with a removable bottom. Lay a piece of plastic wrap on top and press the dough into the pan, making sure the bottom and sides are evenly covered (see opposite). Trim the crust. Prick the dough all over with a fork.

4. Bake for 20 minutes, or until lightly browned. Transfer the crust to a rack to cool.

5. To make the filling, spread the walnuts on a baking sheet and toast in the oven for 8 minutes. Turn off the oven.

6. In a 2-quart saucepan, combine the 1 cup water and agar flakes and bring to boil over high heat. Reduce the heat and simmer until the agar is completely dissolved (see How to Dissolve Agar, page 415). Stir in the maple syrup, rice syrup, barley malt syrup, and salt and return to a simmer.

7. In a small bowl, whisk together the arrowroot, 3 tablespoons water, and vanilla until no lumps remain. Stir into the saucepan and cook for 2 minutes.

8. Turn off the heat and stir in the toasted walnuts. Pour the filling into the cooled tart crust and chill in the refrigerator until firm, about 1 hour.

9. Serve chilled.

YIELD: 6 TO 8 SERVINGS

Pressed Tart Pastry

Place the dough in the middle of a lightly greased tart pan.

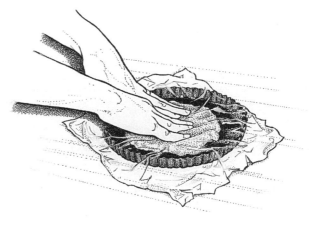

Lay a piece of plastic wrap over the dough and press into an even circle.

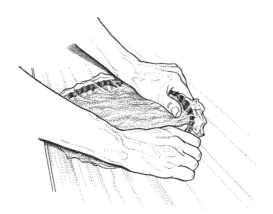

Press the dough up the sides of the pan.

Prick the pastry with a fork and bake until golden brown.

Coconut Cream Tart

I love coconut milk. It is a great staple to have on hand when you want to whip up a simple dessert. And for a scrumptious way to get a little more chocolate into your life, see the chocolate-coconut variation below.

FOR THE CRUST:

4 tablespoons unsalted butter
   or coconut oil, melted
4 tablespoons pure maple syrup
1 cup whole wheat pastry flour
1 cup unsweetened shredded coconut
$1/4$ teaspoon fine sea salt

FOR THE FILLING:

2 (14-ounce) cans coconut milk
   (light or regular)
$1/2$ cup cane sugar
$1/4$ cup agar flakes
1 (2-inch) cinnamon stick
$1/8$ teaspoon fine sea salt
$1/2$ vanilla bean
   or 1 teaspoon vanilla extract
$1/2$ cup cold water
$1/4$ cup arrowroot powder

FOR THE TOPPING:

$1/2$ cup unsweetened shredded coconut
1 tablespoon pure maple syrup
1 teaspoon cane sugar

1. Preheat the oven to 350°F. Lightly grease a 9-inch tart pan that has a removable bottom with butter or coconut oil.

2. To make the crust, combine the butter and maple syrup in a mixing bowl. Allow the mixture to cool, then add the flour, coconut, and salt. Stir well to combine.

3. Press the dough into the pan with moist fingertips (see page 411). Use your thumbs to press the dough into the fluted sides of the pan. There will be enough dough to completely fill the pan. Prick the dough several times with a fork.

4. Bake for 20 minutes, or until golden brown. Transfer the tart shell to a rack to cool. Turn the oven off.

4. To make the filling, combine the coconut milk, sugar, agar flakes, cinnamon, and salt in a saucepan. If using, split the vanilla bean in half lengthwise and scrape the seeds onto a plate. Add the seeds along with the pod to the pan and bring the mixture to a boil over medium heat. Otherwise, simply add the vanilla extract. Reduce the heat to low and simmer for 6 to 8 minutes, stirring occasionally, until the agar dissolves (see How to Dissolve Agar, page 415).

5. In a small bowl, combine the cold water and arrowroot and whisk until smooth. Pour into the pan and simmer, whisking constantly, for 1 minute. Remove the cinnamon stick and vanilla pod. Pour the filling into the tart shell. Set aside to cool.

6. To make the topping, combine the coconut, maple syrup, and sugar in a heavy skillet over medium heat. Stir constantly until the coconut turns golden brown, 4 to 6 minutes (take care, because coconut can burn easily). Transfer the coconut to a plate and let cool. Sprinkle the topping over the tart and refrigerate until firm, about 1 hour.

7. Serve chilled.

YIELD: 6 TO 8 SERVINGS

VARIATION: CHOCOLATE-COCONUT CUSTARD

Add $1/2$ cup unsweetened cocoa powder to the filling ingredients. Increase the amount of cane sugar to $2/3$ cup and add an additional $1/2$ cup Sucanat.

USING TART FILLINGS AS PUDDINGS

Using any of the tart recipes in this chapter, you can choose to serve the filling on its own, as a pudding. If the agar has made the filling too firm, purée it in a blender or food processor with a little water or juice and it will turn into a mousse. Pour the pudding into individual serving cups and chill before serving.

Lemon Tart with Toasted Almond Crust

Here is my variation of a wonderful lemon tart that my dear friend Myra Kornfield developed during the years we spent cooking together at Angelica Kitchen in New York. I made my first lemon tart about seventeen years ago using a sunflower crust. Although the filling was flavored with lemon juice and lemon zest, I did not yet know about the amazing powers of turmeric, which lends the custard a sunny yellow hue, the color egg yolks impart to a traditional tart. My old tart had a great lemon flavor but not the lemon look—it turned out sort of brown.

Since I think coconut and lemon are fabulous together, I decided to base the filling on coconut milk. I also add yogurt for a little bit of richness. You can substitute soy yogurt if you like.

FOR THE CRUST:

1 cup slivered almonds

4 tablespoons unsalted butter or coconut oil, melted

4 tablespoons pure maple syrup

1 cup whole wheat pastry flour

1/4 teaspoon fine sea salt

FOR THE FILLING:

1 (14-ounce) can coconut milk

1 1/2 cups water

1 cup cane sugar

4 tablespoons agar flakes

1/8 teaspoon turmeric

1/2 cup freshly squeezed lemon juice

1 1/2 tablespoons finely grated lemon zest

2 teaspoons vanilla extract

1/4 cup arrowroot powder

1/2 cup plain whole milk yogurt

1. Preheat the oven to 350°F. Lightly grease a 9-inch tart pan that has a removable bottom with butter or coconut oil.

2. Spread the almonds on a baking sheet and toast for 8 minutes. Set the almonds aside on a plate to cool before grinding them to a fine meal in a mortar, food processor, or clean coffee mill.

3. In a bowl, combine the butter and maple syrup. Allow the mixture to cool slightly, then add the almond meal, flour, and salt. Stir well to combine.

4. Press the dough into the tart pan with moistened fingertips (see page 411). Use your thumbs to press the dough into the fluted sides of the pan. There will be just enough dough to completely fill the pan. Prick the dough several times with a fork.

5. Bake for 20 minutes, or until golden brown. Transfer the tart shell to a rack to cool. Turn the oven off.

6. To make the filling, in a saucepan over medium heat, combine the coconut milk, 1 cup of the water, sugar, agar, and turmeric and simmer until the agar dissolves. Stir in the lemon juice, lemon zest, and vanilla. Raise the heat and bring to a boil.

7. Dissolve the arrowroot in $1/2$ cup water, then stir into the saucepan and cook for 1 minute, or until the mixture thickens. Remove the pan from the heat and whisk in the yogurt until the mixture is creamy smooth. Pour the filling into the tart shell and cool at room temperature before refrigerating until firm and chilled, about 1 to 2 hours.

8. Serve chilled.

YIELD: 6 TO 8 SERVINGS

HOW TO DISSOLVE AGAR

Agar, a natural sea gelatin, is sold in bars, flakes, and a concentrated powder. Of the three, I prefer the flakes because they are the most widely available and most convenient to work with. To use it, agar must first be dissolved by boiling it in liquid.

Simply stir or whisk the flakes into whatever liquid the recipe calls for, bring the mixture to a boil, and simmer for about 5 to 8 minutes. (Keep in mind that agar can lose its strength if it is boiled too hard or for too long.) Some flakes will probably sink to the bottom, so you will have to stir the agar for the first couple of minutes to incorporate them. To see if the agar is ready, dip a metal spoon into the mixture and examine it. If you see any flakes, keep simmering and stirring; if it's completely clear, then it's ready to use.

Apple Crumb Tart

This maple-scented dessert crosses a cozy apple crumble with a sophisticated fruit tart.
If you're not averse to using butter, try melting some and substituting it for the oil.
It will give you an even better tasting crust and topping.

FOR THE CRUST:

$1/2$ cup whole wheat pastry flour

$1/2$ cup unbleached all-purpose flour

$2 1/4$ teaspoons maple sugar or Sucanat

$1/2$ teaspoon baking powder

$1/8$ teaspoon fine sea salt

$4 1/2$ tablespoons pure olive oil
    or melted unsalted butter

$1/3$ cup cold water

FOR THE FILLING:

$1 1/2$ pounds apples, such as Golden Delicious,
    Gala, Winesap, or Mutsu,
    peeled, cored, and sliced into $1/8$-inch-thick wedges

2 tablespoons pure maple syrup

2 tablespoons maple sugar or Sucanat

1 tablespoon arrowroot powder

1 teaspoon freshly squeezed lemon juice

$1/2$ teaspoon ground cinnamon

FOR THE TOPPING:

1 cup whole wheat pastry flour

$1/3$ cup maple sugar or Sucanat

$1/2$ teaspoon baking powder

$1/8$ teaspoon fine sea salt

5 tablespoons pure olive oil
    or melted unsalted butter

1. Preheat the oven to 375°F. Lightly oil a 9-inch tart pan with a removable bottom.

2. To make the crust, whisk together the flours, maple sugar, baking powder, and salt in a medium bowl. Drizzle in the oil and stir with a wooden spoon until just mixed. Add the water

and stir lightly to form the dough into a ball. The dough should have a marbled appearance. Place the dough between two sheets of wax paper or parchment and roll into a 10-inch circle, $1/8$-inch thick. Transfer the dough to the tart pan. Press the dough into the rim and trim the excess dough by rolling the pin across the rim of the pan. Refrigerate the crust while you prepare the filling.

3. In a large bowl, combine the apples, maple syrup, maple sugar, arrowroot, lemon juice, and cinnamon and toss well.

4. To make the topping, in the same bowl that you used for the crust dough, combine the flour, maple sugar, baking powder, and salt and mix well with a whisk. Add the oil and toss with your fingertips until the mixture resembles wet sand with pebbles.

5. Remove the tart pan from the refrigerator and fill with the apple mixture. Spread the crumb topping evenly over the filling.

6. Bake for 50 minutes, or until the apples are bubbling and the topping is nicely browned.

7. Cool the tart for at least 20 minutes.

8. Serve warm or at room temperature.

YIELD: 6 TO 8 SERVINGS

Baked Apples with Nut Stuffing and Cider-Raisin Sauce

This comforting dessert is almost like an inverted apple crisp—instead of topping the fruit with an oat mixture, we're stuffing it.

6 baking apples, such as Rome, Cortland, or Mutsu
Juice of half a lemon
$1/2$ cup raisins
$1/2$ cup brown sugar
$1/3$ cup chopped walnuts
$1/3$ cup whole wheat pastry flour
$1/3$ cup rolled oats
$1/4$ cup light sesame oil
    or unsalted butter at room temperature
1 teaspoon ground cinnamon
$1/2$ teaspoon ground ginger
$1/4$ teaspoon fine sea salt
1 cup apple cider
$1/2$ cup water
2 cinnamon sticks
1 teaspoon vanilla extract

1. Preheat the oven to 350°F.

2. Core the apples. Peel a $1/2$-inch band of skin around the tops of the apples and sprinkle with lemon juice.

3. Scatter the raisins on the bottom of a baking dish and place the apples on top.

4. In a larger bowl, combine the brown sugar, walnuts, flour, oats, oil, cinnamon, ginger, and salt. Fill each apple with some of the stuffing.

5. In a saucepan over high heat, combine the cider, water, cinnamon sticks, and vanilla and bring to a boil. Pour the liquid into the pan around the apples, not over them.

6. Bake the apples for 45 minutes, basting every 10 to 15 minutes, until tender.

7. Use a slotted spoon to transfer the baked apples to a platter. Pour the pan juices and raisins into a saucepan and reduce over high heat until slightly thickened. Pour the sauce over the apples.

8. Cool for about 15 to 20 minutes before serving.

YIELD: 6 SERVINGS

VARIATION: BAKED APPLES WITH CARAMEL SAUCE

If you want to gild the lily, try topping the baked apples with this ultra-easy caramel sauce, which is also excellent over ice cream.

To make the dish, omit the raisins from the original recipe and bake the stuffed apples in water rather than in cider. Transfer the baked apples to a platter and proceed to make the sauce.

In a saucepan over medium heat, combine $1\frac{1}{2}$ cups brown rice syrup, $\frac{1}{2}$ cup maple syrup, $\frac{1}{2}$ cup soy or dairy milk, 2 teaspoons vanilla extract, and 1 teaspoon cider vinegar. Bring to a boil. Reduce the heat to as low as possible and simmer, uncovered, for 8 to 10 minutes. Drizzle the warm sauce over the apples, or serve on the side.

Pear-Cranberry Crisp

You can use this nubby, all-purpose vegan crisp topping in combination with any seasonal fruit. Try substituting peaches and blueberries in the summer, apples and raisins in the winter, or strawberries and rhubarb in the spring.

FOR THE FILLING:

3 pounds pears, peeled, cored, and sliced

$1/2$ cup fresh or frozen cranberries

$1/2$ cup apple or pear juice

3 to 4 tablespoons pure maple syrup

2 teaspoons arrowroot powder

1 teaspoon vanilla extract

1 teaspoon ground ginger

$1/8$ teaspoon fine sea salt

FOR THE TOPPING:

1 cup rolled oats

1 cup whole wheat pastry flour

1 cup coarsely chopped pecans (or almonds or walnuts)

$1/3$ cup light sesame oil, canola oil, or softened unsalted butter

$1/3$ cup pure maple syrup

1 teaspoon vanilla extract

$1/2$ teaspoon fine sea salt

1. Preheat the oven to 375°F.

2. To make the filling, toss together in a large bowl the pears, cranberries, apple juice, maple syrup, arrowroot, vanilla, ginger, and salt.

3. To make the topping, combine the oats, flour, pecans, oil, maple syrup, vanilla, and salt in a separate bowl and mix well.

4. Pour the fruit into a 2-quart baking dish and cover with the topping. Cover the dish with foil (shiny side down).

5. Bake for 40 minutes. Uncover and bake for 15 minutes more, or until the topping is crisp and golden and the fruits bubbling.

6. Serve warm. YIELD: 6 SERVINGS

Puddings

Lemon Rice Pudding

This is the easiest rice pudding ever. Cooked on top of the stove, the ingredients are just simmered and stirred until the plump arborio rice absorbs the coconut milk and turns creamy and suave. And the addition of lemon juice and zest really packs a pucker!

You can dress up the pudding as a parfait, layered with fresh raspberries or diced pineapple and topped with sweet toasted coconut.

  4 cups coconut milk
  2 cups water
  1 cup arborio rice
  1 cup cane sugar
  $1/2$ teaspoon fine sea salt
  1 vanilla bean
  $1/2$ cup freshly squeezed lemon juice
  2 teaspoons finely grated lemon zest

1. In a medium heavy-bottomed pot, combine the coconut milk, water, rice, sugar, and salt. Split the vanilla bean lengthwise and scrape the seeds into the pot. Drop in the pod in as well. Bring to a boil over high heat, then reduce the heat to low and simmer for 40 minutes, stirring occasionally to prevent sticking.

2. Remove and discard the vanilla bean. Stir in lemon juice and lemon zest.

3. Pour the pudding into a serving bowl or individual cups and chill for 1 hour before serving.

YIELD: 6 TO 8 SERVINGS

Almond Custard with Mixed-Berry Parfait

This recipe is loosely based on a traditional Provençal custard made with eggs, milk, and semolina flour. My version substitutes arrowroot and agar for the eggs and sweet almond milk for the dairy.

The flavor of almond milk is only as good as your almonds. Always buy fresh, whole almonds and store them unpeeled. You'll be able to taste the difference if you blanch and peel the nuts right before you make the custard.

FOR THE SAUCE:
4 cups mixed fresh berries
1/3 cup cane sugar or maple syrup
Freshly squeezed juice of 1 lemon
1/2 teaspoon vanilla extract

FOR THE CUSTARD:
4 cups water
2 cups whole almonds, peeled
  (see How to Peel Almonds, page 377)
1 cup plus 2 tablespoons pure maple syrup or honey
1/2 cup agar flakes
1 teaspoon almond extract
1 vanilla bean
1 1/2 cups cold water
1/2 teaspoon fine sea salt
7 tablespoons semolina flour

1. To make the sauce, combine the berries, sugar, lemon juice, and vanilla in a bowl. Refrigerate for 2 hours or overnight.

2. To make the custard, combine the water and almonds in a blender and blend until smooth. Strain through two layers of damp cheesecloth and squeeze to extract 1 quart almond milk. Discard the solids.

3. Pour the almond milk into a 3-quart saucepan. Add the maple syrup, agar flakes, and almond extract. Split the vanilla bean lengthwise and scrape the seeds into the milk. Bring to

a simmer over medium heat, then lower the heat and whisk continuously for 2 to 3 minutes, until the agar dissolves (see How to Dissolve Agar, page 415).

4. In a separate saucepan over high heat, combine the cold water, salt, and semolina flour and whisk constantly until the mixture thickens. Turn off the heat and add to the almond milk, stirring to combine.

5. Pour the custard into a 2-quart pan and refrigerate until set, about 30 minutes.

6. In a food processor, purée the custard until creamy. Layer the custard and berry sauce in individual wineglasses and serve immediately or refrigerate.   YIELD: 4 TO 6 SERVINGS

Chocolate Mousse

The sweet spiciness of cinnamon tames the slight bitterness of the chocolate and lends a warming note to this Mexican-inspired mousse.

> **2 (14-ounce) cans coconut milk**
> **1 cup plus 2 tablespoons Sucanat**
> **1/2 cup agar flakes**
> **1/2 cup unsweetened cocoa powder**
> **1 teaspoon vanilla extract**
> **1 teaspoon ground cinnamon**
> **1/8 teaspoon fine sea salt**
> **3/4 cup cold water**
> **1/4 cup arrowroot powder**

1. In a saucepan over high heat, combine the coconut milk, Sucanat, agar flakes, cocoa, vanilla, cinnamon, and salt. Bring to a boil. Reduce the heat to low and simmer for 6 to 8 minutes, stirring occasionally, until the agar dissolves (see How to Dissolve Agar, page 415).

2. In a small bowl, whisk together the cold water and arrowroot until smooth. Whisk into the saucepan and simmer for 1 minute, or until the mousse thickens.

3. Pour the mousse into a 2-quart dish and let cool at room temperature for 15 minutes. Refrigerate for 30 minutes, or until firm.

4. Transfer the mousse to a food processor and purée until creamy.

5. Serve chilled in individual cups or wineglasses.   YIELD: 6 SERVINGS

Fruit Kanten

Over the last 25 years, kanten has become a standard vegan dessert, and with good reason. This wobbly, Jell-O–like dessert is fat-free, yet has an intense fruit flavor.

To make it, you can use any type of fruit juice, nectar, or herbal tea. Those that are more acidic, such as pineapple or strawberry, may need more agar. Here's the test: Once the agar is dissolved, place a spoonful on a plate in the freezer. Check it in 5 minutes to see if it has set. If it is runny, you'll need to add a bit more agar.

You can use any fruit you like. Keep in mind that while soft fruits, such as pears, berries, and melons, are best left uncooked, you might want to cook firmer fruits, such as apples, before pouring over the kanten.

> 4 cups fruit juice
> 1/4 cup agar flakes
> 1/2 vanilla bean
> 2 tablespoons cold fruit juice
> 1 tablespoon arrowroot powder
> 3 cups ripe fruit, such as pears, peaches,
>   or nectarines, peeled and diced,
>   or whole berries

1. In a 2-quart saucepan, combine the juice and agar flakes. Split the vanilla bean in half lengthwise and scrape the seeds into the saucepan. Drop in the bean, too. Bring to a simmer and cook gently until agar is dissolved, about 8 minutes (see How to Dissolve Agar, page 415).

2. In a small bowl, combine the fruit juice and arrowroot and blend well. Add it to the saucepan, stirring well, and cook for 1 minute. Remove and discard the vanilla bean.

3. Place the fruit in an attractive serving bowl, pour on the cooked juice, and allow to cool to room temperature, about 20 minutes.

4. Refrigerate until set.

5. Serve chilled.

YIELD: 6 TO 8 SERVINGS

Strawberry-Apple Kanten

3^1/$_2$ cups plus 2 tablespoons cold apple cider
1 pint strawberries
^{1}/$_4$ cup agar flakes
1 tablespoon arrowroot powder

1. In a blender, combine 1 cup of the cider and 1 cup of the strawberries and liquefy. Strain through a fine mesh strainer or cheesecloth to get 1^1/$_2$ cups strawberry juice.

2. In a 2-quart saucepan, combine the strawberry juice, 2^1/$_2$ cups cider, and the agar flakes and bring to a boil. Reduce heat and simmer until the agar dissolves (see How to Dissolve Agar, page 415).

3. In a small bowl, combine the remaining 2 tablespoons cider and arrowroot powder and mix well. Add to the saucepan and simmer for 1 minute. Pour into a shallow 2- to 3-quart-capacity pan and refrigerate.

4. While the kanten is cooling, slice the remaining cup of strawberries.

5. In a blender or food processor, blend the chilled kanten until creamy. Fold in the sliced strawberries and serve.

YIELD: 6 TO 8 SERVINGS

PRALINES

Pralines add a crispy crunch when served with kantens, hot cereal, ice cream, or any smooth, comforting, custardy dessert.

1 cup slivered or sliced almonds or pecans
2 tablespoons pure maple syrup
2 tablespoons maple sugar

Preheat the oven to 350°F. In a small bowl, combine the slivered or sliced almonds or pecans, pure maple syrup, and maple sugar. Mix well. Spread the mixture on a baking sheet and bake for 30 minutes, stirring occasionally. Scrape the pralines onto a plate and let cool until crunchy.

YIELD: ABOUT 1 CUP

Brownies and Cookies

My mother used to say, "Peter darling, never arrive empty-handed when someone invites you to their home!" A tin of homemade cookies is just the present to bring along. To give something made from our own hands is to share the joy in our hearts and express our love and appreciation. Isn't that the reason we become cooks and chefs in the first place? Here are a few of my favorite cookie and brownie recipes.

Chocolate Chip Brownies

These bars are everything a brownie should be: chewy, gooey, and packed with chocolate.

>   1 cup canola oil
>   1 cup pure maple syrup
> $1/2$ cup soy milk
>   1 tablespoon vanilla extract
>   1 cup whole wheat pastry flour
>   1 cup unbleached all-purpose flour
>   1 cup unsweetened cocoa powder
> $3/4$ cup cane sugar
> $1/2$ cup Sucanat
>   2 teaspoons baking powder
> $1 1/2$ teaspoons fine sea salt
>   1 cup lightly toasted walnuts, chopped
>   1 cup semisweet chocolate chips

1. Preheat the oven to 350°F. Lightly oil a 12-by-17$1/2$-inch jelly-roll pan.

2. In a medium bowl, combine the oil, maple syrup, soy milk, and vanilla. Whisk to combine.

3. In a separate bowl, sift together the flours, cocoa, sugar, Sucanat, baking powder, and salt.

4. Fold the dry ingredients into the wet mixture with a rubber spatula, taking care not to over-mix. Fold in the nuts and chocolate chips.

5. Pour the batter into the pan and smooth the top with a moistened spatula. Bake for 30 to 35 minutes, until surface cracks appear and the brownies are not quite set. Do not overbake—the brownies will set as they cool.

6. Transfer the pan to a rack to cool, then cut into 20 bars.   YIELD: 20 BROWNIES

Oatmeal-Raisin Cookies

$2/3$ cup raisins
$1^2/3$ cups shelled walnuts
1 cup rolled oats
$1^1/3$ cups brown rice flour or whole wheat pastry flour
$1^1/2$ teaspoons ground cinnamon
$1/2$ teaspoon fine sea salt
6 tablespoons melted unsalted butter, canola oil, or corn oil
$1/2$ cup pure maple syrup
$1/3$ cup brown rice syrup
2 teaspoons vanilla extract

1. Preheat the oven to 350°F. Lightly grease 2 baking sheets or line them with parchment paper.

2. Soak the raisins in 2 cups warm water for 10 to 15 minutes. Spread the walnuts and oats on an ungreased baking sheet and toast them in the oven for 8 minutes, stirring occasionally.

3. In a food processor fitted with a metal blade, combine half of the toasted walnuts and oats and grind to a fine meal. Add the remaining walnuts and oats, flour, cinnamon, and salt. Pulse a few times to combine.

4. In a bowl, whisk together the butter, maple syrup, brown rice syrup, and vanilla. Add the dry ingredients and stir to combine. Drain the raisins and stir them in.

5. Drop rounded tablespoons of batter onto the baking sheets 2 inches apart and bake for 15 to 18 minutes or until lightly browned.

6. Let the cookies cool on the baking sheets.   YIELD: ABOUT 18 COOKIES

VARIATION: CHUNKY DATE-NUT DROP COOKIES
    Substitute 1 cup pitted chopped dates for the raisins and $1^2/3$ cups roughly chopped almonds or cashews for the walnuts.

Sesame-Currant Cookies

These crunchy little gems are perfect for dunking.

> 3/4 cup firmly packed dried currants
> 1 cup whole wheat pastry flour
> 1 cup rolled oats
> 1 cup white hulled sesame seeds
> 1/4 teaspoon fine sea salt
> 6 tablespoons pure maple syrup
> 6 tablespoons melted unsalted butter,
>   pure olive oil, or melted coconut oil
> 1 teaspoon vanilla extract
> 1 to 2 tablespoons water (optional)

1. Preheat the oven to 350°F. Lightly grease 2 baking sheets or line them with parchment paper.

2. Soak the currants in warm water to cover for 10 minutes. Drain.

3. In a food processor fitted with a metal blade, combine the flour and oats and grind to a fine meal. Transfer the meal to a bowl. Add the sesame seeds and salt and mix well.

4. In a separate bowl, whisk together the maple syrup, butter, and vanilla. Add the dry ingredients and the currants and mix well with a wooden spoon to form a thick dough. If the dough is too dry, add water, 1 teaspoon at a time.

5. Moisten your hands and form the dough into walnut-sized balls. Place the balls 3 inches apart on the cookie sheets and gently flatten into 2-inch rounds.

6. Bake for 15 to 18 minutes, rotating the baking sheets halfway through for even baking, until cookies are golden brown.

7. Transfer the cookies to a wire rack to cool until crisp.

YIELD: ABOUT 2 DOZEN COOKIES

Toasted Almond Cookies

1 cup whole almonds
2 cups unbleached all-purpose flour
    or 1 cup whole wheat pastry flour and
    1 cup unbleached all-purpose flour
$1/4$ teaspoon fine sea salt
$1/8$ teaspoon baking soda
$1/2$ cup pure maple syrup
$1/2$ cup melted unsalted butter,
    coconut oil, or pure olive oil
1 teaspoon vanilla extract
$1/2$ teaspoon almond extract
1 teaspoon finely grated orange zest
$1/2$ cup sliced almonds

1. Preheat the oven to 350°F. Lightly grease 2 baking sheets or line them with parchment paper.

2. Spread the whole almonds on an ungreased baking sheet and toast in the oven for 8 minutes.

3. In a food processor fitted with a metal blade, combine the toasted almonds, flour, salt, and baking soda and grind to a fine meal.

4. In a bowl, whisk together the maple syrup, butter, vanilla, almond extract, and orange zest. Add the almond mixture and sliced almonds and mix well with a wooden spoon.

5. Moisten your hands and form the dough into walnut-sized balls. Place the balls 3 inches apart on the baking sheets and gently flatten into 2-inch rounds.

6. Bake for 15 to 18 minutes, rotating the baking sheets halfway through for even baking, until cookies are golden brown.

7. Transfer the cookies to a wire rack to cool.

YIELD: ABOUT 2 DOZEN COOKIES

Seasonal Menus
for Lunch and Dinner

Composing a menu can be a creative challenge.

There are no hard-and-fast rules to follow, but a few guidelines can help. Most important is what produce is in season. Visit the farmers' market and see what looks good, whets your appetite, and stimulates your imagination. Create a meal that suits the weather, your mood, or the occasion. Consider how much time you have to prepare the dishes and if any can be made ahead of time. Keep the meal interesting, balancing colors, flavors, and textures. For example, a rich, hearty stew goes well with a simple grain dish and a crisp salad. A creamy soup complements whole-grain bread and quickly sautéed vegetables. A simple fresh fruit dessert rounds out an elaborate dinner, while you might go all out and bake a pie when the other dishes are quick to prepare. The following menus are merely suggestions.

Spring

Summer

DINNERS

Pizza Vegano (page 270)

Crazy Chopped Salad with Basil Vinaigrette (page 82)

Farfalle with Fresh Summer Ragout (page 168)

Slices of fresh watermelon

Black Bean and Bell Pepper Chili with Seitan (page 67)
  with Soy Sour Cream (page 391)

White Corn Arepas from Hominy (page 308)

Cucumber, Watercress, and Red Onion Salad with Mint (page 84)

Chocolate Mousse with fresh raspberries (page 423)

Autumn

LUNCHES

Autumn Miso Soup (page 40)

Nori Maki (page 286) with Sweet Ginger Tofu (page 263)

Garlicky Braised Greens with Toasted Pumpkin Seeds (page 135)

Apple, Fennel, and Walnut Soup (page 50)

Sea Vegetable Salad with Roasted Peppers and Radicchio (page 88)

Barbecued Tempeh Sandwich Filling (page 279)
  with Whole Wheat Sandwich Bread (page 318)

DINNERS

Savory Millet and Sweet Potato "Polenta" with
  Smothered Peppers and Onions (page 204)

Italian-Style Baked Beans with Garlic and Sage (page 251)

Spicy Mustard Greens with Cumin (page 137)

Baked Apples with Nut Stuffing and Cider-Raisin Sauce (page 418)

Crudités with Yogurt Cream with Curry and Mint (page 390)
Chickpea Vegetable Curry (page 256)
Basmati Rice Pilaf (page 194)
Apple-Ginger Chutney (page 371)
Coconut Cream Tart (page 412)

Winter

LUNCHES

Rutabaga Soup with Sizzling Spice Oil (page 56)
Spinach-Mushroom Quiche (page 274)
Potato, Beet, and Belgian Endive Salad with Toasted Hazelnuts (page 90)

Posole (page 71)
Basic Vegan Skillet Corn Bread (page 350)
Celery Salad with Pickled Plum Vinaigrette and Toasted Walnuts (page 92)

DINNERS

Broccoli-Mushoom Soup (page 52)
Sourdough Rye (page 332)
Wintry Root Vegetable Risotto with Red Beans (page 210)
Curly Endive Salad with Garlic Croutons and Mustard Vinaigrette (page 93)
Walnut Tart (page 410)

Seitan Bourguignon (page 63)
Garlic Mashed Potatoes (page 120)
Braised Red Cabbage with Apples (page 130)
Crispy Pickled Vegetables (page 368)
Spice Cake (page 402) with Thick Yogurt Cream (page 407)

Sources

BRIDGE KITCHENWARE
214 East 52nd Street
New York, NY 10022
212-688-4220
www.bridgekitchenware.com
High-quality cookware and utensils

DEAN & DELUCA
560 Broadway
New York, NY 10012
800-221-7714
www.deandeluca.com
Heirloom beans, chestnut flour,
specialty products

FBM BAKING MACHINES INC.
2666 Route 139
Carnbury, NJ 08512
609-860-0577
fbmbongard@aol.com
French and German dough-proofing
baskets, dough cutters, baking peels

GOLD MINE NATURAL FOOD COMPANY
1947 30th Street
San Diego, CA 92102
800-475-FOOD
High-quality traditional whole foods
including umeboshi, miso, Nama Shoyu,
Celtic sea salt, grains, beans, kombu,
hiziki, other sea vegetables, books

KALUSTYAN'S

123 Lexington Avenue

New York, NY 10016

212-685-3451

Beans, spices, grains, urad dhal, international products, especially Indian

KING ARTHUR FLOUR/
THE BAKER'S CATALOGUE

P.O. Box 876

Norwich, VT 05055-0876

800-827-6836

www.kingarthurflour.com

Organic flours and a complete line of baking equipment

MAINE SEAWEED COMPANY

P.O. Box 57

Steuben, ME 04680

207-546-2875

Wild-harvested sea vegetables

MENDOCINO SEA VEGETABLE COMPANY

P.O. Box 372

Navarro, CA 94563

800-964-2270

Fresh and dried sea vegetables

MIRACLE EXCLUSIVES

64 Seaview Blvd.

Port Washington, NY 11050

800-645-6360

www.miracleexclusives.com

Grain mills, pressure cookers, general cooking and baking equipment

MOUNTAIN ARK TRADING CO.

120 South East Avenue

Fayetteville, AR 72701

501-442-7191

Organic grains, beans, tools, equipment

ORGANIC WINE COMPANY

1592 Union Street, Suite 350

San Francisco, CA 94123

www.ecowine.com

Wonderful selection of French and Italian wines

SUR LA TABLE

1765 Sixth Avenue South

Seattle, WA 98134-1608

800-243-0852

Traditional marble mortars and pestles, enamel-coated cast-iron cookware, high-quality stainless-steel cookware and utensils

Suggested Inspirational Reading

Bertolli, Paul, with Alice Waters. *Chez Panisse Cooking.* New York: Random House, 1988.

Bianchini, Francesco, et al. *The Complete Book of Fruits and Vegetables.* New York: Crown, 1976.

Bugialli, Giuliano. *Bugialli on Pasta.* New York: Simon & Schuster, 1988.

Coblin, Annemarie. *Food and Our Bones.* New York: Penguin Putnam, 1998.

de Langre, Jacques. *Sea Salt's Hidden Powers.* Magalia, CA: Happiness Press, 1994.

Fallon, Sally. *Nourishing Traditions.* San Diego: ProMotion Publishing, 1995.

Goldstein, Joyce. *The Mediterranean Kitchen.* New York: William Morrow, 1989.

Grey, Patience. *Honey from a Weed: Fasting and Feasting in Tuscany, Catalonia, the Cyclades, and Apulia.* New York: Lyons & Burford, 1986.

Hazan, Marcella. *Marcella Cucina.* New York: HarperCollins, 1997.

Jacobs, Leonard, and Barbara Jacobs. *Cooking with Seitan.* New York: Japan Publications, 1986.

Johnston, Mireille. *The Cuisine of the Sun: Classical French Cooking from Nice and Provence.* New York: Vintage, 1976.

Katzen, Mollie. *Vegetable Heaven.* New York: Hyperion, 1997.

Kaufman, Klaus, and Annetlies Schoneck. *The Cultured Cabbage: Rediscovering the Art of Making Sauerkraut.* British Columbia: Alive Books, 1997.

La Place, Viana. *Unplugged Kitchen.* New York: William Morrow, 1996.

Lynch, Kermit. *Adventures Along the Wine Route.* New York: Farrar, Straus, and Giroux, 1988.

McGee, Harold. *On Food and Cooking: The Science and Lore of the Kitchen.* New York: Collier Books, 1984.

Madison, Deborah. *Vegetarian Cooking for Everyone.* New York: Broadway, 1997.

Meyer, Danny, and Michael Romano. *The Union Square Café Cookbook.* New York: HarperCollins, 1994.

Ohsawa, George. *Zen Macrobiotic Cooking.* Oroville, CA: Macrobiotic Foundation, 1965.

Ohsawa, Lima. *Macrobiotic Cuisine.* New York: Japan Publications, 1984.

Olney, Richard. *Simple French Food.* New York: Atheneum, 1983.

Pellegrini, Angelo. *The Unprejudiced Palate: Classic Thoughts on Food and the Good Life.* New York: Lyons Press, 1997.

Peterson, James. *Vegetables.* New York: William Morrow, 1998.

Sass, Lorna. *The New Soy Cookbook.* San Francisco: Chronicle Books, 1998.

Silverton, Nancy. *Breads from the La Brea Bakery.* New York: Villard, 1997.

The Good Cook Series. New York: Time-Life, 1981.

Verge, Roger. *Vegetables in the French Style.* New York: Artisan Books, 1992.

Index

About the Authors

PETER BERLEY is a private chef, caterer, and cooking instructor. The former executive chef of the world-renowned Angelica Kitchen restaurant in New York City, he holds classes at the Institute of Culinary Education, the Natural Gourmet Institute for Food and Health, and the Miette Culinary Studio. He is a contributor to *Cooking Light* and *Fine Cooking* magazines and the author of *Fresh Food Fast*. He lives with his family in Dobbs Ferry, New York.

MELISSA CLARK is a food writer and cookbook author. A regular contributor to the *New York Times* and *Food and Wine*, she has written fourteen cookbooks and is at work on her fifteenth, a collaboration with chef Daniel Boulud. She lives in Brooklyn, New York.